BɛT
2.00
Nov'78

THE PEERLESS LEADER
WILLIAM JENNINGS BRYAN

William Jennings Bryan
As Secretary of State

THE PEERLESS LEADER
WILLIAM JENNINGS BRYAN

BY PAXTON HIBBEN

INTRODUCTION BY CHARLES A. BEARD

NEW YORK / RUSSELL & RUSSELL

FIRST PUBLISHED IN 1929
REISSUED, 1967, BY RUSSELL & RUSSELL
A DIVISION OF ATHENEUM HOUSE, INC.
L. C. CATALOG CARD NO: 66-27099

PRINTED IN THE UNITED STATES OF AMERICA

The first twenty-one chapters of THE PEERLESS LEADER:
WILLIAM JENNINGS BRYAN were completed by Paxton
Hibben before his untimely death. The book as it stands was
completed by C. Hartley Grattan, after consultation with those
close to Mr. Hibben, among them Claude Bowers and Harry
Elmer Barnes who were familiar with Mr. Hibben's plan for
the book. Mr. Grattan and the publishers wish to thank Miss
Ida Zeitlin for editorial assistance and Miss Elizabeth Gilman
for checking detail. They regret that it has been exceedingly
difficult to sift from the mass of Mr. Hibben's correspondence
and notes the names of those to whom he would have undoubtedly made acknowledgment of advice and aid. It has seemed
wise, therefore, rather than to publish a faulty list, to make
this blanket acknowledgment.

THE PUBLISHERS

"Where is McKinley, Mark Hanna's McKinley,
His slave, his echo, his suit of clothes?
Gone to join the shadows, with the pomps of that time,
And the flame of that summer's prairie rose.

"Where is Cleveland whom the Democratic platform
Read from the party in a glorious hour?
Gone to join the shadows with pitchfork Tillman,
And sledge-hammer Altgeld who wrecked his power.

"Where is Hanna, bulldog Hanna,
Low-browed Hanna, who said: 'Stand pat'?
Gone to his place with old Pierpont Morgan,
Gone somewhere . . . with lean rat Platt.

"Where is Roosevelt, the young dude cowboy,
Who hated Bryan, then aped his way?
Gone to join the shadows with mighty Cromwell
And tall King Saul, till the Judgment Day.

"Where is Altgeld, brave as the truth,
Whose name the few still say with tears?
Gone to join the ironies with Old John Brown,
Whose fame rings loud for a thousand years.

"Where is that boy, that Heaven-born Bryan,
That Homer Bryan, who sang from the West?
Gone to join the shadows with Altgeld the Eagle,
Where the kings and the slaves and the troubadours rest."*

VACHEL LINDSAY.

------
* From " Bryan, Bryan, Bryan," in *Collected Poems*, by Vachel Lindsay, reprinted by permission of The Macmillan Company, Publishers.

CONTENTS

PAGE

Introduction   xiii

PART I: THE HOUSE OF BONDAGE

CHAPTER

I.   1860   3

II.   Raccoon Township   11

III.   Egypt   22

IV.   Salem   34

V.   Escape   44

PART II: AMBITION

VI.   1874   55

VII.   Whipple Academy   65

VIII.   Illinois College   79

IX.   Chicago   89

X.   Ascent   99

PART III: REALIZATION

XI.   1890   113

XII.   Congress   125

XIII.   Washington   136

XIV.   Capitol Hill   148

XV.   Poised   162

CONTENTS

PART IV: SPRING TIDE

CHAPTER | | PAGE

XVI.   1896   175

XVII.   The Enemy's Country   189

XVIII.   Cuba Libre   202

XIX.   Kansas City   213

XX.   Falter   224

PART V: CLIMAX

XXI.   1904   237

XXII.   Democracy Goes Conservative   250

XXIII.   Around the World to Madison Square Garden   259

XXIV.   1908   276

XXV.   Toward Prohibition   289

PART VI: NEW LIFE

XXVI.   Baltimore   301

XXVII.   In the Cabinet   319

XXVIII.   The Lonely Leader   351

XXIX.   Sixty Years Old   368

XXX.   Redemption   388

Bibliography   409

Notes   423

Index   439

Peerless Leader

LIST OF ILLUSTRATIONS

William Jennings Bryan as Secretary of State *Frontispiece*

FACING
PAGE

Mary Baird Bryan 38

The Hon. Silas Bryan 38

Aunt Mollie 39

Bryan's Sister Fanny 39

At Whipple Academy 70

At Illinois College 70

In Law School 70

Cousin Lizzie Jones 71

Cousin Hiram Jones 71

Mrs. Bryan at the Time of Her Marriage 116

The First Bryan Campaign Poster 116

Mr. and Mrs. Bryan With "Gentlemen of the Press" 117

Mr. and Mrs. Bryan at Red Hook 117

The Silver Knight of the West, 1896 182

Judge Cartoons Bryan's "Fantastic Try," 1896 183

"An Anarchist, A Blasphemer, and the Anti-Christ" 198

As They Viewed Bryan in "The Enemy's Country" 199

The Political Situation of 1908 278

Now Fat and Opulent, Less and Less the Crusader 279

Bryan's Return from Europe 296

FACING
PAGE

Bryan in 1908, before the Office of the *Commoner*   297

Secretary of State William Jennings Bryan, at His
    Desk   ·332

Brother Charley Accepts the Vice-Presidential Nomi-
    nation, 1924   333

"The Sun May Be Eclipsed, but the Democratic Party
    Never"   396

The Judge's Bench at the Scopes Trial   397

In Memory of Paxton Hibben

Only a few short years ago was it my good fortune to meet Paxton Hibben, but within that brief span we had many long conversations on the office of the biographer—as well as cabbages and kings. Possessing an extraordinary knowledge of history, politics, and human nature, Mr. Hibben was under no delusions about the slippery character of excursions into the literature of personalities. With gusts of sparkling laughter, he disposed of professional undertakers who lay out the letters, papers, and documents of deceased persons with the design of giving them immortality and pleasing widows. Nothing in the annals of printing amused him more than the full-length portraits of Lodge and Roosevelt, drawn, draped, and coloured by the eminent authors themselves so that posterity might not overlook their amplitude. With what avail?

But, being a man of poise, Mr. Hibben did not at once jump over to the other side and conclude that the "new" school of biographers had discovered some final words. He knew that the stature of Napoleon was not in reality diminished by folios containing authentic accounts of his follies, mistakes, weaknesses, and childish conceits. Paxton Hibben was equally aware of the commercial origins to which most of the "newest" sex biographies could be traced—sex being, next to stomach, the lowest common denominator of the human race. "There's millions in it." While he loved to thwack magnificent hypocrites over their moral knuckles, he did not look upon the successful retailing of scandal as the noblest achievement of man. A student of social history

and social processes, Mr. Hibben believed that any note-
worthy biography must be closely related to the intellectual
currents of the age in which the character portrayed actually
lived and worked.

Since these, in general, were the views of Paxton Hibben
with respect to the office of the biographer, it seems fitting
that this introduction should be devoted to expanding them
—without committing him to the outcome. Those familiar
with Western literature well know that, broadly speaking,
biography runs parallel with historical writing—beginning
with heroes and ending with statistics; from Alfred the
Great, warrior and patron of learning, to Calvin Coolidge,
civilian and economist. As late as 1840, Thomas Carlyle
could write: "Universal History, the history of what man
has accomplished in this world, is at bottom the History of
the Great Men who have worked here." That seems easy
until some interloper asks: "Who are the Great?" and adds:
"When?" Metternich saving monarchy from the flood or
James Watt changing the face of industry with his steam
engine? Bespangled Ludendorff marching from blaze to
blaze or shabby Lenin brooding in Switzerland over the tides
in human affairs?

Whatever the upshot here, it is certainly true that the
biographies of warriors and politicians (and frequently their
lady friends, mistresses, and dictatresses) did long furnish
the staples of history. But such biography was more than
hero worship. Usually it was also partisan politics. In
glorifying our heroes we magnify our party and belittle our
opponents, flatter ourselves and make Lilliputs out of our
foes. What a pleasing occupation! Twisted, turned, purled,
and embroidered, such is the animus from which many a
stately memoir proceeds. Pride, conceit, and damnation in
hand-tooled bindings! In fact acres of biographies can be
correctly located in the curve of emotions—praising our

friends and banging our enemies, with more or less documentary material as exhibits and alibis.

No doubt the classical example under this head is the splendid life of George Washington written by John·Marshall whose reddest anger could be sheathed in ice. Now, John Marshall was a very great man. Of course it is possible to show that his education was slight, that his clothes were seedy, that he played cards for money, and that he had a Rotarian eye for good real estate. So did many of his contemporaries who began in obscurity and ended in oblivion. In truth Marshall was a grand Federalist politician—as much of a politician as Bryan or Roosevelt—and he wrote a story of Washington which was in gross and detail a Federalist stump speech, couched in the austere language of jurisprudence, with appropriate damnation of Thomas Jefferson and his agrarian faction woven into the very warp and woof. Though the Sage of Monticello was quick to get the drift of the argument, an innocent youth who reads Marshall's work to-day will miss the point as smoothly as he misses the political economy of *Gulliver's Travels*. But Marshall's Life was a great biography, not to be compared with the compilations of Professor Jared Sparks, who was small enough to think that he was doing Washington a favour by correcting his bad grammar and misspelt words.

Such political biography held the field almost undisputed until near the edge of the Twentieth Century when "scientific historians" came riding up to the fray. Then the protective fur began to fly. These newcomers said that they were not interested in bolstering up or putting down parties, causes, sects, and factions. Their business, they announced, was to discover the truth about people, ideas, and things—to find out "how it actually happened." Well, this was certainly a menace to heroic proportions and political perfection, for these searchers, armed with writs of assistance, pried into dust-covered papers and printed volumes of documents not included in "definitive biographies," making total wrecks of many noble traditions.

While the scientific historians were getting under way, political economy and democracy were mopping up the remnants of feudalism—with its Cœur de Lions and Don Quixotes—and proclaiming the era of calculation and common clay. Necessarily, the intellectual climate of this age was unfavourable to heroic stature. Moreover most of the outstanding figures of trade and manufacturing, in the first generation at least, came up from the ranks, from poverty to riches, from log cabins to palaces. So biography was yanked down out of Olympus. Caught between the scientific historians and the promoters of democracy, it lost its Jovian gilt. Indeed, far back, Napoleon himself discovered that he did not dare to call himself the son of God because it would make the fishwives of Boulogne laugh.

As a later phase of democracy and prosperity, opened the epoch of armchairs, cigarettes, sweets, soft lights, and fiction. Whether intelligence of any kind, when, as, and if, can survive it is as yet undecided by the Delphic oracles. To this upshot, I think, Paxton Hibben would agree with his characteristic: "Quite so, my friend, but——"

CHARLES A. BEARD.

PART I

THE HOUSE OF BONDAGE

"And it shall be, when thy son asketh thee in time to come, saying: What is this? that thou shalt say unto him: By strength of hand the Lord brought us out from Egypt, from the house of bondage. . . .

". . . they were sore afraid: and the children of Israel cried unto the Lord . . .

"And Moses said unto the people, Fear ye not, stand still, and see the salvation of the Lord, which he will show you today. . . .

"The Lord shall fight for you, and ye shall hold your peace."

CHAPTER I

1860

JOHN MORRISSEY was twenty-nine in 1858—no longer young for a prize fighter "whose days and nights," said the *Herald*, "are spent in carousing and other carnal pleasures." But his fight with the "Benecia Boy" for the championship of America and a purse of the staggering sum of $5,000 was the first big fight in nine years, and the newspapers were full of it. The *Herald* gave up its entire front page to the mill. The *Tribune* and *Harper's Weekly* devoted column editorials to it. *Leslie's Weekly* printed whole pages of pictures of ringside scenes and the barroom orgies that followed. All in all, the Morrissey-Heenan fight was one of the great events of 1858.

So also was the first trip of the Overland Mail stage, fetching the post from California by way of Tucson in the astounding time of ten days. The publication of *The Courtship of Miles Standish* was an event too—five thousand copies sold before noon of the day of issue.

But out in Illinois none of these epochal occurrences created a ripple. There two men were doggedly plugging away from Freeport on the north to Jonesboro in the heart of "Egypt," travelling sometimes by train and sometimes by boat, but more often by buggy over rough, dusty roads to address thousands of farmers who came from miles around and stood for hours in the hot afternoon sun of Indian summer to hear them. And that was what interested the people of Illinois.

They talked about slavery, these two men. They talked about the Constitution and the decisions of the Supreme Court. They even talked, guardedly and with evident reluctance, about what might happen if the people of the

United States should decide in their majesty that the institution of Negro slavery would have to end. And in what these two men had to say on that subject there was an undercurrent of threat, an undertone of tramping feet and beating drums. . . .

One of the men was only five feet two, but with a massive head and a deep bass voice and a certain handsome opulence of appearance, a certain assured air of a man of the world. The other was more than a foot taller—ugly, uncouth, with a shrill voice and a gray Scotch shawl about his shoulders in the chill October mornings. Both men were tremendously in earnest. Sometimes they lost their tempers and called one another hard names. But in the main they spoke with the restraint of men discussing a desperate, perhaps an irremediable, situation that went to the very roots of what manner of government the people of the United States lived under in that day.

It was in Egypt that the debates came to an end, in mid-October—Egypt, that point of Illinois thrust deep in the very flesh of the South, between Kentucky and Missouri—Stephen A. Douglas's own adopted country, Egypt, peopled with spare, taciturn, suspicious men of the mountains of Virginia and Kentucky and Tennessee, agape to find themselves become overnight prosperous prairie farmers in what seemed to them a land flowing with milk and honey. That is why they called it "Egypt." Southerners they were—Democrats of the type that made up the mob that swept Andrew Jackson into the White House. They were for Stephen A. Douglas to a man.

In Egypt, the Little Giant boasted, he was going to "trot Lincoln out." So when the last debate took place at Alton the steamer *White Cloud* was chartered to fetch a boatload of Douglas rooters from St. Louis, and the railroads—always the friends of Judge Douglas—ran half-fare excursions to swell the crowd. In the milling jam of men waiting the beginning of the speeches, one man thrust aloft a quart bottle of whisky and screamed an invitation to the "Douglas boys" to come and drink. . . . On the speakers' platform were gathered

all the leading Democrats of Egypt to do their hero honour. . . .

The Hon. Silas Lillard Bryan, of Salem, Marion County,
was only thirty-six. But he was nothing if not a leading
Democrat. For six years he had represented the whole
northeastern section of Egypt in the Illinois State Senate.
Back in 1853 the Hon. Silas Bryan voted for Stephen A.
Douglas for the United States Senate, and he was going to
vote for him now. He knew Abe Lincoln, did Silas Bryan—
Lincoln had been elected to the House when the Hon. Silas
Bryan was in the Senate of the Illinois General Assembly.
The Hon. Silas had very little use for Abraham Lincoln or
any of his kind. Few who dwelt in Egypt had.

That memorable campaign of 1858 was not the first time
that the Hon. Silas Bryan had had the opportunity of voting
for Abraham Lincoln for the United States Senate, or had enjoyed the occasion to vote against him. Three years previous, Lincoln controlled all but four of the votes in the
General Assembly necessary to send him to Washington.
Unhappily those four were Democrats of the Hon. Silas
Bryan's own brand. Party was stronger with them than
principle. Under the circumstances there was no way for
Lincoln to be elected. So he stepped aside in favour of
Lyman Trumbull.

But the Hon. Silas Bryan would not vote for Trumbull
either. Seven times he sat there with pursed lips, in frowning
disapproval of Trumbull's anti-slavery Democracy, and cast
his vote for that noisy, swashbuckling Irish soldier of
fortune, Major General James Shields, who once all but
fought a duel with Abraham Lincoln—with cavalry broad-
swords of the largest size. . . .

It was over there, just across the Mississippi from Alton. . . .
Perhaps Abe Lincoln was thinking of that duel as he faced
the howling crowd of "Douglas boys" in mid-October,
1858. . . .

Just the same, Lincoln's friend Trumbull was elected to
the Senate in 1855, despite the Hon. Silas Bryan. And now
here was Abe Lincoln again, once more running for the

Senate himself. Well, the Hon. Silas Bryan thought no better of him now than he had three years before. For the Hon. Silas was not one to blow hot and blow cold. When his mind was made up, it was made up.

"No use pounding on the log," he would snap at the lawyers pleading their cases before him on the Circuit Bench. "The coon's out."

He meant that argument was futile. Judge Bryan had reached his decision.

Judge Bryan had reached his decision also in the campaign of 1858 long before the Lincoln-Douglas debate at Alton. And when election day straggled from darkness, cold, wet and raw, the Hon. Silas Bryan recorded his decision with due solemnity at the polls.

What amazed him and the rest of the Democrats of Egypt beyond measure was that this time Abraham Lincoln carried the State of Illinois by 4,085 votes. Had there been popular election of Senators he would have packed his carpet bag for a protracted stay in Washington in 1859, instead of two years later. True, the Hon. Silas Bryan was a great believer in the popular election of Senators. But this was an exceptional case, of course. So he voted against Abraham Lincoln, the people's choice, with a good conscience. And Lincoln was defeated.

"Senator Douglas has achieved a signal triumph," wrote Horace Greeley in the New York *Tribune*. About Abraham Lincoln he said nothing. By and large, Old Abe got little enough out of his senatorial campaign beyond a badly shattered law practice.

Yet, somehow, Lincoln, would not down. Silas Bryan and the other Southern Democrats who peopled Egypt could vote against him as often as they liked—but there he was always bobbing up again, just as he had been bobbing up constantly in almost every campaign since he had been a clerk in a country store at New Salem, a quarter of a century earlier.

The senatorial contest with Douglas was hardly over before this curiously undiscomfited man Lincoln was admitting to

Jesse Fell that he would like to be President! First one
newspaper then another spoke of it: Abraham Lincoln for
President in 1860.

To men like the Hon. Silas Bryan, with legitimate political
aspirations of their own, the idea was preposterous. After all,
the newspapers putting forward the suggestion were mostly
small-town papers, in that vast, diverse Middle West that
had never yet conceived a clear, sharply chiselled thought on
any subject, social, political, economic, or religious. Who
were they, anyhow, these people who had straggled over the
sparsely settled prairie lands of Indiana, Illinois, Kansas,
Nebraska, and Iowa, where they dwelt with so little homo-
geneity in such fierce individualism? Relatively few were
Virginia, Kentucky, and Tennessee mountaineers, like Silas
Bryan and Abraham Lincoln. Who were the others—and why
had they come?

An intrepid, yet baffled, people, they seemed, ready to un-
dergo every physical hardship to escape the more difficult
problem of inner adjustment. Incapable of mental supple-
ness, once they were confronted by the commercial development and the orgaanied exploitation arising along the Atlantic seaboard they could neither adapt themselves to
changing conditions nor resist the trend of social and economic life. So they fled before a reality they could neither
face nor fight. And conscious of this they brought with
them to this new land a spirit of profound mistrust—of
themselves, of their neighbours, above all, of the East they
had left behind them—a sense of frustration that left them
uncomprehending but resentful.

To people of this mind, a figure at once groping and
shrewd, pliable under compulsion yet yielding no essential,
came to be a reflection of themselves. Their voice. To these
people the slavery question was nothing. A red herring
designed to befool the electorate. They were not to be misled
by it. The slogan of the Free Soilers expressed exactly the
thought of these Mid-Westerners: "Free Soil, Free Speech,
Free Labour, Free Men." They meant it in precisely that
order. Even Kansas barred Negroes by its Constitution.

Illinois forbade Negroes to come into the state on pain of being knocked down to the highest bidder at public auction to pay the fine imposed by law for violating the prohibition.[1] What interested the people of the Middle West was not the slavery or the Negroes, but themselves, and their freedom from the commercial and industrial exploitation of the East. Abraham Lincoln stated their fears for them, simply and clearly, as he had a way of doing. He spoke of the danger of ". . . the supplanting of the principles of free government and restoring those of classification, caste and legitimacy."

That, not slavery, was the issue as Abraham Lincoln saw it. It was the issue, too, as hundreds of thousands saw it throughout the great Middle West, where they had sought and found refuge from the relentless march of Eastern commercialism. They had fled once. Well, this time they would stand their ground and fight.

So, on May 16, 1860, forty thousand of them flocked to Chicago and tried to get into the Great Wigwam in Lake Street that could hold only ten thousand. To the Republicans who came from the East, to whom slavery appeared as the issue, the nomination of William H. Seward, the astute, the immaculate, was "pretty much a certain thing."[2] Men politically as sagacious as John Bigelow and William Cullen Bryant had not a doubt of the outcome.

But the West knew better. To the West Seward was Wall Street, and the West feared and hated Wall Street as long ago as 1860.[3] It was what they had fled from; and it was now reaching out again to subjugate them. Perhaps if they had had no man of their own, they might have succumbed and in the end moved farther West—to Kansas or Nebraska or Iowa. But the West did have a man of its own. For years he had been going among them, making speeches, running for office and occasionally holding one, talking, debating, making friends in a simple, neighbourly way. As much as they trusted anyone, they trusted him. At least Abraham Lincoln understood the angle of vision of these strangely thwarted and bewildered folk who were his own people. He understood it because it was his angle of vision, too.

So the West chose him. The West chose Abraham Lincoln. And the West made him President.

Rapidly it grew into a legend in Illinois and all through the Middle West—a legend that by the time youths born at this period reached adolescence had become to be as immutable a pattern of life as the story of Joseph.

It was the story of the son of a Southern mountaineer who had made his home in the newer lands of the Middle West. He began early to make political speeches and to aspire to elective honours. He studied law, but used the law as a stepping stone to political preferment rather than as a profession. His whole political approach was Jeffersonian, individualistic, hostile to vast combinations of wealth. He sought a Federal job, and was refused. He served in Congress, not without honour. He debated up and down the country-side with one of the leading political figures of the day. He tried to be elected to the Senate of the United States and was defeated. One night, in the darkness of a box car, where neither man could see the other clearly, he confided to Henry Villard his ambition to be Senator—to be President. He was even a soldier in a war in which he saw no fighting.

And finally, after long and arduous effort, "this huckster in politics," as Wendell Phillips called him, was nominated at Chicago by those who hated Wall Street and the whole commercial and industrial East, for the Presidency of the United States, in a "riot of sound that defied description."

Of the youths in whose lives this Lincoln legend was fore-doomed to play a capital rôle one was born to the Hon. Silas Bryan just two months before Abraham Lincoln was nominated in Chicago. For good and sufficient reasons this boy was named William Jennings.

He, too, was the son of a Southern mountaineer, and in due time he, too, made his home in the newer lands of the Middle West. He began early to make political speeches and to aspire to elective honours. He studied law, but used the law as a stepping stone to political preferment rather than as a profession. His whole political approach was Jeffersonian, individualistic, hostile to vast combinations of wealth. He sought a Federal job, and was refused. He served in Congress, and not without honour. He debated up and down the countryside and in magazines and newspapers with the foremost political figures of his day. He tried to be elected to the Senate of the United States and was defeated. One night, in the darkness of their bedroom, he confided to Millard Fillmore Dunlap his ambition to be Senator—possibly President. He was even a soldier in a war in which he saw no fighting.

And finally, after careful and astute preparation, he also was nominated, at Chicago, for the Presidency of the United States, amid vast acclaim, and by those who hated Wall Street and the whole commercial and industrial East.

So far as he could see, every single step had been placed with meticulous care in the very footprints of Abraham Lincoln.

Yet there was something missing. Perhaps times had changed. Perhaps the lives of human beings do not invariably follow immutable patterns.

Or perhaps there was something lacking in the man.

CHAPTER II

RACCOON TOWNSHIP

THE Hon. Silas Lillard Bryan was possessed by a great ambition. All his life he longed to be a country squire living on an estate of which he would rent the land to tenant farmers while he went to Congress.

He came by his ambition naturally enough. For the Bryans were of those two hundred thousand Scotch-Irish immigrants who suddenly began to flood America in 1718 and for a generation scattered to the farthest reaches of the New World, infusing a new element into the blood of the Founding Fathers. Thrifty to the verge of miserliness, vigorous, hardy, industrious, the Scotch-Irish added to these qualities a conviction that they were always right, rooted in the persuasion that their affairs were conducted by direct divine intervention.

At first blush, it is true, there did appear to have been some mistake about this. For when the immigrants began to arrive they found all the good holdings along the seaboard in the hands of the ungodly and nothing left for God's favourite children but the sterile mountain country toward the Western frontier in Tennessee, Kentucky, and Ohio. As there seemed to be nothing to do about it for the moment they shouldered their axes, their seed potatoes, the newly invented rifle, and a few modest belongings wrapped up in a bed quilt, and trudged off along the almost impassable roads, their women folk following behind. So far as the Scotch-Irish were concerned, the glory of being pioneers was dust and ashes. It was a state of affairs to be remedied as soon as possible.

Among these, the Bryans found themselves pushed up summarily into the foothills of the Blue Ridge Mountains, at the edge of the princely domain of Lord Fairfax. The nearest town was Sperryville—a dozen houses. From its barren heights the disillusioned Scotch-Irish looked dourly down upon the broad acres, the deer parks, the indolent slaves, and the generous manors of the rich and well born, where a constant stream of gentlemen and ladies attended by their bodyservants seemed to come and go as to open house. To the newly arrived, sombrely religious immigrants from Ireland, fortified by one or another of the narrower Calvinist creeds, the prosperity of the roisterers and blasphemers who had got there first[1] was an affront to a stern God. Economic and religious factors became inextricably interwoven in their minds. The Bryans, "believing emphatically in a prayer-hearing and prayer-answering God,"[2] kept the burden of their prayers that they, an elect people, might do at least as well in the world as the rich and well born who held the whip hand of government in the Old Dominion, and who persecuted the newcomers relentlessly as dissenters from the Church of England.[3] Especially were Baptists harried and tormented—and both the Bryans and the Lincolns were Baptists.

The Scotch-Irish did more than pray about it, however. In due season, when the Colonies were free from British rule at last, and the hour of reckoning appeared to be at hand for the luxurious, easy-going folk of the Virginia lowlands, these hard-bitten mountaineers voted for Andrew Jackson for President of the United States and had the satisfaction of seeing one of their own breed swept into the White House, followed by a gloating, cheering mob of just such as they.

That year Silas Bryan turned seven.

He had been born in a double log cabin, where the basement was living room, dining room, and kitchen, with a huge fireplace at one end. The floor above boasted four tiny rooms where father, mother, and the four girls slept. The six boys slept in the attic. It was a hard life, and when Silas Bryan was six his mother, Nancy Lillard, gave it up. Two years later, Silas Bryan's father, John Bryan, gave it up, too. By this time they had moved to the banks of the Kanawha in western Virginia, where the land was poorer and the work harder.

On the whole the childhood of Silas Bryan left just two indelible impressions upon him. He recalled the vast estates of the Virginia country squires that lay between the Blue Ridge Mountains and Richmond, with their fertile land, their deer parks and their commodious mansions. Back in Sperryville, he would go to the edge of a clearing and look down upon them, spread out before him like a map. To the barefoot, undernourished boy clad in a single garment, they were the symbol of success in the world. He dreamed of owning just such another himself, one day—deer park and all. It was a dream that persisted all his life, and that, in a way, he realized.

The second childhood memory that stuck to Silas Bryan, and to many another like him, was the triumph of Andrew Jackson. It was in a very real sense his triumph, and that of all the defrauded who had come too late to the land of Great Opportunity. The Lord of Hosts at last led His chosen people to victory. By the sheer weight of their numbers the illiterate, austere, resentful mountain folk wrested the government of the country from the hands of the rich and the well born. While he was yet a lad Silas Bryan saw the meek quite literally inherit the earth through the lowly instrumentality of the ballot. A steadfast conviction of the infallibility of the process remained with him all his life, as immutable as if it had been set down in Holy Writ.

He handed it on to his children as the most precious of all possible legacies.

As he grew older, orphaned and bandied about from relative to relative, one other principle developed from the youthful experience of Silas Bryan. He perceived more and more clearly that the one transcendent advantage which the rich and the well born possessed over the humble who so greatly outnumbered them lay not in their slaves or their deer parks or the prodigality of their mode of life but in their superior education. Who would beat them must beat them on their own ground. Education was a tool essential to the achievement of any kind of success. Wherefore Silas Bryan set out to get himself the best education he could manage.

There was very little of this commodity to be had in the South anywhere in 1830, at least by the poor but honest. And there was none whatever to be had in the mountains of West Virginia. Public schools were as yet undreamed of, and illiteracy ran high among the Scotch-Irish immigrants. They were far too busy taming the wilderness to make the acquaintance of any book save the Bible. Besides, young Silas Bryan had to work for his board and keep. There was no magic about being an orphan that entitled him to go to school, even if there had been a school to go to. On the other hand, he was free. If he did not like it at Point Pleasant he could move farther West. From Maine to Florida a steady stream was flowing uphill from the Atlantic seaboard to the Mississippi Valley—afoot, on horseback, in wagons, by rafts on the rivers, or by canal boats on the newly built waterways of Pennsylvania and New York. They were of all kinds, except rich. They were of every blood and every cast of political thought and every religious conviction, or none at all. Never since the beginning of history had so many people of such differing origins and backgrounds jumbled themselves together in a common enterprise to make up that "Western type which in politics and industry became ultimately the American type."[4]

The Bryans were among them. Silas Bryan's brother William was the first to go. He settled near Troy, Missouri. Of Silas's sisters, Jane and Martha went to Gallipolis, Ohio. Nancy married George Baltzell, and they set up housekeeping at Walnut Hill, in Marion County, Illinois. When he was eighteen it came Silas Bryan's turn. There was an academy near Troy, where his brother William lived. That was what Silas Bryan wanted. There he could get the education he coveted. So the year the whole Ohio valley was ablaze with bonfires and barbecues and log-cabin parades for the election of "Tippecanoe and Tyler, too," Silas Bryan swept down the river past William Henry Harrison's home at North Bend, carrying with him a somewhat discordant baggage in his inflexible Baptist convictions and his dream of a vast estate with a deer park, a commodious manor, and a seat in Congress. Other baggage he had none.

There were two types of the mountain people who moved West in those days: the Thomas Lincolns and the Silas Bryans. The former were an amiable, good-for-little lot, who moved because they could not make a living where they were. They were always moving. In a sense the Silas Bryans, also, sought escape from reality—a pot of gold at the foot of a rainbow. But there was a difference in dynamics. The Bryans moved because they did not like the kind of living they made where they were.

Silas Bryan came as near as most men to the achievement of his ambition. The Illinois State Senate had to do duty for Congress, it is true. But he did own broad acres before he died; he did keep open house in a way; he wore a tall silk hat and mutton-chop whiskers and was very dignified and aloof—a personage in the community. He even managed the deer park. But it was rather a scraggly affair, and with the Hon. Silas Bryan's frugal and abstemious habits his open house bordered on the austere—family prayers thrice a day and a reading of the Bible in the evening, instead of punches and whist and the conscious interplay of sex in highly romantic trappings of the authentic South. But what Silas Bryan achieved of his ambitions was, as with the general run of mankind, precisely what he was capable of achieving and no more. For the Hon. Silas Bryan was at bottom a Puritan with only a very small corner of the soul of a cavalier.

Within a year and half the modest academy at Troy, Missouri, had given Silas Bryan all it could. So he bade his brother William good-bye and crossed into that part of Illinois already dubbed "Egypt," where his sister Nancy lived. It was not Nancy Baltzell, with her "motherly care and prayers,"[5] that Silas Bryan came to seek in Raccoon Township at nineteen, however. There was a Methodist college just a few miles through the woods from Nancy's "cultured and refined home."[6] It was that college that Silas Bryan had in mind.

He would have preferred, of course, to receive his collegiate instruction at the hands of sound Baptists rather than the less austere followers of John Wesley, who conducted the tiny college in the wilderness, six years younger than Silas Bryan himself. Lebanon boasted only two hundred souls and McKendree College only twenty-one students; there were but three besides himself in Silas Bryan's graduating class— one student for each professor. The Reverend Erastus Wentworth, the president of this institution of higher learning, was set down by his contemporaries as "a genius with literary tastes and acquisitions."[7] In time these led him to the broader field of editing the *Ladies' Repository*, and *Golden Hours*, which described itself as a refined magazine for boys and girls. In Silas Bryan the Reverend Erastus Wentworth inculcated the rudiments of Mental and Moral Science.

The entire faculty of McKendree College consisted of Methodist ministers. Indeed, Raccoon Township was as much a Methodist community as Sperryville had been a Baptist one. The very year Silas Bryan's father moved from the Blue Ridge Mountains to West Virginia the great Lorenzo Dow halted his covered wagon on Walnut Hill and preached from the text: "The end of all things is at hand; be ye therefore sober, and watchful unto prayer."[8] He was wrong. It was not the end but the beginning of all things in that part of the world.

Nor were the inhabitants of Egypt as watchful unto prayer as they might be. They danced the Irish Trot all night to the tune of "Hell Up the Wabash" or the "Devil's Dream"[9] and consumed a vast amount of corn whisky in the process. The operations of sex attraction were swift and fatal. Many a lad of seventeen married a girl of fourteen, and the two faced sixty to seventy years of married life and a family of ten children with the hardihood of sheer youth. Divorce was almost unknown, and a divorced woman was "looked upon with suspicion and contempt by all."[10] There were even said to be a great many witches in that part of Egypt just south of McKendree College.[11] But as there was also a famous witch master who knew how to get bewitched cows out of mud holes by laying the open Bible on their backs[12] the community felt safe.

With such godless goings on as this Silas Bryan, of course, had no truck. However, that education he set such store by came hard. He cut wood every Saturday, worked as a farm hand during vacation, and a little later taught school at Walnut Hill to earn the money to pay for it. He and another lad built themselves a shack in the woods near the college and kept bachelor quarters together to save board and lodging. They did their own cooking, and Silas fell ill of it. It began to look as if he would never achieve that education, after all.

So Silas Bryan entered into a solemn compact with his Creator. If Divine Providence would so prosper him that he might live and secure his degree from McKendree College, he for his part would offer up a prayer to God three times a day for the remainder of his life, no matter where he might be. God did prosper Silas Bryan. He did graduate from McKendree College, nine years after he had come West in quest of an education. It is perhaps the most characteristic thing in the man's whole life that, to his dying day, he scrupulously kept his vow.

If Silas Bryan had any minor vices, aside from a fondness for practical jokes and a passion for singing when he could not carry a tune, there is no record of it. True, he chewed tobacco; but everyone did in that day and neighbourhood— except the women. They took snuff. Even tobacco Silas Bryan foreswore when dyspepsia came upon him in his middle years. Some of the girls he taught in the subscription school were older than he—full blown, deep bosomed, disturbing; and kissing was common enough.[13] But education was Silas Bryan's mistress. He was a single-track individual to whom promiscuity of any kind was repugnant.

Religion came nearest to being Silas Bryan's vice. Yet even in that he was too self-conscious to yield to the more boisterous evidences of the descent of the spirit upon the troubled soul of man customary in the fall camp meeting in southern Illinois. Almost every pious person shouted a little toward midnight, when waves of emotional excitement swept over the hundreds of men and women crowded against one another in the dim light of the great revival shed and sent them grovelling in ecstasy on the floor—or perhaps apart, out among the saplings, where there was no light at all.[14] There was a fine reserve about Silas Bryan that would not permit him to give himself, unrestrained, to all and sundry.

Silas Bryan was twenty-six when he rounded the first corner of his career by graduating from McKendree College. For a penniless young man ambitious to go to Congress the law was the one open door. There were less than a hundred and fifty lawyers in Illinois, and reading law was a more or less perfunctory affair. But even an ambitious young college graduate has to live. So Silas Bryan returned to school teaching while he looked into Blackstone.

There were still no public schools in Egypt.[15] What education the youths and maidens of Marion County had meted out to them with a ferrule was paid for by subscription and administered in somebody's abandoned log cabin, with puncheon floor, slab seats for the pupils, and hewn logs as desks. Everyone studied aloud in a droning whisper, and geography was taught by singing crude rhymes.[16] The teacher was despised by pupils and community alike as a weakling who took to the effeminate business of teaching because he could not do a man's work in a man's world. It wounded Silas Bryan's pride, so he set about agitating for public schools. Shortly he found himself elected county school superintendent.

It was Silas Bryan's first taste of public office, and he was tremendously elated by it. He conceived himself an authority on education forthwith. For years he would visit the nearest available school as regularly as Friday afternoon rolled around, sit on the platform by the teacher's desk, and deliver himself of a homily sprinkled with quotations from the Book of Proverbs. The school children loved these visits. It meant no lessons while the great man talked.

Eleven years after Silas Bryan had floated down the Ohio

without one broad copper to rub against another he was admitted to the bar of Marion County. There Lyman Trumbull was an occasional practitioner, and Abraham Lincoln's friend Joseph Gillespie, and Sidney Breese, "the Webster of Illinois."[17] He had come far, had Silas Bryan. He was a man of consequence in the community, with the future clear before him. But he was unmarried, and a man in public life at twenty-nine was expected to furnish society those indispensable gauges of respectability, conservatism, and seemly behaviour, a wife and children.

The step need not, of course, be taken impetuously. A commendable prudence might profitably be yoked to passion, with a weather eye on political advantages to be gained and, perhaps, not too far distant, that country seat with its deer park. For practical considerations such as these, no family in Raccoon Township so recommended itself to the attention of Silas Bryan as that of Israel Jennings.

Born prior to the Revolutionary War, Israel Jennings had moved to Kentucky about the same time that Thomas Lincoln had. When Illinois became a state he moved once more and was the second man to purchase cheap government land in Marion County. In due time he became the largest landowner in the county, a politican who served his terms in the Illinois General Assembly at Vandalia, and a Democrat of the kind Andrew Jackson turned into postmasters. Once, when Israel Jennings first arrived in the Illinois wilderness, one of his daughters died, and he had to fell a tree and hollow it out to make a coffin for her. Old Israel Jennings figured that when his time came there would be no one in the puny generation of his offspring able to perform so considerable a feat. So he went to St. Louis and fetched him back a metal coffin to have handy about the house.[18] For forty years he kept it, and when he died was buried in it. Nothing went to waste in the household of Israel Jennings.

Eight children had Israel Jennings in all, and countless grandchildren. Of his sons the most prosperous by far was Charles, whose thousand acres of prairie land hardly com-

pensated for a large family of girls who had to be married off
to someone. It was a rare opportunity for an ambitious
young man like Silas Bryan. Here were wealth, position,
political influence, and widespread family connections, all
in the person of Mariah Elizabeth Jennings, daughter of
Charles and granddaughter of old Israel and one of the pupils
in Silas Bryan's school. Not only that, but Mariah Elizabeth
Jennings even at seventeen possessed distinct qualities of her
own. There was in her little of that hard acquisitiveness of
the men of her family. She loved music and clung to the
richer emotional experiences of the worship of God according to the rite of John Wesley. Even when the preacher read
out the hymns two lines at a time, and the congregation sang
the two lines and then waited for the reading of the next two,
her emotional response to the sound of human voices blended
was not dissipated. She was tall, straight, upstanding—the
type of the mountain woman—with brown hair, gray eyes, a
large nose, high cheek bones, and the freshness of youth as
her chief attraction. What eagerness there was in the courtship of Silas Bryan and Mariah Elizabeth Jennings was hers.
He was cautious, conscious of his superior years and learning,
treated her as a child. But in him she saw the potential
great man, on that account distant and reserved, whose
handmaiden she would be glad to be.

For Silas Bryan the match was excellent from every
point of view. Old Israel Jennings was proud of his new
grandson—he saw not a pin's difference between their respective outlooks upon life. Nor indeed was there. The same
year he was married, with the backing of the Jennings family
and its connections, Silas Bryan was elected to the Illinois
State Senate, and he and his youthful bride moved to
Salem, the county seat. The Hon. Silas Bryan was thirty.
But he was well on his way.

Success had its price. The very year of the Lincoln-
Douglas debates, when Democracy rode triumphant for the
last time, the Hon. Silas Bryan in its train, he recorded in
the family Bible the deaths within a week of two of his
children:

Virginia and John both had whooping cough as the primary disease. Inflamation of the lungs set in with Virginia and inflamation of the bowels with John,

set down the meticulous mind. Then the heart spoke:

I make the above record this 10th day of February 1858 in great distress of mind about my beloved children not feeling that I can ever be reconciled to their loss or that the Lord will ever bless me hereafter with children that will give me so much satisfaction as these precious children. Thank God that I feel that I am their father still and that I will be with them soon.

They had died just at Christmas, almost two months before. But under the Hon. Silas Bryan's aloof, precise, stern mask of pride, the wound was still bleeding.

For the remainder of his days Christmas brought no joy to Silas Bryan.

CHAPTER III

EGYPT

THE year 1860 was election year, and by March 19th, the political pot was already boiling. The soured and lonely man in the White House was too old to succeed himself, even if he had wanted to. The field was open to favourite sons, and there was a plethora of them.

For four years the Hon. Stephen A. Douglas of Illinois had worked hard to be the Democratic nominee. There was, in fact, very little that he had not done to win the coveted prize, for the Democratic nomination in 1860 was equivalent to election. There was no other political party worthy the name. The old Whigs were as dead as Henry Clay, so long their leader. The Know Nothings had fallen into a somnolence from which they were not to be awakened for half a century. The newly launched Republican party had given no signs of formidable strength with Fremont as candidate. It was as plain as any political fact ever is that the next President of the United States would be chosen at the Democratic national convention at Charleston, South Carolina, a month later. Already the Northern newspapers complained that the Carolinians were preparing to gouge the delegates by charging $5 a day for room and board. Perhaps, had the hotel rates been less, the convention might not have adjourned when it did, and the Hon. Stephen A. Douglas might have been the candidate of a united Democracy and sixteenth President of the United States. By such slender threads hangs the fate of nations.

But on Monday, March 19, 1860, the Hon. Stephen A. Douglas was clearly worried. He scurried about the Senate chamber with a genial smile and a hearty hand grip, adroitly attempting to put out little sparks that kept flaming up

22

in that powder mill that was the Thirty-sixth Congress.
There was, for example, the Hon. Jefferson Davis of Mississippi pressing "a bill to sell arms to the States," from the
arsenals of a still united nation. What a thing to do, with
everyone so jumpy over a possible armed conflict between
the states! The Hon. Stephen A. Douglas and the Hon.
Jefferson Davis had precious little in common. Throughout
the Charleston convention to come the Hon. Jefferson
Davis was to receive precisely one vote, and no more, for
the Democratic nomination for President of the United
States, while the political fortunes of Senator Douglas rose
and fell and were lost forever.

Then there was that stubborn, hot-headed tailor, the Hon.
Andrew Johnson of Tennessee, who insisted on consideration
of the Homestead Bill; and in the House of Representatives,
Experience Estabrook, Delegate from the Territory of
Nebraska, presenting a bill to make Nebraska a state,
cleverly hidden away in whose more obscure clauses was a
provision to grant alternate sections of the public land to
financial interests in the East "for the construction of certain railroads therein." Everything that was going on in the
nation's capital that 19th of March, 1860, was a source of
anxiety to the Hon. Stephen A. Douglas of Illinois and
portentous to the future of the country.

But out in Illinois Mariah Elizabeth Bryan on that day
gave birth to her fourth and then only living male offspring.
Silas Bryan wanted to call the boy William after that
brother to whom Silas had first come West twenty years
previous, in Troy, Missouri. But the child's mother wanted
him named Jennings, for old Israel. As there were sound
practical reasons for that, he was called both.

A sturdy youngster, he sat on the floor of the tiny Salem
house whose joists the Hon. Silas Bryan had himself hewn,
and widened his mouth by sucking his fist, while Silas Bryan
made speeches for the Hon. Stephen A. Douglas. The reverberations of the bitterest campaign the country had yet
known were only so much bewildering noise to young William
Jennings Bryan; muddy-booted farmers coming and going

with a great clatter; a vast deal of loud talking that meant nothing; a strained air of stimulation that even a child could feel. Then, suddenly, in place of all this hubbub, ominous quiet, more awesome still; men whispering together in dark corners; men coming and going furtively; an electric atmosphere of suppressed excitement; and after a long time the rolling of drums, the thump of marching feet along the dusty road.

As the child grew older and began to put little things together in his mind it seemed strange that there were no able-bodied men about—a world of women and old men and children. Mostly of women. Women tortured by anxiety; dry eyed with grief; black robed and sullen in despair. A world in which boys and girls alike played all day at being soldiers, and old men sat in the sun on the horse blocks around the court-house square, garrulously reminiscent of other wars, their toothless mouths filled with queer-sounding words: Cerro-Gordo, Churubusco, Chapultepec.

The conflict between the states was not an event apart from the lives of those who dwelt in Egypt. It was their lives. War was on three sides of them, in Missouri and Kentucky. Above all it was in their hearts and minds, omnipresent. For the sympathy of the Bryans' neighbours was with the South. The war, according to "Black Jack" Logan, the Indian-blooded Congressman from Cairo,[1] was "a damned abolition crusade." He even raised an "Egyptian Corps" for the Confederate army and took it as far as Paducah himself,[2] before he decided suddenly to accept a commission as brigadier general in the Union army and do his personal fighting on the other side. Later General Logan became a worthy running mate to the Plumed Knight—the man who "snatched the mask of Democracy from the hideous face of rebellion." The story ran about the Court House of Salem that the Hon. John Martin, a sterling Democrat, would go into the brick safe in his office and hallo for Jefferson Davis to his soul's content and then come out and become bustling and assiduous in support of the Union. He, also, received a brigade in the Union army.

There were many who wanted to join Egypt to the South and made no bones about it.[3] Resolutions were openly adopted declaring that:

the interest of citizens of Southern Illinois imperatively demand at their hands a division of the State. We hereby pledge ourselves to use all means in our power to effect the same, and attach ourselves to the Southern Confederacy.[4]

Some political genius on another occasion moved to

seize the money in the hands of the Sheriff to defray the expenses of arming and equipping soldiers for the Southern army.[5]

But while many a soldier for the Southern army was armed and equipped in Egypt, it was not habitually done out of the public funds.

So far as the Bryans' own Marion County was concerned, the rolls of its men serving in the Union forces are copiously sprinkled with the laconic notation: *Deserted*. One whole regiment recruited in Egypt had to be arrested, disarmed, and placed under guard. When the draft was finally resorted to there were riots in southern Illinois that made those of New York pacific demonstrations by contrast.[6] The Federal authorities found it difficult to make men fight for what they did not believe.

They did their sanguinary best, however. "Every Democrat who did not openly and actively support the Administration and the war was labelled a venomous 'copperhead,' at once a Southern sympathizer and a traitor to the Union."[7] As the copperhead is a particularly poisonous snake indigenous to southern Illinois the meaning was clear. It was by no means easy walking for Silas Bryan and his fellow Democrats of Egypt. All sorts of dignitaries of the party of Andrew Jackson—including even judges and former state senators, like the Hon. Silas Bryan himself—were arrested wholesale, held without trial for months, only to be released just as arbitrarily, without exoneration. Less prominent Democrats were simply taken out and flogged by bands of "Union Regulators,"[8] or warned to leave the country.[9] As for the guarantees of the Bill of Rights they were laughed at.[10] General Burnside's whiskers earned him no more enduring fame than his action in suspending the publication of two Democratic newspapers* by military order. It took all Abe Lincoln's tact to still the storm that swept his state over the affair. Poor old Abe was no longer a hero among his own people.[11] One gathers that the people who had made Abe Lincoln what he was took little pride in the job.

The Democrats of Egypt were bitter, but they were not supine. Brutality was a game two could play at. The Knights of the Golden Circle, an organization with many of the features if not quite the earning power of the Ku Klux Klan of half a century later, reached into every county of southern Illinois. It did what it could not only to resist the swift trend to centralization which the Republican party was hatching in the incubator of war, but to pay off a few political and personal grudges into the bargain.

Union men were seized and whipped and sometimes driven from their homes; in numerous instances they were shot down, even in their own homes, by rebel sympathizers.[12]

War, in short, was hell long before Gen. Sherman discovered it.

The Hon. Silas Bryan, however, had a canny sense of what was impending. He had served eight years in the Senate of the Illinois General Assembly, and it was time to move up a rung in the political ladder, anyhow. A seat on the circuit bench was not only more profitable but a vast deal safer in war time than one in the legislative chambers at Springfield, or Washington, either. Not that either was any too secure for a Democrat as the war progressed. Once the Hon. Silas Bryan was driving along a lonely country road when a boy in a field warned him that a band of Union Regulators was just ahead, attending to the case of an obstinate Democratic farmer. The Hon. Silas Bryan was well known, and the outlook was far from reassuring. He reined in Mike, the old

---

*The Chicago *Times* and the Jonesboro *Gazette*.

white horse, stepped stiffly out of his buggy, placed his tall
silk hat on the ground, and knelt by the roadside in prayer.
God heard him.

It was about the time that William Jennings Bryan was a
year old that the Hon. Silas Bryan became Judge Bryan of
the second judicial circuit including the whole northern end
of Egypt. It was not that he retired from active politics or
in any sense abandoned the principles of Andrew Jackson,
which he regarded as at once the sole guide to political health
for the distracted country and the sole road to the political
preferment of the Hon. Silas Bryan. In this respect he
differed from such impudent opportunists as General John A.
Logan and General John Martin. But Silas Bryan knew a
storm when he saw one, and the war between the states was
a storm a prudent mariner would do well to ride out under
bare sticks.

True, the midwar elections of 1862 were encouraging to
the Democrats of Illinois. They gained a sweeping victory,[13]
and throughout the land those high in authority looked
upon the amazing career of the rail splitter in the White
House as ended. In the House of the Illinois General Assembly a resolution pronounced the war a failure and called
for an armistice between North and South to discuss terms
of peace.[14] In the end the Governor had to prorogue the
Legislature to choke off heaven only knew what treasonable
action by the President's own state. Judge Bryan rubbed his
hands with satisfaction. In June, 1863, with the military
outlook at its blackest, forty thousand Democrats, Judge
Bryan among them, assembled in the state capital and
declared the "further offensive prosecution of this war
tends to subvert the constitution and the government, and
entail upon this nation all the disastrous consequences of
misrule and anarchy."[15] Their idea was that such disastrous
consequences to this nation could be conjured by making it
into two nations.

All of these developments were not simply vague unco-
ordinated happenings passing over the head of a child too
young to grasp their significance. Elsewhere in the country

they might have proved no more. But the bitternesses
aroused in Egypt by war on the very doorsills of the inhabitants persisted long after the events themselves had
passed into history. They were what men, and women too,
talked about as young William Jennings Bryan grew up.
They constituted the sombre background of his childhood
and youth.

As the war between the states drew to a close and William
Jennings Bryan came gradually to a certain consciousness of
what was going on, the savagery all about him became intensified. Guerrilla warfare was open and merciless.[16] Bands
of "Butternuts" raided Egypt from Missouri; bands of
Union Vigilantes retaliated upon local Democrats with buck-
ets of hot tar and a ripped feather bed, with blacksnake
whips, or more handily with a bight of hempen rope flung
over a low-hanging bough. Thousands of terrified Negroes
from the invaded states flooded Egypt, overrunning the
country, homeless, pathetic, unwanted. On their heels came
the returning soldiers, swaggering, drunken, barbarous, possessed by a lust for all the good things of life they had been
deprived of so long—comfort, food, women, power. Driven
like a wedge into the South, where the great open highways
of the Ohio and Mississippi rivers met, Egypt caught it all.
The backwash of war. The sinister underside of killing men
wholesale. Poverty. Misery. Disease. Maimed and crippled
men. Wretchedness. Cruelty. Want. And, above all, the
minds of men brutalized and disordinate, loosed from the
secure moorings of custom and habit.

It was in the midst of such things as these that the childhood years of William Jennings Bryan were passed—the
swiftly hardening mould in which the man is cast. Even
after the war was over and the men folk had straggled home
to fill the court-house square again every Saturday, William
Jennings Bryan's world still remained a world of women.
For with the advent of two more children during the war the
little house in town grew too small for Judge Bryan's growing family. The time had come, if ever, for the long-dreamed-
of country place. So Judge Bryan bought him 488 acres a

mile from town, and built the long-dreamed mansion—a
prison-like structure of brick—and set off fourteen wooded
acres for the long-dreamed deer park.

It had its disadvantages. The children were more or less
isolated, cut off from the common play of town youngsters.
Also, there was no little work connected with the pretentious
new house and the sheep and the horses and the cows and
their calves and the chickens—not to speak of the deer.
Everyone had to do his share of it, and that kept the children
from running about the neighbourhood. They could not go to
school in town, either. It was too far. So it was Mariah
Elizabeth Bryan who did the teaching as well as the housework, the churning, the putting up of preserves and the
general chores about house and garden, and the childbearing
to boot. The Judge's circuit comprised five counties, and he
was away a great deal more than he was at home. Those who
enclosed the childhood and boyhood of William Jennings
Bryan within their circle were almost exclusively women,
and what is perhaps equally significant, women older than he.

There was his mother—"a woman of many praiseworthy
traits" among which frugality ranked highest and an iron
hand in the discipline of the children only slightly lower. "A
remarkably strong-minded, clear-headed Christian woman,"
said the neighbours. There was little of softness about Mariah
Elizabeth Bryan. There was Aunt Jane Cheney, Silas Bryan's
oldest sister, one of those who had gone West—to Gallipolis,
Ohio—when Silas was a boy, back in Virginia. She was "the
idolized aunt around whom all the nieces and nephews clus-
tered, who regarded her as an elderly saint." With her spruce
black silk dress with a white collar and a black cape, her
hair parted primly in the middle above a round face, a comb
standing high at the back, Auntie was the sort of person of
whom everyone said: "She was never heard to utter an un-
kind word against any of God's creations."[17]

Closer to Willy Bryan, there was Mollie Smith, the orphaned daughter of Silas Bryan's sister Martha, who had
gone to Gallipolis, too, in the old days, and died there. Silas
Bryan adopted Mollie; she lived with the Bryans, doing all

the lighter housework, helping with the children, even taking a spell at teaching them when Mariah Elizabeth was too busy with more urgent matters[18]—which was often. Little blue-eyed, roly-poly Mollie Smith with her round face and her blonde ringlets and that short upper lip, which makes so much for prettiness if not for beauty, she was just as much older than Willy Bryan as Silas Bryan was older than his wife. So the difference in their ages did not seem so great to either of them. Which was important.

And finally there was Willy Bryan's older sister—so daring, so popular, so handsome, so much the leader among all the Salem youngsters. Willy adored her. He slept in the trundle bed with her—the trundle bed that during the day was hidden under the magnificent canopied walnut bedstead of Judge and Mariah Elizabeth Bryan. Old Judge Bryan was dyspeptic and addicted to a nap after midday dinner. It was Fannie who conceived the idea of pasting paper on his bald head to keep the flies off. It was Fannie who taught Willy to crawl along the baseboard of the fence of the Salem house, out of range of their mother's eagle eye, to run off from lessons to play with the town children. It was Fannie, the tomboy, who led in all the mischief and all the games and who attracted to the Bryan place what boys came there. There was something in Fannie that William Jennings Bryan lacked and in his secret heart reached out for and grasped, vicariously, through her. She knew what she wanted. She was sure of herself.

Thirty years later, when William Jennings Bryan had swept the Chicago convention off its feet with his golden voice, it was to Fannie he came in his triumph. Straight to Salem, to Fannie.

"My parents were quite strict with me," said William Jennings Bryan, years later, "and I sometimes considered the boys more fortunate who were given more liberty."[19] There is a poignant wistfulness in this admission by one who took the Fifth Commandment as seriously as did William Jennings Bryan. It would have been of little use, however, to deny the stern discipline and severe economy that ruled in the Hon. Silas Bryan's country seat with its deer park. Everybody knew it. "Judge Bryan was pretty strict," said Willy's playmate, Judd Green. "I guess he brought up his boys under closer rules than most of our fathers did."

He did indeed. Silas Bryan had had none too easy a time of it in his own early years. It never occurred to him that his children were not fully as accountable to the mandates of an austere God as he. The Book of Proverbs was his favourite out of all the Bible.[20] "Foolishness is bound in the heart of a child; but the rod of correction shall drive it from him." So Silas Bryan believed; and, as he believed, he did. When Judge Bryan came home from holding court in distant counties he brought his offspring catechisms as presents. And they had to be learned by heart, those catechisms. Judge Bryan himself attended to that in person, on Sundays.

Silas Bryan moulded Mariah Elizabeth Jennings in his own image. It was a gradual process, but none the less complete. She was tall and gaunt, as he was, with a large nose, brown hair brushed severely straight, cold gray eyes, and a strong jaw. The youthful freshness, her chief attraction ten years before, when Silas Bryan married her, soon went. Women did not long remain young in that day or those surroundings, and life was not easy on Mariah Elizabeth Bryan. In return, she was not of a stock to take life easily, either. Old Israel Jennings was a shrewd, hard, successful man, and her father was another. Life itself was hard in that slattern county-seat town with its thousand inhabitants, its hogs running loose in the muddy streets, and its wooden sidewalks always out of repair. Only in the high emotionalism of religious service, with its annual revivals, did Mariah Elizabeth Bryan ever know release from the drudgery of unending toil and the drabness of unchanging days.

To this one sure comfort Mariah Elizabeth Bryan clung with pathetic tenacity. Judge Bryan was a pillar of the Baptist church in Salem, "a most devout man," said his neighbours, "and a truly God-fearing Christian." He was no bigot, however. One could, after all, fear God under almost any auspices. But Mariah Elizabeth Bryan was of other stuff, and younger, besides. She could not face life on any such plane as foreordination and the remainder of the unyielding Calvinist creed implied. It was too barren for the teeming emotionalism of a young woman married to an older man.

So for twenty years, while Silas Bryan attended the Baptist church with exemplary regularity, his wife went to the Methodist church—and little William Jennings to the Sunday schools of both.[21] As Mariah Elizabeth Bryan approached forty the wellsprings of sentiment in her dried up. Quietly one day she joined her husband's church. The flame had guttered out.

To Mariah Elizabeth Bryan religion brought a certain serenity among so many cares and responsibilities, a placidity, or at least a sureness of herself. "Mother did not have the educational advantages Father had secured," wrote her distinguished son.[22] Nevertheless, she absorbed Silas Bryan's confidence in education as the means to all ends. Just what education might consist of she was no more certain in her own mind than anyone else in the Middle West of her day. It was, as she conceived it, the inculcation regardless of consequences of a given number of lessons laid down in schoolbooks. Thought was bewildering and led to unnecessary embarrassment in answering questions not in the book. One took the word of William Holmes McGuffey for the authentic character of his selections, from the story of George Washington and the cherry tree to the startling pronouncement that *killing people* did not make Alexander a truly great man. It was not so much literature William Jennings Bryan learned from his mother's teaching, as life. And the life he learned was a static affair of irrefrangible rules and an undeviating trajectory. No subsequent experience ever quite succeeded in impressing upon the mind of William Jennings Bryan a different view of the course of man.

But if William Jennings Bryan's mother was the voice of Authority to him, she was also something else. In those fearsome childhood days when war and alarms and rumours of night riders and the Ku Klux Klan and momentous social and moral upheavals filled the world without with nameless

terrors, the flame of emotionalism still burned fitfully in
Mariah Elizabeth Bryan. She found time, even with all her
work, to play the piano a little and to sing a great deal—
hymns, for the most part, with their heart-swelling, releasing
fervour, and such war-time ballads as "Farewell, Mother,
you may never press me to your heart again." Little Willy
Bryan would stand by the piano listening, big eyed. All his
life these songs ran through his head.[23] Their sentimentality
coloured his whole existence. Somehow or other, broken toys
could be mended and agonies obliterated by an emotional
miracle. So the Methodists taught. So Mariah Elizabeth
Bryan believed. And so little William Jennings Bryan came
to believe, too.

It was his earliest and his most enduring equipment for
the battle of life.

CHAPTER IV

SALEM

BILLY BRYAN sat on the worn, tobacco-stained steps that led up to the bench where Judge Silas Bryan dispensed justice in Salem Court House. No one paid any attention to the round-faced, black-haired rather oversized boy, and he had no eyes for anyone but his father. When the clerk called the Court to order, Judge Bryan bent his head to the wooden table before him, dropped one knee to the dusty floor, and prayed aloud.* Sometimes, when Court ran past noon, Judge Bryan would bow his head again, half kneel, and pray once more—this time silently, carrying out his vow of twenty years ago. And whenever some peculiarly knotty point of law came before Judge Bryan it was his habit to step into the dingy little room behind the bench and pray for light. Unfortunately either the Lord was imperfectly versed in the intricacies of Illinois law or the higher courts were godless bodies, for Judge Bryan's decisions were frequently overturned on appeal. A Peoria lawyer once twitted him on it.

"I see, Judge, that the Supreme Court has reversed the Lord in six cases," he laughed. "What have you got to say about it? I thought you always decided your cases under divine direction."

Judge Bryan looked the man over from head to foot with quiet dignity.

---

*In his *Memoirs* William Jennings Bryan denies that his father habitually opened Court with prayer, a fact which is of itself interesting. There is overwhelming evidence, however, that this was Judge Bryan's practice. It should be here stated that William Jennings Bryan's *Memoirs* were not written by him but were hastily compiled and never revised by Mr. Bryan before his death. Data obtained by writers on Mr. Bryan from his *Memoirs* alone, without other corroboration, cannot be depended upon.

"The Supreme Court, sir, is wrong," he said. And he turned on his heel and walked away.

He was immensely proud, was Silas Bryan, tall and lean, almost a giant in the high silk hat in which he kept his mail, his bandanna handkerchief, and notes of little purchases to make at the general store. He liked to refer to his grandfather as "a man of excellent parts, an influential citizen, who ranked with the successful planters and representative men" of Virginia. It was a great trial to the Hon. Silas Bryan that he did not know his grandmother's name. As for the Lillards, his mother's people, the Hon. Silas was fond of recounting how they were an "old American family of English origin," and his mother herself, he said proudly, "a remarkable woman, abundant in resources." He was nine when she died, and he recalled, in fact, little of her. The humble, crowded, double log cabin of his barren childhood was transformed by the magic of success, in prevalent American fashion, into "a large tract of land"—what one might call, if one were so inclined, an ancestral estate. Of himself Judge Bryan was content to hear that he brought "to the bench the ability, erudition and dignity characteristic of the learned and accomplished jurist."

And when the Fourth of July rolled around, the mellifluous voice of the Hon. Silas Bryan was heard in the land declaiming the principles of the Declaration of Independence in polished and resounding periods of the old school, while Willy Bryan, on the outskirts of the crowd about the speakers' stand, listened, his heart swollen with pride, poking the dust with his bare toes.

To Willy Bryan, observing and pondering, the auspicious career of his distinguished father became a model of achievement. There was in it a sort of predestination of greatness for the boy. "Ancestry counts," wrote William Jennings Bryan sententiously in later years. It did with him. He never questioned his father's eminence, nor is there any evidence that the Hon. Silas Bryan had any doubts on the subject, either. In another less unstable period, under other and less swiftly shifting social, political, and economic conditions, Judge Bryan might in fact have turned out to be as conspicuous a political figure as he conceived himself. Certainly he was no less able than scores of others in the Middle West he so perfectly impersonated. It was the war and its prodigious consequences that played the mischief with Silas Bryan, as with many another potential statesman in that day of rapid and bewildering readjustments.

For the war between the states had proved to be in very truth the revolution Alexander Stephens called it. Nothing was the same after Appomattox. Even slavery was transmuted, not destroyed, as that farsighted Carolinian, James H. Hammond, predicted:

The man who lives by daily labor and scarcely lives at that, and who has to put out his labor in the market and take the best he can get for it; in short, your white class of manual laborers and operatives, as you call them, are slaves [he said]. Your slaves are white, of your own race; you are brothers of one blood. They are your equals in natural endowment of intellect, and they feel galled by their degradation. If they knew the tremendous secret, that the ballot-box is stronger than an army with bayonets, and could combine, where would you be? Your society would be reconstructed, your government reconstructed, your property divided, not as they have mistakenly attempted to initiate such proceedings, by meeting in parks, with arms in their hands, but by the quiet process of the ballot-box.[1]

In his own groping way, Silas Bryan, too, grasped something of this and passed on to his son a passionate faith in the divine right of the people—"the laboring and toiling millions,"[2] he called them—to decide anything whatsoever. It was he who, in the Illinois Constitutional Convention, moved "that all officers to be provided for by the new Constitution, in the executive, legislative and judicial departments, shall be elected by the people."[3] With eyes turned backward, the Hon. Silas Bryan was still voting for Andrew Jackson.

"Too much government in republics is the rock upon which they founder," he thundered,[4] in the Constitutional Convention.

Many of our people have been . . . taught to look to government to educate their children, instead of doing it themselves. They have trusted to government to build their railroads, canals, eleemosynary institutions, instead of permitting capital in the hands of the citizens to seek its own investment and the lame and the halt to share the spontaneous benevolence of their fellow men.

In the view of Silas Bryan, the fierce individualism of the early pioneers was the way of salvation, and there was no other. The whole idea of state-built roads, harbours, ports, railroads, or anything else was, "an exploded policy," he said, "dead in both State and National politics."[5]

In the confusing emergence of so many new factors in the political and social life of the country the Hon. Silas Bryan inclined to lean more and more heavily upon the Lord as his shepherd. He presented the Constitutional Convention with a petition from the citizens of Marion County praying that the Legislature of Illinois be forever forbidden, by the Constitution of the state, from permitting the Bible to be removed from the public schools,[6] and he fought valiantly —and successfully—to have the prayers offered at the opening of each day's session printed in full in the report of Proceedings.[7] The very mention of woman suffrage sent cold chills down the Hon. Silas Bryan's spine. As for the rights of married women:

That interest, sir [he said], has passed along for six thousand years without any other constitutional provision than what is to be found in the hearts and admiration of their husbands.[8]

If Silas Bryan had his way, married women would remain the property of their husbands for another six thousand years. He declared:

There is a power behind the throne in this country that will vindicate the white race [he declared]. The people will finally decide that our government is for the white race.[9]

Representing "a county in which there are more miles of the Illinois Central road than any other county of the State," he pronounced the people of Illinois "opposed to the State engaging in public improvements." Government in general, he maintained, and the government of the United States in particular, had its roots in "the influence of the Christian system."[10] And according to the Hon. Silas Bryan, the Christian system was every man for himself and the devil take the hindmost.

The Illinois Constitutional Convention of 1869 was the high-water mark of Silas Bryan's career. In the pages of its proceedings he wrote his autobiography and his political epitaph alike. The war between the states had been, as he saw it, the triumph of the common people over those aristocrats upon whose great plantations he had looked down with envy as a boy, a triumph ordained by the will of God through the influence of the Christian system. The voice of the people was the voice of God, and an elected official a chosen vessel.

It was in the atmosphere of such political concepts as these that William Jennings Bryan passed his tenth birthday and set out—in tow of Fannie—to attend school at "the Old College," a semi-private school in Salem, that had failed as a female seminary.

"Well, little man," said the teacher, looking the new pupil over. "What do you mean to be when you grow up?"

"President of the United States," gravely replied Billy Bryan.[11]

And perhaps he did.

The circle of female influence that ringed William Jennings Bryan about throughout his childhood was rather enlarged than broken by his going to school. Whenever he had to speak a piece on Friday afternoon—some lugubrious selection from McGuffey, with a conspicuous moral—it was sentimental little Mollie Smith who trained and encouraged him.[12] Long ago, when he was very little, she had taught him to say:

> God is great and God is good
> And we thank Him for this food.
> By His hand must all be fed—
> Give us, Lord, our daily bread!

Mary Baird Bryan

The Hon. Silas Bryan

Aunt Mollie

Bryan's Sister Fanny

Even after she married the father of one of Billy Bryan's boyhood playmates, she still cajoled him and spoiled him with the worship of a lonely girl who was love hungry. To William Jennings Bryan, Mollie Smith was a more approachable mother—nearer his own age, less harassed by the cares of a large family. All his life he remained devoted to this emotional girl cousin within the penumbra of whose tenderness he had grown up. And when William Jennings Bryan, at the summit of his fame and power, dispensed the offices in the gift of the President of the United States, he made Mollie Smith postmistress of Salem.

It was Mollie Smith, too, who brought the first romance into young Billy Bryan's life. Mollie's bosom friend was Hester Williams, younger than she, the passionate, full-blooded, strikingly handsome daughter of the Campbellite preacher. The two girls would take Billy buggy riding behind old Ben, Billy sitting on the little folding seat backed by the dashboard, close between two pairs of robust legs, brushed by their skirts, stirred by the pleasant warmth of their bodies. He could look up at the high colour of Hester's dark cheeks, at her glowing eyes. She was the woman he was going to marry when he grew up.[13] He knew that. Unfortunately Hester could not wait. That vibrant life-evoking and life-giving quality in her that so troubled young Bryan had to be satisfied. She married the sheriff.

With school came still another woman, but of a very different sort—Mary Putnam Reed Lemon, a mountainous person, so dark that she was reputed to be of Indian blood, like "Black Jack" Logan. A wheel horse of education in Marion County whose motto had always been "Spare the rod and spoil the child," and whose boast that no child entrusted to her care had ever been spoiled. To her the mark of culture was the broad "a," and when she said "Bahptist" and the boys mocked her she laid about her with a heavy hand.

Mrs. Ben Lemon was not without her aura of romance. Her daughter had married a Pole, namesake and descendant of that John Sobieski who distinguished himself by fighting against his own country, then becoming its king, and who finally attained immortality by halting the advance of the infidels under the very walls of Vienna. An enthralling, semi-legendary figure to the lads of Salem was Mrs. Lemon's son-in-law, claimant to the Polish throne. Billy Bryan's mind faltered at the thought of Mrs. Lemon's gigantic figure, willow switch changed to knout, meting out punishments in the royal palace at Cracow.

She had her own claim to glory, however. In the days when Abolitionists were hardly safe in Egypt, she had been uncompromising on slavery and, after the war, militant against the exclusion of Negro children from public schools. She was as positive now on the perils to the younger generation of the wave of licence sweeping the country in the wake of war. She prayed over her charges and exhorted them to report in one another any leanings toward that loose deportment which she proclaimed to be the budding of sin.

Of Billy Bryan she made an ardent convert. One day in class his hand shot up. Mrs. Lemon's eyes gleamed in anticipatory triumph.

"Well, Billy, what have you noticed?"

"Maria Wolff's got her legs crossed," he reported breathlessly.

If Maria Wolff was a brand to be saved from the burning, William Jennings Bryan saved her.[14]

One other woman completed the female circle that enclosed the childhood of the Hon. Silas Bryan's eldest son: Mrs. A. V. Beville, his Sabbath-school teacher. "He is still to me one of my boys," she declared long afterward, when fame had come to her pupil. And she proudly related how once when she was ill he had come to see her, "asking in a deep voice, 'Are you better?' The simple question was very characteristic of him," she added. A romantic soul was Mrs. Beville, who also recounted how young William Jennings Bryan as a mere boy had set his heart upon going to Oxford. There appears to be no corroborative evidence of this exotic ambition.

Mrs. Beville, too, was "a woman of strong Christian

character."[15] They all were, those women who hemmed young Bryan in. Even blithe, irresponsible little Mollie Smith became at last county president of the White Ribbon Army and an indefatigable church worker.[16] It was the one social outlet for the women of the small towns and the country districts that, together, made up the vast empire between the Alleghenies and the Pacific, the Great Lakes and the Gulf, as the last quarter of the Nineteenth Century opened. Even reading was hardly a female accomplishment in that part of the world. For one thing, the women were too occupied with childbearing and housework, and had they not been there was nothing to read but the Bible. Five thousand agents of the American Bible Society[17] visited every house in Illinois, Bible in hand; the state stood second or third in the Union in "the Bible cause."[18] No other book—not even Henry Ward Beecher's sermons—was peddled with anything like this assiduity. To be brought up among women, as William Jennings Bryan was, meant to have one's cultural outlook bounded on one side by the Book of Genesis and on the other by the Revelation of St. John the Divine. The Bible was the exclusive source of all human knowledge, past and to come.

With men it was otherwise. They also went to church, but there were few like Billy Byran's Uncle Russ, who tended the stock scales beside the railroad track for thirty years and was never on a train in his life. And proud of it. The men for the most part read a weekly newspaper, went to auctions and cattle sales, drove to town on Saturdays, and occasionally attended court. Many of the more enlightened even belonged to the Grange, where economic and political questions were discussed. Above all there was politics. Where two or three were gathered together there was politics in their midst. They stood about the court-house square, boots bespattered with mud, whips safely in hand [whips cost money and were easy to steal], Adam's apple moving up and down as they chewed tobacco, faces bronzed and sparsely bewhiskered, hands gnarled and hairy, clothing painstakingly mended, and discussed in drawling voices the corruption of the Grant Administration—the "epoch of gift enterprises,"[19] as Charles Sumner called it.

As William Jennings Bryan, with infinite pains, began to push his way free of the imprisoning circle of women that had developed his boyhood it was into the field of politics that he emerged. He never entered another. These two domains marked the frontiers of his life, as they might also have delimited the lives of many another born at that period —Theodore Roosevelt, Nicholas Murray Butler, Charles Evans Hughes, Clarence Darrow. There was this difference, however. These others had access to so much of the accumulated wisdom of the centuries as was generally available in that day. William Jennings Bryan had not. It was not entirely his fault. It was a circumstance inherent in the America of which he was the perfect product, the America of the Middle West, where sentimentality took the place of knowledge and evangelism was the motive force of action.

William Jennings Bryan was twelve when his father stood at last on the top rung of the ladder of his ambition. After twenty-one years of unbroken office holding as a pillar of the Democratic party, the Hon. Silas Bryan received the coveted nomination for Congress in a district so overwhelmingly Democratic that defeat was unthinkable. To make assurance of victory doubly sure, he was also endorsed by the Greenback party. Nothing but genius in ineptitude could lose him a seat in Congress.

Yet he lost it, and to that renegade Democrat, General John Martin, to boot.

His father's campaign was William Jennings Bryan's first direct contact with politics. He went to all the meetings he could, saw his father on the platform, the focus of all eyes, listened to the interminable flowery speeches, drank in the applause. There is a legend that at a rally at Centralia little Billy Bryan took part in his father's campaign:

His little body became a perfect volcano of enthusiasm. Finally he mounted the platform and began to talk. Many laughed outright at the idea and all smiled. He was undaunted, however. He did not appear to see his auditors nor to hear their laughing remarks at the

start. As he proceeded the laughter ceased. In forcible and eloquent
language, with the energy and diction of the born orator, he pursued his argument. . . . The audience became quiet and attentive,
then wildly enthusiastic. Cheer upon cheer rent the air. . . . When
he closed there was a tumult of applause and he was carried from
the platform and about the town on the shoulders of the cheering
men.[20]

The tale is apocryphal. But when it appeared William Jennings Bryan pasted it in his scrapbook, nevertheless.

That his father should not be elected was inconceivable to
young Bryan. It was inconceivable to the Democrats of the
district too, and when Silas Bryan managed to achieve defeat his political career ended forever then and there. The
Democratic party had no seats in Congress to throw away.

For the Hon. Silas Bryan, the campaign of 1872 was that
day of reckoning that comes to every man, sooner or later.
It caught him between the two major forces of his life, ambition and acquisitiveness. The campaign assessment was the
modest sum of $500, but to Silas Bryan $500 was $500, and
there was nothing modest about it. He tried to convince himself that the election was a certainty, anyhow, that he
could have his cake and eat it too. The Democrats of the district spat tobacco juice through their teeth and said bitterly
that Judge Bryan was too "nigh" to part with the money
necessary to elect him.

They wronged him. All his life Silas Bryan had fought
political corruption. What he loathed in the Grant régime
was its shocking, its colossal, venality. He could not conform
to it. There was no compromise in the man. When the
crucial moment came he refused to put up a cent, and General
John Martin, who ten years before had been halooing for Jeff
Davis, was elected by 240 votes.

It was a lesson in practical politics that William Jennings
Bryan never forgot.

CHAPTER V

ESCAPE

FOR forty-five years William Jennings Bryan was constantly making speeches and in the course of them reaching for illustrations from the stock of goods on the shelves of his mind. Rarely did his hand meet an incident of his boyhood. He recalls hunting rabbits with Henry Webster, Mollie Smith's stepson. But he did very little of that. He remembers almost nothing of his school days, not even the formidable Mrs. Lemon's name. By a curiously Freudian metamorphosis he calls her Mrs. Lamb. He dwells with a certain unction upon the joys of attending Sabbath school twice every Sunday.[1] But what particularly sticks in his mind is the hard labour incident to the farmer's care-free life.

I can see myself engaged in this drudgery, my nose running, my fingers numb, and possessing feelings for which the Sunday-school songs I knew did not furnish fitting expression,[2]

he says

Of what went on in the great world outside the confines of Egypt, Billy Bryan seems to have known nothing. He was eleven when the Chicago fire took place, and President Grant had the effrontery to send Federal troops into the sovereign state of Illinois, uninvited. He was fourteen when the Beecher-Tilton scandal shook the homes of the godly to their foundations, throughout the land. Neither catastrophe touched William Jennings Bryan. Even the licking he got when the teacher discovered W J B neatly cut with a jackknife in a brand-new desk left no impression of which he ever spoke.

The boys and girls of the neighbourhood went bobsledding

44

down the hill on which the Bryan house stood. It seemed a very lofty eminence to Billy Bryan then. But in later years

I wondered how the hill could have seemed so high [he said]. Perhaps it was due to the magnifying power of time, for all the hills in the neighborhood have shrunk, and the streams that seemed deep appear shallow.

Phenomena like what he called "the magnifying power of time" puzzled William Jennings Bryan all his life. They seemed to him to partake of the miraculous.

Billy Bryan played town ball with the other boys, but Boston Ring was his best game. He played for keeps and amassed with keen zest a great store of marbles. He liked accumulating things. He went on hay rides with the girls, where his sister Fannie was the life of the party. But Billy Bryan, when all is said and done, was never deeply interested in girls. He had been so much among women all his early life that he came to be in a sense immune to the allure of sex through familiarity—like a gynæcologist or a priest. In a day, too, when a good fist fight was as much a mark of the male as pants, Billy Bryan would not fight. Not that he was a sissy, or afraid, either. He was strong enough to thrash much older boys. But he could see no more sense in fighting than a woman could. He could not feel that it proved anything. Also, he disliked swearing.[3] The grossness and the meaninglessness of it shocked and irritated him as it would a woman of that age. His closest friend among boys was Jackie Chance, who was intensely religious and passionately devoted to music. When Billy Bryan had bolted his mother's frugal breakfast he would rush over to the Chances' and consume a huge plate of buckwheat cakes to top off with. He had the appetite of a sultana. And on precious Saturday afternoons when he might have stolen away to go swimming, or hooked a watermelon and eaten it all warm and succulent just out of the sun, Billy Bryan met with half a dozen other lads in a vacant storeroom to debate. They made believe they were the Senate of the United States.

William Jennings Bryan was the Senator from Illinois.

As Billy Bryan passed puberty and swung into the troubled waters of adolescence he found himself in an adolescent world. America issued from the war between the states an entity. The hold-overs from the Old World in social, political, and intellectual outlook became atrophied during the isolation of the conflict. The nation emerged uncertain, crude, bewildered by conflicting influences, shoved now this way, now that, by warring interests, unable to take stock of itself yet driving ahead with terrific velocity. Or was it backward?

In this period of flux men were freer to exercise what native capacity they possessed and what equipment life brought them. Some rode the wave of opportunity with appalling adroitness and success—James G. Blaine, Collis P. Huntington, Marshall Field, P. T. Barnum, J. P. Morgan, Mark Twain, Cyrus McCormick, T. DeWitt Talmage, John D. Rockefeller, John L. Sullivan, August Belmont, Dwight L. Moody, and countless more. Others there were, however, to whom the ancient process of trial and error, the painstaking accumulation of data from which to construct a clear-headed philosophy of life, was still the sound way of progress. Which course any American lad in the 'seventies was to follow depended less upon anything within himself than upon where he was born and the people among whom he lived.

William Jennings Bryan enjoyed no such opportunities for observation and judgment as fell to the lot of Theodore Roosevelt, for example, or Woodrow Wilson. In Salem, Marion County, Illinois, it was the custom to equip a young man with a set of formulæ drawn from the Book of Proverbs and McGuffey's Readers and turn him loose in the world to do or die. There was no problem, he was taught, that could not be solved by Divine Providence or political action. Preferably both. It was inevitable, therefore, that when his father's defeat proved politics a broken reed young William Jennings Bryan should turn to religion. There was nowhere else to turn.

He had started out in life with the ambition to be a preacher—the guests at Silas Bryan's house accorded the greatest deference were preachers. But when Billy Bryan witnessed his first baptism by immersion he changed his mind. The disappearance under the water of the candidate for celestial honours and the highly emotional singing and groans and cries of "Glory!" from the onlookers frightened him.

"If I am a Baptist preacher will I have to do that?" he asked, wide eyed.

He was assured he would. From that moment forward the faith of his fathers lost its allure for William Jennings Bryan. Nevertheless, he could not altogether escape. The golden age of corruption of Grant and "Smiler" Colfax, of Belknap and Babcock and Jim Fisk, of Crédit Mobilier and corners in gold, of speculations in Erie and "Whisky Rings," and shameless plundering of the public treasury, had their reaction in the panic of 1873. And with the panic came a tremendous revival of religion in Illinois.[4] Others besides the boy Bryan turned to God when confronted by practical difficulties they could not understand or do anything about.

A sharp tightening of moral lines suddenly supplanted post-war depravity, or seemed to. The Methodists formally inveighed against the growing fondness for social and public amusements. "The theatre, the circus, the ballroom, or the wine-party," they declared, "confessedly lead to spiritual death."[5] Sunday newspapers and Sunday trains were snares of Satan. Bands of women invaded saloons to pray and sing hymns. They even purchased the barkeeper's entire hellish stock and destroyed it publicly in the streets until the gutters ran beer and whisky,[6] while boys of Billy Bryan's age stood around and jeered—or cheered. That summer Judd Green and Billy Bryan were water boys for the harvesters on Judge Bryan's estate—and in those days harvest hands were furnished whisky as well as water. But Billy Bryan would not carry the whisky jugs to the men in the fields. It was wrong he felt. So the two boys arranged a division of labour. Billy carried the water and Judd the whisky, and they went their rounds together.[7]

It was that same year that the tide of religious revival reached Salem. Every church felt it, but none more than the

Cumberland Presbyterians. For it was on the rock of re-
vivalism that the Cumberland group had split from the
older Presbyterians after "that great divine visitation" in
the Cumberland country of Kentucky and Tennessee in
1800.[8] They were strict, of course:

No visiting, pleasure-riding, cooking, strolling through the
woods, no whistling, no travelling, except to church, no conversation, or reading, except on religious subjects, was tolerated.[9]

Yet where doctrine, not conduct, was involved, the Cumberland Presbyterians leaned to relative modernism. Christ
died, they held, to save all mankind, not a select few; infants
were not, by the mere fact of their infancy, doomed to everlasting hell fire.[10] Theirs was, on the whole, quite the least
gruesome of the Christian faiths preached in Marion County
in William Jennings Bryan's youth. It was also the most
popular with the younger generation.

The Reverend Henricks was a big man with a deep bass
voice and an irresistible attractiveness to women. He captivated sixteen-year-old Fannie Bryan quite as effectively as
he did the more sophisticated ones, and to the Cumberland
Presbyterian church William Jennings Bryan followed his
sister, as he had followed her implicity all his life.

It was a new and a troubling experience for the boy Bryan.
The revival services were held in the evenings, and night
after night Billy Bryan hurried feverishly through his chores,
broke away from his playmates and his family at any cost,
and ran the three quarters of a mile, his footsteps on the
plank walk echoing his heartbeats, to the dim-lit church.[11]
He was intoxicated by the whole proceeding, gave himself
up to it utterly. The crude intimacy of these confessions
wrung from grown men and women shaken by a sort of lust
to reveal what was most secret within them; the terrific
power of the human voice, of words spoken in exaltation,
and, more pregnant still, the breathless, expectant silences,
these held young Bryan spellbound. For the first time in his
life he felt himself of transcendent importance in the hot

excitement of all these people so eager to yield themselves, while the Creator of the Universe Himself leaned down from His high heaven and sought to become possessed of the very being of this fourteen-year-old boy.

William Jennings Bryan had no will to resist, no thought of struggling to hold back anything of himself. His surrender was complete, without mental or physical reservation. And all his life he cherished the memory of the precious experience as a woman might cherish the memory of her abandonment of herself to a lover.

Whatever may have been his faults the Hon. Silas Bryan was a man of rare personal integrity in his conviction that every individual was and should be the captain of his own soul. And what he preached he practised. When his son and daughter exhibited a desire to join the Cumberland Presbyterians instead of the Baptists he merely said:

"You children will have to form opinions of your own. I hope they will be right."

"I never knew until after his death that he was disappointed that I did not become a member of his own church," wrote William Jennings Bryan,[12] long years afterward. He would have to be a singularly insensitive person not to know it. But, of course, he was.

The act of joining a church neither that of his mother nor that of his father was by far the most momentous event in the life of William Jennings Bryan up to that hour. It was his first break for liberty from the tutelage of the women about him and the overshadowing influence of his father. He was amazed and perhaps a bit disconcerted to find how easy it was to escape these constricting forces. It did not occur to William Jennings Bryan, then or later, that save for his father's insistence upon individual freedom and the responsibility that went with it, he could never have done the thing. In short, the iron ring in which William Jennings Bryan felt himself enclosed was not real, after all, but a fantasy of his own creation. He did not see this, however. Having created the fantasy he dwelt in it. All his life he was never quite at ease in a world of reality. The fact played havoc with him, and with countless thousands who placed their faith in him, as well.

Having won independence in matters religious, independence in other respects followed swiftly and with weighty consequences for William Jennings Bryan. He was to go to college, of course. No son of Silas Bryan should lack what Silas himself had won with such sacrifice.

I do not recall that I ever did decide to go to college [said William Jennings Bryan]. It was decided for me by my parents and when I was too young to fix the day. [13]

From the first, Silas Bryan had hit upon a modest Baptist college at Liberty, Missouri, where the costs of instruction were not exorbitant and the results reasonably predictable.[14] But young Bryan suddenly decided not to be a Baptist, and a strictly sectarian education at once became impossible.[15] What with six children and a deer park to maintain, the question of expense was a major one with Silas Bryan. In the end, therefore, what determined the college William Jennings Bryan was to attend was the presence at Jacksonville, Illinois, of Silas Bryan's second cousin, Dr. Hiram K. Jones.

Dr. Jones was born in the same Blue Ridge country of Virginia four years earlier than Silas Bryan.[16] He was an alumnus and trustee of and a lecturer in Illinois College, boasted a lucrative practice as a physician, and was childless. It was a combination too providential to be overlooked by one with Silas Bryan's firm belief in the providential direction of human affairs. William Jennings Bryan would go to Illinois College, would live in the Christian home of Cousin Hiram and Cousin Lizzie, and would run the doctor's errands, tend his furnace in winter, and mow his lawn in summer for his board and keep. He would receive a first-class education at little or no cost. The Hon. Silas Bryan rubbed his hands with satisfaction. The arrangement could not begin too quickly to please him.

So the year William Jennings Bryan turned fifteen he was packed off to Jacksonville to prepare for Illinois College at Whipple Academy.

To Will Bryan—no longer Billy now—the occasion was epochal. Had he been able, then or later, to look back upon his completed fifteen years many things of which he never did gain a very clear vision might have been as plain as the nose on his face. There was, for example, the sinister influence of those fear-ridden war and post-war years, when prominent Democrats like the Bryans were of the hunted class, to whom almost anything might happen. So far as conscious memory went they seemed to have been wholly obliterated. But what William Jennings Bryan had yet to learn was that human experience is like matter, indestructible: one is not a balance struck between what is called good and what is called evil, but the sum of both. All his life William Jennings Bryan was engaged in the attempt to match one experience against another in the hope that both would disappear. They never did.

On the eve of his departure for Jacksonville young Bryan was trying to match his father's prominence as a member of the Illinois Constitutional Convention and a candidate for Congress against the slumbering consciousness that there had been a day when Judge Bryan climbed out of his buggy and knelt by the roadside in prayer to be saved from bodily harm. He could not do it. Sternly "reared in 'the fear and admonition of the Lord,'"[17] fear was a large part of William Jennings Bryan's mental equipment. He could not be free of it, try as he would.

Then there was the physically pinched, emotionally stunted life of the farmer. Drudgery, William Jennings Bryan called it. Silas Bryan was relatively a wealthy man,[18] but it profited his son nothing. The Bryan boys—there were three now—had to work like any other farmer's sons. And throughout Egypt there were thousands of farmers, with the number growing daily, who for all their toil could boast nothing better to live in than a miserable hovel

with barely room to stand up in, with never a flower or a shrub near, without the kindly shade of a tree; a bare, bleak, wretched abode, fit for nothing but the squalid and the pigs—[19]

and nothing to look forward to but bankruptcy and the grave. It was a life to escape if one could, and with all his heart William Jennings Bryan wanted to escape it. He found a brief refuge in the emotionalism of religion only to learn that, even for the converted, life went on much as before when the first flame had died down.

William Jennings Bryan looked about him. To the pitiless eyes of adolescence the Bryan place was not one of the "most tasteful homesteads in southern Illinois,"[20] but a huge, gloomy, brick prison set in a straggling group of ill-kept trees. The farm was not a "country seat,"[21] but so many acres rented out and shiftlessly cultivated. His father was a disappointed, covetous old man suffering from dyspepsia; his mother a gaunt, stern woman tired with too much childbearing, too much housework. It was a hard, ugly life among hard, ugly people of deep-bitten prejudices, sullen suspicions, obstinate hatreds. Before William Jennings Bryan left Egypt forever, much of this unyielding, tenacious quality in those among whom his childhood was passed had come to be immedicably part of him.

Yet he was still young enough to grope with eager hands for something else. He read aloud to his father William Cullen Bryant's "To a Waterfowl," and a lump rose in his throat and his heart swelled when he came to the lines

> "He who, from zone to zone,
> Guides through the boundless sky thy certain flight,
> In the long way that I must tread alone,
> Will lead my steps aright."

Yes, that must be so, he thought. What he had to do first was to get away, to escape the crushing weight of the ugliness, the meanness, the cruelty all about him. He must be free.

But what William Jennings Bryan did not realize then, or perhaps ever, was that freedom is a thing of the spirit that dwells not in outward circumstance but within the human mind.

PART II
AMBITION

53

"I had great admiration for Bryan because of his sterling qualities as a man and because of his ability to state what he had to say in a forceful and eloquent manner, and because I believed he had the moral courage to stand by his principles. The week that I spent with him gave me the opportunity to know the man intimately. I had access to his library and conversed with him every day. We walked and drove together, and in the course of our conversation we covered many topics. I found that he was fairly well versed in law; that he had studied Blackstone and Kent and the English precedents, but that he was utterly ignorant of almost everything else except the Bible and the evils of intemperance; that his library contained almost no books whatever of value to a man fitting himself to be President of the United States or even a member of a State Legislature. I also found that, while his personality was charming, whatever ability nature may have endowed him with had been badly dwarfed and crippled by a narrow education, and that he was not big enough to overcome his training by continuing his investigations of men and affairs after he entered public life."

R. F. Pettigrew.

CHAPTER VI

1874

FOR half a century Illinois College was an outpost of New England in the Middle West. As alien as a missionary compound in China, the college before the war was "the fountain and hotbed of ultra abolitionism"[1] in that part of the world. The Hon. Silas Bryan would as lief have consigned his eldest son to hell as to an institution presided over by the Reverend Edward Beecher.

But much had changed since the last ragged Confederate soldier turned his face homeward to break his cavalry mount to the plough again. Time had been when the Hon. Silas Bryan would have lost his reason over the spectacle of the Hon. Blanche K. Bruce, a distinguished coloured citizen of Floreyville, Mississippi, in the seat so long occupied by no less a person than Jefferson Davis. Yet there he was, large as life and twice as black, in the front row of the Senate under the very nose of the Vice President of the United States. And the Hon. Silas Bryan somehow survived.

Illinois College too had changed. Where once it had been a bulwark of Abolition, now it was equally a stronghold of free trade. And of that the Hon. Silas Bryan heartily approved. Much of the early importance of the college had dwindled, however. It was hardly to be compared with the Illinois Industrial University at Urbana with a faculty of twelve, and two hundred and ninety-seven undergraduate gentlemen and eighty-three undergraduate ladies, as the catalogue put it, or that mammoth department store of education, the University of Chicago, sponsored by the Hon. Stephen A. Douglas, and boasting a faculty of twenty-seven and over five hundred students. The faculty of Illinois College was a modest group of eight. There were only sixty students in the college proper and seventy-eight in Whipple Academy. Nevertheless, the flag of high morality was nailed to the masthead of the institution at Jacksonville.

We avow that we mean to build on the foundation of apostles and prophets, Jesus the Christ Himself being the chief cornerstone [President Sturtevant declared]. We deny the possibility of providing for the necessities of a Christian community on any other basis.

And that, also, the Hon. Silas Bryan approved.

To William Jennings Bryan, however, Jacksonville meant principally the great world outside of Egypt. And what a world it was, to be sure! The Beecher-Tilton trial had just drawn to its ignoble close. President Grant had just written across the back of a letter charging his own personal private secretary with colossal crookedness: "Let no guilty man escape"—and then proceeded to use all the mighty machinery of the Presidency to see that Orville E. Babcock did escape. The head of the St. Louis whisky ring provided the President of the United States with "sylphs" for his entertainment,[2] and horseflesh as well; and the leading figure of the Republican party, his pockets bulging with the spoils of the Little Rock and Fort Smith Railroad, drew a red herring across the trail of corruption by declaiming against the South:

I here before God, measuring my words, knowing their full extent and import, declare that neither the deeds of the Duke of Alva in the Low Countries nor the massacre of St. Bartholomew, nor the thumbscrews and engines of torture of the Spanish Inquisition begin to compare in atrocity with the hideous crime of Andersonville.[3]

It was the fashion of the day. Every political crook caught with his arms elbow deep in the public coffers promptly raised a great halloo that all Democrats were traitors, rebels, and murderers, and unfit to be trusted in public office. And not a community in the country, confronted daily with problems of the most vital concern, requiring honesty and integrity to solve, failed to shout itself hoarse and go high-stepping down the street the moment the bands began to play and the

torchlights to flicker in a political parade. It was an era when
oratory was all a man required to attain to any exalted
position.

This was fortunate indeed for young William Jennings
Bryan. For about all he fetched with him to Whipple Academy from his five years' schooling at Salem was a pleasing
personality, a magnificent physique, reasonable good looks, a
voice holding promise of remarkable depth, resonance, and
carrying power, and the ability and willingness to recite
pieces in public on every conceivable occasion. In short, the
equipment of the perfect orator.

True, before Will Bryan set off, the Hon. Silas Bryan called
his son in and solemnly presented him with the two largest
volumes (excluding the family Bible) in his modest library.
They were a Greek and a Latin lexicon. William Jennings
was, his father charged, to use the former six and the latter
five years. There was to be none of this modern nonsense
about replacing the classics by science. The classics were the
symbol of education as Silas Bryan conceived it. One might
never be able to read either Latin or Greek without a dic-
tionary at one's elbow, but that was of minor consequence.
There was a magic in mere contact with ancient literature,
in the opinion of Silas Bryan, that marked off the gentleman
from the boor. One might be born with it, like the Virginia
planters of the days before the war; one might achieve it, as
Silas Bryan himself had done. Failing either of these, a young
man of ambitious parentage stood an excellent chance of
having such culture thrust upon him.

Had he considered it necessary the Hon. Silas Bryan could
have given his son a few valuable pointers on politics, as well.
Perhaps he deemed it superfluous. No native of Egypt had
much to learn in the field of political technique or anything
to speak of in the way of political illusions to lose. Senator
Hoar of Massachusetts, staunch Republican though he was,
put the general situation as clearly as anyone:

I have seen five judges of a high court of the United States driven
from office by threats of impeachment for corruption or malad-

ministration [he said]. I have seen in the State of the Union foremost in power and wealth four judges of her courts impeached for
corruption, and the political administration of her chief city become a disgrace and a by-word throughout the world.*

I have seen the chairman of the Committee on Military Affairs
in the House, rise in his place and demand the expulsion of four
of his associates for making sale of their official privilege of selecting
youths to be educated at our great military school.† When the
greatest railroad of the world binding together the continent and
uniting the two great seas that wash our shores, was finished, I have
seen our national triumph and exaltation turned to bitterness and
shame by the unanimous reports of three Committees of Congress
—two of the House and one here‡—that every step of that enterprise had been taken in fraud.

Had young Bryan cherished any doubts of the accuracy of
this picture he could have resolved them by reading the
reports of the impeachment proceedings against General
William W. Belknap, President Grant's Secretary of War.

It was the last note struck by the Senator from Massachusetts that rang clear in the ears of the people of the
Middle West—that remark about the railroads. Not five
years before, the Hon. Silas Bryan had himself laid it down
in his didactic way that "every dollar that had been put in
the lines of that road§ had become a producing dollar. It
has made the dollar of the people along its line worth two
dollars." Trying to make a dollar worth two dollars was one
of the chief pursuits of the Mid-West farmers, but they made
little hand of it where the railroads were concerned. The
Hon. Silas Bryan was not long in changing his mind about
the railroads, and in this he was at one with the vast majority
of his neighbours between the Alleghenies and the Rockies.
Those once beneficent highways to the markets of the world
suddenly loomed a gigantic octopus with long arms of steel
outflung to strangle the agricultural communities. No one

---

*New York under Tammany.
†West Point.
‡In the Senate.
§The Illinois Central Railroad.

had ever given him anything, said the farmer; he had fought for every foot of land he owned and every depreciated greenback dollar he possessed. But to the railroads, with insane prodigality, two hundred million acres of land had been presented out of the public purse—an area greater than the whole of New England, New York, New Jersey, Delaware, Pennsylvania, Maryland, Ohio, and Indiana,[4] greater than France and England and Belgium combined, greater than the entire Japanese Empire—and all of this without so much as "Thank you."

If the farmers of the Middle West looked upon this stupendous largess with a jaundiced eye they were little to be blamed. For it was their votes that had sanctioned this colossal bounty, and no sooner was it effected than the very railroads they had thus endowed turned upon them and exploited them with discriminatory rates, rebates, and secret favours to large shippers until the rural goose that had laid the golden egg had its neck well wrung. And as if this were not enough, because the tremendous national asset of these millions of acres, the property of the whole people, had been wantonly dissipated, the cost of running the government had to be met by a tariff that fell with crushing weight on the farmer—a tariff, as Manton Marble wrote, that was "a masterpiece of injustice, inequality and false pretense."[6]

On the whole the farmers of the Middle West felt, and not without reason, that they had been handed the bedaubed end of the stick to hold.

They say it is too hard to give fifty bushels of corn (an acre of corn) for a pair of boots, simply to satisfy tariff monopolists [wrote Abe Lincoln's old law partner, Bill Herndon]. They are down on railroads and rings, and conspiracies, and monopolies, and *treason* against the general welfare.[7]

They were indeed.

Not one single feature of this situation escaped William Jennings Bryan. It was the one thing he had heard every day of his life for fifteen years. Around the Salem Court House the gaunt, laconic farmers of Egypt talked about it with a bitterness that was the more intense as they felt themselves incapable of concerted action in the premises. Not that they did not try. Two years before young Bryan left Salem for Jacksonville, 761 new granges sprang up in the state; 704 new ones the following year. Hardly a rural community lacked its organization of farmers, to whose meetings men and women alike drove long miles over execrable roads. There was all the fascinating secrecy and ritual and gaudy trappings of quality dear to the American heart about membership in the Grange—that pomp so sadly missing in the arid Protestant religious sects. Even the women could rise from "Maid" to "Shepherdess" and from "Gleaner" to "Matron."[8] Great mail-order houses sprang up in Chicago for the sole purpose of catering to these groups of embattled farmers, and especially their embattled wives. There was far more excitement over the menace of the railroads and the iniquities of the tariff throughout the Middle West than ever there had been over slavery—and with sound reason. If the equivalent of $50 for a pair of boots was not a sound reason, what was?

As the Presidential campaign of 1876 approached, the farmers of the Middle West felt the grip of Eastern business organization upon their throats and were panic-stricken. They were "agin' the gov'ment" all along the line. From Indiana, Illinois, Iowa, Kansas, Nebraska, they flocked to the Democratic Convention that June, a meagre supply of "battle-scarred and blood-stained greenbacks"—the only money these Westerners had known for a generation—securely pinned to red flannel undershirts. They were stewing with wrath, not merely at the corruption of the Grant Administration—these farmers were realists not moralists— and not solely over the high-handed conduct of the railroads and the impudent robbery of the tariff, either. But they felt upon their backs a last straw in iniquity in the alliance of the government in Washington with the financial interests of Wall Street. As they saw it, these were the same financial interests that had profited by the enormous grants of public land to the railroads; that were even then profiting by the flagrantly unequal schedules of the tariff; and that now, through the banks, were "trying to contract the currency down to such a point as to allow the banks to practice extortion upon the people of this country," as that adroit political weather vane, the Hon. John A. Logan, put it.[9] Enough was enough, said the farmers of the Middle West. They had had enough.

For what the government at Washington was up to at this moment was taking away from the people of the West, not only from the farmers but from the city merchants and the factory workers as well, "the best money they had ever known"[10]—the greenbacks. Wanted to make gold the sole legal tender! They had never seen a gold piece in their lives and did not care if they never did see one. The "battle-torn, blood-stained 'greenback'" had been plenty good enough during the hard years of the war—what was the matter with it now? Who wanted anything else as currency, anyhow? The bankers of Wall Street, of course. And they wanted gold because it was they who had the gold, locked up in their own vaults. And if gold were made the only legal tender, then the farmers and the labourers would have to come with their greenbacks, that represented long hours of toil in field and factory, and buy gold of the bankers of Wall Street who had never done a stroke of honest work in their lives—and pay perhaps twice the value of it, reckoned in sweat.

So they argued, the people of the West. And who shall say they were altogether wrong? For when they borrowed the money to develop the vast prairies that were the real substantial wealth of the country, what they received was not gold but greenbacks. And what they now proposed to pay back was these same greenbacks. Why not? they asked. The larger aspects of the financial situation meant nothing to the Western farmer. He had not borrowed his money in Europe—he had borrowed it at the bank on the corner of the court-house square. If the Wall Street banker had borrowed abroad and was expected to pay in gold, that was his risk. "Having unloaded his sixty-cent dollars on the West," said the Chicago *Tribune*, he "can hardly object to being paid in the same kind of currency."[11]

But he did object. And that, not civil service reform or the return of home rule to the South, was the real issue of the campaign of 1876. Silas Bryan himself was a dyed-in-the-wool "greenbacker" and made no bones about it, either. There was not a farmer in his part of the world who had not heard how, when "bankers, brokers, capitalists, merchants, manufacturers," hard hit by the panic of 1873, ran blubbering to the government, "beseeching the President to increase the currency by every means in his power, and declaring that unless the government came to the rescue nothing could save the country from bankruptcy and ruin,"* the President did come to the rescue of these business men of the East. Even in defiance of the law, the Secretary of the Treasury printed $26,000,000 in greenbacks to relieve Eastern bankers.[12] But now that the farmers of the West stood in desperate need of the same kind of help they were laughed at. They did not see the joke.

"This country," wrote Senator Poland, "is fast becoming filled with gigantic corporations wielding and controlling immense aggregations of money and thereby commanding great influence and power."[13]

Yes, commanding even the government of the United States, said the Western farmers. They went to the Greenback Convention at Indianapolis in May with blood in their eyes. But that foxy old manufacturer, Peter Cooper, who looked like a farmer but had amassed his fortune by shrewd trading, captured the Greenback Party. The Democratic Convention at St. Louis was the only hope left to the Western farmers. It was a forlorn one.

It was aboard a train filled with these bitter, disillusioned, leaderless, and inarticulate Mid-Westerners that William Jennings Bryan climbed one day toward the end of June, 1876, to attend his first national political convention. He was sixteen. He had spent one year at preparatory school and

---

*So Senator Oliver P. Morton, of Indiana, declared.[14]

felt himself very much a man. His father and mother were in Philadelphia, agape at the wonders of the Centennial Exposition. Will Bryan was free to do whatever he liked. The one thing he wanted to do was to go to that convention; and he did it.

It was a ravishing experience. Never since the days of Douglas had the Democrats been so buoyed by hope, so carried away with enthusiasm.[15] Young Bryan was caught up in the excitement and tossed this way and that by it. There they all were, the great of the party of Jefferson and Jackson: Peter Cooper's son-in-law, the Hon. Abram S. Hewitt—the wily old hatmaker had a foot in both camps; Gen. Roger A. Pryor, putting aside for the moment a suit charging the Rev. Henry Ward Beecher with adultery and perjury to do his duty as a citizen; David B. Hill, only thirty-three, but already a man of political promise in the Empire State; and over and above all that "strong, heavy, raw-boned man with a firm jaw, clear and determined eyes, and awkward manners,"[16] Honest John Kelly of Tammany Hall.

William Jennings Bryan watched the "Tammany Special" sweep by, its locomotive named "John Kelly" and its fifteen palace cars decorated with flags and flowers—the last one bearing a huge picture of Honest John himself on either side.[17] —and was thrilled to his finger tips. At the convention hall Marse Henry Watterson, of lionlike head, wielded the gavel. Miss Phœbe Cozzens addressed the assembled delegates on the burning topic of woman suffrage, dressed to the minute in yards and yards of billowy skirts and an enormous bustle. August Belmont, the astute representative of the House of Rothschild, offered a resolution calling upon all true patriots to trample underfoot and extinguish forever the smouldering ashes of distrust, rancour, and animosity between two sections of our country. The grandiloquent text smelled of Manton Marble, the brilliant rhetorician of the New York *World*, but it lacked the carrying power of Horace Greeley's "clasp hands across the bloody chasm." The tall sycamore of the Wabash, the Hon. Dan'l Voorhees, furnished the oratory and

Blue Jeans Williams the comic relief of the breath-taking occasion. Both were from Indiana.

But Will Bryan could not get in. He ran from door to door in a tremor of excitement, snatching tantalizing glimpses of the proceedings, catching broken fragments of the speeches. Finally a policeman shoved him through a window where, clinging perilously to the sash, he looked down with beating heart upon the vast assemblage.[18] Honest John Kelly was speaking. Men on the floor screamed and hissed at him, shook their fists, tried to howl him down. But he stood there solid, his massive body immovable, his thick neck swollen in the effort to make himself heard.

And he was heard:

Do not be blinded by your passions, but be led by your reason, for if you are beaten in the coming canvass, it is the end, in my opinion, of the Democratic party. I believe sincerely also that it will result in the destruction of our government [warned the spokesman of Tammany Hall]. If this convention nominates Mr. Tilden as their candidate for the Presidency, they will regret it.

He went on to point out that in the last three campaigns Eastern candidates had led the Democracy to defeat after defeat. It was the turn of the West, he said. He urged that the nomination be "given to the Western people."[19]

The farmers of the West rose in their seats and cheered and cheered. So, too, did the lad in the window.

But Mr. Tilden was nominated.

CHAPTER VII

WHIPPLE ACADEMY

WHEN William Jennings Bryan settled down in Jacksonville as a Middler at Whipple Academy he knew little or nothing of what manner of person he was and a vast deal too much of what manner of person the Hon. Silas Bryan wanted him to be. In a vague sort of way the lad Bryan looked to politics as a career and to two such arc lamps of political achievement as his father and Abraham Lincoln as guides. Playing at being the United States Senate with a few boys of the Salem High School, Will Bryan sometimes took the name of the Hon. Thomas F. Bayard of Delaware as his[1]— little foreseeing that this patrician descendant of the Chevalier Bayard and scion of the house of Peter Stuyvesant would three times be a candidate for the nomination for President of the United States* and finally content himself with the post of Secretary of State. There was something at once incongruous and prophetic in the choice.

Of this, however, William Jennings Bryan divined nothing. He carried with him from Salem two qualities already crystallized to a certain immutable hardness: he believed in himself—he, the man child, brought up among women, by virtue of his sex and his seniority and the heritage of his father's position and authority, he saw himself a creature of destiny. Second, from every association throughout childhood and youth William Jennings Bryan had come to believe in the theory, at least, of democracy. To him quite literally, as to old Silas Bryan before him, the voice of the people was the voice of God. Grounded in Fundamentalism as he was,[2] he would cheerfully have submitted the Westminster Catechism to popular vote and abided the result.

*In the Democratic conventions of 1876, 1880, and 1884.

With these two convictions firmly woven into the fabric of his subconscious mind William Jennings Bryan left the deer park behind him and stepped out into the wide, wide world without serious misgiving.

The game of being United States Senators never grew to be a popular sport among the sons of Marion County's hard-headed, close-fisted farmers. They took their politics straight, not vicariously. But Jacksonville was different. For Jacksonville regarded itself seriously as a centre of Eastern refinement in a crude, uncultured land. Thither came the intellectual Titans of the day: Wendell Phillips to lecture on the Lost Arts; Henry Ward Beecher and Theodore Tilton to follow one another on the same platform—Jacksonville was nothing if not broad-minded. And when no one else was available there was always that distinguished Platonist, Dr. Hiram K. Jones, to oblige with an evening devoted to "Man: Spirit, Soul, Body."

The object and aim of all philosophical research, concerning the living, is the essential *form* existing, or which is the same, the ideal actual. This is the *real* [he would proclaim, looking up at a corner of the ceiling with a birdlike air]. The soul, and the spirit through the soul, adumbrate and form a body consonant and conformable to the nature and quality of their conjoint disposition and energies.[3]

All Jacksonville agreed that they did indeed.

To the end of his days William Jennings Bryan looked upon the rare privilege he was thus accorded in his early youth of intimate association with the great man as "one of the best bits of good fortune that has fallen to my lot."[4]

Dr. Jones was a man of the highest character, of great learning and lofty ideals [William Jennings wrote in after years]. Dr. Jones was the head of the literary circle of the city and for some years a lecturer at the Concord (Massachusetts) School of Philosophy. His speciality was Plato. Possibly no scholar of his day was more thoroughly acquainted with the work of the great Greek philosopher.[5]

Nor was this solely young Bryan's view of Cousin Hiram. Dr. Jones, according to the local historian, was "an enthusiastic student of Plato and was justly regarded as the ablest and wisest interpreter of the eminent philosopher in this country."[6]

Yet curiously enough Dr. Hiram K. Jones had no Greek to speak of. His acquaintance with the eminent philosopher was through the somewhat constrained medium of the Bohn translation, while his interpretations consisted principally in the startling discovery that "the dialogues of Plato are practically Christian in their character."[7] Nevertheless, as far East as the capital of transcendentalism, Dr. Hiram K. Jones was indeed hailed by such profound, if murky, intellects as Bronson Alcott as "the reviver of the study of Platonism in his time and land,"[8] and "welcomed by the choice company of thinkers in Concord, and Mr. Emerson,* then beginning to withdraw himself more and more from public discourse because of failing memory."[9] In short, Dr. Hiram K. Jones and Bronson Alcott were kindred spirits.

He was also, according to his admiring young cousin and disciple, a devotee of microscopy "and he often called me in to examine the specimens upon which he was working," Bryan says.[10] Older and less impressionable heads in Jacksonville laughed not a little at Dr. Jones's pretensions to science; they said his famous collection of microscopic slides was a stock set about which he knew little or nothing.[11] But to young Bryan Cousin Hiram was the very embodiment of scientific knowledge. So limited and casual a contact with science William Jennings Bryan experienced at Jacksonville. He never improved upon it; and if in later years he came to regard science with a certain tolerant contempt it must be here set down that all the science he ever knew was not much above that rating.

It may hardly be fairly laid at the door of William Jennings Bryan that he was one of only seven in his class refusing to be exposed to what meagre acquaintance with science a

---

*Ralph Waldo Emerson.

Western institution of learning purveyed in that day. That was the Hon. Silas Bryan's doing.[12] Against his father's edict, however, young Bryan evinced none of the rebellion of a curious and acquisitive mind. His was not, on the whole, that kind of a mind.

Nevertheless, there was a general atmosphere of quest for truth, or something respectable resembling it, about Illinois College not without its effect upon young William Jennings. He did not immediately join a church in Jacksonville. He was not certain whether he would at all or not. In those adolescent years so full of doubt for the soundest— the years of which Walt Whitman could write:

> The question O me! so sad, recurring—What good
> amid these, O me, O life? —

the Presbyterian convert from Egypt suffered his questionings, too. He wanted someone to go with them—someone sure not by authority but by conviction. He cast about him.

One there was who stood preëminent, a figure at once to enchant and appall, master of words and of men through the instrumentality of words—gallant, fearless, triumphant, incomparable, who could challenge God and compel the homage of the pastor of Plymouth Church—Robert Green Ingersoll. Trembling at his own audacity, yet impelled by the ferment within him that must somehow be stilled, William Jennings Bryan wrote the Great Agnostic. Who can doubt the workings of Divine Providence? Bob Ingersoll never saw young Bryan's letter. A secretary sent a stereotyped reply, enclosing a printed copy of one of Colonel Ingersoll's addresses.

I scanned it with eagerness and found that he had expressed himself about as follows: "I do not say that there is no God, I simply say I do not know. I do not say there is no life beyond the grave, I simply say I do not know" [William Jennings Bryan recounts]. And from that day to this I have asked myself the question and have been unable to answer it to my own satisfaction, how could anyone find pleasure in taking from a human heart a living faith and substituting therefor the cold and cheerless doctrine, "I do not know."[13]

He, for one, could not. William Jennings Bryan asked no questions of life, then or ever.

"I passed through a period of skepticism when I was in college," he says. "It was at this period that I became confused by the different theories of creation."[14]

Nor did he ever get them straight.[15]

In his Whipple Academy days he read, too. For the first time in his life William Jennings Bryan tasted the secret sweets of romance—the thrilling adventures of a beautiful quadroon—soft, starlight Southern nights—passion—the heavy odour of jasmine—"there my young heart yielded to the influence of Love—a first and virgin love!" But to young Bryan it was not fiction.[16] He turned to where Mayne Reid had written at the end: "The book is founded upon an actual experience." Yes; it was all true—except the names, of course. They would have to be changed.

History came the same way, through Jacob Abbott's enthralling phantasms. Young Bryan chose the women to read about. Queen Elizabeth and Mary Queen of Scots he read twice. There was that chapter on "Elizabeth's Lovers." "Nothing is stated, not even the most minute and apparently imaginary details, without what was deemed good historical authority," wrote the author. And William Jennings Bryan believed and was glad the world was so wonderful.

He read Lowell's poems, too, and even Shelley's. Two weeks he spent with eight volumes of Grote's *History of Greece* on his desk, and then took them back to the library. But Samuel Slick's adventures in England young Bryan enjoyed hugely. When he read fiction, as fiction, Dickens was his favourite. There was something about the way everything comes right in the end with Dickens that struck William Jennings Bryan as essentially true to life.

He spent three weeks, too, at the feet of George Bancroft in an atmosphere thick with the theological interpretation of history. Had the Hon. Silas Bryan's indoctrination of the divine guidance of human affairs required other sanction, here it was. From Bancroft, William Jennings Bryan came away convinced beyond cavil of the direct influence of God in bringing to fruition the American experiment in government. It was a faith that never wavered.

Beyond these books, however, young Bryan did little of what he called "indulging in reading."[17] His real training, he says, was in the debating society, Sigma Pi.[18] He hardly knew his way about Jacksonville before he was maintaining in a debate (which he lost) that professional men are more useful to society than mechanics, and reciting "The Three Black Crows" as a select reading. In the art of declamation it is recorded that William Jennings did himself and the society credit.[19] Essays he dodged, however[20]—he would offer to do declamations instead.[21]

Yet he had no grace of oratory at this time.[22] Professor Hamill, who taught elocution, rhetoric, history, and English literature, thought lightly of young Bryan as a speaker—he inclined to timidity[23] and his enunciation was poor.[24] Only his baritone voice was extraordinarily fine. There was a reverberating quality to it[25] that entranced his hearers whatever he was saying, and a carrying power that was astonishing. It was a great temptation to young Bryan, that voice. He could so easily substitute it for content in his speeches. Indeed, at first he did, hiding a certain vacuity behind the words of other men. His first year at Whipple Academy, he declaimed Patrick Henry's "Give Me Liberty or Give Me Death" in a prize contest. The judges decided the latter would be appropriate.[26]

But young Bryan's belief in himself was not dimmed. They made fun of him in the Sigma Pi meetings: "Bryan's pathetic address moved all to tears," the secretary recorded ironically.[27] And again:

Bryan, in the course of the debate, brought down the house by saying: "The President of the College is for free trade, our ex-President is for free trade, and *I myself* am for free trade."[28]

Yet gradually it was borne in upon his classmates that William Jennings Bryan ranked opinions in precisely this

At
Whipple
Academy

At
Illinois
College

In Law School
(Bryan is in upper left-
hand corner)

Cousin Hiram Jones

Cousin Lizzie Jones

order of importance. Some respected his candour. Others thought he should have been a student at Yale.

With no pronounced success attending his scholastic efforts and even less his budding career as a boy orator, Will Bryan sadly missed Mollie Smith's undisguised worship. It was not that Will Bryan doubted himself. But he was not as yet immune to the human craving to have others share his confidence. Queen Elizabeth and Mary Queen of Scots were all right in their way, and not to be despised. But an adolescent had need of something more tangible. There was a quiet luxury about Jacksonville, with its "elegant mansions, the homes of the wealthy and learned,"[29] with which this country lad, his pants frayed and shiny and baggy at the knees, felt himself out of keeping and self-conscious. He wrote his father for five dollars to buy him a new pair of pants. But the Hon. Silas was not to be moved by his son's plea. "Down here in Salem, in Marion County, your old home, the people measure a man's ability not by the length of his trousers, but by the breadth and depth of his brains," he wrote. "Your mother, when you get home, will attend to your trousers for you."[30] It was mortifying. He padded his accounts to cover purchases of sweets. But canny old Silas caught him up in that, too. Poor Will seemed to be destined to humiliation and defeat.

It was Cousin Lizzie and her sister-in-law, Dr. George Jones's wife, who took Will Bryan in hand when he needed it most. Cousin Lizzie was far from a beauty, "with her quaint primness and stiff little side curls,"[31] and was old enough to be young Bryan's mother; but her influence "upon my ideas and ideals" William Jennings Bryan found it difficult to calculate.[32] From the circle of women that had inclosed him throughout his childhood at Salem he passed straight into another at Jacksonville. It was his salvation. He forgot the doubts and questionings that had driven him momentarily to seek help of Robert Ingersoll; he forgot his slick pants and his farmer boy's hands that seemed always in the way; he forgot his poverty and the tight hold Silas Bryan kept on the purse strings. Cousin Lizzie had faith in him. Well, he

would show them all! He went out to the farm of his classmate, Granville Hulett, and in the big woods stood on a
stump while Gran Hulett sat on the ground as audience and
critic. And William Jennings Bryan practised speech making over and over again, until his hands no longer bothered
him, until he could get his words out clearly without half
trying, until he was neither self-conscious nor hesitating.

After he had been in Whipple Academy a year William
Jennings Bryan was ready. It was Cousin Lizzie who sug-
gested his subject for the declamation contest—Virginia
French's stirring poem:

"Together!" shouts Niagara his thunder-toned decree. . . .
"Together!" cry the people, and *together* it shall be
An everlasting charter-bond forever for the free!
Of liberty the signet seal, the one eternal sign,
Be these *united emblems*—the Palmetto and the Pine.

And William Jennings Bryan of Salem won third prize.
He was launched.

"During his college course, he was president of all the
classes and societies to which he belonged, and showed evidence at every turn of unusual ability,"[33] said the Chicago
Tribune, when William Jennings Bryan was nominated for
the Presidency of the United States in 1896. The American
tradition! Yet as a description of William Jennings Bryan in
his student days it is misleading. Will Bryan moved slowly,
without striking brilliance, but with a diligence and pertinac-
ity which commanded respect. He would have made an excellent guard on a football team, but athletics did not interest
him[34]—he was strong as an ox, and he saw no sense in exercise for its own sake.[35] Saturdays, instead of playing baseball, he made a little extra money "by clerking in a hat
store," as he put it.[36] So Abraham Lincoln had been clerk
in a country store at New Salem, forty-five years before.
The Lincoln tradition was always in the back of William
Jennings Bryan's mind.

The fragrant spring days when the Seniors of Illinois
College paraded the streets of Jacksonville singing "Baby

Mine" under the windows of the "Jail for Angels"—as the Jacksonville Female Academy was called—wearing silk hats and carrying slender canes, while the Juniors sported white plug hats with black bands, William Jennings Bryan waited on customers in Goltra's hat store and pounded away at German, which he hated, and geometry, which he liked. His chief recreation was solving mathematical problems for the Jacksonville *Journal*.[37]

Partly because he had been two years at Whipple Academy and was generally known, and partly because he lived with so important a person as Dr. Jones, who annually explained the facts of life to the fledgling collegians in "a very valuable course of Lectures on Physiology which all students are expected to attend,"[38] William Jennings Bryan was president of his class in Freshman year. He served conscientiously. When the customary "horn spree" took place he led his class and went to jail with the rest of the ringleaders.[39]

But William Jennings was no more a prince of good fellows in Jacksonville than he had been in Salem. His was the sterling worth that finds its supreme recognition in being chosen a vice president—and vice president of his class he became in Sophomore year,[40] when his classmates had looked about them a bit. It was not that young Bryan was unpopular, exactly. But he knew what he wanted among young men who had come to college to find out what they wanted. They resented a little what seemed assurance in him, when it was only confidence in the integrity of his purpose. Of himself it may be doubted if he was ever quite sure. The probity of his aim he never questioned. He made few friends, but close ones. One fight he did have, and only one—on a trip to Alton to attend a baseball game between Illinois and Shurtleff colleges. It was characteristic of Bryan that he picked an upperclassman to have it with. There is no record of who won.

As William Jennings Bryan grew older he grew better looking. He was above average height, his face, a little pale and thin still, cut by a wide, thin-lipped mouth; dark, flashing eyes under heavy brows; big nose; square chin; black hair, meticulously slicked down.[41] A romantic figure that would

have set the hearts of matinée devotees going pit-a-pat had
he been an actor. No; William Jennings Bryan was not a lad
to be overlooked. Nor had he any intention that he should be.

His Freshman year in the college proper, young Bryan
improved a little on his previous record, bringing delight to
the heart of the Hon. Silas Bryan by splitting the second prize
in Latin prose with Thomas Antie of Petersburg. It was not,
after all, a very distinguished showing. But it was William
Jennings Bryan's solitary classical achievement. He pleased
himself vastly more and brought delight to the heart of
Cousin Lizzie by reciting on the stage of Strawn's Opera
House[42] a selection from Felicia Hemans and winning the
whole of the second prize in declamation thereby. Permitted
to select his own prizes, William Jennings Bryan chose the
Bible and Shakespeare.

With his new-found self-confidence young Bryan began
to venture more and more into the debates held by Sigma Pi,
stoutly maintaining that a Representative is not duty
bound to uphold all the principles of his party,[43] that skepticism had done more toward hindering the progress of man
than superstition,[44] and that Catholicism is more dangerous
to the United States than Communism.[45] The Catholic menace was a burning topic among the staunch Congregationalists of Illinois College.[46] Young Bryan even heard without ill
effects the chaplain of Sigma Pi read a paper on "Science
and Religion" wherein "it was very clearly shown that
religion advances hand in hand with science."[47]

It was in Sophomore year that William Jennings Bryan
found his feet firm at last upon the heights. He won first
prize with an essay on "Idleness,"[48] which smacked strongly
of McGuffey's Fourth Reader. In speaking of this production in later years he quietly altered its title to "Labor."

Creeds may differ and yet each proves its position by the Bible,
[he wrote] but upon this subject there is no room for doubt. The
dignity as well as the necessity of labor pervades every page of
Holy Writ.

Which, of course, settled the matter.

It was precisely these debates in which young Bryan occasionally shone and in which he exhibited marked improvement as he hammered away at them that brought William Jennings the greatest good fortune of his life. For from time to time the two rival literary societies of Illinois College held open meetings, and to these the young ladies of the Illinois Woman's College and the Jacksonville Female Academy came by invitation in large, fluttering, giggling ecstatic groups of feminity, duly rendered the more romantic and desirable by the strictest of chaperonage. And it was just at the beginning of his Junior year in college, when progressive successes had lent young Bryan a certain flaunting arrogance vastly irritating to his classmates but entirely alluring to the female fair, that no less than forty of the dear creatures assembled to hear the best of Sigma Pi perform.

There was to be ice cream and cake afterward and a great sighing and furtive touching of hands and exchanging of sheeps' eyes and whispered words of endearment. It was, in short, a memorable occasion, and the climax of the programme was Henry Clay's expert pronouncement on the subject of ambition, appropriately declaimed by William Jennings Bryan.[49] Among the quota furnished by the Jacksonville Female Academy to this altogether disquieting audience was a demure young miss who had just come to Jacksonville from the Monticello Academy at Godfrey, in Madison County—a slender, rather small young lady, with soft, dark brown hair and "grey-brown eyes with a searching expression and a calculating glint, not unmixed with humor."[50] A very self-poised young lady, "not beautiful, as beauty goes,"[51] but a "woman such as good men believed their sainted mothers to have been"—in a word, "the personification of American womanhood."[52] Or so, at least, she seemed to the orator of the evening.

There was a salutory mocking coolness about Mamie Baird. It was not the first time she had seen young Bryan, and she found him "neat, though not fastidious in dress." He stood firmly and with dignity, she thought. She was not a little amused at the extent of his smile. "That man can whisper in his own ear," someone said. But Mamie Baird found this "a cruel exaggeration."[53] On the whole, she rather liked him.

And William Jennings Bryan liked her. It was a new incentive to him, and a new source of encouragement as well. In some ways he was doing remarkably well—in the matter of winning prizes, for example. But in others, unaccountably, he had not had the success he hoped for. Since his election to the presidency of his class in Freshman year, he had somehow failed to command the suffrages of his fellow students. Even in the very small circle of the membership of Sigma Pi, where politics were rampant, William Jennings Bryan in eight elections had been unable to capture anything higher than the thankless office of critic. For a young man with an ambition, brought up in an atmosphere of political activity, young Bryan had displayed no striking political talents. What he required, he felt, was someone to counsel and suggest, someone to point out his errors and advise improvements. And for this just such a cool-headed, humorous, sensible, and articulate a person as Mamie Baird was indispensable to him. Easily the head of her class in the Academy, she managed to be popular at the same time. Ambitious and self-reliant, she maintained close and intimate friendships with no sacrifice of her independence. She had a quality of being able to measure a situation, a question, or an individual with unerring common sense. There was about young Bryan a little too much of the crusader, of the evangelist, to be altogether serene or sure of himself, however sure he might be of his ability. They are by no means the same.

Mamie Baird was exactly what Will Bryan needed.

Young Bryan went about it in the time-honoured way— seeking to achieve new distinctions, new trophies of prowess, with which to dazzle his chosen woman. He suddenly took a spurt in every field. He was made financial manager and later associate editor of the college paper.[54] He managed at last to be elected vice president of Sigma Pi.[55] And he was appointed one of five contestants for the Junior Oratorical Prize, the laurel crown of collegiate achievement. The winner would represent his college in the intercollegiate oratorical contest which, throughout the Middle West, was and still is so signal a distinction.

William Jennings Bryan's oration was on Individual Power. He showed that "those who had given to the world the great ideas were the men who had made preparation." He himself had.

I left nothing undone that would contribute towards success. I had had in mind for nearly five years the honor of representing the college in the oratorical contest [he relates]. This vision was before me and my work as a declaimer, as an essayist, and in the delivering of orations was to this end.

I was successful.[56]

It was late at night before the judges rendered their decision. Lights were out in the Jacksonville Female Academy and Mamie Baird was tucked away in bed, even if she was not asleep. Will Bryan could not wait till morning to apprise her of his triumph; they had arranged that if he should win, he would pass by the "Jail for Angels," dragging his cane along the picket fence.

So at three o'clock in the morning of that soft May night the stillness of Jacksonville's streets was shattered. "Clack-clack-clack-clack . . ." went his cane along the pickets. And Mamie Baird sat up suddenly in bed, her eyes shining. He had done it! She sank back on her pillows and fell asleep with a sigh of content.

But it was not all glory. When the final test came and at Galesburg the following October William Jennings Bryan for Illinois College delivered an oration on Justice, the prize he won was the second prize.

I do not feel as I thought I would [he wrote Mamie Baird]. I prayed that humility might be given with success. My prayer is answered, for I cannot feel that I am anything more than I was before, and as I look over the possibilities of life, I can honestly ask in the language of Lincoln's favorite hymn, "Why should the spirit of mortal be proud?"

In truth, William Jennings Bryan stood face to face with himself in that hour in a way in which it is given few men to stand so early in life. That destiny of which he had been so sure—possibly it was not as certain as he thought. He recalled a dream that had come to him:

I could see my name very distinctly occupying the second place, but I could not make out the name of the man who was awarded the first prize.[57]

It was not material. What lay at the bottom of William Jennings Bryan's mind was that he was perhaps doomed to be second in all things, to dream and struggle and toil and hope and then just miss winning. Perhaps in his secret heart that was what he wanted most to do: to finish his course without faltering; to fight a good fight; to keep the faith—and to fail. Yet it was disconcerting. He could not quite admit it to himself. Somehow he must reconquer his shaken self-esteem.

So with the fifty dollars of his second prize, William Jennings Bryan bought a tiny ring, a garnet set in gold. With it safe in his pocket he marched boldly up to Mamie Baird—he so big and she so little, smiling up at him. And he put the ring on her finger.

It was during the campaign of 1896 that she lost it.[58]

CHAPTER VIII

ILLINOIS COLLEGE

THE campaign of 1880 engulfed William Jennings Bryan. He read every word of the dramatic scene at Chicago in June where Garfield, dexterously outmanœuvring Roscoe Conkling, captured the Republican nomination for himself— a dark horse. He smiled over the stupidity of Conkling's arrogance and watched Garfield loyally voting for John Sherman for thirty-six ballots while quietly working for himself. It was a classic in political technique by no means lost on young Bryan. What he admired most was the consummate adroitness with which Garfield emerged from the contest with the whole-hearted support of Sherman. Garfield, said Sherman, had "a great head and a great heart."[1] He had a great head, at all events, and he knew the value of a tactful speech at the right moment. The incident was filed away in young Bryan's mind for future reference.

Many things happened to William Jennings Bryan that memorable year besides his formal engagement to Mamie Baird. Just a little too soon to learn of his son's oratorical triumphs or of his engagement either, Judge Bryan passed to his eternal rest and lay in state in the Marion County Court House, where he had been a distinguished figure so many years. In that hour his fellow citizens forgot that Silas Bryan had been bigoted, remarkable principally for a certain lack of culture and broad outlook upon life, and alternately ruled by avarice and ambition. They recalled only that in an age when politics and dishonesty were synonymous Silas Lillard Bryan had passed his life in politics and remained an honest man. He may have guided his course by beacons behind rather than before him. No doubt he did. But throughout his days he believed passionately in those principles of

the Declaration of Independence he was wont to declaim
so sonorously at Fourth of July celebrations. If they found
little practical application to his own life, Silas Bryan was in
that respect no different to the rest of his countrymen.

To Marion County folk, Will Bryan was only Judge
Bryan's oldest boy home from college, when the political
tom-toms began to beat that summer. Besides, he was not
old enough to vote. However, for his father's sake the local
Democratic Committee agreed to give young Bryan a chance
to do a little speaking if he wanted to. He did want to.

There was nothing glamorous about William Jennings
Bryan's initial political effort. He was to speak at a farmer's
picnic in a grove near Salem. When he arrived there were
four men present. Two were other speakers; one had the
gambling concession for the picnic; the fourth owned the
grove. Nobody else came.[2]

Later young Bryan had better luck. They put him on the
programme for a Saturday-night rally at the Court House,
when all the farmers from the country about would be in town
and the torchlights would smoke and gutter and the most
distinguished Democratic leaders obtainable would grace the
platform. William Jennings Bryan talked an hour and a half,
and when the crowd broke up and men in overalls and
hickory shirts pushed their way through swinging doors they
said to one another:

"Well, Billy Bryan's got a nice voice, but he ain't the
man his father was—and never will be."

Back in Congressman William McKendree Springer's
district, when college opened again young Bryan found the
going easier. Many an Illinois College lad was being used in
the country schoolhouses scattered all over the district and
Will Bryan had no difficulty at all in getting an assignment
to speak. He and Millard Fillmore Dunlap were sent out to
the Buckhorn schoolhouse one night, not so far from Jacksonville. They lost their way and were taken for Republicans
coming to break up the meeting—a good deal of the spirit of
the days following the war was still alive in the country districts of Illinois—but they finally reached the place. The

presiding officer rejoiced in the name of Timothy Flynn, and when he saw how young the speaker of the evening was he took Bryan aside and offered him a nip from a hip flask.

"Well," he said dubiously, when William Jennings refused, "do the best you can, anyhow. You can give 'em hell—there ain't a Republican in the audience."[3]

Young Bryan did.

That night when he and Dunlap lay abed in the dark in Dunlap's house in Jacksonville, William Jennings Bryan suddenly spoke his thought aloud.

"I am going to the Senate," he said. "I am going to the Senate first, and then . . ."

His voice trailed off. But both boys knew what was in William Jennings Bryan's mind. They lay long awake thinking of it.[4]

William Jennings Bryan took the defeat of General Hancock much as a modern college student takes the loss of the great football game of the year.

They tell us we are dead. *In memoriam* has appeared in every Republican journal throughout the land. How they long to plant the cypress over our final resting place! But, gentlemen, they sing their solemn dirges too soon [he thundered]. The Democrats may have been slaughtered, but like the oxen of the sun, which the companions of Ulysses butchered, the hides crawl after their tormentors.[5]

And curiously enough the young man was right. In the very next election following Garfield's triumph the Democrats crawled after their tormentors to some purpose.

William Jennings Bryan had other things on his mind besides politics that year. There was the difficult business of seeing Mamie Baird, for example. It was one thing to be engaged to an inmate of the "Jail for Angels" and another to manage any intercourse whatever with the lady. The rules of that institution were based on the assumption that no young girl could be trusted and were calculated to preserve the purity of American womanhood *vi et armis* if need be. "Your daughters," parents were notified, "are not to receive permission from you to visit, to receive company, to carry on correspondence in violation of our general regulations."[6] All of which made William Jennings Bryan's courtship exceedingly trying.

Mamie Baird's father was a retired country storekeeper in a town of some two hundred inhabitants, thirty miles from Jacksonville. An only child of moderately well-to-do parents, she had ambitions of her own and was eager to go to college. She took vocal lessons, which cost $25 extra, and art (consisting principally of china decoration), which cost $12.50 more.[7] On Washington's Birthday she read a paper on "Webster's Eulogy on Washington" which was described as "highly instructive, and displayed excellence of style and originality to a rare degree."[8] She was deeply impressed by Bronson Alcott's lecture to the young ladies of the Female Academy, in which he advised them to keep a diary and told them "what to put into it."[9] Mamie Baird began a diary at once. None of these attainments, however, helped her to get off to go buggy riding with the young man of her heart. It was Will Bryan's friend Gran Hulett who accomplished the miracle.

Gran Hulett and Will Bryan were rivals throughout their six years together in Whipple Academy and Illinois College in all things except girls. They were so close in scholarship that at the end there was not a pin's difference between them, and in one famous debate in Sigma Pi, when William Jennings Bryan fiercely assailed Prohibition, Hulett worsted him badly.[10] So sharp was the struggle between the two and so deeply did it cut into Bryan's mind that when he came to write his *Memoirs* half a century later he mispelled Hulett's name—as he altered the name of his first terrifying schoolteacher at Salem, and of his professor of elocution at Illinois College. Will Bryan never did like that elocution professor.[11]

According to popular belief at the time, legendary since, Mamie Baird used to climb out on a balcony of the Female Academy, swing out on a limb of one of the giant elms close to the building, and slide down to the waiting arms of her sweetheart. There was precisely the right amount of romance in such a procedure to satisfy the cravings of the Victorian mind—and not a doubt Mamie Baird would have done just that if she had had to. But Gran Hulett was a "trusty" of Professor Erastus F. Bullard, the dragon who presided over the "Jail for Angels" and had the run of the place. Hulett would let Mamie Baird out the cellar door in the early dusk and let her in again when the moonlight buggy ride with Will Bryan was over.[12] Indeed, everyone conspired to promote the romance. Professor Tanner, who taught Latin and rhetoric in the college and was intensely sentimental, invited the two young people often to his house, where they could see one another to their hearts' content, unmolested. It was he who finally married them.[13] Cousin Lizzie did her part, too, and there were fortnightly meetings of a young people's reading club, where little or no reading was done, and picnics along the bluffs of Maivaise Terre Creek, that the Morgan County folk called "Movestar."

Of course Mamie Baird was caught stepping out to go buggy riding with young Bryan. As punishment she was sent home before the end of her first year at Jacksonville—put on the train by the irate principal of the Academy in person. It is not recorded that young Bryan suffered any penalty for the disaster he had brought upon the young lady. That was the way of the Victorian world. But one thing may be said for William Jennings Bryan: he faced the music without flinching. When Professor Bullard put Mamie Baird on the train to send her back to her parents Will Bryan was hidden in the baggage coach ahead. He went with her. Hand in hand[14] they faced her father together. When William Jennings Bryan emerged from the trying interview with John Baird he was an engaged man. Nothing further was said about the escapade.

Shortly afterward he visited her again, this time at her parents' home and with their permission. The one chance they had to be alone, however, was when she drove him to the station in her phaëton. As they drove along they came upon a man trying to repair a broken harness.

"Wait a minute," said young Bryan. "I'd better help that man."

"Don't bother with him," begged Mamie Baird. "I know the family. They're shiftless. You'd only waste your time."

What she meant was "our time." They drove on a little way, then Bryan put his hand over hers on the reins.

"Stop, please," he said. "I must go back. He needs me."

He went back [wrote Mamie Baird, forty-five years later]. And while he repaired the dilapidated harness, the all too short hours of our visit passed. That might serve as an epitome of his life.

The next year Mamie Baird returned to the Jacksonville Female Academy and was graduated at the head of her class. William Jennings Bryan's record was not so brilliant as hers. In most of his studies he ranked second.[15] Geology and science in general, such as was given—only a term each[16]—held him back. But he had two terms of De Tocqueville on American Government, and in that and moral philosophy he ranked 100 per cent.—"the acknowledged hero of his class."

Thus in the end he managed to divide scholastic honours with Gran Hulett—Bryan the Valedictory and Hulett the Salutatory. William Jennings Bryan never quite achieved the clean-cut victory he worked so hard to attain. He hoped to be editor of the college paper; he was only associate editor.[17] He was vice president of the Interstate Oratorical Association and at the annual banquet responded to the toast of "The Girls,"[18] but he was never president. Bitterest disappointment of all, after William Jennings Bryan had slaved and schemed and played politics to the best of his ability for six years, "his inordinate ambition to become president of Sigma Pi was doomed to defeat."[19] He was made chaplain, instead.[20]

It did not occur to William Jennings Bryan, then or ever, that anything might be wrong with his system. His was the accepted American view of life: One worked for definite ends, consciously visualized—to win a certain prize; to obtain a college degree; to be elected to a specific office; to amass a fortune; to be buried with imposing honours in a national cemetery under an elaborate monument. America was the creation of men who went about the business of life in this practical fashion, not of those who sought knowledge for its own sake or truth because lies and hypocrisy repelled them. The spirit of inquiry—the scientific spirit—that was abroad in the world in the 'seventies and 'eighties, no more than brushed the mind of William Jennings Bryan with its wings. Even that slight touch he felt only on the side of his nature immune to change—the emotional side, where belief was belief and all else damnation. It could not stir him.

I think it would be just as easy for the kind of God we believe in to make the earth in six days as in six years or in six million years or in six hundred million years. I do not think it important whether we believe one or the other [he said].[21]

Fact did not interest him. Faith was sufficient.

No impulse, no influence he received during his six years in Whipple Academy and Illinois College was in the slightest degree calculated to alter the fixed conception of what is a life well lived that William Jennings Bryan fetched with him to Jacksonville from the narrow circle of women who moulded him first in Salem, and the acquisitive materialism of his father. Among his fellow students, sons of the Middle West, success was measured by the achievement of such feats as the winning of prizes, the capturing of honours. The showy, florid, superficial attainments of men like Professor Tanner and Dr. Hiram K. Jones made the former president of Illinois College and the latter a trustee and Jacksonville's most famous figure. There were men of worth and courage, as well: Sturtevant, whom Lincoln trusted; Rufus Crampton, a thorough man and a straight thinker. But no gaudy honours came to them, and them William Jennings Bryan neither sought out nor knew. He was content with his Sunday school, his debating society, his buggy rides with Mamie Baird.

"Success, glory, and honour have been placed as the rewards of the diligent," he proclaimed.

He was diligent.[22]

As his college career drew to a close it became imperative for William Jennings Bryan to decide what he was going to do. Silas Bryan was dead, and his law office in Salem in charge of two of William Jennings Bryan's cousins. There might be a place there. One of the cousins had gone to the Union College of Law, in Chicago. It was as good a thing to do as any. Already the college *Rambler* joked a bit about a possible law firm of Bryan, Drennan and Tomlinson. After all, for what else was he so well equipped, with his golden voice, his facility as a speaker, his quickness in debate, his ability to hold an audience?

In May of his Senior year, William Jennings Bryan made up his mind. He "intends to study law, making it the stepping stone to the arena of politics," the *Rambler* announced.[23] At the class dinner his was the toast to "Our Lawyer."[24] The class history poked fun at Bryan's fondness for peanuts; but it also recorded that "law and politics are his friends, and he intends to court them as soon as other things will permit."[25] The one other thing was his engagement to Mamie Baird.

It was appropriately romantic that she should deliver the Valedictory at the Jacksonville Female Academy and he at Illinois College. Of hers, nothing is known. But the final oration of William Jennings Bryan as an undergraduate is the epitome of his outlook upon life at twenty-one. It was— indeed, it would be—upon "Character."

It is a slow but sure growth in which every thought and action lends its aid. To form character is to form grooves in which are to flow the purpose of our lives [he said]. This we are doing each day, consciously or unconsciously. There is character formed by our association with each friend . . . by every object toward which our affections go out, yea, by every thought that flies on its lightning wing through the dark recesses of the brain. . . . As little reason have we to murmur if in after-life we discover a character deformed by the evil thoughts and actions of to-day—as little reason have we to impeach the wisdom of God if our wild oats, as they are called in palliation, leave scars upon our manhood, which years of reform fail to wear away.[26]

Which was, after all, as sound psychology as if it had been written by Sigmund Freud. One may call it sin or faithlessness to one's self. But the wages is death.

Throughout his college course the mind of William Jennings Bryan dwelt in the realm of those abstractions common to the general run of mankind. These formed the theme of his public utterances: Individual Power, Justice, Eloquence. Around them he massed a phalanx of truisms—"knowledge which everybody would admit,"[27] as Henry Ward Beecher put it. And having laid a foundation of incontestable truths— or what passed as truths to the average mind—he brought them to bear upon his audience with all his excited heart and feeling. It had been the formula of oratorical success from time immemorial. It was the very structure of that prodigious growth just then emerging from small beginnings at Fair Point, on Chautauqua Lake. Essentially characteristic of America, this confidence that a mere sonorous recital of axioms is the equivalent of thought was what William Jennings Bryan took with him from Illinois College as the furniture of an adult mind.

His Commencement was not, however, all triumph. There was what was known as a "bogus programme" of the exercises surreptitiously printed by the wits of the class and circulated among the audience. And while William Jennings Bryan delivered his Valedictory with impressive earnestness they read it and giggled and nudged one another.

This cute youth hopes some day to secure a position as page in the U. S. Senate, a place which he is admirably fitted to fill, as well from his convenient size as from his natural disposition and talents [it read]. It sounds well to hear him say: "Cromwell, I charge thee fling away ambition!" in view of the fact that his college life has been one continuous endeavour to secure place and power. . . . He will talk and gesticulate concerning character in a forcible manner. His conscientious principles (we suppose) have impelled him to blarney the boys on different occasions in order to secure their votes.

There is a cruelty in youth that is not without is accompaniment of salutory candour.

If young Bryan's classmates feared that his engagement to Mamie Baird would lead him to marry at once and take a job with Millard Fillmore Dunlap in a local bank they little knew their Mamie Baird. She had been intensely ambitious for herself: had even dreamed of a career. But now all of that was sunk in the future of her man. Not that Mamie Baird conceived herself in any Tennysonian rôle of yearning passiveness. She saw life as a mutual undertaking of two who loved each other dearly, between whom there could never be question, not by any conscious sacrifice on the part of either, but because their minds would come gradually to flow in a common channel.

Nothing must ever be allowed to shake our confidence in each other [he wrote her]. If we keep no secrets from each other we cannot wander far from the right path.[28]

Nor did they.

With these two, emotion was no taskmaster but a tool to work with; marriage no sentimental relationship but a joint enterprise. If William Jennings Bryan, by his good looks, his magnificent physique, his incomparable voice, his resistless magnetism, was supremely fitted to walk the quarterdeck in gold braid, megaphone in hand, Mamie Baird was not resentful. She rejoiced.

For, unseen in the pilot house, she charted the course of their ship.

CHAPTER IX

CHICAGO

A VAST and stately town," wrote Edward A. Freeman. "In that great city I could see or hear of nothing older than the fire." Sir Henry Irving was slightly less exuberant. He came from the depot, he says, "through piles of lumber, and back streets filled with liquor bars, and decorated with flaming posters, to fine stately thoroughfares, crowded with people, past imposing buildings marked with architectural dignity, to the Grand Pacific Hotel."

True, the Pennsylvania Railroad was doing its best to persuade the public to stop using that horrid word "depot." Even the splendid depot at Pittsburgh was to be called a "station." Very elegant was the Pennsylvania Railroad in 1881, with its twenty-six hour Limited between Chicago and New York, meals actually served on the train. No longer would the clanging dinner bell at eating stops tumble the passengers out for fifteen minutes for dinner.[1] Other railroads into Chicago, consumed with jealousy, countered with a rate war. William Jennings Bryan could have travelled to New York, spent two whole days there, and returned to Chicago, all for $9.[2] So tremendous an adventure never suggested itself to Will Bryan, however. He was saving his money to get married.

The Chicago for which Will Bryan and Gran Hulett took train from Jacksonville was an "elegant city of over half a million inhabitants,"[3] boasting seventy-two miles of stone sidewalks and eleven miles of concrete ones, not to speak of almost two hundred miles of improved streets.[4] There was an Art Institute and an Athenæum and McVicker's "beautiful temple which bears his name, as handsome a place as any of the character in the country."[5]

A highly moral town, too, was this Western metropolis that
had so swiftly outstripped Cincinnati and St. Louis. The
tabernacle of Moody and Sankey at LaSalle Street and
Chicago Avenue was a very redoubt of righteousness. The
godly of Chicago severely rebuked the Reverend H. W.
Thomas, pastor of one of the largest Methodist churches, for
holding among other convictions that no sane man would believe all of the Bible. He was found guilty of heresy. Even
Carter Harrison, the newly elected Democratic mayor, was
moved to raise his voice in protest against what he called
shameless attacks upon the good name of Chicago:

Some of our own people [he complained] have been made to
believe that this city is a sink of festering crime. . . . As Mayor of
Chicago, proud of its good name, I cannot silently permit that this
name be tarnished by the slanders of men who, had they lived 1800
years ago, would have sold their Master for thirty pieces of silver.

A mass meeting was promptly called to have saloons closed
at midnight and their number limited to one for every five
hundred inhabitants.[6] But nothing came of it.

Chicago was the great world to William Jennings Bryan in
a way that Jacksonville never had been. He had hardly arrived before the National Farmers' Alliance met there to oppose all monopolies, favour an income tax, denounce free
railroad passes, demand regulation of railroad rates, and declare the adulteration of food equivalent to counterfeiting.[7]
The employees of one of the railroads struck for an increase
of wages to twenty cents an hour and won their demands.[8]
Speculation in breadstuffs attained such proportions that the
"scenes at the Board of Trade at the height of the excitement
have been simply indescribable"[9]—this wild gambling in
grain was a national scandal, trailing ruin in its wake. Yet
thirty thousand American tourists spent fifty million dollars
in Europe that same summer.[10]

Garfield died, and the citizens of Chicago hanged his assassin in effigy[11] while thousands followed an imposing cata-
falque through Chicago's streets.[12] Men who had never given
the contingency a thought found their grief over the Presi-

dent's death sharply intensified by the vision of Roscoe
Conkling's errand boy in the White House.

So many redoubtable events dismayed young Bryan. The
walls of the secluded little world of Illinois College and Dr.
Hiram K. Jones's Christian home suddenly expanded as by
magic, leaving this twenty-one-year-old lad naked and com-
fortless among strangers. Chicago furnished the only direct
contact William Jennings Bryan ever did have with that
industrial America, already growing with such appalling
speed. He shrank from it as a woman might, never seeking to
understand it, always a little fearsome of the complexity of its
problems. Even that very first morning, when he and Gran
Hulett arrived, Will Bryan was awestruck and apprehensive
of the great city. One person he knew in it, at least by reputation. Him he sought out straightway.

"A quiet, sincere, frank, honest American gentleman,"
said a memorial of the Chicago Bar Association.[13] "Lyman
Trumbull was one of the very great men of the nation."
He was precisely that when Will Bryan came to ask his help
in the fall of 1881. Cousin to those Jonathan Trumbulls who
seem to be hereditary governors of Connecticut, descended
on his mother's side from Increase and Cotton Mather, Lyman Trumbull was, as Joseph Medill grudgingly described
him, "a man of great ability, undoubted integrity, and stain-
less reputation, pure as the driven snow and nearly as cold."[14]
Secretary of State of Illinois at twenty-eight, Lyman Trumbull spent thirty-two years in public life without ever once
making the most infinitesimal concession to expediency or
yielding a jot of his convictions in support of any cause or
for any reason whatever, good or ill. He was one of those to
whom Honest Abe wrote frequent cryptic letters marked
very confidential, with the persons mentioned in them indicated only by initials and the little caution at the end—
"Do not let my name be known in the matter." They disagreed on many points, did Lincoln and Trumbull. But if
there was man or woman whom Lincoln trusted implicitly
Trumbull was he. "He could have been President instead of
Hayes or Garfield or Harrison," said Joseph Medill. But

there is a price a man pays to be President of the United States that Lyman Trumbull did not have in his purse. Nothing in his long life so grieved Trumbull as to see Abraham Lincoln pay that price by making Simon Cameron his Secretary of War.[15]

Lyman Trumbull had been Judge of the Supreme Court of Illinois, Congressman, United States Senator, candidate for Governor, tendered the ambassadorship to Great Britain. He draughted the Thirteenth Amendment to the Constitution of the United States and introduced the Freedmen's Bureau and Civil Rights bills, the three measures designed to secure forever the gains to humanity of the war between the states. He was one of the "seven traitors" vilified and excoriated because he would not vote to impeach Andrew Johnson. His name was cut deep and clean in the tablets of his country's history. He was approaching seventy and was of that breed who grow more radical as they grow older.

To be sure there was little enough in common between the Hon. Silas Bryan and the Hon. Lyman Trumbull at any time. But, after all, Silas Bryan did learn something from the war between the states, and one of the things he learned was what manner of man that selfsame Lyman Trumbull, against whom he had voted so zealously for the Senate in 1854, really was. Once having seen the light the Hon. Silas Bryan was not the man to temporize. In 1871, when the shattered Democratic party was casting about for a standard bearer, it was no other than Silas Bryan who suggested Trumbull as "the Providential man for the present crisis." He did even more. He offered, himself, if Trumbull were willing, to promote the choice by a hopeful Democracy of the Hon. Lyman Trumbull for President of the United States. Lyman Trumbull did not reject Silas Bryan's overture. But in the excitement of his own campaign for Congress, the matter appears to have slipped the Hon. Silas Bryan's mind. It did not slip his son's mind, however. And when William Jennings Bryan, ten years later, discussed with his family the best place to study law, the fact that Judge Trumbull was the leading figure of the Chicago bar was a factor of weight. Nothing much was ever allowed to lie fallow with the Bryans.

On the other hand, this was not the sole reason why William Jennings Bryan finally matriculated at the Union College of Law. He had little choice in the matter. Judge Bryan was dead, and the master spirit of the law firm of Bryan, Jennings & Bryan—all in the family—was Will Bryan's cousin, Charles Edgar Jennings, a man of "intense and absolute fixity of purpose," those who knew him said; with "a dominating resolve to rise and make his influence felt."[16] In a word, a true Jennings. He had gone to the Union College of Law, and that, he decided, was where Will Bryan would go, too. When Will Bryan completed his law course, he would come back to Salem and enter the firm in his father's place. That was settled.

In formulating this programme for his cousin, Charles Edgar Jennings neglected two important factors. One was William Jennings Bryan and the other was Mamie Baird. Neither had the remotest intention of settling down to a country law practice in Salem, Illinois. Both were firmly convinced that there were far greater things in store for William Jennings Bryan than ever Egypt would offer. But one law school was, on the whole, more or less like another; so they made no point of the matter at this time. Leaving his beloved with her family, Will Bryan marched resolutely off to Chicago, high hopes in his heart.

The Union College of Law was Chicago's oldest law school. In time it came to have a certain distinction as the law department of Northwestern University, but when William Jennings Bryan entered it was only as they received their degrees that the law students realized that they were part of a larger institution of learning. The fact was printed on the diplomas. There was a faculty of four and forty-three students in Will Bryan's class, two of them girls. Class hours were from eight to ten and four to six so that the students could work the better part of each day in some Chicago law office. It gave them practical experience and helped them to earn a little money toward the price of tuition.

It was a job of this sort that William Jennings Bryan sought in the office of the Hon. Lyman Trumbull. As Trumbull was a generous soul who bore no malice, young Bryan was duly installed at the office boy's desk. He copied pleadings in longhand, filled the inkwells, and swept out the office, all for five dollars a week. But back in Salem, and even in Jacksonville, it had a sonorous sound to say that William Jennings Bryan was reading law in the office of the great Lyman Trumbull. Young Bryan missed no opportunity to say it.

Of the law as a means of livelihood William Jennings Bryan learned nothing whatever from Lyman Trumbull and little enough from law school. The Hon. Lyman Trumbull was Professor of Constitutional and Statute Law and Practice in the United States Courts, in the law school of Chicago University; but that was, after all, a rather specialized subject of scant utility to a young man ploughing his way through Blackstone and Kent. Trumbull was a lawyer's lawyer—he might have helped Bryan at fifty; he was no use to Bryan at twenty-one. What drew the two together was not law, or even politics, about which young Bryan was so enthusiastic and old Trumbull so tolerantly disillusioned—but Henry Trumbull.

Henry was the youngest of Judge Trumbull's sons. Brilliant, indolent, lovable, unstable, he drank and played cards and got into trouble at Yale and was fetched home to study law under his father's eye, in Will Bryan's class. For such a lad, the circumspect conduct and strict moral views of an upstanding young man like William Jennings Bryan were precisely what was needed, or so thought Lyman Trumbull. So young Bryan came often to the Trumbull house at Oakland, and Henry Trumbull and Will Bryan were inseparable.

It did neither of them any good. Certainly, for a son of Trumbull there was no way of salvation through Bryan's unquestioning faith that "one can be convicted of sin, and, in a spasm of repentance, be born again."[17] There was something just a little too easy and evasive of all responsibility about this smug procedure of throwing the entire burden on

God. Lyman Trumbull had a philosophy of his own, less positive perhaps, certainly less facile, but also less naïve:

> Whilst ever ready to acknowledge my own imperfection and impotence, I suppose I know nothing of, or at best see but as through a glass dimly, that change of heart of which the converted speak, and which comes of a faith it has not been given me to possess,[18]

he wrote. To William Jennings Bryan this was unthinkable. Religion was "the only basis of morality."[19] He could conceive no other. Never before in his life had he come into intimate contact with a man like Lyman Trumbull, who had different standards, or Henry Trumbull, who, without pretensions to conspicuous virtue, could grasp in an hour what it took Bryan weeks to master.[20]

In this incongruous association, therefore, Henry Trumbull's very weaknesses came to be William Jennings Bryan's strength, and Lyman Trumbull's anxiety for his son justification of William Jennings Bryan's faith. Had Bryan required demonstration that the race is not to the swift nor the battle to the strong, here it was. He emerged from his intimacy with the Trumbull family, his horizon not enlarged but constricted. His was plainly the way of righteousness and of reward. If the facts of human experience failed to accord with one's theory of life the remedy was not to modify one's theory but to alter the facts.

Applied to the law so empiric an approach was not helpful. It left William Jennings Bryan far from the head of his class, grounded only in certain broad, resounding principles of jurisprudence, useful, perhaps, to a lecturer but scarcely calculated to weigh with hard-headed juries. It in no wise impaired his value as a political orator, however; quite the contrary, in fact. Since it was as a political orator, in class and out, that William Jennings Bryan sought to make his mark at the Union College of Law, he was well satisfied. In the very first of the fortnightly meetings of the College Literary Society, with the help of Henry Trumbull and Dan Kagy, of Salem, Will Bryan managed to be elected the orator of the occasion. Bryan selected "Eternal Vigilance is the Price of Safety"[21] as a subject.

I have been deeply moved by the lethargy of our people [he wrote Mamie Baird]. The perpetuity of a nation I think depends more upon the character of its people than upon the principles which underlie its government, and observing the inaction of our people, the carelessness with which they elect their representatives and neglect the administration of justice, I am wrought up to such a pitch that I cannot hold in.

It was all strongly reminiscent of that highly emotional discourse on Character with which William Jennings Bryan had regaled his classmates of Illinois College. But as his new classmates had not heard that, his oration was an instant and signal success.

Nevertheless, William Jennings Bryan was not popular. His fellow students had come to law school to be lawyers, not Senators. They resented Bryan's attempt to turn the classroom into a political debating society. William Jennings Bryan had no desire to be included in the little groups of students who gathered about scrubbed deal tables in German beer gardens and argued points of law over a stein of Pilsener. In any event, he was not asked to join them. He had his own little group of intimates—Gran Hulett, studying medicine; Dan Kagy, of Salem; Adolphus Talbot, whom he had first met at Galesburg; and his own younger brother, Charley— old acquaintances, not new. They met every Sunday after church and dined together, each taking turn as host. One Sunday when it was Will Bryan's turn, he asked the others what they would have.

"You're host, Will," said Gran Hulett. "You do the ordering."

"All right," said Bryan. "Let's all have apple dumplings." They ate it.

"Now what?" asked Bryan.

"Go ahead and order, Will," said the others.

"All right. Apple pie."

They ate that, too. When they had finished no one had any room for more food.

"I figured," Bryan confided to Gran Hulett, with his wide smile, "that two orders of apples would fill us all up and I could save a little on the meal."[22]

In many ways there was a good deal more Scotch than Irish in the make-up of William Jennings Bryan.

It was almost four miles from where Will and Charley Bryan roomed, far out on the South Side, near where the growing industrial town of Hyde Park began, to the Law School. But Will Bryan habitually walked it to save fare on the cable car. Every morning, too, he walked three blocks for his breakfast, to a place where he could get three buns for ten cents, instead of two. He wore a black alpaca coat, a very low collar with a black string cravat tied in a careless bow, parted his hair far over on the right side, and let his beard grow. He looked like Moody and talked like Moody, his classmates said. Not a few of them wondered what Bryan was doing in law at all.

None of this disturbed William Jennings Bryan. He appeared to be not only insensitive to criticism, but good-natured about it. There was within him a profound conviction that he was right that was like an armour. Added to this was his desire to claim the lady of his heart as soon as possible—just so soon as he was making $500 a year, he said.[23] Between the two, during the two years he spent in Chicago, William Jennings Bryan dwelt in a little world of his own which nothing of the feverish, slipshod, ruthless growth of that grandiose city penetrated. He might as well have been in Heidelberg.

He saw Mamie Baird as often as he could and wrote her regularly—grandiloquent letters, sometimes with a sort of clumsy badinage in them, more frequently running to high-flown oratorical phrases that could be used later in speeches—and were:

Oh, memory, God given garden of the soul, where flowers once planted will forever bloom. May we scatter on thy sacred soil only seeds of kindness, truth, and love. Seeds watered by the dews of Heaven which may blossom and bear fruit through eternal years.

Before William Jennings Bryan graduated from law school he made a trip to Kansas City, to look the ground over as a possible place to launch his career as a lawyer. But Kansas City seemed too big to begin in. He was overawed by the place and decided against it. Of one thing William Jennings Bryan was certain: he was not going back to Salem to be his father's son for the rest of his life. In the end he decided to return to Jacksonville, where what reputation he had made in college was at least his own and those who might be of assistance to him were friends, not relatives.

William Jennings Bryan fetched back from Chicago with him scarcely more than he had brought there two years previous: assurance a little more firmly grounded; self-sufficiency more fully developed; a growing sense of righteousness; and a conviction of his own destiny. The knowledge of the law he obtained was negligible. But from Lyman Trumbull, William Jennings Bryan carried away the germ of an idea he was never altogether to lose: fear of monopoly and all forms of concentrated wealth—plutocracy, he came to call it—to be fought without quarter as the implacable foe of free institutions, by "laws limiting the amount of property to be acquired by devise or inheritance"; by government ownership, if need be, of "monopolies affecting the public interest"; by every possible means, as one might fight an epidemic of cholera, or the bubonic plague, or any other unclean and destroying thing. For in the twilight of his days, the Hon. Lyman Trumbull came to believe in human brotherhood and equality of rights as the way of salvation. And in the light of the faith of this gentle old man William Jennings Bryan was vouchsafed a vision.

The close of William Jennings Bryan's law course was not without its bitter lees. He had set his heart upon being Valedictorian of his class, as he had been at Illinois College. But the class would have none of him. He was defeated by one vote. Furiously Bryan and his friends charged that the election had not been fair and demanded another. They had their way.

And William Jennings Bryan was defeated again.

CHAPTER X

ASCENT

WILLIAM JENNINGS BRYAN'S decision to settle in Jacksonville was an error.

He recognized it himself in due time, but meanwhile four precious years were lost in an unrequiting struggle to earn a living. That was one thing young Bryan, in common with every American of his age, found he had first to do: he must demonstrate his manhood to himself and the world by running up butcher's bills, then paying them. Thoreau could write as seductively as he pleased about plain living and high thinking: that formula might do very well for Walden. But in the Middle West it was not respectable. The chief difference between the schools of philosophy at Concord and Jacksonville was that Bronson Alcott lived unashamed off the earnings of his talented daughter Louisa May, while Dr. Hiram K. Jones had to make his own living before anyone would listen to him on the subject of Plato or anything else.

Fortunately for Will Bryan, Hiram K. Jones, looking more like the late Silas Bryan than ever, was at the height of his fame in 1885. It could hardly be said of him, as of poor Bronson Alcott, that his "listeners decreased steadily in numbers but never entirely deserted him."[1] The philosophical appetite of the Athens of the West was more robust than that of Concord—the reputation and the influence of Hiram K. Jones only increased with the years. However, as Emerson was dead and Alcott stricken with apoplexy, Dr. Jones had nothing further to gain by the annual pilgrimage to the capital of transcendentalism. Instead, the very summer young Bryan returned from law school his distinguished cousin founded the American Akadémé in Jacksonville, Illinois,

and the intellectual world of the Middle West beat a path
to his doorstep. The purpose of the Akadémé was "the ele-
vation of the mind from the sphere of the sensuous life into
that of virtue and justice, and into communication with the
diviner ideas and natures."[2]

True, the motto of the Akadémé was Lucretia Mott's
somewhat simpler dictum: "Truth for authority, not
authority for truth."[3] William Jennings Bryan never quite
understood what this meant. How could one come by truth
more surely than upon the authority of such minds as that
of Hiram K. Jones? All his life he had been taught to respect
the authority of wiser heads than his own—his mother, old
Silas Bryan bucklered with the Book of Proverbs, swarthy
Mrs. Ben Lemon, Mrs. Beville, his Sabbath-school teacher,
General James C. Black, who had given young Bryan priceless advice on how to capture an audience, President Tanner
of Illinois College, Judge Trumbull. And now, more distinguished than any of these to the mind of William Jennings
Bryan, and to the mind of many another as well, Dr. Hiram
K. Jones. In his presence the seekers of culture in the Middle
West "sat in that conventicle, in that holy chapel, in that
church where the message came from beyond and descended
straight from the throne," as one of them describes it, "listening to the illuminated words of the great thinker and
great man."[4] If the authority of such as these was not final,
what was? So argued William Jennings Bryan. And in the
hothouse atmosphere of the exotic mental exercises of the
American Akadémé such lucid, specific, realistic ideas as he
had borrowed for a moment from Lyman Trumbull withered
and died.

Nevertheless, certain practical advantages did indubitably
accrue from the renewal of young Bryan's almost eight years
of intimate relationship with the family of Hiram K. Jones.
Dr. Jones was still—indeed, more than ever—a leading citizen of Jacksonville, a trustee of Illinois College and president
of its Alumni Association. In all three capacities he was
closely associated with Judge Edward P. Kirby. So there was
no difficulty at all about arranging for desk room in the law

offices of Brown, Kirby & Russell, where Will Bryan could pick up what legal business he might.

It was little enough. When William Jennings Bryan cherished visions of all Jacksonville flocking to the office of the brilliant orator of the Class of 1881, to have their cases pleaded before respectful judges, deeply moved by the golden voice and florid rhetoric of the young attorney, he was dwelling still in a fantasy world where what he wanted to be true must of necessity be true. It was a distinct shock to William Jennings Bryan to learn that nothing in life is quite so ephemeral as academic honours.

Young Bryan's first case in court was the defence of a horse thief. None other than Gran Hulett was the plaintiff—it was his father's horse.

"Shame on you," he said to Bryan, when the culprit had been sentenced to seven years' imprisonment, "for defending a man you knew to be guilty!"

"Every man is entitled to some defence," Bryan replied, a little nettled. "If I had not helped him he might have been given ten years!"[5]

"When I got upon the floor my fright all left me and I never spoke with more fluency and earnestness than I did that day," he wrote Mamie Baird. And he quoted the Jacksonville *Courier:* "W. J. Bryan was highly complimented on Monday for his success in his first speech before a circuit Court jury." Bryan wrote the item himself and turned it in at the *Courier* office. But of that he said nothing to Mamie Baird.

He had a keen appreciation of the value of publicity, had William Jennings Bryan. He was always ready to make speeches at church and Sunday-school picnics, into which he would adroitly "inject a reference to my being a lawyer,"[6] as he put it. Then when he came back to town in the evening he would go over to the office of the Jacksonville *Journal* and sit down and write out a little account of each speech, referring to himself as "a promising young lawyer," or, if the speech happened to be political, as "one likely to go far in the political world."[7]

Nevertheless, even with all of this, the way of the law in Jacksonville was tedious. His first six months William Jennings did not even make living expenses and had to draw on his father's estate.[8] One month he took in only $2.50.[9] Most of his business settled down into collections for Dr. Jones and Dr. Jones's patients.[10]

The days passed wearily. There was a continuous tread upon the stairs [he says], and I would turn to the door each time I heard a hand upon the knob, only to find that the visitor had turned into the office of Mr. Brown, Mr. Kirby, or Mr. Russell. They had clients enough and were busy all the time, but the chair that I had been careful to provide and place at my desk stared at me vacantly.[11]

He planned to buy Mamie Baird a gold thimble for Christmas—if he had the money. "That statement 'If I have the money' does not sound very well." he wrote her wistfully, "but I do not hide even my poverty from you."[12]

Russell moved to Minneapolis, and Bryan hinted to be taken into his office. But Russell was noncommittal. Next William Jennings wrote his law-school classmate, Henry Trumbull, whose father had sent him to Albuquerque, suggesting a law partnership—a connection with Lyman Trumbull's son would be well worth moving even to the Territory of New Mexico. Nothing came of that, either.[13] Bryan tried to induce Richard Yates, the son of Illinois's war governor, who had been the prize orator for Illinois College two years before Bryan, to enter into partnership with him. A son of Governor Yates would be almost as good as a son of Lyman Trumbull. Unfortunately, Yates refused. "A slight difference in regard to the division of the first year's fees prevented that partnership," he explained.[14] The whole step-by-step process of professional advancement irked and irritated William Jennings Bryan. He was convinced that there was a royal road to success somewhere and that he was missing it.

One thing Bryan felt he did lack: personal popularity. He set himself to gain it, with methodical thoroughness. He joined the Y. M. C. A. and was assiduous in his attendance.

But he could not resist accepting a 2 per cent. commission
on all collections he made for the organization, and was surprised to find that the members looked upon his association
with them as one of business rather than good fellowship.[15]
He taught Sunday school in the First Presbyterian church,
and even subscribed $10 toward the purchase of a number 6
plush chair for the pulpit. For the first—and last—time in
his life he went in for athletics. He was particularly good at
jumping backward, a feat in which there was little competition. Also, he played baseball on a team organized by
the younger members of the Morgan County bar. He was
not especially adept at the game, but the bleachers extracted
endless delight from his flowing beard. He wore it, he explained, to give himself "a more elderly and dignified appearance,
not a disadvantage in dealing with a certain class of clients,"
he added seriously. For one who made a practice of using
humorous illustrations in speeches or debate he was singularly
lacking in sense of humour where he himself was concerned.
He kept close touch with collegiate activities and received a
Master's degree for an oration on "American Citizenship,"
three years after graduation. In short, William Jennings
Bryan neglected no means he could think of to keep himself
in the public eye. But the swift progress to success he had
dreamed failed to materialize.

The campaign of 1884 furnished young Bryan his best opportunity to achieve distinction. Both conventions were held
in Chicago that year, the Republican first. Feverishly young
Bryan followed every step of the proceedings, noted in his
mind the names of the leading delegates: Mark Hanna, William McKinley, J. B. Foraker, Henry Cabot Lodge. He
read with amusement the speech of Theodore Roosevelt, of
New York, in enthusiastic—and successful—support of the
Hon. John R. Lynch, a coloured delegate from Mississippi,
for temporary chairman of the convention.

Bryan saw very clearly that between the Republicans and
the Democrats who would nominate Grover Cleveland there
was no difference whatever—Cleveland would make the
best Republican President the country had had since Lin-

coln, as in fact he did. Only the Hon. Benjamin F. Butler, appropriately attired as for a ball in a white cravat and dress coat, and representing a million and a half labouring men,[16] stood for anything at all. To William Jennings Bryan the opportunity seemed tremendous for some man to step forth the champion of the disinherited and inarticulate millions, farmers and workers, of the Middle West and sweep to victory on a clear-cut issue of the exploited masses arrayed against a cynical and predatory class. Bryan itched to be in the thick of just such a fight.

It was all he could do to get to the Democratic convention at all, so hard up he was. He did manage it, however, and one of Carter Harrison's ballot-box stuffers passed him into the hall.[17] For the second time he saw Honest John Kelly, pale and nervous in a battered suit, beaten and disregarded;[18] for the second time he saw the Democratic party, dominated by August Belmont, turn to New York for its candidate, when the great body of dissatisfied men and women who should have constituted a victorious Democracy dwelt in the West. One high light there was in the whole affair for young Bryan—"the exquisite beauty of Bourke Cockran's speech."[19] He listened, enraptured, to a type of oratory he had never before heard, diction, a phrasing, an elegance, a passion that might have belonged to Pitt or Fox, as distinct as day and night from the stodgy pedantism of Daniel Webster and Henry Clay in which young Bryan had been steeped. Here at last was one to match Robert Ingersoll—a very magician of eloquence, swaying like a great tree caught in a whirlwind as the tumultuous current of his words beat down resistance and swelled the hearts of those who heard him. Young Bryan watched the vast audience, alternately agitated and stilled, as a field of standing barley is swept by gusts of summer wind. There was something terrible and divine in the power of the spoken word to move men as Bourke Cockran first arrested their attention and then held them enthralled.

William Jennings Bryan came away from the convention, exulting. "Amid shouts and screams Tammany's defeat was

put on record," said the *Herald*.[20] Bourke Cockran's plea had
failed. For all his matchless eloquence, there was something
missing, and Bryan knew what it was. There was no conviction behind the beautiful façade of diction. The tremendous
drive of evangelizing purpose was not there. The spirit of the
crusader was lacking. These Bryan was confident he had. He
might never be able to charm audiences as Bourke Cockran
could. He might never achieve a perfection of form to catch
and hold his hearers breathless. But he could drive. He could
learn to make men and women do as he bade them.

The problem of his future opened clear before William
Jennings Bryan as he took the train from Chicago back to
Jacksonville. There was no use waiting any longer to get
married. On the contrary, Mamie Baird could help him. He
knew what he had to do and was certain he could do it: he
must master the art of taking command of the minds of
men, not through the impact from without of his ideas upon
theirs, seeking to convince them against their will, but from
within, divining what was in their minds and expressing it
for them. His strength would be the strength of a thousand
men, because his heart beat with theirs. "Effectiveness in
speech is measured by earnestness," he said.[21] That was the
secret: "eloquence is heart speaking to heart."[22] And William
Jennings Bryan possessed it.

He and Mamie Baird were married at Perry, on October 1,
1884. They had known each other five years. There were
neither secrets nor pretense between them.

I am sorry your throat is worse. My dear, that troubles me.
Can't you cure that? Does it come from Catarrh? I have a recipe
which I am trying. Equal parts of Golden Seal, alum and borax.
Don't know what effect it will have [he wrote her the year before
they were married]. In regard to the dress, I rather like velvet
though your objection may be sufficient. Don't they wear velvet
in Summer?

And just before the wedding:

I am practicing on "and with all my worldly goods I thee
endow," so as to make it duly impressive. If you dare to laugh when
I say that, I won't kiss you when he tells me to salute my bride.

They could afford to joke about his poverty: a comfortable home awaited them, on College Hill in Jacksonville, with her parents.

The wedding ring William Jennings Bryan gave his wife was engraved: "Won 1880. One 1884."[23] After the ceremony they drove to the station in her phaëton. This time, however, there were no stops to fix anyone's harness. Charley Bryan had been his brother's best man, and he followed the bridal pair on their honeymoon to St. Louis, telling everyone on the train that they were newly married.

They returned from a short visit in Salem in time for Bryan to make a number of speeches for Cleveland in the bitterest campaign the country had yet seen. Most of Bryan's political activity was in Congressman Springer's district, and he had every reason to cherish hopes of recompense when Cleveland was elected. None came. It was discouraging. William Jennings Bryan needed money; he was recently married and there was to be a baby. He had, of course, something still left of his father's estate and his father-in-law was reasonably well off. The young couple was in no danger of want. But Bryan needed not so much the money as to make money. It was the symbol of success in that Middle West from which he sprang and in which he dwelt. He might be invited to deliver the addresses at innumerable important meetings, acclaimed as an accomplished public speaker and treated with outward deference by the leading men of the place on such occasions. It meant nothing. No one knew better than William Jennings Bryan that if he could not turn his talents into cash, the very men who flattered him to his face for his oratory would despise him in their hearts. Even Henry Ward Beecher was admired and applauded in that Middle West less because he was known throughout the world as a matchless preacher than because he had amassed a million dollars.

William Jennings Bryan had made a mistake in beginning in a community where his early promise had been so brilliant. Even his friends were commencing to pucker their foreheads and say: "Ah, yes. In college everyone predicted a great future for him!" And then quickly to change the subject. There was no escaping the incongruity between the growing fame of William Jennings Bryan as a popular speaker always in demand at church affairs, political meetings, and even on civic occasions, and William Jennings Bryan the lawyer, engaged in the niggardly business of buying up farms at tax sales on commission for Fill Dunlap's bank, collecting bills on time payments, and acting as assignee in bankruptcy —an occupation more like pawnbroking than the law. Bryan hated it. He went into all sorts of dubious financial ventures in the hope of a lucky strike that would mark him as a man of substance, a success in the eyes of his neighbours. A deposit of coal was discovered near Jacksonville, and William Jennings Bryan became one of the chief promoters of the enterprise. He sold the first load of coal mined at public auction in the court-house square of Jacksonville with an eloquent appeal to investors to support a local industry. The mine turned out to be a pocket. Bryan waited three years for some tangible recognition of his political services in two Presidential and three congressional campaigns. When nothing was forthcoming, he put his pride in his pocket and went to beg a job as Assistant United States District Attorney of an old friend of his father whom Cleveland had made District Attorney at Springfield. He was put off with vague promises, perhaps because in his letters of application he persisted in misspelling the District Attorney's name. Still undismayed, a few months before leaving Jacksonville he applied to Congressman Springer for the office of Recorder of Deeds for the District of Columbia, a position bringing in an income of some fifteen thousand a year.

I notice in the papers that Recorder James M. Trotter is very sick [wrote Bryan]. I have been thinking over it and have concluded to make the sacrifice and accept the position if it should become vacant and our President should offer it to me. . . . I believe I could attend to the duties of the office. I know I am honest. The reason I wish the office is that the salary is good. . . . I believe that the President has the good of his party and above all his country at heart. . . . He was wise in appointing a colored man to succeed Douglass and if he thinks it better to offer the office to another colored man I will believe him right. . . . You will please not allow the fact that I am an applicant to be known either to the press there or the people here. . . . I am glad to note a constant growth in the Cleveland sentiment. . . .

Bryan was not called upon to "make the sacrifice." Mr. Trotter recovered.

Jacksonville, as I soon saw, was a settled community [he says]. I went West to seek larger opporutnities to practice law.[24]

William Jennings Bryan was, in fact, twenty-seven before he came reluctantly to the realization that he was foredoomed to mediocrity in Illinois. He did not really know enough law to be a success at it, nor was he sufficiently interested in the law as a vocation to master its technique. In a newer country, he figured, where the competition was not so sharp and less legal acumen was demanded, he would stand a better chance. But where?

It was at this auspicious moment that one of the collection cases that made up the bulk of his legal business took William Jennings Bryan to Kansas. On his way he stopped off at Lincoln, Nebraska, to see his old law-school classmate, Dolf Talbot, a rising young railroad attorney. Together they talked it over.

Again and again in after life, Bryan went out of his way to protest that "no thought of politics ever entered my mind," as he put it, in deciding his removal to Nebraska. "How could it," he would add, "when Nebraska was a Republican state?"

He was disingenuous. The same fall that William Jennings Bryan moved to Lincoln, the Hon. John A. McShane, a Democrat, took his seat in Congress representing the very district which Bryan had chosen as his field of political activity. In fact that particular district in Nebraska had already furnished the first break in the solid phalanx of Republican representatives in the newer country of the Middle West. William Jennings Bryan had to blaze no untried trail; it was enough that he follow. The whole of Nebraska was trembling in the balance, the prey of a far-reaching agrarian unrest that might lead the states west of the Mississippi into any political camp. It was the opportunity of a young man if ever there was one.

And no one better than William Jennings Bryan knew how specious and transparent was his claim that political considerations did not actuate his move to Nebraska. What is significant is that he should have persisted in trying to cover up his real motives. "I entered politics by accident," he asserted, not once but a hundred times. He liked to believe that. He liked to believe that Divine Providence had suddenly summoned him, reluctant, from a career as a successful lawyer and bade him take up the defence of the friendless and the downtrodden. To Bryan's mind this amiable fiction lent his career the character of a crusade and added strength to his spirit and depth and conviction to his voice. It was not a personal idiosyncrasy. It was the accepted manner in which all Americans approached the performance of what they desired, and what they intended to do—a lingering relic of Puritanism in the American mind that habitually prefaced self-appreciation with the phrase: "If I must needs glory, I will glory of the things which concern mine infirmities."

When William Jennings Bryan, on the third anniversary of his wedding, left his wife and child behind him in Jacksonville while he made a home for them and cleared a field of action for himself in Nebraska, he had reached a decision. The practice of law, save as a convenient means to an end, was behind him. Henceforth his career was to lie in the world of politics, and no time was to be lost about it, either. Once and once only, taken off his guard, William Jennings Bryan spoke out his real thought:

Certainly from the time I was fifteen years old, I had but one ambition in life, and that was to come to Congress. I studied for it. I worked for it, and everything I did had that object in view.[25]

Which was precisely the reason why, all of his life, William Jennings Bryan so persistently maintained that nothing of the sort was in his mind.

PART III
REALIZATION

"It is a poor head that can not find plausible reason for doing what the heart wants to do."

William Jennings Bryan.

CHAPTER XI

1890

WHEN William Jennings Bryan pulled up stakes and began life over again in Nebraska, he turned his back upon the real problem in the America of his day and set jauntily off down a political bypath that led nowhere.

There were excellent precedents for this, congenitally American. No real American could divest himself of the historic conception of the United States as a land of inexhaustible opportunity. The lesson was written in the McGuffey Readers and inculcated from childhood in every schoolboy that the heroic rôle was flight. If economic conditions grew intolerable in one community the thing to do was to pack up and go elsewhere. The foot of the rainbow was always a little farther West, and those who threw up the sponge in the battle of life and went in quest of the pot of gold were called "pioneers." Monuments were built to them.

Plainly, however, no economic problems were solved by this procedure. Instead, more problems seemed to arise, as ancient as Nebuchadnezzar. Preëminently there were two: The plight of the farmer who toiled long hours, fed the world, and had a constitutional objection to a diet of his own grass; and the plight of the industrial worker who ate what bread he could get in the sweat of his face and wrested mighty little else out of life.

Just at the moment William Jennings Bryan was reaching the conclusion that Jacksonville held no future for him two men emerged who sought to deal with these problems in a spirit of reality, not romanticism. They were Henry George and John Peter Altgeld. Each man stood squarely for the vast inarticulate mass of the disinherited; and each man attracted to himself a compact, devoted following. The year before Bryan moved to Lincoln, Henry George, an obscure California printer a decade previous, left Theodore Roosevelt a poor third in the race for Mayor of New York. That same summer, in St. Louis, in Chicago, and all along the lines of the great transcontinental railways, there flamed an industrial struggle so sanguinary that in another country it would have been called a revolution. In Haymarket Square in Chicago a sudden bloodletting revealed in the flash of an exploded bomb the extent of the fear and the depth of the hatred that marked the conflict. That doughty warrior, General John A. Logan, promptly proposed to increase the United States army by 20 per cent. so as to handle striking workmen with celerity and dispatch. The business interests and the press of the East applauded the idea. In the West, however, there was less enthusiasm. General C. H. Van Wyck, Senator from Nebraska, refused to permit soldiers to be used "to 'put down the people' and sustain Jay Gould and his confederates as the army used to be employed to sustain slaveholders."[1] A great gulf opened between the West and the East on either brink of which men snarled at one another in distrust and bitter animosity.

For an ambitious young man whose heart beat in tune with oppressed humanity it was a moment to be up and doing. But William Jennings Bryan had more important matters in hand. He had worked hard to be Chancellor Commander of the Knights of Pythias at Jacksonville, and the prize seemed at last just within reach when he decided to move to Lincoln. Bryan was torn with doubt. If he announced that he was on the point of leaving Jacksonville for good he would, of course, never be elected Chancellor Commander, never enjoy the distinction of being a Past Chancellor Commander, nor the material advantages of the position. Yet he hated to deceive his fellow Knights. True, there was nothing final about his move as yet, he told himself; he might not like Nebraska. After all, the whole venture was only an experiment. There was always the possibility that he would return to Illinois.

So William Jennings Bryan kept his tongue discreetly between his teeth, and by so doing was duly elected Chancellor

Commander of the Knights of Pythias in Jacksonville, and in due time, also, installed. Once that was out of the way he departed for Nebraska with a good conscience. It was an excellent stroke. The Knights of Pythias were the strongest fraternal organization in Lincoln. Past Chancellor Commander Bryan had a standing from the very first.

The political career of William Jennings Bryan had begun. It was none too promising. Politics in Nebraska toward the end of the 'eighties might appropriately have been classified as a gainful occupation, win or lose. The Hon. John M. Thurston, the leading Republican, was employed by the railroads crossing the state to see to it that the Republican party sponsored no legislation inimical to railroad interests; the Hon. J. Sterling Morton, the leading Democrat, was employed by the same railroads to perform the same function with respect to the Democratic party. By this happy arrangement all questions affecting the railroads might well have been entirely removed from politics, to the distinct advantage of both politics and transportation, had it not been for the farmers of Nebraska.

As farmers they were not conspicuously successful. They still used brush harrows and were satisfied with three-inch ploughing, with the result that every dry spell had the effect of a drought, and the wails of the horny-handed tiller of the soil were heard in the land with depressing regularity. The Nebraska farmer, however, was no more inclined than anyone else to blame himself for his troubles. To his mind the railroads and the banks between them held him in a sort of peonage. As there was plainly no relief to be obtained from politicians frankly the hired men of railroads and banks the Nebraska farmer stepped out into politics on his own account—a circumstance that greatly upset the calculations of old-line political leaders.

No one was more upset by this highly irregular conduct on the part of the "Alliance men," as the farmers in politics were called* than the Hon. J. Sterling Morton. A copperhead

* From the Farmers' Alliance.

as reactionary as any who managed to survive Reconstruction days, a free trader of the Cobden Club,[2] an aristocrat and a suave public speaker, the Hon. J. Sterling Morton was in appearance and cast of mind as completely the Southern gentleman of the days before the war as only one born in New York and raised in Michigan knew how to be. He was also perennial candidate for every office from Congressman to Governor,[3] and Democratic boss of Nebraska. True, the Democratic party was, as is its habit, split into two warring factions in Nebraska. But when William Jennings Bryan arrived, it was to the Hon. J. Sterling Morton that he reported for duty ten days after he reached Lincoln.[4] And the Hon. J. Sterling Morton graciously took the sprouting young politician under his wing.[5]

It was not, however, until the election year of 1888 that Bryan found opportunity to display his oratorical wares in the new field. Meanwhile he established himself, made friends, worked up another collection business as a lawyer, fetched his family from Jacksonville, and set up housekeeping in a house built by his father-in-law, and made speeches whenever anyone would give him the chance.[6]

He was twenty-seven—the golden age. He was slim and straight and handsome, after the manner of an actor or a fashionable young clergyman, with a wealth of black hair that he flung back with a quick movement of his head when he spoke, snapping dark eyes, and a mobile face. Young Bryan was so much cleaner looking than the usual politician of the day that he stood out at once in any political gathering. People liked him immediately. Even Charles G. Dawes, an ambitious young Republican as Bryan was an ambitious young Democrat, liked him. Dawes's law office was on the fifth floor and Bryan's on the third of the same building. The two would get together while waiting for clients and talk politics. Bryan even proposed that they make a little money and secure a little free advertising by staging debates on public questions—he was willing, he said, to take either side of the argument.

Spring rolled around, and the political pot began to

Mrs. Bryan at the Time of Her Marriage

The First Bryan Campaign Poster

Mr. and Mrs. Bryan with "Gentlemen of the Press"
at Upper Red Hook, N. Y., in 1896

Standing left to right: J. W. Cutright, Perry Walton of the New
York *Evening World*, Harry Walker of the New York *Journal*,
Charles M. Pepper of the New York *Herald*, A. Maurice Low of
the Boston *Globe* and the London *Chronicle*, Richard V. Oulahan
of the United Press, Edward Graham of the Associated Press, and
Martin Hutchins of the New York *World*.

Mr. and Mrs. Bryan at Red Hook
During the Campaign of 1896

simmer. A rally was advertised at a town[7] in the western
part of Nebraska at which a prominent Democrat from another state was to speak. Bryan ran over to hear him. It was
his vice. Where another man would go to a baseball game
or a prize fight or call on a girl Bryan went to a political
rally. At this one there were a brass band and a torchlight
parade and banners and gangs of shouting boys and a committee of local dignitaries with long streamers on their
coats to mark them off from common folk. There was everything, in fact, for a highly successful meeting but the speaker
of the evening. He had missed his train. In despair the committee went through the train asking if a political speaker
were aboard. Instantly Bryan was on his feet, volunteering.
The committee were a little dubious. He looked very young.

"Can you make a speech?" one of them asked.

William Jennings Bryan smiled his engaging smile.

"I'll try," he said.

As there was no one else he was given the chance. He spoke
for two hours. He was witty. He told apt little stories. He
used bright quotations. When he made a gesture to sit down
the audience shouted for more, until finally William Jennings
Bryan swung into an exalted, rhythmic peroration that lifted
his crowd to its feet as by magic and set them roaring with
emotion and enthusiasm.

Bryan reached home at daybreak and waked his wife.

"Mary," he said, sitting on the edge of the bed, "I have
had a strange experience. Last night I found I had power over
the audience, I could move them as I chose. I have more than
usual power as a speaker. I know it. God grant I may use it
wisely."

And he knelt down and prayed.[8]

The next day he wrote out an account of how W. J. Bryan,
Lincoln lawyer, had successfully taken the place of the
missing speaker at a large Democratic rally and captivated
his audience. He sent it to the Lincoln and Omaha papers.

William Jennings Bryan was right. He did have power
over an audience. There were those even in that day who
claimed that Bryan could sway a crowd more completely

than Robert Ingersoll.[9] Perhaps it depended on the kind of
crowd.

> In his youth Bryan must have had a skillful teacher in elocution
> and must have been a docile pupil [said the Hon. Champ Clark]
> Some passages from his orations are gems and are being used as
> declamations by boys at school—the ultimate tribute to American
> eloquence.[10]

Those who disliked Bryan's political principles called i
"high-school oratory."[11] Grudgingly, however, they admitted
its effectiveness. Certainly the farmers of Nebraska had
never heard the like of it before. It was something, moreover
that William Jennings Bryan had never produced before
either, with all his oratorical honours in college and law
school.

For here for the first time in his life William Jennings
Bryan was free. Back in Salem he would have been Judge
Bryan's son to the end of his days. He had had the sense
to see that early. Nor in Jacksonville was it likely that he
could have come into his own. There were scholars in Illinois
College of the calibre of President Sturtevant and Professor
Milligan who knew their history and their economics as
William Jennings Bryan never had and never would. In his
heart he stood in awe of men of this type and their precise
sufficient knowledge. But of what use, he argued, was such
knowledge if those who possessed it could import it only to
drowsing students in a classroom, with thoughts on the next
football game or the girl in the blue tam-o'-shanter? "A
orator," said Bryan, "is a man who says what he thinks
and feels what he says."[12] He did precisely that. How a man
came by what he thought did not bother him in Nebraska
it had in Illinois. There were no supercilious college professors in his audiences to smile in tolerant politeness. Th
Nebraska farmers leaped to their feet instead and cheered

William Jennings Bryan found attending the National
Democratic Convention at St. Louis in 1888 as the proté
of the Hon. J. Sterling Morton a very different business
seeing the show from a window sill. Nevertheless, there we

certain similarities. Once more he heard Marse Henry Watterson, his mane a little grayer, read the platform. Once more
he listened to a woman—not the same one—plead for equal
rights for women.[13] Once more he heard the iniquities of the
Republicans denounced in sonorous phrases and saw the
embattled Democracy of the nation choose a Governor of
New York as its standard bearer. He might have been asleep
twelve years. One thing alone impressed Bryan. Instead of
Honest John Kelly fighting a howling mob to be heard,
there was the Hon. John W. Daniel of Virginia, with the face
of an Indian, four times wounded at the battle of the Wilderness, balancing himself precariously on his crutches while he
held an impatient audience with the grandiloquent periods of
days gone by.

When the Republicans met at Chicago, the Hon. Marcus
Alonzo Hanna essayed in vain to compass the nomination of
John Sherman, while enemies of Blaine (and he had them
aplenty) did their best to persuade William McKinley to
emulate Garfield and capture the presidency by betraying
his friend.[14] McKinley was handicapped, however. He could
not make as good a speech as Garfield. In the end it was
Andrew Carnegie who dictated by cable from Skibo Castle
the nomination of the Hon. Benjamin Harrison of Indiana.[15]
The Republican ticket, said the Hon. John O'Leary, "has
no more chance than a snowball in hell."[16] The pièce de
résistance of the electoral struggle was a campaign *Life of
Ben Harrison* by the author of *Ben Hur*. William Jennings
Bryan was shocked. *Ben Hur* was his favourite novel.
The slogan of the Democrats was "Grandpa's Pants Won't
Fit Benny." They were mistaken. They did.

Bryan was more than merely active as a delegate to the
Nebraska State Convention at Lincoln that year. The Hon.
J. Sterling Morton put him on the resolutions committee;
and when there was a lull in the proceedings Bryan was called
upon to make a speech. He did himself proud, with his wife
there in the gallery to hear him, and etched his name in the
memory of every delegate present. It was Bryan, too, who
moved to make the nomination of the Hon. John A. McShane

for Governor unanimous. He was so ubiquitous, in fact, that when a victim was sought for sacrifice as candidate for Lieutenant Governor, W. J. Bryan of Lincoln was mentioned.

But Bryan was nobody's fool. He knew as well as the next man that no figure in political life is quite so dead as an unsuccessful candidate for Lieutenant Governor. William Jennings Bryan was far from ready to be interred. He meant to go to Congress in his own good time. But he was far-sighted about it. He brushed the nomination for Lieutenant Governor aside and took off his coat and went to work with might and main to elect the Hon. J. Sterling Morton to Congress. Thus, in case Morton failed again, as he always had, it would be plain to everyone that a stronger man had better be found.

William Jennings Bryan knew right where he could put his hand on that stronger man when the time came.

Bryan stumped thirty counties for Cleveland and eleven for Morton. Everywhere he spoke he made an instantaneous good impression. And when he came home from each trip he never forgot to write out little accounts of his meetings and his speeches, and send them in to the Lincoln and Omaha papers.

When the election was over and the Democracy had gone down to defeat as usual, one Democrat at least was considerably better off. William Jennings Bryan had been a resident of Nebraska only a year, but already he was as widely known as many a politician who had lived in the state all his life and a great deal more favourably than most. Aside from his mellifluous voice and his striking, clean-cut appearance, one quality permanently endeared Bryan to the farmers and especially their wives—his Gargantuan appetite. They might not understand very well just how the tariff affected the farmer, but they knew when a man liked the food they set before him. Where another man might cherish a predilection for a well-turned ankle William Jennings Bryan's eyes gleamed and his face lit up at the sight of a dish of buttered radishes or a fried chicken or a plate of green corn. As there were more well-laden tables in Nebraska in that day than well-turned ankles Bryan's weakness was by no means a negligible factor in a growing popularity. Many a prairie housewife stood with hands complacently clasped under her apron and watched the young man eat with undisguised satisfaction. It flattered her.

Satisfying as it was in other respects, campaigning from one end of the state to the other was none too good for the law business. Lincoln was four times the size of Jacksonville, and the state capital besides. "The push and enterprise of Western people is opening up untold resources, developing all branches of business and making it possible for every young man and woman to make his mark," wrote a Lincoln booster.[17] It was true. The year William Jennings Bryan settled in Lincoln, a million dollars was spent in building in a town of 43,000 inhabitants—the Palace Livery Stable alone cost $20,000. Lincoln also boasted an atmosphere of culture springing from the State University with its little coterie of self-conscious intellectuals. Indeed, with the acquisition of the Seventh Day Adventist College, Lincoln was "one of the most important educational centres in the United States,"[18] or so it claimed. Then there was the ancient rivalry between Omaha and Lincoln ready to be turned to advantage by an up-and-coming resident of Lincoln. All in all there were quite a number of approaches to success open to a promising young pleader at the bar. The most obvious of these was to practise law industriously until success knocked at the door.

Had he remained in Illinois, William Jennings Bryan would probably have had to pursue this course whether he liked it or no. In college and law school he had no choice—he was a diligent, not a brilliant, student. One of the things he admired and was not a little envious of in Henry Trumbull was the ease with which young Trumbull seemed able to accomplish whatever he undertook. To William Jennings Bryan's way of thinking there was nothing admirable about the slow but sure method of progress. It was a hindrance to be overcome as speedily as might be. Plodding smacked too much of the effete East—in fact, Bryan felt that there was something almost un-American about it. In the West men rose to fame and fortune overnight, and those who lingered behind, building with laborious care, were mere laggards, forswearing their birthright in a land of opportunity. William Jennings Bryan had no mind to be one of these.

Nevertheless, he did have to move swiftly. He had no capital and a hit-or-miss law business would not maintain his growing family forever, while he traipsed about the country making speeches for nothing at county fairs and church gatherings. Politics must be made productive at once.

Like any other political figure long in leadership, the Hon. J. Sterling Morton had a world of enemies whose intentions to destroy him were excellent. Their chief handicap was that they had no one to put up against him. A brilliant young speaker bent upon politics as a career was precisely what they required. There were just two relatively minor matters, however, that would have to be settled before the door of political preferment would swing wide open before William Jennings Bryan. The first of these was that the Hon. J. Sterling Morton had given Bryan his first chance and still regarded the young man as a faithful henchman. Would Bryan let himself be a flail in the hands of Morton's enemies? The anti-Morton faction lost little sleep over this detail. Long familiarity with politics furnished them with the correct answer.

The second matter at issue was more serious. Prohibition had suddenly laid its devastating hand on the politics of Nebraska. With Omaha the proud possessor of the third largest distillery in the United States and brewing its chief industry the prohibition agitation was no laughing matter. Every man who aspired to elective office had to take his stand one way or another, William Jennings Bryan among them.

Not that the liquor interests cherished any prejudices against those who did not drink. They were broad-minded on the subject. A man might be as "dry" as he liked in the sanctity of his own home if his vote was cast in the proper sense when occasion required. William Jennings Bryan's personal dislike of strong drink was not necessarily a cross laid upon him.

It was at the Democratic State Convention at Omaha in
1889 that William Jennings Bryan resolved both doubts in
the minds of the anti-Morton leaders to their entire satisfaction. As a member of the resolutions committee he adroitly
adapted the principles of Jefferson and Jackson to the needs
of the present hour:

We regard with distrust the various forms of sumptuary legislation and accept a well regulated and carefully guarded license law
as the most peaceful solution of the liquor question.

This, the liquor interests felt, was as it should be—within a
year, 240 licenses were issued in Omaha alone, or one to
every 350 inhabitants. Bryan's handling of the prohibition
menace was regarded as masterly.

Even so, William Jennings Bryan might not have profited
by the situation save for one little circumstance. The bankers' and business men's organization of Omaha, in charge
of the fight against prohibition, was maintained by assess-
ments levied upon its members, and an assessment of $1,200
was charged against the Hon. W. J. Connell, Republican
Member of Congress for the Omaha-Lincoln district. Now
the Hon. W. J. Connell was what was known as "a sopping
wet," and he felt that that fact, together with his vote in
Congress, was all that might reasonably be required of him.
He refused to pay.

At this juncture the Hon. James E. Boyd, a wealthy business man of Omaha and a leader in the anti-Morton faction
in the state's Democracy, stepped into the breach. He would
like to be Governor, he told the bankers' and business men's
organization. But he wanted to be Governor, not just run for
the office. He would be as "wet" as they liked if they would
back him. True, he was not much good at making speeches;
but he knew the best man in Nebraska at that game—young
Bryan, of Lincoln. Now if the bankers' and business men's
organization would back him, Boyd, for Governor, he would
in his turn put up the $1,200 assessment Connell had re-
fused to pay, and William Jennings Bryan would receive the
nomination for Congress, to do the speech making for the

campaign. That was the Hon. James E. Boyd's straight-forward, businesslike proposition. It was promptly accepted by the liquor interests.

On July 30, 1890, at Lincoln, four names were proposed for Congressional nomination. On the second ballot William Jennings Bryan was chosen.[19] The Hon. J. Sterling Morton was surprised and a little amused at the smoothness with which his enemies within the party organization had managed to beat him with one of his own men. It is a long political road, he reflected, that has no turning. A score was chalked up against young Mr. Bryan for future settlement.

There was one little formality, however, that William Jennings Bryan had to comply with before the support of the bankers' and business men's organization, which meant election, would be forthcoming. He would have to be plain-spoken and explicit on the subject of prohibition. He was.

I want you to understand thoroughly my position on prohibition [he said]. Although I do not touch liquor myself, I do not endorse the prohibition amendment.[20]

The liquor interests were satisfied.

W. J. Bryan is not a dodger [commented the Ohama *World-Herald*, the Boyd organ, editorially]. He never fails to announce that he is against prohibition. He tells this to small groups of farmers where prohibition may be in favour as readily as he tells it to city audiences where it is not.

Some twenty thousand fraudulent votes were cast in the election that fall. The election was so scandalous, in fact, that the Hon. James E. Boyd had to take the result all the way to the Supreme Court of the United States to be declared Governor over the Populist who had really been elected, and a special investigation by the Legislature of the State of Nebraska disclosed mammoth frauds on the part of the liquor interests.

But William Jennings Bryan was elected to Congress by a plurality of 6,713.

He had bowed the knee to Baal.

CHAPTER XII

CONGRESS

THE election of William Jennings Bryan to the Fifty-second Congress was not quite the triumph it seemed. He was over eight thousand votes short of a clear majority in his district. What saved Bryan was the saloon.

Throughout the campaign, when he was at home on Sunday, William Jennings Bryan would dismiss his Sabbath-school class a little early so as to run over to Omaha and meet the boys in the bar of the Paxton Hotel to keep track of how things were going. At first the Anti-Saloon League was not a little disturbed by these equivocal associations on the part of a hitherto exemplary character. A young prohibition worker had his office in the Burr Block with Bryan and Charley Dawes. He had been baptized William Eugene, but he came to be known to fame as "Pussyfoot," Johnson. He argued with Bryan frequently about prohibition, but he made no headway. Bryan did not believe in it. For the Anti-Saloon League he kept tab, too, upon William Jennings Bryan's excursions into Omaha's underworld. He might have spared his pains. Beyond learning that Bryan did in fact visit the back room of Ed Lathrop's saloon and like resorts where frailer sisters "sat for company" and political workers of humbler rank frequently drank more than was good for them, there was nothing to report on William Jennings Bryan. He never drank anything stronger than sarsaparilla. It may be doubted if he knew there was a woman in the place.[1]

William Jennings Bryan did not confine his political activities to making the rounds of the saloons of Omaha, however, He had been brought into the campaign to do the speech making, not the hand shaking, and no one in the history of

Nebraska ever did a better job. He covered every crossroads town in the district with more than eighty speeches in all, and staged eleven joint debates with W. J. Connell, his Republican rival, besides. The first of these, in Lincoln, was a little trying. Bryan was nervous to the point of nausea.[2] But long before the series ended the best Connell could do by way of rejoinder to Bryan's sallies was to call him "the boy orator of the Platte."[3] The name stuck. At the final debate Bryan presented his rival with a copy of Gray's "Elegy Written in a Country Churchyard," with an appropriate speech, and received in his turn from admiring friends a floral offering with the words "Truth" and "Eloquence" picked out in pansies.[4]

It required something more than truth and eloquence, however, for William Jennings Bryan to be elected to Congress. He had to satisfy two types of disgruntled voters who had yet to learn that their griefs were basically identical: farmers and labourers. Only the previous December, at St. Louis, representatives of both groups had gathered to form a new political party. They adopted a programme that sounded like nothing so much as the very platform Bryan himself was running on,[5] including pledges to fight capitalistic encroachments and to return the country to its historic practice of using silver as well as gold as legal money. When Bryan spoke at country meetings the farmers often asked him why he was not running as a Populist. He spiked their guns by admitting candidly that there was little difference between his views and the platform of the People's party. Other traps were set for the young man. He met them all with consummate adroitness. Charged with travelling on a pass given him by the railroads, Bryan confessed he had done so. "But since I have been a candidate for public office, I have paid every nickel of my fare," he declared.[6] A rumour was launched that he belonged to the A. P. A.,* a particularly virulent anti-Catholic organization. Had the story been true it would have been worth votes to Bryan, in Nebraska. He threw them away. "I respect every man's

---

*American Protective Association

right to worship God according to his own conscience," he gave out, in a public statement.[7]

One slip he did make, and it plagued him mightily. "I am tired of hearing about laws made for the benefit of men who work in shops," he told a group of farmers.[8] The farmers cheered lustily. So were they. But back in the factory districts of Omaha the statement did not have quite the same heroic ring. The workers swallowed it, however, because Bryan promised them the saloon.

President Canfield, of Nebraska University, wrote Louis F. Post:

We have just elected a young man to Congress of whom I am sure you will get good reports before long. His political courage is great. When he was speaking in his own campaign, he invited questions from his audience and when they came he answered them frankly and boldly. I recall a question as to what he would do to protect the sugar beet interests in this region, and he replied:

"I will not vote in Congress to injure my own constituents for the benefit of others, nor will I vote to injure others for the benefit of my own constituents."[9]

The Lincoln *Herald* summed Congressman Bryan up more succinctly:

Able, brilliant, young, magnetic, hopeful, candid, honest, and poor.[10]

Chiefly William Jennings Bryan was hopeful. He had more than a year in which to prepare himself for the illustrious career he planned in Washington. The law had never been an exacting mistress; he kissed her good-bye without a pang. While his name remained on the door of his office with Dolf Talbot he never essayed the serious practice of law again. One thing Bryan grasped: the tariff was the dominant question of the day. If he would make any mark for himself in Congress he must master the intricate business of specific or compensatory duties added to *ad valorem* rates, of the difference between the cost of wool growing in Australia and the United States, of agricultural schedules, sugar bounties,

duties on binding twine, reciprocity provisions, and the rest
of the complicated machinery devised by William McKinley,
Jr., "the guardian angel, in the halls of Congress, of the industries of the country," to wet-nurse these infant industries
far into lusty manhood.

General ideas on the beneficence of free trade, absorbed
from old Silas Bryan and confirmed by President Sturtevant
of Illinois College, were all right for the crossroads meetings,
but they would not do for Congress. The lawmakers of the
nation were not dealing with a principle. They were beset
by clamorous citizens representing every imaginable commerce who looked upon government as designed to advance
their personal fortunes. It was the American credo. That was
what government of the people, by the people, and for the
people meant. Business men, prosperous by virtue of thump-
ing governmental bounties, thought of themselves as industrial giants for whom the desert had rejoiced and blos-
somed as the rose. They were disposed to be virtuously indignant should anyone propose to deprive them of their sub-
sidies, quite as if an impious hand had been laid upon the
flag or American womanhood traduced. It was not merely
that these gentlemen might make less money without protection. They were not greedy. The agitation for free trade
struck deeper. What haunted the American business man
was the fear that, in a world-wide competitition for which he
was in no wise equipped by education or experience, the il-
lusion of his amazing cleverness might be shattered. His
attitude toward tariff reform was not economic. It was emotional.

If the hard-headed (as he conceived himself) business man
was emotional on the subject of the tariff, those farmers and
labourers, perennial victims of the policy of protection, who
had organized the great, loose, blundering, voiceless group at
St. Louis in 1889, may be forgiven a tendency to become
wrought up over the same question. Ever since Abe Lincoln
had put it into words for them the farmers and workers of
the West felt, too, that "inasmuch as most good things are

produced by labor it follows that all such things of right belong to those whose labor has produced them." They put their conviction into a single phrase: "Equal rights to all and special privileges to none," and set forth like so many crusaders to make it come true.

With so much feeling beclouding the tariff issue from both sides Bryan was in his element. If anyone knew how to give emotional expression to a practical matter it was William Jennings Bryan. There were, however, certain basic factual data that he must become familiar with before tackling the tariff specialists who had passed the McKinley bill. These he set himself to acquire with the same methodical diligence with which he had won collegiate honours in Jacksonville. He wrote to Professor Milligan of Illinois College for the books he should read. "I didn't know he had it in him to work so hard," remarked the astonished professor.

Without Mrs. Bryan he never would have, either. She had been admitted to the bar to help him with his law; and now that the law had given way to politics, precisely as they had planned, she had one side of the desk and he the other, as they worked together in complete partnership and harmony. Her mind was more analytical than his, and it was through her eyes that William Jennings Bryan saw and understood as much as he did of the political problems he had to deal with. Together they went to Mexico and fetched back a collection of cutlery selling for less across the border than in the United States, where it was manufactured. To William Jennings Bryan this was the tariff in a nutshell. He found it more convincing than a shelf of works on economics. So did the bulk of his audiences.

There were, of course, other things going on in the world during that year between Bryan's election and his taking his seat in Congress. They did not seem important to him. True, he went to Iowa and made speeches to help Boies to be elected Governor. Iowa was next door to Nebraska, and it was good politics to make a friend of Uncle Horace. But when eleven Italians were taken by a mob from a New Orleans jail and lynched, Bryan was not interested in the affair. The Italian navy, being considerably more imposing than the navy of the United States, the government of the United States reluctantly paid $25,000 for the lives of those Italians, which was not, on the whole, expensive.

At the other end of the world, a gallant and tragic figure looked his last upon the snow-clad peaks and shot himself in the American Legation at Santiago de Chili. And that, too, brought the nation to the brink of war. In Brussels, another figure, less heroic, an empire within his grasp, shot himself also, fear stricken at the threshold of power. Charles Stewart Parnell, idol of a race of mighty men, married Mrs. O'Shea at last and sank to his long peace, a broken spirit. General Sherman died, and George Bancroft and James Russell Lowell. A famine in Russia slew its millions. In New York a madman set off a bomb under a millionaire. In Brooklyn a statue of Henry Ward Beecher was unveiled, facing City Court, where he had stood trial for adultery. What were they —pride, power, place—when death beckoned?

All through the West, people were singing about a "picture that is turned toward the wall," and boys whistled shrilly *Ta-ra-ra-ra-boom-der-é*. Denman Thompson's *Old Homestead* completed a run of four years; Edwin Booth gave another farewell performance of *Hamlet*. John Drew became a star, and Ada Rehan played in *The Prodigal*. "Miss Rehan is getting old," said the critics. In England *Hedda Gabler* was produced, and Barrie wrote *The Little Minister*. There was talk of a World's Fair, to be held in Chicago—"now generally acknowledged to be the typical American city." Robert G. Ingersoll abandoned his anti-Christian lectures. They no longer paid. "Perhaps, after all, we are a Christian people," commented *Leslie's Weekly*. Perhaps we were.

No one of these happenings was within the range of William Jennings Bryan's vision. One matter alone absorbed him: how to lay securely the foundations of his political future.

To all appearances Bryan had no future in Nebraska. He had no personal following, and being a Democrat under a Republican administration, no hope of patronage by which to create one. The Republican postmasters were postmasters because they could be depended upon as unflagging party workers—the mail of many a Democrat was held up for days, when it was delivered at all. William Jennings Bryan's earliest political lesson, taught him by no less a person than the Hon. Benjamin Harrison himself, was that to the victor belong the spoils. He never forgot it.

Elected by a minority over a thousand votes greater than his plurality above his Republican opponent, it was clear that someone had the whip hand of Congressman Bryan. If he had any doubts as to who it was, all he had to do was to cast an eye at the other two Congressmen elected from Nebraska the same year. Both were Alliance men—Populists, as they began to be called. The dullest political observer could see plainly that William Jennings Bryan had only one hope in the world of being reëlected to Congress: he had to go out and gather in Populist votes as fast as ever he could.

That is precisely what William Jennings Bryan did.

If there was one thing the farmers and small shopkeepers and labourers and idealists and cranks and reformers and men of vision and zealots of every complexion who made up the St. Louis group were ready to fight, bleed, and die for, it was what had been called from time immemorial "easier money." That had been the slogan of victory of the followers of Andrew Jackson. It was what old Silas Bryan had campaigned for in 1872. As late as 1878 a million votes were cast for that one specific thing. Political weather vanes like General John A. Logan and dyed-in-the-wool Republicans like Oliver P. Morton stood like rocks for the principle of a more elastic medium of exchange. It might be state banknotes. It might be greenbacks. It might be silver. What it was was of no consequence. What was important was that there should be enough of it. The men and women of the great open spaces, the mines and the factories of the country, who did the country's sweating, were and always had been sick and tired of having to buy at a pawnbroker's premium the money with which to pay their debts. Said the Topeka *Capital*, a Republican journal:

The business of the country needs more money and the people want as much as possible of it made of silver.[11]

There was virtually no disagreement on this head. Nineteen states had declared unequivocally for silver as a primary currency,[12] and the United States Senate had put the stamp of its approval on its free coinage.[13]

It was not William Jennings Bryan who was the fiery champion of the free and unlimited coinage of silver in 1891, but the Hon. William McKinley, Jr., of Ohio. He hardly had words to express his indignation that, in 1873, silver had quietly been dropped as a coinage medium. It was, he said, "dishonouring one of our precious metals, one of our own great products." McKinley was deeply stirred by sinister proposals "to contract the circulating medium and demonetize one of the coins of commerce, limit the volume of money among the people, make money scarce and therefore dear." These nefarious attempts to repudiate America's own precious metal, said McKinley, had "increased the value of money and diminished the value of everything else—money the master, everything else its servant."[14]

William Jennings Bryan himself could not have put it better. In fact, in 1891, he could not have put it at all. He had not the vaguest idea what all the fuss about free silver meant, and he was too busy trying to puzzle out what the tariff meant to bother his head with currency problems. What Bryan did understand was that since 1888 the Populist vote in Nebraska had been gaining with bewildering rapidity, while the Democratic vote had as steadily decreased,[15] and, further, that the Populist farmers of Nebraska, whose votes he would have to have to be reëlected to Congress when the time came, were fanatic on the subject of silver. It was not simply a panacea to them, it was a rallying cry, a symbol, a religion. The simplest way to win the Populist vote was to come out for free silver.

Accordingly, two months before William Jennings Bryan left for Washington, before 453 delegates to the Democratic State Convention at Grand Island, he sponsored a resolution that promptly played the mischief with the Democracy of Nebraska.

We favor the free coinage of silver [it read], and that it be made a full and legal tender for all debts, public and private, and we denounce as unjust and dishonest the provision of the law recently enacted allowing parties to stipulate against payment in silver and silver certificates, thus setting up a standard for the rich man and another for the poor man.[16]

The last phrase was greeted by prolonged and frantic cheers. It was William Jennings Bryan's own, expressing exactly his whole view of the silver issue. To him it was not an economic question. It was sentimental—the poor of this world to whom God had promised the Kingdom, despised and oppressed by the rich. Lazarus at the gate of Dives.

But William Jennings Bryan did nothing by halves. He went on in his speech to bid openly for Populist support and to nominate J. H. Broady for Judge of the Supreme Court. Broady he designed to be the personal representative of the new leader of Nebraska's Democracy, Congressman William Jennings Bryan.

On the whole the Hon. William Jennings Bryan was well content. He had won his first recognition under the ægis of J. Sterling Morton. He had been elected to Congress on the ticket with Morton's enemy, the Hon. James E. Boyd. Now he dropped Boyd and erected his own machine with Judge Broady in charge. Bryan had written into the Democratic platform of the state a plank to which the leaders of the Nebraska Democracy were unalterably opposed, and himself taken a position diametrically counter to that of Grover Cleveland, the head of his party. He had blasted the recently united Democracy of Nebraska into warring factions once more and opened its gates to the wooden horse of Populism. As a politician, William Jennings Bryan was coming on. There was not very much more that even the most active young man could do. So William Jennings Bryan set off to Salem to see Fannie before he went on to Washington.

The Fifty-second Congress was overwhelmingly Democratic. Even the Hon. William McKinley, Jr., lost his seat in the House and chairmanship of the Ways and Means Committee. The strength of the Republicans, who had manned the first billion dollar Congress, was cut in half by the popular rebuke administered to what George William Curtis called "a tariff at which even Henry Clay would have blushed."[17] It did not take Congressman Bryan a week to figure that with seventy-nine new Democrats and eight new Populists in the House a first-term member could hardly be subjected to the customary contumely. There were too many of them. For a man who was up and doing there were bound to be some fat pickings in the way of Committee assignments. William Jennings Bryan felt that the Ways and Means Committee best suited his talents and went about the business of securing the appointment with his habitual thoroughness and dispatch. He importuned every Democratic organization before which he had spoken in the past four years to write recommending him for that assignment. A Kansas City man described the procedure:

Bryan spoke in Kansas City some time ago [he said]. He made a good speech of the kind, and he had the cheek to demand his pay. When he was elected, he demanded from the club under whose auspices he spoke an endorsement. A meeting was held and the endorsement was sent. It was subsequently repudiated. Bryan worked every State in the West for support.[18]

And when William Jennings Bryan arrived in Washington he worked the newspapers too.

The young Congressman is everywhere. In the hotel rotundas he is pointed out more frequently than many old Congressmen [said a dispatch from Washington in the home papers]. It is conceded that Bryan will be on the Ways and Means Committee in any event.[19]

There was something naïve and altogether charming about this picture for home consumption of William Jennings Bryan conspicuous in hotel rotundas, while the Bryans carefully counted the pennies in Cotton Bride's modest boarding house on Capitol Hill. Nevertheless, luck was with Bryan. The one man he knew in Washington was William M. Springer, for whom he had made speeches back in Jacksonville, and Springer was a contender for the speakership of the House. It was a close fight, and Bryan loyally stuck by Springer.

On the night before the finish Springer sent word to Crisp that he and his faithful band would go in a body to Crisp *provided* he would make Springer chairman of the Ways and Means Committee, and also make William Jennings Bryan, a first-timer from Nebraska, a member thereof. Crisp declined, but next morning on the first ballot he came so near defeat he sent a trusted friend to Springer and accepted his proposition.[20]

Back in Nebraska, Bryan's supporters preened themselves. Here was prompt recognition of the genius of the "young man eloquent," as they fondly called him. "I have been told that no other new member has been thus honoured," wrote Mrs. Bryan proudly.[21] But how it was done she does not say.

The first real meeting of the House was on January 5, 1892, and on January 6th Congressman Bryan rose to speak. No time was to be lost in making a reputation. The bill was to appropriate money to transport grain given by the farmers of America to their famine-stricken Russian brethren.

What right have we [asked William Jennings Bryan] to provide for the carrying of the products of Nebraska to the suffering inhabitants of foreign lands when we had not the authority last year to aid the distressed citizens of Nebraska?

Russia, he declared, was "one of the most despotic of nations." He was opposed to appropriating anything to help "those subjects of the Czar who bear the double burden of want and persecution."[22] He had his way.

Out in Nebraska, they were a little taken aback.[23]

There appears to be no sentiment of sympathy or feeling of humanity in Congressman Bryan's make up [said an editorial].

CHAPTER XIII

WASHINGTON

THE Boy Orator of the Platte was by no means the youngest member of the Fifty-second Congress. The Hon. Joseph W. Bailey of Texas was almost three years younger, and there were half a dozen others of the same age as William Jennings Bryan or less. The Hon. William Jennings Bryan was not the most compelling figure in the House, either, albeit he was admittedly a very handsome young man. The newspapers, when they spoke of him at all, compared his appearance to that of the late Samuel Jackson Randall, sometime Speaker of the House, as he was when he first came to Congress at the age of thirty-six, a quarter of a century before.[1] The Associated Press found Bryan "in person, features, voice and gestures" like the Hon. William McKinley, Jr.[2] William Jennings Bryan hardly considered this a compliment. The New York *Times* said he resembled John G. Carlisle. Bryan liked that even less.

Beside Sockless Jerry Simpson of Kansas, or the Hon. Henry Plummer Cheatham, a representative of the Grand Old Party from the sovereign state of North Carolina, William Jennings Bryan paled into insignificance. Congressman Cheatham was officially described as "a bright mulatto."[3] In the same class, in point of distinction at least, may be placed the Hon. Henry Cabot Lodge, the scholar in politics, and his colleague, the Hon. George Fred Williams, whose subsequent ambition to be King of Albania narrowly missed realization. There was Tom Watson, too, the Populist firebrand from Georgia, and John Lind, a lonely Republican from Democratic Minnesota, predestined to notoriety if not fame through an unequal encounter with Latin-Americans whose subtlety was over the head of the Swede. The Mexicans called him "*El Machado*," ostensibly because he had lost an arm. But there was also a scurrilous implication in the nickname. Portly, pompous Czar Reed had been returned to the ranks as a mere member of the minority, while frail, studious little·William L. Wilson of West Virginia replaced the Hon. William McKinley, Jr., absent by request of his constituents, as authority on the tariff. One other striking figure there was—a soft-voiced, gentle, kindly old man whose clothes fitted him badly but whom everyone loved for what he was, not what he seemed. Silver Dick Bland, of Missouri, said Champ Clark, "amid the splendours of Washington retained the rural manners and simple tastes of his earlier years." He had been in Congress so long that pages who had known him when he came were now older than William Jennings Bryan.

The Bryans' third child was not nine months old when they arrived in Washington, which rather handicapped Mrs. Bryan. When the congressional ladies asked her what committees she would like to serve on she replied with some asperity: "The only committee I know anything about is domestic relations."[4] That was a gross understatement. Almost every afternoon she met her husband after the adjournment of Congress and went with him to Arlington Cemetery where phrase by phrase, gesture by gesture, they went over the speech that was to make William Jennings Bryan known throughout the land. And weeks before William Jennings Bryan had made any impression whatever on his colleagues, his wife was already recognized as "a woman of rare mental endowments. She might be safely credited with at least half of all there is good and honest and successful in the Nebraska man," wrote Dan Quin, early in 1892. And he added: "No man with such a faithful true intelligence at his side would ever stray far from his reservation."[5] Nor did Bryan. He had reached the saturation point so far as women were concerned early in childhood: he looked upon women precisely as another woman might, but with no feeling of rivalry. Women were just so much furniture to William Jennings Bryan.

Not that the Bryans were hermits. They attended the first White House reception, Bryan conspicuous in a frock coat and Mrs. Bryan wearing a "high-necked, big-sleeved black cashmere dress, not even fashionably cut or made." But they were entirely unembarrassed by the unconventionality of their attire or the attention it attracted. Mrs. Bryan received with Mrs. Springer, who took the newcomer under her wing; and every time Congressman Bryan rose to address the House, if only to offer a petition against the manufacture and sale of cigarettes (of which he presented half a dozen), he could look straight into the eyes of Mamie Baird, sitting there in the gallery, ready to nod approval of the effect he was making or to shake her head if she felt he was overdoing it. Mrs. Bryan had organized the Sorosis Club in Lincoln,[6] but she was not an avowed suffragist.[7] Her instrument of self-expression was William Jennings Bryan. "Her judgment is excellent," said the Washington *Post*, "and the work of her mind is seen in the revision given to Mr. Bryan's speeches."[8]

Hardly had Congress settled down to work before Bryan was off making speeches here and there. He told the young Democrats of Philadelphia that there were in the West "thousands who had never 'bowed their knee to Baal.' While some of us do not agree with him on the silver question [he added], we all admire the matchless courage of Grover Cleveland who, when President, dared to do what he thought was right and risk the consequences."[9]

Hard upon the heels of which Bryan attended the convention of the Populists in St. Louis, where Cleveland was roundly denounced as a tool of Wall Street, and the free and unlimited coinage of silver, government ownership of railroads, the abolition of national banks, an income tax, and the direct election of Senators by the people were pledged. William Jennings Bryan was at home in both gatherings.

The Hon. William Jennings Bryan had been in Washington three months and a half when he could contain himself no longer. In less than a month the Democracy of Nebraska would assemble at Omaha to choose delegates to the Democratic National Convention at Chicago. If William Jennings Bryan wished to be a delegate it was high time he distinguished himself in some striking manner to justify his being in Congress at all. The moment had come for Congressman Bryan to be up and doing.

Accordingly, on March 16, 1892, he summoned every resource he possessed—the background of unyielding faith in the processes of Democracy that he had of his father; the long perfection of his technique as a public speaker; the readiness at retort and the adroitness in handling embarrassing queries that fifteen years of debating had developed; the superb physique, the fine head, the golden voice—he threw them all into the great adventure like some prodigal virgin hot upon surrender. Mamie Baird sat in the gallery scarcely daring to breathe. She gripped the arm of her seat so hard that she split her glove.[10] But there was no occasion for her to shake her head.

BRYAN DOWNED THEM ALL

gloated the New York *World*, in huge headlines.

To-day, almost with the effect of an ambuscade, the Democrats uncovered a ten-inch gun, and for two hours shelled the surprised enemy so effectively, that the protectionist batteries [the New York *Times* reported] were silenced.

The *National Democrat* was exultant over Bryan's effort:

It should be read in every home in this broad land as an educational argument. For brilliancy, wit, repartee and information it will compare favorably with anything that has ever been delivered in the halls of Congress.[12]

William Jennings Bryan "now for the first time drew to himself the attention of men of every party throughout the United States," Professor Peck records.

This speech has been a revolution. No new member has received such an ovation in years [said the *World*]. Mr. Bryan's speech was the talk of the town to-night.

And so it was. In the bar of the House there was such
jubilation among the Democrats as had not been seen for a
generation. Bryan was dragged there in triumph. He had,
he said, been nervous before he began to speak—"a sort of
stage fright," he called it. After three hours of an amazing
feat of memory, quoting without notes intricate statistics
and complicated tables of figures, heckled by the ablest
debaters the Republicans could muster, counter attacking,
parrying, evading, keeping the discussion always on his own
ground, it was hardly to be wondered at that "he grew faint
and seemed about to swoon"[13] when the strain was over. In
the bar they offered him a drink of whisky—it was flowing
freely.

"I never use it," said Bryan simply. He took a glass of
buttermilk instead.

It was, however, a wet night for the Democracy of the
capitol.

Yet in point of fact Willam Jennings Bryan brought to
light no new law of economics in his speech. He indicated
no undiscovered angle from which to view the ancient question of free trade. He displayed a mere familiarity with the
technical weaknesses of the McKinley tariff, the property of
every assistant professor of political economy in the land,
however rare in Congress. It was his year of intensive work
upon the tariff that made Bryan's speech that March afternoon "the greatest and most brilliant he ever delivered," as
Champ Clark called it. But in Bryan's estimation there was
something else, of greater importance. He had given evidence,
to an extent unexampled since Lincoln spoke at Gettysburg,
of a facility at translating the practical problems of life into
terms of emotion, where they could be, if not solved, at least
exorcised. This was his triumph. He had, he was convinced,
carried his audience away with his eloquence.

He had done nothing of the sort. Probably no audience in
the world was so little amenable to the impact of sonorous
phrases as the House of Representatives of the United States.
What had set Bryan aside as "the most eloquent tribune that

the people have had in this hall"—so proclaimed Champ Clark—was not his eloquence but his knowledge. For years the capitol had been cluttered with men who could declaim on the subject of free trade. Not since John C. Calhoun died, however, had there been a man who could speak effectively on the subject, who knew so well what he was talking about.

It was precisely this intimate inside acquaintance with the tariff as a factor in American politics which William Jennings Bryan had gained in his year of study that proved to be of the first importance to Bryan and scarcely less so to the country at large. It was not, after all, so much he, however, as Mrs. Bryan who saw with lightning clearness that the tariff as a political issue was at the end of its long, tortuous road. Protection, let the Bryans and their like say what they might, had been absorbed into the very essence of the American republic as certainly as if it had been inserted as a principle in the Declaration of Independence or embodied as the supreme law of the land in the Constitution. For a young man whose political career was just opening to bank on free trade, or even the compromise of "tariff for revenue only,"[14] were political suicide. A younger generation was coming up to whom the tariff question would appear as settled as slavery. If Bryan expected to go farther in politics he would have to find a new issue.

At this critical juncture in his career fate threw William Jennings Bryan into the company of the Hon. Richard Parks Bland. "Silver Dick" had just what Bryan was looking for.

Not that Bland had invented the free coinage of silver as a political issue, or discovered it, either. Even the Republican platform of 1888 declared flatly for "the use of both gold and silver as money." But there was about Silver Dick Bland an almost childlike faith that through the unlimited production of silver dollars control of the affairs of the nation could somehow be wrested from the economic overlords of the East and returned to the West where men were men and women were their wives. He believed in it as only a simple, credulous soul could. Free silver was Bland's religion.

There was something in Silver Dick's earnestness and the sincerity with which he preached his faith that fired the imagination of the young Nebraskan. There were obvious practical advantages, too, in thrusting silver to the fore as an issue. Bryan's congressional district had been revamped, and Omaha was no longer in it. It would be the farmers and not the saloon keepers who would reëlect Bryan if he were to be reëlected, and the farmers were for silver.

So the very day of his triumph as what the New York *Times* called "the best tariff speaker in ten years," William Jennings Bryan buttonholed Representative Bailey of Texas and asked him to recommend some good books on the money question. "I am going to take up the subject right away," he said. And when the House adjourned, at the moment all Washington was talking of Bryan's great speech on the tariff,[15] Bryan and Bailey went down to a bookstore together where the Texan picked out a course of reading on bimetallism for his Nebraska colleague.[16]

A month later William Jennings Bryan appeared before the Nebraska Democracy, at Omaha, a champion of "the free and unlimited coinage of silver."[17]

"Cheap money is the fruit of cheap statesmanship," retorted the Hon. J. Sterling Morton, contemptuously.[18] Bryan's free silver plank was voted down.

But the galleries, Populist filled, cheered Bryan—"Whoop-e-e! Yow! Whoop!"[19] His renomination was secure. He was even suggested as a candidate for Vice President of the United States, on a ticket with Calvin Brice, of Ohio, until someone found that he was still too young.[20] Next he was put forward for the governorship.[21] But the Hon. J. Sterling Morton had his eye on that job; Bryan did not have a look-in. In the end, preceded by a brass band, and in the same carriage, drawn by four white horses, with the Hon. J. Sterling Morton, William Jennings Bryan drove to the convention, where he was duly renominated for Congress by acclamation. He wrote his own platform, however.[22] It contained the free silver plank, rejected by the Democracy of his state and condemned by the Presidential candidate of his party.

William Jennings Bryan was thus left in isolated grandeur, badly in need of friends. He therefore jumped at the opportunity to make the Independence Day speech at Tammany Hall where in a brand-new frock coat he sat on the platform beside the Hon. Richard Croker, surrounded by Sachems wearing huge collars of blue velvet with stripes of gold and flaming badges of the Tammany Society. It was a little embarrassing, however, to have the braves roar, "What's the matter with Wilson? He's all right! Who's all right? *Wilson!*" when Bryan rose to speak. They thought he was William L. Wilson.

"When I go home I will tell the Democrats of Nebraska that New York is all right. Tammany Hall is a great organization and it is solid for the ticket," said William Jennings Bryan.

By the time Bryan finished his speech the audience realized their earlier error.

"Hoorah for O'Brien!" they shouted.

Back in Nebraska the Democratic party was magnanimously disposed to let Bryan manage his canvass as he thought best. He had no chance of reëlection, anyhow.

Mr. Bryan wants to run for Congress again and has an idea that it will be a shrewd stroke of policy in him to favor free silver and thus catch some of the independent vote [explained his chief backer, Mayor Sawyer of Lincoln]. The Democrats do not favor free silver but are willing to keep their hands off and let Bryan pitch into any sort of campaign he likes.[23]

Bryan was right. In his district the Hon. J. Sterling Morton, running for Governor on a "gold" platform, was snowed under by 5,500 votes, William Jennings Bryan on a "silver" platform carried the district by just 140.

It was a hard pull. Bryan repeated his feat of the previous canvass by debating his Republican rival. But Judge Allen W. Field was a man of very different calibre to the unhappy Connell. He stammered a little, however, and the contrast to Bryan's golden voice and magnificent sweep of sonorous words was too great a handicap to overcome. On the other hand, no less distinguished a pair than the Hon. Joseph B. Foraker and William McKinley, Jr., invaded Bryan's district. As McKinley was a far more forthright prophet of free silver than Bryan, it hurt.[24] Indeed, Bryan's enthusiasm for the white metal seemed to many a little sudden. He was kept busy explaining to suspicious audiences of Alliance men that he had been too occupied with the tariff to give proper attention to monetary problems during the past session of Congress—he even begged and obtained a certificate to that effect from the silver members of the Coinage Committee of the House of Representatives.[25]

They pestered Bryan in a thousand ways, those Populists. He began to ask himself whether it was worth it to concede so much to them. Especially were they pertinacious about his support of Cleveland for President. They could not see how, if Bryan were sincere, he did not come out for General James Baird Weaver. True, Bryan had been for Uncle Horace Boies rather than Cleveland or David B. Hill.[26] But when Cleveland was chosen at Chicago Bryan accepted the convention's decision. It was of his creed that the majority must rule. Cleveland, Bryan held, was wrong on the silver question. But he was a Democrat, and Bryan was a Democrat, and so Bryan must support Cleveland whether he agreed with him or not.[27] To the Nebraska farmers this was childish reasoning. Not a meeting passed at which some tall, gaunt, rasping-voiced Populist did not point it out.[28]

To meet it Bryan developed a story which he used constantly, of an old Baptist lady (so he put it) who got to shouting at a Methodist camp meeting. The astonished Methodists asked her how she, a lifelong Baptist, could behave in such a manner.

"That's all right," said she. "I was born a Baptist, but I have strong Methodist tendencies."

"I was born a Democrat," Bryan would add, "but I have strong Alliance tendencies."[29]

Frequently they quizzed him on the currency question, and when they did Bryan was lost. For the Nebraska farmers knew the gospel of Silver Dick Bland from alpha to omega, and they saw quickly that Bryan did not. He took refuge in a candour that won them wholly.

"I don't know anything about free silver," he said at a meeting at Auburn, on September 22, 1892. "The people of Nebraska are for free silver and I am for free silver. I will look up the arguments later."[30]

What William Jennings Bryan could not tell his Populist hecklers was that he had the best of all reasons to be for free silver. His campaign expenses were being paid by the silver mining and smelting barons of the Rockies. For Bryan had been in a quandary when his nomination came to him. If he went with the Hon. J. Sterling Morton's crowd of gold Democrats he could never in the world carry his district of Populist farmers. His campaign in 1890 had cost him only $400,[31] but that had been because the Hon. James E. Boyd and the liquor interests of Omaha had supplied a well-filled barrel. Now these altruistic civic influences regarded Bryan's "silver" platform with a fishy eye. He could not raise a nickel from them. Yet Bryan was desperately pressed for money, and the campaign he planned was a costly one.

Bryan's man Friday, Judge J. H. Broady, was in charge of his campaign,[32] and shortly after Bryan's nomination Judge Broady turned up in the office of the Hon. Charles S. Thomas, of Denver, attorney for the leading silver mine owners and smelters of Colorado. He bore a confidential letter from the Hon. William Jennings Bryan. "He was badly in need of funds for his campaign," Bryan wrote Senator Thomas, "with no prospect of securing anything in Nebraska, and asking if I could be of any assistance to him. He added that whatever I did would, he hoped, be a strictly personal affair. He also asked that any contribution secured should be made to Judge Broady, thus keeping his name out of the picture." Senator Thomas had no difficulty in raising $2,000 among his clients, exclusive of his own contribution.

This sum was paid over to Judge Broady, and no doubt used by him in compliance with Mr. Bryan's directions [Senator Thomas says]. Mr. Bryan waited until he saw me after the campaign to make his acknowledgments, explaining that he did not feel safe in making any written acknowledgment of the receipt of the money.[33]

There were silver barons in Salt Lake City, as well. Judge Broady made the rounds.

Bryan's secretiveness respecting the $4,000 more or less spent by the silver interests to elect him to Congress had something of old Silas Bryan, something also of the evangelist, but most, perhaps, of the woman in it. There was no reason why Bryan should not have admitted openly the source of his campaign fund. The manufacturers of the country had been shaken down to the tune of some three million dollars four years before, to elect Harrison and maintain the McKinley tariff.[34] Almost as much was being spent to elect Cleveland the same year Bryan ran.[35] Torchlight parades, brass bands, railway fare, and printing cost money, and everybody in Lincoln knew that Bryan had none. Obviously it came from somewhere.

But a certain craftiness inheres in the small-town life of the Middle West, especially in respect of money matters, of which Silas Bryan himself had furnished a striking example. It had its religious justification too—let not thy left hand know what thy right hand doeth applied to other things besides charity. With Bryan, however, it was probably the enduring influence of the circle of women that, in his childhood, put its mark upon him for life. He was secretive as a woman is, reluctant to trust anyone, least of all herself.

The vote was so close that the result of the election was not known for several days. While the returns still looked as if Bryan had been defeated Mrs. Bryan was invited to a luncheon.

I knew the wife of our opponent would be there, and the majority of the women were Republicans [she writes]. I felt at first I could not go—am afraid I cried a little—but my pride let me dry my eyes, dress as nicely as I could, and go to congratulate our enemy. I had a little speech ready. The successful candidate's wife was there, surrounded by friends, all happy and smiling.

Shortly after I came I was called from the room. Word had been telephoned up from headquarters that later returns gave the election to Mr. Bryan by 75 votes. What a load off my heart! I could smile too. . . . I did not make my speech of congratulation.[36]

At the final meeting before election Bryan's admirers again presented him with a floral tribute.

This time it bore only one word: "Eloquence."

CHAPTER XIV

CAPITOL HILL

IN THE brief span of four years the Hon. Grover Cleveland, twice President of the United States—the first Democrat to occupy the White House since the war between the states and the only President to be reëlected after a defeat—was relegated to that innocuous desuetude he had himself invented. The leadership Cleveland was too headstrong to retain fell to the magnetic Representative from Nebraska, just turned thirty-three. The process by which this came to pass is intricate, perhaps dull as well. But it is what is known as democracy.

Both Cleveland and Bryan were elected by minorities. The Populists—the disinherited, the terrible meek—held the balance of power. William Jennings Bryan knew this, and cut his coat according to his cloth. But if Grover Cleveland had an inkling of whose votes sent him back to the White House in 1892 he showed no signs of it. The money of the bankers and financial leaders of the East paid his campaign expenses.[1] To them Cleveland felt he owed his fealty, as perhaps he did. In full honesty he discharged his debt.

Grover Cleveland hated Bryan, but he did not belittle him. He knew from the first between whom the conflict lay. To look at the two men when the struggle between them began in 1893, Bryan had all the advantages. Cleveland was fifty-six, corpulent, apoplectic,[2] choleric,[3] and suffering from cancer of the throat.[4] He wrote ably, but, with an artificial jaw of vulcanized rubber and no palate, he was distinctly handicapped as a public speaker.[5]

Bryan, on the other hand, was handsome as a god to some tastes, finely set up, teeming with energy and eagerness, and possessed of a capacity to sway men by the power of his voice, the sweep of his words, and the charm of his manner that no man in America equalled. No one of these qualities is a negligible factor in any walk of life. Taken all together they constituted a rare political equipment to which intellectual profundity would have added little.

Above all, William Jennings Bryan stood in the broad light of relative candour. He was not, it is true, shouting from the housetops who had paid his campaign expenses. But neither was anyone else in that day. Bryan had been elected on a platform calling for the free coinage of silver, an income tax, drastic revision of the tariff downward, and direct election of Senators by the people. He dodged none of these issues.

Cleveland's course was, when all is said and done, tortuous. Elected on a clear mandate to attend to the tariff and leave the money of the country severely alone,[6] he had not yet even packed his trunks to return to Washington before his financial backers foreclosed their mortgage on the White House. What these gentry demanded and what they proposed to obtain without further nonsense or delay was that the United States should be placed permanently upon the same financial footing as England, with gold and gold alone the basis of all currency then or thereafter to be issued, forever and ever, amen. The idea may have been excellent. But the manner in which the financial giants of the day went about it certainly earned them no political laurels.

The truth is that it was by no means a simple matter. Both gold and silver had been the joint bases of the money of the United States for some threescore years and ten. As nothing out of the way had happened during that period, the average citizen could perceive no reason whatever for all the fuss about gold. He rarely saw any of it, anyhow. The whole pother struck the man in the streets and the man in the country roads as something academic. He was inclined to oppose change as the average man always opposes change.

So the problem before "Cleveland and the Eastern financiers who agreed with him,"[7] as Professor Rhodes puts it, with curious inversion, became the extremely delicate one of persuading the citizen of modern means that his own particular bread and butter was in some miraculous way bound up with a unique gold standard for the paper dollars he received in his pay envelope. What made the problem peculiarly difficult was that nothing of the sort was the case.[8]

Now the bankers, to whom the question of gold was indubitably important, might have set about the education of the farmer, the small-town banker, the country storekeeper, and the men and women of modest and timorous outlook, to their point of view. It would have required relatively little effort. But the financiers of the East preferred the ancient weapons of those of guilty conscience: intrigue, and force. To both of these methods of procedure the President lent himself with a completeness that made it difficult for the people at large to regard him as honest. William Jennings Bryan, whose world was all black or all white, found it impossible.

Undeniably there were certain dubious aspects to the President's course. He had not yet taken office, for example, when he began negotiations with that distinguished Democrat, August Belmont, representative of the House of Rothschild, for the sale by the United States—of which Cleveland was not yet President—of an issue of gold bonds which the Congress had not yet authorized. The bonds, Belmont pointed out, "should be sold abroad if they are to serve the purpose at all."[9] The purpose was clear. Marketed abroad, the credit of the nation would be engaged. There could be no going back upon the action. One bright morning the country would suddenly awake to find itself upon a single gold basis, without act of Congress or vote of the people or any of the other irritating and frequently uncertain operations of popular rule. Not Henry Clay in his palmiest days ever conceived anything half so adroit. Naturally, Mr. Cleveland's correspondence with the House of Rothschild was highly confidential.[10]

But Grover Cleveland's financial friends were hardly naïve enough to put all their eggs in a single basket. The public could not be altogether damned, or hoodwinked either. It was most desirable that a chastened frame of mind be induced in the country at large in order that humble men and women of no financial sagacity might be disposed to place their fate in the hands of those more experienced and to trust their leadership. In short, if God in His wisdom should see fit to visit a panic upon the land, the scourge might not prove to be wholly without its providential features. In the ensuing fright and confusion the silver bugaboo could be disposed of once and for all and everybody be happy.

No sooner said than done. A circular was promptly drawn up and sent out to key banks throughout the land, with the knowledge and consent of the Secretary of the Treasury.

The interests of National Bankers require immediate financial legislation by Congress. Silver, silver certificates and Treasury notes must be retired and the National Bank notes upon a gold basis made the only money [read this peremptory and ambitious document]. You will at once retire one third of your circulation and call in one half of your loans. Be careful to make a money stringency felt among your patrons, especially among influential business men. Advocate an extra session of Congress for the repeal of the purchase clause of the Sherman law, and act with other banks of your city in securing a large petition to Congress for its unconditional repeal, as per accompanying form. Use personal influence with Congressmen; and particularly let your wishes be known to your Senators. The future life of National Banks as fixed safe investments depends upon immediate action, as there is an increasing sentiment in favor of governmental legal tender notes and silver coinage.[11]

With how much of the detail of this "conspiracy—one of the cruellest and most scandalous in the history of the Republic," as it was described in England, Grover Cleveland was cognizant is not certain. He was no financial genius, and on numerous prior occasions he had been grossly misled by what he termed "lying and treacherous representations."[12] At best Mr. Cleveland was a very sick man who "complained that his mind would not work."[13] It worked sufficiently well, however, to serve the needs of those who, according to the

Hon. David B. Hill of New York, were attempting in every way to spread disaster broadcast throughout the land.

> These disturbers [Senator Hill declared], the promoters of the public peril, represent largely the creditor class, the men who desire to appreciate the gold dollar in order to subserve their own selfish interests, men who revel in hard times, men who drive harsh bargains with their fellow men regardless of financial disaster and men wholly unfamiliar with the principles of monetary science.[14]

Senator Hill was certainly no radical. But the Hon. William Jennings Bryan himself could not have put the situation more succinctly.

Nor was Bryan idle while this was going on. He knew no more of what was afoot than did the country at large. But he did not have to—he knew the forces behind Cleveland.

> I have no doubt from my observation of his course that the financiers put up the money that secured his nomination [he wrote], and I know they furnished large sums of money to secure his election. His Committee spent $900,000 in the State of New York and among the contributors to his campaign fund was the Sugar Trust which gave $175,000.[15]

All of which was true. Even before Cleveland took office, Congressman Bryan was warning the country—not without reason—against the "dictation of the moneyed interests."[16] A week after August Belmont wrote in such confidence instructing Mr. Cleveland just how the projected bond issue had best be managed,[17] William Jennings Bryan was on his feet in the House denouncing any bond issue at all.[18] He went West, too, and got from the silver men all their ammunition of arguments and statistics. He attended the National Silver Conference at Chicago, profiting of the occasion to take mamma and the children to see the World's Fair.[19] What impressed Bryan most at the exposition was not the Midway Plaisance. It was a single gold nugget worth more than three thousand dollars.

"What an outrage that the finder should be able to convert that into money at such an enormous profit!" he exclaimed.[20]

Bryan even journeyed to Springfield to consult Governor John Peter Altgeld,[21] "the guiding spirit in all secret conferences"[22] held by the bewildered, simple folk of the land, overwhelmed by the flood of organized propaganda flowing from the financial centres of the East. When Congress assembled in special session in August, William Jennings Bryan was ready. He knew as much about the silver issue as he would ever know. He had been through the country and seen with his own eyes the unexampled unemployment, the suffering and despair of the great masses of the people. To Bryan, by the sheer logic of democracy these patient, leaderless, inarticulate millions must be right and President Cleveland and his little group of financial mentors must be in error. If this were not so, then was democracy itself meaningless.

On August 16, 1893, William Jennings Bryan rose in the House to put into words all of these nebulous ideas that filled his mind and all the profound emotional reactions that possessed him.

Bryan was pale and cool. There was a slight tremor in his voice. He began to speak over the heads of the members. A pretty young woman in neat brown dress had entered the gallery as he began. The young woman was his wife. He was speaking to her, looking to her, no doubt for confidence.[23]

He had need of all the confidence that Mary Bryan could give him. For on his desk lay the proofs of the speech over which they had worked so hard together, all in type, ready for the *Congressional Record*. And suddenly, as William Jennings Bryan looked about the chamber, he decided that his prepared address would not do at all. He turned his notes face downward and began a wholly new speech.[24]

The empty seats became filled as if by magic [the newspapers reported]. Senators came over from the other chamber until there were not half a dozen in the Senate. . . . The press gallery was full.[25]

It was "the most forcefully persuasive exposition of the argument for silver that has ever been presented before a deliberative body," records Professor Peck.

When a crisis like the present arose and the national bank of his day sought to control the politics of the nation [boomed the deep voice of the Nebraskan], God raised up an Andrew Jackson, who had the courage to grapple with that great enemy, and, by overthrowing it, he made himself the idol of the people and reinstated the Democratic party in public confidence.

When he had done, there were cries of "Vote! Vote!" But the Administration had seen to that. Under the rule of debate no vote could be taken.

If William Jennings Bryan's tariff speech of the year before had made a hero of him, his silver speech raised him at once into the chief figure in the party whose nominal leader was the sick man at the other end of Pennsylvania Avenue.[26] It was "worthy of a Roscoe Conkling, Henry Winter Davis or Alexander Stephens."[27] Bryan was "a second Henry Clay."[28] Congressman William M. Springer was beside himself with pride over his protégé. "It was the greatest speech I ever heard in either branch of Congress," he cried. "It will take rank with the speeches of Clay or Webster or Wendell Phillips."[29] Tom Reed and Joe Cannon rushed up to congratulate a worthy foeman.[30] Silver Dick Bland put his arm on the youngster's shoulder, his eyes filled with tears, as if he were saying: "Here is one mightier than I, whose shoes I am not worthy to bear."

That night, President Cleveland sent for the Hon. J. Sterling Morton, of Nebraska, his Secretary of Agriculture, and gave him the job of chief executioner. Under no circumstances was the Hon. William Jennings Bryan to be allowed to return to Congress.

The extreme silver advocates in the Senate and the House had been busying themselves in an effort to obtain offices for their friends [the President gave out from the White House]. Among these active men none was more industrious in securing places for his followers than Mr. Bryan.[31]

Considering that Cleveland had himself replaced every internal revenue collector, ten elevenths of the collectors of customs, and four fifths of the fourth-class postmasters his first term as President,[32] he spoke with some authority on the spoils system. By similar tactics, now, the President drove through the repeal of the silver-purchase clause, trading jobs for votes[33] regardless of civil service. "A man," said Cleveland, "has never yet been hung for breaking the spirit of a law." It was from his party chief that William Jennings Bryan learned his second lesson in what might be due deserving Democrats.

Out in Lincoln that October, Congressman Bryan faced the music. The President had demanded the young upstart's head on a charger, and the Hon. J. Sterling Morton's organization of "pap-sucking spoilsmen"[34] was prepared to deliver it. For hours the convention was a madhouse, with delegates shouting and screaming and singing "After the Ball."[35] Bryan alone sat in his seat with that familiar set smile upon his face,[36] white with fury, his frame quivering with pent-up indignation.[37] The fight was hopeless, and Bryan knew it. There was more in politics than speeches. There was also the intricate machinery of men held together by a system of rewards and punishments that must be unyielding if it were to be effective. The account of the Hon. J. Sterling Morton was overdue. William Jennings Bryan must pay the reckoning.

The galleries at least were with him. "Give it to 'em! Shoot it into them!" they shouted when he arose to speak.

There was no whining about his speech. He applied the lash and applied it with an unrelenting hand. He declared that . . . he would leave the party and fight the battle of silver under the banner of another party, even if he went alone.[38]

His courage availed Bryan nothing. And yet, disowned and dishonoured by his own party, the current comment ran that "W. J. Bryan was the biggest and most conspicuous Democrat west of the Mississippi."[39]

And so, in fact, he was. The Administration found cold comfort in disciplining "the Chevalier Bayard of the Democratic party of Nebraska."[40] Not merely Bryan's friends, now, but his political adversaries as well hailed him the new leader of the party Cleveland had shattered. Almost a million copies of Bryan's famous silver speech were circulated by the silver-mine owners.[41] His handsome features began to appear in the political cartoons of the day. His name was more familiar throughout the West than those of most of Cleveland's cabinet officers. The star of the sick man in the White House was setting.

For when the coinage of silver dollars had been duly halted at the President's demand, nothing happened. Business conditions grew steadily worse, not better. The depression was world wide, and trying to stem it by legislation was as preposterous as attempting to turn aside a tornado with a fan. The gentlemen of what Cleveland described as "moneyed institutions," so ready to start a flurry to obtain what they wanted, found it one thing to launch a panic and quite another to arrest it. Unemployment assumed gigantic proportions.[42] Industrial unrest increased, and with it bitterness between those who had and those who had not.

All of this was grist to the mill of the Hon. William Jennings Bryan.

The poor man is called a socialist if he believes that the wealth of the rich should be divided among the poor, but the rich man is called a financier if he devises a plan by which the pittance of the poor can be converted to his use [he declared]. This question cannot be settled by typewritten recommendations and suggestions made by boards of trade and sent broadcast over the United States. It can only be settled by the great mass of voters in this country.[43]

He was on solid Democratic ground. The President clearly was not. If anyone were driving the country recklessly along the road to revolution it was not William Jennings Bryan.

He was tireless, too, in pushing the advantage of the independence of his position. All bridges were burned behind him. For a year he had been working on an income-tax law, and that he sprung now, buttressed with a wall of figures on the income tax in other countries, furnished by the Department of State itself.[44]

If there was one thing calculated to fill President Cleveland's financial friends with apprehension it was the very idea of anything so revolutionary as an income tax. "Anarchy," cried the great Joseph Choate—a "communist march" to be halted at once! Robbing the successful of the fruits of their genius for the benefit of the loafers and failures. Who were these hayseeds, anyhow, with their perennial clamour for a more equitable share in the common profits of the national life? They were anarchists, that was what they were. This man Altgeld—a foreigner himself—pardoning three foreign bomb-throwing anarchists who had tried to overthrow the government of the United States by force and violence! And this Socialist, Debs, tying up the railroads, defying the courts—another anarchist! And that old fool Lyman Trumbull, a great man once but in his dotage now, riding his hobby of an inheritance tax! Anarchy!

So they mouthed, the rich and well born of the Eastern seaboard. So they had decried Thomas Jefferson. So they had raved against Andrew Jackson. So they had predicted instant anarchy if Lincoln were elected. "It was not free silver that frightened the plutocratic leaders," Tom Johnson wrote in retrospect. "What they feared then, what they fear now, is free men."[45]

And to an ever-widening multitude of human Americans William Jennings Bryan became with increasing momentum the spokesman of free men. He was speaking constantly, now, in the House. He had nothing to lose by it. Four days after his first income-tax speech he was on his feet again, this time to speak on the tariff.

It was Saturday night, and the word had gone out that the Young Man Eloquent was to have the floor. The galleries were filled. A dense mass of people, congregated in the corridors, clamoured for admission. Congressman Springer, beaming with pride in his protégé, asked unanimous consent that the doors be thrown open and the ladies admitted to seats on the floor of the House, and immediately every possible corner was filled. Beside Bryan, in his own chair, sat little nine-year-old Ruth Bryan, wide eyed in worship.

The spirit of Burke seemed to have revived in Bryan as he thundered forth his brilliant philippic against the crimes of protectionism in sententious periods and measured cadences [wrote an eye-witness]. Henceforth he must be considered a marked figure in American politics. His speech is the talk of the town. . . . At its conclusion the vast concourse of people in the galleries and on the floor united in three stentorian cheers for the speaker.[46]

And well they might. For as the measured cadences drew to a climax the Hon. William Jennings Bryan swung into his peroration:

I rejoice that the people of these once estranged sections are prepared to celebrate the complete union of north and south so beautifully described by the poetess who says:

"'Together!' shouts Niagara his thunder-toned decree. . . .
"'Together!' cry the people, and *together* it shall be
"An everlasting charter-bond forever for the free!
"Of liberty the signet seal, the one eternal sign,
"Be these *united emblems*—the Palmetto and the Pine!"[47]

The Hon. William M. Springer, sometime of Illinois College, smiled. He seemed to have heard that ending before.

But Bryan was only unlimbering his guns. Within a single week in January, 1894, he had spoken four times, and once had taken the Hon. Nelson Dingley completely into camp on facts regarding his own state, of which the gentleman from Maine appeared ignorant.[48]

It was just before the passage of the Wilson tariff bill, with its income-tax rider. Bryan's own proud handiwork, that the Boy Orator of the Platte crossed oratorical swords with the matchless successor of Robert Green Ingersoll. The Hon. Bourke Cockran, of New York, assailed the income tax in a flash of eloquent appeal. Bryan replied instantly.

If this were a mere contest in oratory no one would be presumptuous enough to dispute the prize with the distinguished gentleman from New York; but clad in the armor of a righteous cause I dare oppose myself to the shafts of his genius, believing that "pebbles of truth" will be more effective than the "javelins of error" even when hurled by the giant of the Philistines, he began. When the speech ended appropriately with "Breathes there the man with soul so dead . . ." there came "a great burst of applause which after a moment changed into cheers and shouts. The members on the floor rushed over the chairs and desks to seize Mr. Bryan's hand, and the confusion was so great that the House adjourned."

So at least the New York *World* reported the event.[49] According to the New York *Tribune*, Bryan was a traitor and his Populist speech socialistic.[50]

It was on the great day that the Wilson tariff passed the House, however, that William Jennings Bryan really came into his own. The Hon. William L. Wilson, small and bent and feeble, a few sprigs of lily of the valley pinned upon his lapel, his plain black clothes hanging awkwardly, almost shabbily, upon his bent form,[51] closed debate upon his own bill.

It was a scene unparalleled in parliamentary history in America. The Capitol police were powerless, and the regular police force of the city had to be sent for. It was the greatest crowd ever assembled in the Capitol.[52]

Miss Leiter, the heiress, sat beside Bourke Cockran. Mrs. Cleveland was present, and Cardinal Gibbons "with his little red cap conspicuous among the dark heads."[53]

When Prof. Wilson closed his eloquent appeal to the Democrats to vote for freedom and the Wilson bill, hats, papers and books were thrown in the air, and finally, their youthful blood refusing to calm down, young Harry St. George Tucker and William Jennings Bryan of Nebraska, the one the son of the Tuckers of Virginia, and the other the ardent disciple of the new populistic doctrine in the House, raised the fragile form of Mr. Wilson on their broad shoulders and carried him down the aisle and then, not knowing what to do with their burden, they dropped him into the midst of the crowd of men and women.[54]

It was Bryan's victory, too. None had worked harder for that tariff bill than he. It was fitting that his 180 pounds of corn-fed brawn should bear its author in triumph.

It was the peak, also, of the Hon. William Jennings Bryan's congressional career. Reluctantly he announced that he would not be a candidate for reëlection. The announcement was superfluous. The Hon. J. Sterling Morton had seen to that. It was a pity. They had been so content—he and Mary and the children—in the second floor of Cotter Bride's house on Capitol Hill, with its modest library of "choice standard works."[55] There would be family prayers in the sitting room every morning before breakfast,[56] and Mr. Bryan would read a chapter of the Bible aloud, just as his father had done. And when there was time, a buggy ride behind Silas, the old white horse Bryan had fetched with him from Lincoln. At night he and Mary would read and discuss or perhaps go to a lecture or one of the more serious plays, like *Shore Acres*.

What should he do now? Go back, like Lincoln, to the humdrum of the law, hoping for a turn of the political wheel? Left to himself, perhaps he would have. But William Jennings Bryan was not left to himself. There was Mary—as there had been Cousin Lizzie and Mollie Smith and Fanny, and back of them all the stern figure of Mariah Elizabeth Jennings. Mary was like all of these combined. Her ambition was unquenchable.[57] There was no question of his giving up now.

One sultry day in the gallery of the Senate he sat listening to a dull debate.

"This place has no attraction for me. The other House is closer to the people, more thoroughly permeated by popular ideas," he said suddenly to Willis John Abbot. "But upon a man of such slender means as I the need for going back to his district after two years to seek reëlection at some considerable expense is a serious drag. It interferes with his work, and if he be poor it makes him poorer. The six-year term of the Senate is all that commends itself to me."[58]

It had always been in the back of Bryan's mind, the Senate—ever since the Salem days, when he had played at being the Gentleman from Illinois or Senator Bayard of Delaware.[59] It was of the Senate he had spoken that night to Fill Dunlap as they lay in the dark together. It was of the Senate that he dreamed now.

There was still much to be done, however, before Bryan's term ended. "Silver will lay aside its graveclothes and its shroud," Bryan had predicted. "It will yet rise."[60] It did rise, and the battle of the previous year was fought all over again. Convinced that he had now disposed of the silver question for good and all, the President next tried to drive through Congress the plan to issue gold bonds he and August Belmont had hatched before ever Cleveland stepped into the White House the second time.

But Congress was sullen. Many a Western member had heard from home since voting so blithely to repeal the silver purchase provision, and what he heard filled him with the fear of God and his constituents. Again and again Bryan denounced the bond issue, and this time he was on the winning side. Frantically the Hon. J. Sterling Morton wrote the President that Bryan's stand was ruining Morton's machine in Nebraska.[61] In the clouds lowering above his political future, the Hon. William Jennings Bryan thought he discerned the glint of a silver lining. In a fine frenzy of impassioned exultation he let himself go, just before Christmas of 1894:

"I shall not help crucify mankind upon a cross of gold," he thundred, his vibrant voice reëchoing from the farthest corner of the House. "I shall not aid in pressing down upon the bleeding brow of labor this crown of thorns."[62]

CHAPTER XV

POISED

IN THE spring of 1893, the Legislature of Nebraska had chosen a Senator. The Hon. William Jennings Bryan, just elected to Congress, was in a receptive mood notwithstanding. Had Divine Providence called him to the United States Senate he would have bowed without reluctance to the higher will. Writing her husband's biography in 1896, Mrs. Bryan said: "He received the support of a majority of the Democratic members of the Legislature, but, when it became evident that no Democrat could be elected, he assisted in the election of Senator Allen, a Populist."[1] Just so, forty years before, Abraham Lincoln, lacking four votes to be elected to the Senate, had thrown his strength to Lyman Trumbull.

The difficulty with this striking parallel, however, is that it is not so. In 1893, Bryan received, on the first ballot, two votes in the House and one in the Senate of the Nebraska Legislature. At no time during the sixteen joint ballots subsequently taken did the Hon. William Jennings Bryan receive more than 8 votes out of 130. On six of the ballots he received none at all.[2]

But the Lincoln tradition was more real to the mind of William Jennings Bryan than mere official records. Lincoln had tried for the Senate once and failed. He had tried again, staging the famous debates with Douglas. Again he failed. Two years later Lincoln was nominated for the Presidency at Chicago and elected. The formula seemed infallible to Bryan. He could see no more deeply into the matter.

The Hon. William Jennings Bryan did not, therefore, expect to be elected to the Senate in 1894. He was merely shaping his career after a certain pattern. It was part of this pattern that there should be a series of debates between the candidates in which the issues of the struggle for the Presidency two years later should be ringingly set forth by the champion of the humble. Accordingly Bryan challenged his Republican opponent to debate and waited impatiently for the ensuing fame.

He played in no luck. It was not Lincoln who had given the debates with Douglas what renown they brought, but the Little Giant. The Hon. John M. Thurston, Bryan's senatorial rival, was an amiable gentleman with a good speaking and singing voice, but no giant, intellectual or otherwise. No additional national distinction accrued to William Jennings Bryan from his campaign for the Senate. But a great many useful things did.

The Wilson tariff bill, passed with such boyish enthusiasm by the House of Representatives, emerged from the Senate an example, in President Cleveland's phrase, of "party perfidy and party dishonour." Nevertheless, Cleveland permitted it to become law. But when the silver issue cropped up again, the President lost his temper completely[3] and vetoed Silver Dick Bland's seigniorage bill with a bang. "Where your treasure is, there will your heart be also," quoted the Democrats of the West and South.[4] To them Grover Cleveland's heart was in Wall Street, and so far as they were concerned, there it could stay and he with it. They were through with Grover Cleveland for good and all. They were through with anybody who hailed from within a thousand miles of the corner of Broad and Wall streets. They did not need William Jennings Bryan to tell them that "our Eastern brethren, both Republicans and Democrats, are . . . building up a plutocracy which will make servants of the rest of the people."[5] The tariff, free silver, were but symbols—"hall-mark of revolt."[6] The struggle Grover Cleveland precipitated was more than a clash of political issues. It was the fight of the poor to wring a little something from the rich, the protest of the debtor against those whom he believed to be extortionate creditors, the bitter outcry of the farmer against the grain gambler, the grievance of the individual against corporations.[7] "The people against organized wealth," said Bryan.[8] Democracy against Plutocracy.

It was also, in Nebraska at least, Cleveland against Bryan. And while one issue might in theory have been as good as another to fight it out on, there were the soundest of reasons why Bryan should prefer silver as the battle cry. No one interested in free trade was rushing to contribute substantial sums to the campaign expenses of a young senatorial candidate. Those interested in free silver, on the other hand, were only too delighted to do precisely that thing. The Hon. William Jennings Bryan was, after all, a practical man.

A meeting held in the Paxton Hotel in Omaha toward the end of May, 1894, to organize the Nebraska Democratic Free Coinage League was not, therefore, altogether spontaneous; Judge J. H. Broady was among those present. A state conference was promptly called, and Bryan himself, from Washington, dictated its stand by telegraph:

We favor the immediate restoration of the free and unlimited coinage of gold and silver at the present ratio of 16 to 1, without waiting for the aid and consent of any other nation on earth.[9]

To this sentiment Bryan spoke with the fire of a crusader. Had he been a gaunt rail splitter announcing that a house divided against itself cannot stand, his words could have had no more inflammable appeal. Save for a handful of Federal officeholders, the tight little organization the Hon. J. Sterling Morton had so long captained[10] evaporated overnight. Grover Cleveland was swept aside with contumely,[11] and William Jennings Bryan stepped forth without peer or rival, leader of the new Democracy in the West at thirty-four.

From this position of vantage the course of the Hon. William Jennings Bryan ran with astonishing smoothness. He was no longer a "lame-duck" Congressman, repudiated by the Administration and out of a job. He was the potential voice of some twenty million people living west of the Mississippi. He was the champion of the disinherited, the despairing, the sullen and bitter losers in that tragic year of industrial conflict, who needed but the wrong kind of a leader to break into insurrection.[12] Bryan was, in short, precisely what the silver men of the Rockies had been seeking for many a long day, to replace poor Silver Dick Bland, who lacked personal magnetism,[13] was too old, besides,[14] and and whose badly fitting coat and bagging trousers made him always just a little pathetic.[15]

But the Hon. William Jennings Bryan had to live, too. His congressional career was near its end, and he was practically penniless.[16] If he returned to the practice of law, he could hardly be expected to go gallivanting about the country with a copy of Harvey's *Coin's Financial School* in his coat-tail pocket, explaining the A B C of bimetallism to groups of farmers. A job must be found for the Boy Orator of the Platte which would leave him foot free and yet be dignified enough to supply a certain prestige.

Providentially the Omaha *World-Herald* was in financial difficulties. The paper had been a loyal supporter of Bryan and had come out squarely for free silver, as well. So the Hon. William A. Clark and the Hon. Marcus Daly, of Montana, and their associated silver barons, chipped in to raise a pool, in the neighbourhood of $20,000 to subsidize the *World-Herald* on the single condition that William Jennings Bryan become the paper's editor-in-chief. Accordingly, on September 1, 1894, while still a Member of Congress, the Hon. William Jennings Bryan became editor of a newspaper of standing by grace of the silver dollars of the Western mining men.

It is not to be assumed that the Hon. William Jennings Bryan was in any sense bought by this procedure. Had he been for sale he had better offers—one of $10,000 a year to be general counsel for a railroad associated with the Standard Oil Co. Bryan was sorely in need of money, but he refused it.[17] To the *World-Herald's* pool Bryan's father-in-law also contributed $2,500 and his brother-in-law $500 and others among the sanguine like sums.[18] Moreover, Bryan's salary was only $30 a week; the chief advantage he drew from the arrangement was a forum in which to present his views and

free transportation to be charged against advertising in the
World-Herald. He needed both.

For now the stage was set. When Grover Cleveland should
quit the White House for the last time, on March 4, 1897,
there would be no Democratic party. For Cleveland had forgotten, if ever he knew, the lesson that Jefferson and Jackson
and Polk and Tilden had all been at some pains to master:
that the strength of Democracy lay in a combination of
South and West—either section without the other was im-
potent. It was clear, then, that the man who would reform a
shattered Democracy must do two things: he must infuse
the new blood of the growing Populist strength of the West
into the hardening arteries of the Democratic party, and he
must effect this with the approval of the South.

So far as the West was concerned, looking beyond the
senatorial campaign of 1894, the chances of William Jennings
Bryan to perform the operation were as good as those of
another. But in the South he was unknown. He had two
years, therefore, in which to make a reputation in the cradle
of oratory below the Mason and Dixon line and at the same
time to strike some kind of a morganatic alliance between
Populism and Democracy. It may be doubted if an older
hand at the political game would have undertaken such a job
at any price.

But Bryan, after all, had nothing to lose. There would
always be the law if all else failed, and the Lincoln Round
Table to address on important occasions, and his pleasant
little library, with its hundred or so volumes purchased of
subscription agents in sets bound in half calf, to spend the
evenings in,[19] and perhaps Congress to go back to a little
later—he was still absurdly young. So William Jennings
Bryan rolled up his sleeves and went at it.

He began with Nebraska, for obvious reasons. Unless he
could amalgamate Populists and Democrats in his own state
he stood little chance of being able to do it elsewhere. Bryan's
newly organized Free Coinage League controlled the Democratic Convention in September and Bryan was nominated
for the Senate without opposition. But that was only half his

task. He would have to persuade a gathering of hide-bound, old-line Democrats to endorse the Hon. Silas A. Holcomb, a Populist, for Governor, in the hope that the Populists, in return, would vote for Bryan for the Senate.

William Jennings Bryan strode to the platform radiating confidence. With his golden voice and his ingratiating manner he took possession of his hearers and by sheer force of personality won them to his plan. What is more, he made them stick. For when the votes were counted Judge Holcomb was elected. But William Jennings Bryan ran third.* The Democrats had voted for the Populist, but the Populists had not voted for Bryan. It was his first serious setback. That December no less a person than the Hon. Lyman Trumbull wrote the declaration of principles of the Populist party. "Human brotherhood and equality of rights are cardinal principles of true democracy," a limit to the amount of money that could be inherited, government control of railroads and all monopolies affecting the public interest, free coinage of silver at the ratio of 16 to 1.[21] To these principles, in general at least, the Hon. William Jennings Bryan made haste to subscribe.[22]

Yet Bryan did not thereby become a Populist—he would as lief, in fact, have become a Roman Catholic. Nor did anything so fantastic as the formation of a separate "Silver party" suggest itself to Bryan's mind.[23] To his way of thinking the Democratic party was the Silver party, not because of any magic inherent in silver, but because, as Bryan saw it, the use of both gold and silver meant more money in circulation and thus less pressure upon the farmers and the small business men and the workers to whom a note in the bank was a calamity, not an accommodation. It was of these people in their need that William Jennings Bryan conceived himself the spokesman. "The restoration of silver is only one of the reforms," he declared, "but if the Democratic party cannot accomplish it, it cannot accomplish the others."[24]

In this view of the nature of the struggle at hand Bryan

---

*The vote in the Legislature stood: John M. Thurston 97; W. A. Jones (Populist) 18; W. J. Bryan 17.[20]

was confirmed by his last weeks in Congress. The fight was over that little scheme August Belmont and Grover Cleveland had so confidentially projected three years earlier—the floating, for the first time in the country's history in time of peace, of an issue of gold bonds, through J. P. Morgan & Co. and the House of Rothschild. The New York *World* called the transaction "the most gigantic hold-up to which an honest and credulous President and a panic-stricken Secretary of the Treasury ever permitted a powerful government to be subjected."[25] Bryan was not so certain Grover Cleveland was merely credulous.

What little he understood of the whole proceeding left an indelible impression upon Bryan's mind. To the fear and hatred of the financial East that had come down to him from old Silas Bryan and the close-fisted, suspicious pioneers of Egypt was added this concrete experience.

This is not a contest for the supremacy of one of two metals—it is not a miners' campaign [he said]. It is a fight for the control of the national credit. If the gold standard advocates win, this country will be dominated by the financial harpies of Wall Street. I am trying to save the American people from that disaster—which will mean the enslavement of the farmers, merchants, manufacturers and laboring classes to the most merciless and unscrupulous gang of speculators on earth—the money power. My ambition is to make money the *servant* of industry, to dethrone it from the false position it has usurped as *master*, and this can only be done by destroying the money monopoly.[26]

In short, very much what the Hon. William McKinley himself had said in the days of his youth and enthusiasm,[27] and what Theodore Roosevelt was to say a few years later in slightly terser form.

In was the emotional, not the economic, aspect of the irrepressible conflict impending in 1895 that William Jennings Bryan understood and gave tongue to as he moved across the West and the South, lecturing under the auspices of and with his expenses covered by the Western Silver Miners' Association, with headquarters at Denver.[28] Precisely this emotional approach made Bryan seem "little less than a second Messiah"[29] to the eyes of humble, inarticulate folk journeying frequently all day and half the night to hear the new gospel of "equal rights to all; special privileges to none" presented in silver raiment.

It is unlikely that William Jennings Bryan ever fully grasped the economic roots of the social disorder for which he sought a specific, and in default of another, accepted the free coinage of silver as the slogan of profounder aspirations. "To 'a vast number of our people' *Coin's Financial School* seems to be 'a plain and simple presentation of the argument in favour of sound money,'" he wrote the President, in an open letter.[30] These ingenious little pamphlets with their infantile illustrations contained the whole story of the wrongs of the farmer, the small shopkeeper, and the worker as they themselves understood their wrongs. They were a godsend to Bryan—he had no time now to read up further. Hundreds of thousands of copies, circulated by the silver-mine owners,[31] served as a textbook for Bryan's addresses. His arguments were all in those pages. He was free to swing his audiences out of themselves in flights of almost hysterical emotionalism. David Houston heard Bryan at Fort Worth early in 1895. He wrote:

I discovered one could drive a prairie schooner through any part of his argument and never scrape against a fact or a sound argument [he wrote]. He has impulses, mainly in the field of morals, and is constantly on the alert to get something which has been represented to him as a fact to support or sustain his impulses.[32]

The characterization is as apt in respect of millions of Mr. Houston's countrymen as it was of William Jennings Bryan.

Throughout 1895 and the first half of 1896, Bryan travelled constantly, speaking unceasingly.[33] His platform was a declaration, signed by some thirty Democratic Congressmen just prior to the end of the Fifty-third Congress, that

the money question will be the paramount issue in 1896, and will so remain until it is settled by the intelligence of the American voters.

The declaration was prepared by Silver Dick Bland, but Bryan managed that W. J. Bryan's should be the most prominent signature.[34]

At the Illinois Currency Convention this young defeated Congressman outshone Altgeld the eagle and Governor Stone of Missouri, and when he denounced Grover Cleveland as "the tainted instrument in the hands of concentrated wealth, the official head of the 'communion of pelf'" who had "tried to take the very political life of every David whom the people trusted," one thousand and sixty-seven delegates cheered like insane men.[35] At Memphis, at Atlanta, at Mobile, at Savannah, throughout the South where he spoke, William Jennings Bryan, in his black cutaway coat, old-fashioned low-cut vest, string tie and soft felt hat, left behind him an ineradicable impression that he, too, was of the South, that he understood their needs and had in his pocket the cure for the malady from which they suffered. The Atlanta *Constitution* was lyric in his praise. He made a "splendid impression among Southerners," said the Savannah *Morning News*. It was what he meant to do.

For while, as with Abraham Lincoln, few knew what was afoot, there had been no thought in Bryan's mind since his defeat for the Senate save the Presidential nomination in 1896. The more astute of his silver-mining backers knew it, of course—"his connection with the *World-Herald* was a part of the campaign to secure his nomination," says Senator Gilbert M. Hitchcock.[36] To the *World-Herald* Bryan sent back rough notes for editorials, scrawled in pencil on the backs of envelopes or bits of paper torn from letters, and Richard L. Metcalf put them in shape for publication. Every line looked to Bryan for President in 1896. The senatorial campaign was scarcely over before Jim Dahlman was writing Bryan that he had "begun to talk you for President, and I mean it."

But for the public at large William Jennings Bryan was merely a sort of crusader completely obsessed with the idea of the free coinage of silver, as was many another in that day. He might have ambitions to try again for the Senate. If so, they wished him well. But that he had an eye on the Presidency occurred to no one. The Hon. Richard Parks Bland, who had fought so long with such rare disinterestedness, was the logical man to lead the triumphant silver forces to victory. True, friends wrote Bland warning him that another and a younger man was quietly at work to snatch the prize from him; but Silver Dick just smiled. No one could do that to *him!* And when the contesting silver delegation, from Nebraska, of which Bryan was a member, came out for Bland, Silver Dick felt safe. He would be nominated.[37]

It was not all beer and skittles for William Jennings Bryan. The silver-mine owners were not overgenerous. At Denver, when he spoke, they made up a purse for him of $250. But in El Paso the *Times* ran a little item to the effect that

The expenses of stopping Mr. Bryan here will be paid by popular subscription and all who want to help can leave their contributions at either of the following places: Harper's Book Store, etc.[38]

Once or twice, Bryan had to meet the cost of hiring a hall out of his meagre expense fund. Back in Lincoln his father-in-law's house in which Bryan and his family lived was badly in need of a coat of paint. Thirty dollars a week did not go very far in support of a family of five, even with Bryan absent most of the time.

Yet as the convention crept nearer and nearer, William Jennings Bryan felt a great exultation. He wrote Senator Charles S. Thomas, of Colorado, his chief financial backer:

I don't suppose your delegation is committed to any candidate. If we succeed in getting a sixteen-to-one plank in Chicago our delegation may present my name. Whether it goes further than a compliment will depend upon the feeling of other states. I am not saying this to the public, but write you this in confidence. The state would instruct for me, but I prefer to be a delegate, so that I can help to secure the right kind of a platform.

And in the Omaha *World-Herald* he wrote:

"The Democratic party cannot serve God and Mammon; it cannot support plutocracy and at the same time defend the rights of the masses."[39]

"There's another gyascutus loose!" commented the New York *Tribune*.

PART IV
SPRING TIDE

"Their candidate made a gallant figure wherever he moved, and went up and down the country as no presidential candidate before him had ever done, to give the people his own striking version of the doctrines he preached. To the excited crowds who pressed about him, he seemed a sort of knight errant going about to redress the wrongs of a nation. There could be no mistaking his earnestness or his conviction or the deep power of the motives to which he appealed. His gifts were those of the practised orator, his qualities those of the genuine man of the people. His strong musical voice carried his message to the utmost limits of any throng, and rang in a tone which warmed men's blood. There could be no doubting the forces of conviction which lay back of him . . . the great throngs out-of-doors who cheered . . . with full-throated ardor cheered because they also believed."

Woodrow Wilson.

CHAPTER XVI

1896

BY THE middle of 1895 the Hon. Grover Cleveland stood in precisely the position to which Professor Woodrow Wilson, of Princeton University, assigned him—"a man alone without a party."[1] But he was still President of the United States and as such exercised that autocratic power which only the chief executive of a democracy wields in this day and age. The national machinery of the Democratic party was wholly in his hands. Whoever would take it from the man in the White House must build a machinery in opposition, and build it nation wide.

That was what the Hon. William Jennings Bryan was about.

It took time, energy, and money. All of these Bryan had. He was, of course, poor as a church mouse himself. But the silver-mine owners were not, so that funds were not lacking. Under the impulse of Bryan's activity first one little group, then another, met, made speeches, adopted resounding resolutions and an imposing name—the American Bimetallic League, the National Bimetallic Union, the National Silver Committee, and the like—and then, swiftly they converged into a single broad current capable of carrying the gospel of silver from Montana to Maine.

In all this portentous development, William Jennings Bryan played a capital part. He was, in the first place, the only man of any prominence so placed that he could devote all his time to fostering the silver movement and incidentally his canvass for the Presidential nomination. It was no more than natural that he should occasionally be mentioned as a possible temporary chairman for the Chicago convention,[2] to deliver the keynote speech of the 1896 campaign. What was astonishing was that Bryan appeared to be taken no more seriously for the leading rôle.

"I have my lightning rod up, and my hearing is splendid,"[3] he said.

Only in Nebraska was William Jennings Bryan able to push his ambition to the fore. But even in Nebraska Bryan moved stealthily. Home from his speaking tours at rare intervals he would eat midday dinner—Gargantuan feasts of fried chicken and mashed potatoes drowned in gravy—at the Democratic stronghold, the Paxton Hotel, in Omaha, and discuss with the faithful of the silver crusade just how Nebraska's Young Man Eloquent was going to be nominated at Chicago. Just so Abe Lincoln and Bill Herndon and Norman B. Judd had been wont to talk things over in the dingy office in Springfield the year before William Jennings Bryan was born.[4]

The plan hit upon at last was James C. Dahlman's. An astute politician was Dahlman, sometime Mayor of Omaha. Over and over again he had seen Bryan, as a minority member of the resolutions committee in one or the other of those raucous political wrangles known as the conventions of Nebraska's Democracy, step to the platform and with his youth, his clean look, his magnetism, and his golden voice, gather unto himself delegates who ten minutes before had not given the young man from Lincoln a thought. Nebraska, Dahlman argued, was only a cross section of the United States. What Bryan had done in Nebraska he could do in Chicago, said Dahlman. The Hon. J. Sterling Morton's hand-picked "gold" delegates would of course be seated by President Cleveland's National Committee. But there would be a contesting "silver" delegation from Nebraska, and the Hon. William Jennings Bryan would be among them. There would be an appeal from the National Committee to the body of the Convention, and Bryan would speak. He would sound the silver trumpet, and the rank and file of the nation's Democracy would rise to his call.

The thing simply could not fail.

So sure they were that they had barrels of Bryan buttons made and a hundred "Bryan for President" badges, to be worn by the members of the general staff who frequented the Paxton Hotel conferences and were on the inside of what was afoot.

Meanwhile, everything depended upon the Young Man Eloquent, himself. The silver delegation from Nebraska would be morally, if not specifically, pledged to Silver Dick Bland—the one outstanding figure among the Democratic prophets of free silver. On the other hand there was also the Hon. Henry M. Teller, of Colorado. A Republican since the birth of the Republican party, but a silver man for good and sufficient reasons, he was prepared to split his party wide open on the coinage issue and join the Democrats, if need be, in response to the "great roar of discontent going up in the country to-day," as he put it.[5] It might prove Napoleonic tactics for the Democrats to nominate a Republican to head their ticket. In short, a great many things might happen to ruin the plans of William Jennings Bryan and his backers. After all, who was Bryan beside such veterans of the silver movement as Bland and Teller?

Who indeed? There were moments when William Jennings Bryan asked himself the question—moments, then and all his life, when Bryan was unsure of himself. Rarely did he make a speech of importance that he was not seized with nausea so that at times it was a question whether he could go on or not. In those early days Bryan saw himself a potter's vessel—any might laugh at him who would. But of the righteousness of the cause he championed, neither then nor ever did doubt creep into the mind of William Jennings Bryan to steal away his fervour.[6]

If certain of the silver Democrats were revolving in their minds the advisability of nominating a silver Republican to lead them to victory they were well behind the Hon. Grover Cleveland in "party perfidy and party dishonour." As early as May, 1896, the President seized upon the funeral of his Secretary of State as an appropirate moment to send the dead man's son as a confidential emissary to the Hon.

Charles W. Fairbanks, preparing his keynote speech for the Republican National Convention.

"Mr. Cleveland is going to bolt to your side, providing you give him something to bolt to," Otto Gresham told Fairbanks. And Fairbanks tore up his speech and wrote another to conform to Cleveland's demands. "I have no doubt that it was Grover Cleveland's views, financial and political, that switched William McKinley from . . . soft money to hard money," young Gresham declared.[7] As the crowning act of his political life Grover Cleveland dictated that part of the Republican credo dealing with the supreme issue of the campaign of 1896. It was, however, Melville Stone, of the Associated Press, who wrote the Republican platform. He was the only man present who could spell "inviolably."[8]

That spring Bryan spoke for his friend the Hon. Champ Clark in Clark's district of Missouri, and afterward Clark and he travelled a way together.

"I wish I could disguise you and get you into the Chicago convention as a delegate from Nebraska for a quarter of an hour," Bryan ruminated.

"Why?" said Clark.

"To put my nomination," Bryan answered calmly.

"Are you a candidate?" Champ Clark asked in astonishment. From Missouri, and a Bland man, he was amazed that Bryan should be so frank with him.

"Yes; and I will get the nomination," Bryan replied.

"How will you do that?" Clark persisted, incredulous.

"By the rule of elimination," said Bryan. "Bland will not be nominated because it is too early to nominate a candidate from one of the old slave states. I have no prejudice on the subject, but others have."

And Bryan went on to eliminate Governor Matthews of Indiana, Joe Blackburn of Kentucky, and Adlai E. Stevenson, Vice President under Cleveland, but a staunch silver man. When he had done with his analysis of the field no one was left but the Hon. William Jennings Bryan of Nebraska.[9]

Bryan knew what he was talking about. His two years of

unremitting speech making had borne fruit. He had set out to win the South and he had won the South. In Georgia, Louisiana, Mississippi, and North Carolina—wherever he had spoken—William Jennings Bryan was not without his following. "I perhaps was personally acquainted with more delegates than any other delegate who was mentioned as a candidate," Bryan says.[10] Which would be true save that William Jennings Bryan was not mentioned as a candidate by anybody but himself prior to the convention.[11] Of those who were, Senator Stephen M. White, of California, bluntly eliminated himself.

"I am a Catholic," he said, "and, besides, I am from the Pacific slope."

Even Silver Dick Bland was a bit uneasy. His wife was a Catholic, too, and there was, after all, a good deal of truth in what Bryan had said about a candidate from one of the former slave states.

The Republicans were not so beset. But they had their little problems, too. There was Major William McKinley, Jr., the favourite son of the Protectionists, tarred from head to foot by the silver heresy. "I am in favour of the use of all the silver produce of the United States as circulating medium," McKinley had written in 1890. The silver-mine owners themselves demanded no more. McKinley, said the *Nation*, "has no more idea of the laws of currency than one of his Negro delegates at St. Louis will have of the higher mathematics."[12]

Prospects were far from bright for President Cleveland's banking friends as the time for the national conventions approached in June of 1896.

William Jennings Bryan attended the Republican Convention at St. Louis, ostensibly as a reporter for the Omaha *World-Herald*, but in reality, he says, to foment rebellion in the Republican ranks.[13] It was a pity his mind should have been occupied with other matters, for, as a newspaper man, William Jennings Bryan might well have rejoiced at the dramatic scene when the Hon. Henry M. Teller led the silver cohorts, with banners flying, as they shook the dust of

Plutocracy from their feet. As it was, Bryan's emotions were curiously mixed. The bolt of the silver Republicans was epochal. If now the Democrats would only adopt a free silver platform at Chicago and just stick together! Out of what had appeared the hopeless disintegration of the party of Jefferson and Jackson here suddenly was rebirth. It seemed almost too good to be true.[14]

Bryan's seat was far back in the press gallery. As the silver men marched out of the hall Arthur Wallace Dunn was furiously scrawling bulletins at a desk in the front row. Suddenly someone stepped on the paper on which he was writing. He looked up. It was William Jennings Bryan. He stood there on the desks, straight and tall, his coal-black hair flung back like some young Napoleon watching from the heights of Austerlitz the movements of the enemy before the battle. Below in the hall leather-lunged Republicans were shouting, "Go to Chicago!" . . . "Take the Democratic train!" to the departing silver men. There was a gleam of triumph in Bryan's eye. The least smile of satisfaction flitted across his face.[15]

There were also, however, moments of heart-arresting suspense for the young Nebraskan. One in particular, when Major William McKinley, Jr., appeared to debate whether he could in good conscience forswear his previous record and safely execute a back flip onto a platform of gold. It had been the intention of Mark Hanna to let his candidate keep a foot in each camp. But a delegation drummed up by President Cleveland and representing the moneyed institutions of the land gave the Warwick of Ohio just an hour in which to make up his own mind and McKinley's as well. Hanna was a realist. It did not take him half that time.

Encouraging as it was for the Democrats, the bolt led by Senator Teller had its sinister aspect for the Hon. William Jennings Bryan. It made Teller a stronger contender than ever for the Democratic nomination at Chicago. There was no time to be lost, and Bryan lost none. When Senator Charles A. Towne, exultant over the developments at St. Louis, cried to Bryan: "We are going to Chicago to nomi-

nate Senator Teller! You had better come and help us!"
Bryan replied curtly:

"I can't do it. I am going to be nominated myself."[16]

And to Senators Patterson and Towne and Congressman
Hartman, coming to him as a committee to ask his support
of Teller, Bryan drove home every argument he could think
of against the Colorado man, with all the force he had.

I said to them that I did not regard Senator Teller's nomination
as a possibility . . . and that it was easier to bring the disappointed
Republicans over to the Democratic party than to carry the
victorious Democrats over to the Republican party,

recounts Bryan. There was, of course, no question whatever
of carrying "the victorious Democrats over to the Republican party" of Mark Hanna—and none knew it better
than William Jennings Bryan. But Teller must be disposed
of, and that instantly.

When I stated that I did not believe Senator Teller could be
nominated [continued Bryan], Senator Patterson asked me who
could be nominated, and I told him that I thought I had as good
a chance to be nominated as anyone.[17]

No one could charge William Jennings Bryan with having
let mock modesty stand in the way of procuring what advantage might accrue to his candidacy from the secession
of the silver Republicans. But Bryan was not satisfied.
The Democratic platform must also be one upon which the
Hon. William Jennings Bryan could stand. He saw to that,
too. Charles H. Jones, of the St. Louis *Post-Dispatch*, was
engaged in drawing up that historic document, and to him
went Bryan with his 16 to 1 free silver plank and had it
quietly inserted in the draught of the Chicago platform.[18]

Well content, William Jennings Bryan returned to Nebraska.

But not for long. On the eve of Bryan's triumph, death
stalked to the front of the stage. First, Lyman Trumbull, a
weary old man but valiant, made his way home, undismayed.

"Any distinction I have gained I owe to the man who is buried here," said William Jennings Bryan at Trumbull's grave.[19]

But Clarence Darrow knew Trumbull better.

The socialistic trend of the venerable statesman's opinions in his later years sprang from his deep sympathies with all unfortunates [he said]. He became convinced that the poor who toil for a living in this world were not getting a fair chance. His heart was with them.[20]

It was a point of view that found no lodgment in William Jennings Bryan's moralistic mind.[21]

A few days later the gaunt frame of Mariah Elizabeth Jennings won eternal ease at last. She had not reached her Biblical threescore years and ten, but the tireless engine had run down. All her life she toiled and scrimped and saved, ambition for her husband, for her children, burning like a glowing furnace within her. And when, after all the barren years, the day approached that might, perhaps, have been compensation for her starved emotionalism, God closed her eyes before the curtain rose.

"I went from her funeral to the Chicago convention," said William Jennings Bryan.[22]

There was plenty to do in Chicago. The silver men were in overwhelming majority, but the party machinery, by that curious anachronism characteristic of the American democracy, was still the property of the discredited man in the White House. A contest was both inevitable and farcical.

It served, however, to keep the Hon. William Jennings Bryan occupied in getting himself seated as a delegate instead of free to go about the business he had come there for. It was heartbreaking. Time flew by, and Bryan was as yet only a spectator of the drama in which he had cast himself in the leading rôle. Not William Jennings Bryan, but John Peter Altgeld emerged from the confusion of the preliminary struggle the dominating figure of the convention—luckily for Bryan. John Peter Altgeld had had the misfortune to be born in Prussia. Altgeld was for the Hon. Richard Parks

The Silver Knight of the West—1896

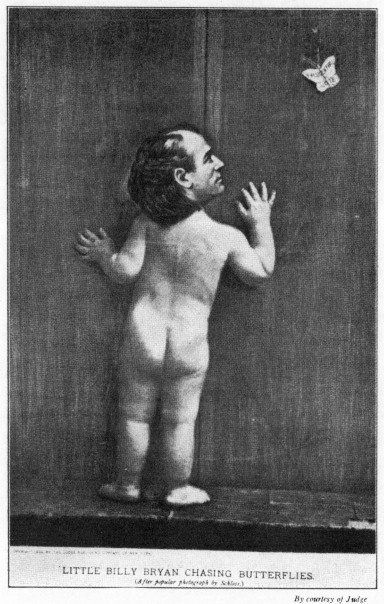

LITTLE BILLY BRYAN CHASING BUTTERFLIES.
(After popular photograph by Schloss.)

Judge Cartoons Bryan's "Fantastic Try
for the Presidency" in 1896

Bland for President, but he was not unwilling to accept William Jennings Bryan for Vice President.[23]

For a moment Bryan was tempted. Silver Dick was no longer young and none too robust. It might be the most practical way.

But William Jennings Bryan had borrowed $100 and sent for Mrs. Bryan to come on from Lincoln. There she was, now,[24] just as in the old days in Washington she had sat in the gallery of the House when he was to speak. No; there could be no turning back.

The plan that had looked so simple and so sure in the Paxton Hotel somehow did not work out, however. The Nebraska Boys with their red bandannas and their band seemed only a drop in the ocean of twenty thousand sweating people packed into the Coliseum and as many more in the streets outside. The Nebraska Boys were outside, too, for their delegation had not yet been seated, and Bryan, who had hoped to be temporary chairman of the convention, or at the very least chairman of the Resolutions Committee, could not even be a delegate until the status of the contesting silver delegations was settled. It was maddening. There was the impatient mass of sweltering men, waiting for the committees to report and calling for speeches—first from this popular idol, then that. It would have been William Jennings Bryan's chance. But he was not there. He was before the Credentials Committee, fighting to be seated in the convention at all. It seemed to Bryan that everything on which he had staked so much had gone wrong. With an access of superstition he changed his room at the Clifton House from Number 13. It was plainly unlucky. A Southern delegate gave him a rabbit's foot. Bryan carried that, too.[25]

Then, when the Resolutions Committee disagreed irremediably over the silver plank, Bryan's chance suddenly came. There were to be three speakers on each side, and William Jennings Bryan was to be one. Now if he could only manage to speak last!

I went to Senator Tillman and asked him whether he wanted to open or close the debate [Bryan recounts]. He said he would like to close and that he wanted fifty minutes. I told him that was too long for a closing speech and that I hardly thought the other side would agree to our using so much of the time in closing. I went back to Senator Hill and presented Senator Tillman's request and he objected to it, as I supposed he would, and said that if Senator Tillman wanted to use so much time as that he ought to use it in opening. I then returned to Senator Tillman and stated the case, and as he, Senator Tillman, felt that he needed more time than Senator Gill was willing to use in closing, he decided to open the debate and left me to close it.[26]

It could not have been more adroitly managed.

The debate was not till the following day, and that night William Jennings Bryan made him ready.[27]

Just before the debate began there was a little Bryan boom, with the Nebraska boys waving their bandannas.[28] To the spectators, it seemed a pathetic eddy in a great current. At the last moment, Clark Howell of the Atlanta *Constitution* scribbled on the back of an envelope: "This is a great opportunity," and passed it to Bryan. Instantly William Jennings Bryan wrote: "You will not be disappointed," and passed the envelope back.

Tillman enraged the audience with his sectional appeal. Hill was didactic, and the crowd was against him. Vilas bored them. They could not hear former Governor John E. Russell, of Massachusetts.[29] As his hour drew near Bryan felt sick at his stomach. He wanted to lie down, he says.[30]

I can see Hill, bald and short, with his pointed nose, and his badger-like ferocity, gesturing with short strokes, as if with a broadsword, as he predicted the disgrace and overthrow of the party [wrote Edgar Lee Masters]. Suddenly I saw a man spring up from his seat among the delegates . . . and with the agility and swiftness of a boxer hurry to the speakers' rostrum. He was slim, tall, pale, raven-haired, beaked of nose. They caught at his coat, as he made his way, as if to bid him God-speed, for he was going to reply to the great Hill of New York.[31]

As he confronted the 20,000 yelling, cursing, shouting men before him, they felt at once the indescribable magnetic thrill which beasts and men alike experience in the presence of a master [wrote Harry Thurston Peek]. Serene and self-possessed and with a smile upon his lips, he faced the roaring multitude with a splendid consciousness of power. Before a single word had been uttered by him, the pandemonium fell to an inarticulate murmur, and when he began to speak even this was hushed to the profoundest silence. A mellow, penetrating voice that reached apparently without the slightest effort to the farthermost recesses of that enormous hall—[32]

"*It would be presumptuous, indeed, to present myself against the distinguished gentleman to whom you have just listened if this were a mere measuring of abilities; but this is not a contest between persons. The humblest citizen in all the land, when clad in the armour of a righteous cause, is stronger than all the hosts of error—*"

Bryan began. There were those who had heard the young Congressman from Nebraska reply to the Hon. Bourke Cockran on the income tax who pricked up their ears. But Bryan went on, unheeding:

"*With a zeal approaching the zeal which inspired the crusaders who followed Peter the Hermit . . .*"

"He was smiling," says Edgar Lee Masters. "A sweet reasonableness shone in his handsome face."[33]

"*The man who is employed for wages is as much a business man as his employers; the attorney in a country town is as much a business man as the corporation counsel in a great metropolis; the merchant at the cross-roads store is as much a business man as the merchant of New York; the farmer who goes forth in the morning and toils all day—who begins in the Spring and toils all Summer—and who by the application of brain and muscle to the natural resources of the country creates wealth, is as much a business man as the man who goes upon the board of trade and bets upon the price of grain; the miners who go down a thousand feet into the earth, or climb two thousand feet upon the cliffs, and bring forth from their hiding places the precious metals to be poured into the channels of trade are as much business men as the few financial magnates who, in a back room, corner the money of the world. . . .*"

*It is for these that we speak. We do not come as aggressors. . . .
We have petitioned, and our petitions have been scorned; we
have entreated, and our entreaties have been disregarded; we
have begged, and they have mocked when our calamity came.
We beg no longer; we entreat no more; we petition no more. We
defy them!"*

A crash of applause followed each sentence. "The tumult
was like that of a great sea thundering against the dykes,"
says Professor Peck. "This orator had met the mood to the
very full. He had found magic words for the feeling which
they had been unable to express."[34]

*"Having behind us the producing masses of this nation and
the world, supported by the commercial interests, the labouring
interests, and the toilers everywhere, we will answer their
demand for a gold standard by saying to them: You shall not
press down upon the brow of labour this crown of thorns, you
shall not crucify mankind upon a cross of gold."*

"When I finished my speech, I went to my seat in a silence
that was really painful," Bryan said afterward. "When I
neared my seat, somebody near me raised a shout, and the
next thing I was picked up—and bedlam broke loose!"[35]

The delegates arose and marched for an hour, shouting, weeping,
rejoicing. They lifted this orator upon their shoulders and carried
him as if he had been a god [wrote Edgar Lee Masters]. At last a
man! Silver Dick must step aside as John the Baptist did of old!

That evening William Jennings Bryan rode quietly home
on the elevated with Millard Fillmore Dunlap and Judge
Thompson, of Grand Island, Nebraska.

"Aren't you afraid that the adjournment of the convention
will spoil your chances for the Presidency?" they asked him.[36]
But he shook his head.

"Don't rush things," cautioned Bryan. "If my candidacy
won't keep overnight it will wilt pretty soon on a canvass."[37]

It did wilt. Bryan did not return to the Coliseum. He had
done all he could. The rest was on the knees of the gods.
From the stage of the convention Mrs. Bryan telephoned
him the result of the balloting.

"It reads a good deal like a continued story," Bryan told the reporters ruefully, "where the hero is always left in a desperate situation at the end of each chapter."[38]

At the close of three ballots Bland still led, but on the fourth ballot Bryan passed Silver Dick.[39] The barrels of Bryan buttons were opened and the buttons distributed, broadcast. One man offered $100 for a "Bryan for President" badge. He did not get it. . . . The Illinois delegation went into a huddle. "'For God's sake, stand by Mr. Bland!' cried an Arkansas delegate, clutching the Governor by the arm. John Peter Altgeld's face was white as death."[40] . . . Men milled about the vast hall, some shouting: "Bryan! Bryan! William Jennings Bryan!" like a sort of barbaric chant. Others paraded bearing improvised banners on which was scrawled: NO CROWN OF THORNS! NO CROSS OF GOLD!

On the fifth ballot the forty-eight votes of Illinois swung from Bland to Bryan. It was all over. . . . Mrs. Bryan stood on tiptoe in the presence of the reporters and kissed her handsome husband. . . . A first wave of admirers found him calmly reading. A little later he went down to the barber shop, and there a second crowd discovered him. This time Bryan smiled through the lather and wept a little over the news of his nomination that he had known hours before.[41]

But out in Lebanon, Missouri, the scene was more bucolic. Silver Dick Bland was not a delegate—to him there was something indelicate about a man being a delegate to a convention that might nominate him for the Presidency. He had refused to go.[42] But when the convention adopted the free silver plank he and young Bryan had worked out together, Silver Dick was certain all was well. Still, he was a little nervous because Allen Thurman, of Ohio, had brought up the fact that Mrs. Bland was a Catholic "and suggested that his religious connections would make him objectionable to many voters in the Western states."[43] So Silver Dick sent for the country physician and asked him to prescribe something that would make him sleep.

The doctor took a bottle or two of sedative out of his satchel and put them on the table.

"Do you think you will be nominated, Mr. Bland?" asked the doctor.

"Yes, I am sure of it," Mr. Bland said. "I do not want it, but it seems to be coming my way."

Just then the news came from Chicago.

Silver Dick Bland walked over to the table and picked up the bottles.

"I will not need medicine now," he said. "I shall sleep all right to-night."[44]

CHAPTER XVII

THE ENEMY'S COUNTRY

I AM a tariff man standing on a tariff platform," declared Major William McKinley, Jr., shortly after his nomination. "This money matter is unduly prominent. In thirty days you won't hear anything about it."

"In thirty days you won't hear of anything else," remarked Judge William R. Day, of Canton, drily.[1]

The desperate aftermath of Grover Cleveland's "bankers' panic" was at hand.[2]

Never within my memory have so many people literally starved to death as in the past few months [said the Rev. T. De Witt Talmage]. Have you noticed in the newspapers how many men and women here and there have been found dead, the post-mortem examination stating that the cause of the death was hunger? There is not a day when we do not hear the crash of some great commercial establishment and as a consequence many people are thrown out of employment. Among what we considered comfortable homes have come privation and close calculation and an economy that kills. Millions of people who say nothing about it are at this moment at their wits' end. There are millions of people who do not want charity but want work.[3]

To these millions the Silver Knight of the West came as the one hope of salvation. To the Rev. Thomas Dixon, Jr., of Virginia, and many another of like breeding and refinement, he was just "a mouthing, slobbering demagogue."[4] It was left to the Hon. John Hay, viewing the situation from a distance, to put his finger on the sore spot:

What if the Baby Demosthenes should get in with his program: free silver; abolition of Supreme Court; abolition of national banks; confiscation of railroads and telegraphs! [he wrote Henry

Adams, from London]. Add to this such trifles as making Debs attorney-general, and you or Brooks Secretary of State![5]

The "gold standard" was, after all, largely a curtain behind which were concealed all the gigantic vested interests, built up with such appalling rapidity under benign Republican rule since the war between the states. It was not the Democratic platform that frightened the successful of the land out of their wits,[6] but that Populist programme drawn up by the Hon. Lyman Trumbull and including such revolutionary items as a graduated income tax and the declaration that "the government should own and operate the railroads in the interests of the people."[7]

A fortnight following his nomination by the Democrats at Chicago, William Jennings Bryan was chosen standard bearer of the embattled farmers of the People's party, in the same building in which Major William McKinley, Jr., had been created, by grace of Grover Cleveland and Marcus Alonzo Hanna, the Advance Agent of Prosperity. No less a person than General James B. Weaver, who four years before had polled over a million votes for President, gave Bryan his blessing.[8] It was a memorable occasion for that body of citizenry whom Bryan called the Great Common People. But from the standpoint of getting himself elected President of the United States it was perhaps a mistake.

William Jennings Bryan did his level best to make it clear that the Populist platform "endorses some policies of which I do not approve"[9] and that his alliance with the People's party was a sort of companionate marriage for the sole purpose of fighting out the monetary issue. But the sovereign voters of the United States are not addicted to reading party platforms, and when a man of the standing of Elihu Root said that Bryan was a Populist,[10] why Bryan was a Populist—and an anarchist,[11] a blasphemer[12] and the anti-Christ,[13] to boot. Marse Henry Watterson had his say, too:

Mr. William J. Bryan has come to Kentucky, and the Kentuckians have taken his measure. He is a boy orator. He is a dishonest dodger. He is a daring adventurer. He is a political fakir. He is not the material of which the people of the United Stats have ever made a President, nor is he even of the material of which any party has ever before made a candidate.[14]

Marse Henry was in error, as more mature reflection on the character of some of the candidates for the Presidency of the United States should have shown him. Bryan missed carrying Kentucky by just 281 votes; had there been no gold Democratic ticket in the field, he would have carried the state hands down.

In their own way the adherents of the Silver Knight of the West were as impassioned albeit less intemperate in the expression of their feeling.

It was a fanaticism like the Crusades [wrote William Allen White]. Indeed, the delusion that was working on the people took the form of religious frenzy. Sacred hymns were torn from their pious tunes to give place to words which deified the cause and made gold—and all its symbols, capital, wealth, plutocracy—diabolical . . . They sang their barbaric songs in unrhythmic jargon, with something of the same mad faith that inspired the martyrs going to the stake. Far into the night the voices rose—women's voices, children's voices, the voices of old men, of youths and of maidens, rose on the ebbing prairie breezes, as the crusaders of the revolution rode home, praising the people's will as though it were God's will, and cursing wealth for its inequity.[15]

In the East what was lacking in emotion was more than compensated by the practical nature of the activities of the opponents of radical change. Bryan had not yet got home from the Chicago convention before James J. Hill, of the Northern Pacific Railroad, wrote J. Pierpont Morgan:

There is an epidemic craze among the farmers and to some extent among those who receive wages or salaries, and people go about even in the cities from house to house talking upon their views in favor of free coinage. I take the liberty of . . . hoping that you will urge those who are to manage the McKinley campaign that they should get to work *at once*. . . .[16]

A man of the financial importance of James J. Hill did not have to "take the liberty of hoping" twice. Hill himself met the Hon. Marcus Alonzo Hanna in New York in mid-August and introduced him to the proper people.[17] The effect was magical. The Warwick of Ohio found his ambition "to go out and buy somebody"[18] realized to the full. He had begun by buying Major William McKinley, Jr., much as a man of sporting proclivities might buy a race horse, three years before McKinley was nominated for the Presidency. The doughty Major was running for Governor of Ohio at the time, and found himself in debt to the tune of some $130,000[19] —a whacking sum, even for the defender of the "financial honour and prosperity of the country"[20] to be owing. The Hon. Marcus Alonzo Hanna came to his rescue. As a result there was not much of anything Major William McKinley, Jr., would not do for his dear friend Hanna throughout the campaign of 1896.

The whole setting and character of Bryan's campaign was the antithesis of "the coarse and under-cover methods"[21] of McKinley's managers. William Jennings Bryan was not readily led. "He was as easy to handle as a baby—and as difficult," said Jim Dahlman, of Omaha, a little ruefully, after the campaign was over. When the Democratic National Committee met to lay out their plans Mrs. Bryan came into the room with her husband and sat down beside him. A certain constraint and embarrassment were evident. Bryan merely swept the company with his engaging smile and announced that Mamma would remain.

"There will be no secrets in this campaign that Mrs. Bryan cannot know," he said simply.[22]

Possibly William Jennings Bryan meant in all honesty that there should be no secrets in his campaign that all the world should not know. Things had begun a bit awkwardly, however, for so sweeping a programme of virtue. There was the fate of poor old Silver Dick Bland, and on top of that the unhappy business of Tom Watson, of Georgia, idol of the Southern Populists. It had been agreed that if the Peoples' party would endorse Bryan for President the Democratic National Committee would withdraw the wealthy, Down-East Yankee banker and shipbuilder who was Bryan's running mate on the Democratic ticket and substitute Tom Watson for Vice President.[23] The People's party did endorse Bryan, but the Hon. Arthur Sewall of Maine was not withdrawn, and there was confusion and recrimination and lost electoral votes in consequence.[24] The whole manœuvre smacked of the sharp practice of politicians, not crusaders.

Then there was the matter of campaign funds. Bryan was no more than nominated before the Republican press was announcing that he had been "employed and carried on the pay roll of the Big Bonanzas for a number of years." According to the Chicago *Chronicle:*

A paid agent of and spokesman for the silver combine, he has not since his retirement from Congress had any other visible means of support. The richest men in the world, the proprietors of the Big Bonanzas, hire orators like Bryan exactly as other men hire fiddlers and value them as highly.[25]

All of which was only partly true. Bryan made no attempt to deny his connection with the silver-mine owners.[26] If he had been paid, he had been paid starvation wages and had given more than value received. He had not been bought. He believed in Free Silver as he believed in the Bible— William Jennings Bryan was no McKinley to shout for bimetallism until he heard his master's voice, and then shout as loudly for a single gold standard.[27] Bryan's silver mining backers put up in all some $228,000[28] or at the rate of three cents a vote polled by their candidate—a pathetic showing for "the richest men in the world." They also paid for the distribution of some 125,000 copies of *Coin's Financial School*[29] and called it a day. Whatever else was done in the campaign was done by William Jennings Bryan, alone and single-handed.

It must be admitted that there was nothing niggardly about the bankers and business men of the East when it came to paying the price of making the country safe for a single gold standard. From the first of August campaign expenses in the stronghold of "honest money" ran "not less than $25,000 a day."[30] They ran, in fact, a great deal more as the election neared. One hundred and eighty-five thousand dollars went to defeat Bryan in his home state—$1.80 for every Republican vote cast in Nebraska. The Democrats had $8,000. Bryan carried the state by 12,000 votes. Over a hundred million campaign documents were sent out from the Chicago Republican headquarters—twenty to every voter in the Middle West.[31] The banks of the country were assessed one fourth of one per cent. of their capital[32] for McKinley's benefit, and men who howled that an income tax was communism paid a capital levy without a murmur. How much passed through the pudgy hands of the Hon. Marcus Alonzo Hanna in those three hectic months can only be conjectured. But the figure probably lay somewhere between four and six million dollars.[33]

"The strain of universal suffrage on the virtue of the country is tremendous," said the Hon. Whitelaw Reid,[34] as he contributed generously to Mark Hanna's barrel.

When William Jennings Bryan began his campaign, travelling in a dusty, crowded day coach, speaking briefly at every stop from the back platform, he had not the faintest conception of the extent and power of the forces he had challenged. Had he set out to destroy the solar system he could not have taken on a bigger job than with the resources he had at hand to captain "the first great protest of the American people against monopoly," as Tom Johnson defined the issue; "the first great struggle of the masses of our country against the privileged classes."[35]

It all seemed so clear to Bryan. "There is nobody on our side but the people," he said.[36] What else was necessary? This was a democracy, was it not?

I assert that the people of the United States . . . have sufficient patriotism and sufficient intelligence to sit in judgment upon every question which has arisen or which will arise, no matter how long our government may endure. The great political questions are in their final analysis great moral questions, and it requires no extended experience in the handling of money to enable a man to tell right from wrong.[37]

It was the whole creed of William Jennings Bryan, and it was, he felt, infallible. "Who shall save the people from themselves?" he cried.[38]

He would. William Jennings Bryan would. He believed it without arrogance or conceit. God had raised him up for that very task. For that he had been born of the loins of the Hon. Silas Bryan, schooled by Professor Hamill in the art of voicing the thoughts of the common people, and initiated into the artifices of practical politics in the stews and groggeries of South Omaha. For that he had come clean through six years of politics and stood before his countrymen a good man, in more complete a sense than any man who had ever before aspired to the Presidency. It was unthinkable that such a one should fail.

Yet William Jennings Bryan was a beaten man before the electoral canvass began. Victory was not in him or of him. The very speech that won his nomination in Chicago was a speech not of triumph but of failure.

"The individual is but an atom," he said. He referred to Peter the Hermit—but Peter the Hermit failed, too. "We defy them!" he cried—but one does not defy a weaker adversary.

Burn down your cities and leave our farms, and your cities will spring up again as if by magic; but destroy our farms and the grass will grow in the streets of every city in the country [he declared]. Our ancestors, when but three millions in number, had the courage to declare their political independence of every other nation; shall we, their descendants, when we have grown to seventy millions, declare that we are less independent than our forefathers?

Every note of the Cross of Gold speech was a note of defence, of question. "You shall not!" cried Bryan at Chicago. Had he been sure of himself and the sweep of the forces behind him he would have thundered: "You shall!"

He could not. Nowhere in William Jennings Bryan's thirty-six years had the constituents of success made their appearance. An environment of Southern sympathizers, beaten in their struggle; of poverty-stricken farmers, crushed in their conflict with the railroads, the boards of trade, the banks—the abortive career of the Hon. Silas Bryan as model; the baffled ambitions of Mariah Elizabeth Jennings as inspiration; the cohibited circle of women imprisoning his boyhood in their suppressions as the stage-setting of his youth. Even back of childhood lay a long tradition of defeat: the Scotch-Irish immigrants, come to the New World because they could make no place for themselves in the old one, quitting the Eastern seaboard because they were neither shrewd enough nor strong enough to wrest the best holdings from the earlier arrivals. The very religious belief of William Jennings Bryan was a faith of submission, rooted in fear and founded upon acceptance of man's unworthiness.[39] William Jennings Bryan was of those meek who may inherit but will never conquer the earth.

Byran's strength was in the West and the South, as had been Lincoln's and Jackson's and Jefferson's before him. He had no hope of the commercial East. But he could afford to ignore it. With the West and the South he could win as Lincoln and Jackson had won; but Bryan must lose no state west of the Mississippi or south of the Mason and Dixon line. The strategy of the campaign should have been clear, and perhaps it was clear. But in the mind of William Jennings Bryan other elements of the situation were of greater importance.

All Bryan's life his rule of conduct was to take his friends for granted and seek to make friends of his enemies.[40] This was impeccable Biblical procedure, and Bryan's world was God-guided. His was an "optimism based upon factors confessedly outside of human control."[41] To the little circle gathered about the marble-topped table in Silas Bryan's parlour the direct intervention of Divine Providence in human affairs was as fixed as the law of gravity, and God's instrument to register His will, the Common People.[42] The assumption that in any part of the land the popular verdict was foregone were an impious denial of the power of the Almighty to perform a miracle at His will. No such assumption was possible to William Jennings Bryan. In a consistent, albeit futile gesture, therefore, he resolved to invade "the enemy's country"[43] and formally accept his nomination at Madison Square Garden—"the champion of Lazarus at the gates of Dives."[44]

They were a strange caravan setting out from Nebraska to beleaguer the Jericho of the Money Power, like Joshua of old. There was William Jennings Bryan himself—"a rather engaging young man with a prominent nose, an extremely wide thin-lipped mouth, a smile that was almost a grin, a black alpaca coat, a 'boiled' shirt, a low collar and a 'string' tie, who talked with the utmost freedom to the newspaper men about himself, his political ideas," et cetera.[45] And there was Mamma, "not pretty, not fascinating, not especially stylish, not demonstrative nor flattering, but sensible, remarkably observant, calm and sincere."[46] Her soft brown hair had a few silver threads in it, the newspaper men noticed.[47] "Besides the newspaper correspondents our party consisted of Mrs. Bryan and myself," Bryan wrote afterward. He said nothing of the Hon. Richard Parks Bland.[48] But loyal old Silver Dick was there, too, with no necktie and his trousers bagged at the knees, as usual. When they came to Canton they all went to call on Major William McKinley, Jr., to the vast embarrassment of the major.

"You should have been nominated," said McKinley bluntly, to Silver Dick Bland. "You were the logical candidate and the strongest man your party had."[49]

Standing by, William Jennings Bryan smiled his broad, benign smile. He said nothing.

It was an amazing Odyssey. If William Jennings Bryan hoped for miracles he also performed them.

Never in our time was another such as he [wrote Ted Lowrie]. He likes it all! The early rising, the crowded days, the bands, the turmoil, the shouting and applause. He doesn't mind the queer food because he eats only milk toast in towns that don't have a first class Presidential postmaster. He can sleep anywhere and at any time.[50]

At Valley Junction, Iowa, two or three hundred had gathered to meet Bryan's train at six in the morning. Bryan was shaving, but hastily washed the lather off his face, dressed, and got off the train. The reporters followed, dressing on the station platform, to the amusement of the crowd. There was a procession up Main Street, headed by the Valley Junction Silver Cornet Band of two fifes and a drum. They stopped at a café for breakfast, and crowds gathered to peer through the windows at Bryan consuming "two cavernous bowls of milk and toast." [51]

The whole environment evidently depressed Bryan [Lowrie records], for he preached to his audience, scarcely talking politics at all.

He would often do that. Far more than a politician seeking votes, William Jennings Bryan was the evangelist of a new hope for the helpless and disinherited.

Over and over again, just as Bryan was crawling into his berth after twenty-two hours of speech making, some whiskered individual would poke his head between the curtains and say:

"You know me, Mr. Bryan. I am old man Mullen's son—J. P. Mullen is my name. You remember when you was up to our town there was a big crowd of people in the street, and I stuck my head out of the window and yelled, 'Hooray for Bryan!' and you looked up at me and waved your hand. I am that fellow." [52]

Nine times out of ten Bryan did remember him and could add little details to prove it. The baggageman on the accommodation train in which Bryan travelled would run all the way back to the rear platform to hear every speech. There was always something new in each one. Frequently he spoke twenty times a day: occasionally thirty. [53] Once half a dozen men and some "dear old ladies in sunbonnets" were running alongside the cars calling for Bryan. He was shaving and called back that he could not come out. But they persisted.

THE SACRILEGIOUS CANDIDATE.

No man who drags into the dust the most sacred symbols of the Christian world is fit to be president of the United States.

By courtesy of Judge

"An Anarchist, a Blasphemer, and
the Anti-Christ," 1896

THE ASSASSIN.

By courtesy of Judge

So he stuck his head out of the window just as he was and shook hands with all of them. Neither he nor the people outside seemed to think there was anything unusual in the performance. It was not undignified. It was just friendly and simple, and lacking in all pretence.[54]

When John Hay, who had never heard Bryan speak, wrote Henry Adams:

> The Boy Orator makes only one speech—but he makes it twice a day. There is no fun in it. He simply reiterates the unquestionable truths that every man who has a clean shirt is a thief and should be hanged, and there is no goodness or wisdom except among the illiterate and criminal classes; that gold is vile; that silver is lovely and holy . . .[55]

he painted an enduring picture, not of William Jennings Bryan, but of John Hay.

The thermometer stood at ninety-seven in Madison Square Garden. The building was packed, the streets outside jammed with the cavilling, egocentric, cynical inhabitants of the metropolis. Demosthenes and Cicero in one would not have satisfied them.[56] They came to hear the Boy Orator, shrug their shoulders, and depart commenting: "Not so much!" So they had treated Lincoln, also.

William Jennings Bryan had no clue to this temper in his audience, and none to give him one. He was uncomfortable, out of element, daunted, and so defiant. That power over vast aggregations of men and women that had come to be as much a part of his equipment as his voice deserted him in the face of this heterogeneous multitude whose mood was wholly captious. He was like the prince in the fairy tale, when the wind blew off the cap which rendered him invisible to the eyes of the giant. Bryan's familiar Biblical phrases that among the Western farmers brought them up shouting with enthusiasm[57] fell on ears long untuned to such language. Governor Stone of Missouri bored the sweating crowd to curses with a rambling introduction. When the Young Man Eloquent from Nebraska at last rose to read his speech—

and read it badly[58]—any votes he might have captured in
New York with his youth, his golden voice and his magnetism
were lost. William Jennings Bryan's invasion of "the
enemy's country" was more like Napoleon's invasion of
Russia than the crusade of Peter the Hermit.

An Englishman described Bryan in Washington, with
impartial eye.

With the faint blue stubble on his face, and his long, grizzly
hair, he suggests an actor to the British mind. But you could not
mistake him for a bad actor [wrote G. W. Steevens]. No one
listened to the first speaker. Suddenly above the periods of the
orator and the whistling of the wind, the band crashed out: "See
the Conquering Hero Comes." Instantly the whole park awoke. A
forest of little American flags sprang up and waved furiously. . . .
Shrieks became delirium. . . . For a moment the square figure
stood perfectly still. Then slowly he reached out his hand like St.
Paul in the Bible. Still very slowly he raised his arm above his
head and made—one, two, three—in each direction of the crowd.
Gradually silence crept over the mass of heads and then the
orator opened his lips. . . .

As I splashed home I saw the four-horsed carriage, with the
nodding helmets of the mounted police, driving rapidly off with a
yelling escort of devotees. And I saw the black, square figure turn
from side to side, buoyant and elastic, glad and exultant over the
popular applause.[59]

Far more the Warwick than Mark Hanna, it was Grover
Cleveland who elected Major William McKinley, Jr. "Would
you die for the Majah?" John Hay wrote Henry Adams.
"Mr. Cleveland would."[60] It was Cleveland who stimulated
the organization of a "gold" Democratic party financed out of
the same pockets that poured forth Mark Hanna's limitless
treasure. "Bryan," wrote John Hay, "has succeeded in scaring
the Goldbugs out of their five wits." There were no lengths
to which they would not go and did not go to smash the
Silver Knight of the West and all he stood for. In Tennessee
an attempt was made to poison Bryan.[61]

As the month of November drew near, capitalists resorted to
the very effective device of carrying large orders to manufacturers

on condition that these orders should be executed only in case of Mr. McKinley's election. In this way notice was served on artisans that if they voted for Mr. Bryan they would be voting to deprive themselves of work [wrote Prof. Peck]. At the end of the week preceding the election many employers of labor in paying off their workmen gave them notice that they could not return to work in the event of Mr. Bryan's success.[62]

Insurance companies intimated to Western debtors that if McKinley were elected, extensions of five years on mortgages would be granted. The banks throughout the country exercised every conceivable form of pressure. . . . From the pulpits, Bryan and his platform were denounced in terms rarely heard within the four walls of the house of God.[63] . . . Negroes were imported from the South by trainload, at $5 per head, to vote for McKinley—in one district with 30,000 voting population, 48,000 votes were cast. The very graveyards were robbed of the names on their tombstones to be enrolled as voters for an honest dollar.[64]

"O God, keep him humble!" prayed Mrs. McKinley for her son.[65]

As his long, wearying journeyings ended, William Jennings Bryan also prayed.

"To me the news of my defeat was a relief," he told Louis Post. "Before the news came I literally and sincerely prayed the Lord to let this responsibility be averted; nevertheless, not my will but Thine be done."

His prayer was answered.

CHAPTER XVIII

CUBA LIBRE

WE HAVE submitted the issue to the American people, and their will is law," telegraphed William Jennings Bryan to Major William McKinley, Jr., when the election returns were finally in.[1]

The gentlemen of the Eastern seaboard who had contributed so generously to Mark Hanna's barrel certainly hoped so. Even in Chicago, the night of the election the principal bankers and merchants of the city played "Follow the Leader" over sofas, chairs, and tables, upstairs and down, in the Chicago Club, and wound up dancing in one another's arms in a delirium of relief.[2]

The celebration was premature.

Almost the last words of Mr. Bryan before the declaration of the polls were to the effect that if he were beaten this time he was ready to begin work at once on the campaign of 1900,

recorded the Englishman, Steevens.[3]

Many a solid citizen, profoundly shocked at the methods by which the victory of McKinley was achieved, besought Bryan to go to Washington and claim the Presidency on the ground that the Republicans had won by fraud. But William Jennings Bryan had no taste for the rôle of a second Coxey. Instead he issued a trumpet call for the campaign of 1900:

In the face of an enemy rejoicing in its victory, let the roll be called for the next engagement. I urge all friends of bimetallism to renew their allegiance to the cause. If we are right, as I believe we are, we shall yet triumph.[4]

Even McKinley was more than chary about touching the currency question, upon the basis of which, if any-

thing, he had been elected—it was over three years before
he summoned courage to make gold, irrevocably and im-
mutably, the standard money of these United States. By
that time the discovery of gold in the Klondike and the
perfection of the cyanide process of extracting gold from
ore had already attended to the matter.[5]

What was not settled by the election of 1896, or indeed,
so far as one could see, in the way of being settled, either,
was what Bryan called "the fight between the money power
and the people."[6] On the contrary, feeling was sharpened
and embittered by the contemptuous ruthlessness of Mark
Hanna. It was all very discouraging for Grover Cleveland
and his "gold bug" friends who had sacrificed everything
to poll some ten thousand less votes than the Prohibitionists.
They had accomplished nothing save to make William Jennings Bryan "the undisputed leader of his party"[7]—the
last thing they wanted. As the fact of that leadership with
all it implied of menace to the settled order of things became
more apparent, it was borne in upon the best minds of the
country that almost anything might be preferable to the
fright, not to speak of the expense of the campaign of 1896—
even war. A party conducting a victorious war was not
usually in peril of being turned out of power. War might,
in the long run, be a political expedient meriting serious
consideration.

It was not a new idea. In the brief sixscore years of its
existence the United States had proved to be the most belli-
cose nation on the globe, with something like a hundred
wars to its credit.[8] Not a generation had passed without its
sanguinary conflict, and when in February, 1895, the Cubans
again renewed their struggle for freedom from Spanish rule,
under the very noses of the newspaper-reading public of the
United States, the Americans were like a reformed drunkard
at the swinging doors of a saloon on a hot summer day.
Even President Cleveland toyed with the seductive prospect,
and in his last annual message pointed out that between
thirty and fifty million dollars in American capital were involved in the fate of Cuba. "It cannot be reasonably assumed

that the hitherto expectant attitude of the United States will be indefinitely maintained," said he, with cryptic significance. "The United States is not a country to which peace is necessary."[9] With that secrecy with which the Hon. Grover Cleveland seemed to think the business of a democracy best conducted, he tried to open negotiations, in the closing hours of his administration, for the purchase of Cuba from Spain, for $100,000,000.[10] Altogether, it was plain that some sort of reckoning with Spain over Cuba was imminent before ever Cleveland left the Presidency—"under a greater burden of popular contempt than has ever been excited by a public man since the foundation of the government."[11] War with Spain was, in fine, one of the numerous skeletons Major William McKinley, Jr., found in the White House closets.[12]

President McKinley was not distinguished as a politician albeit a decided improvement on his predecessor. But the Hon. Marcus Alonzo Hanna was a political realist if ever there was one. It did not take him two minutes to see that what the Republican party had to do, and do without delay, was to remove Willaim Jennings Bryan from public life, come and cost what might. If so distinguished a conservative as Whitelaw Reid could say of Bryan that "when a man polls as many votes as he has received for the Presidency, I suppose there must be something in him,"[13] it was clearly time something were done about it.

The trouble was that, despite the unequal electoral vote, Bryan had come perilously near being elected. Everyone who studied the figures, as all of Bryan's followers did, was aware of it. He had received almost a million more votes than Grover Cleveland polled four years before, and that in spite of the active opposition of the President of the United States and the nominal leader of his party. No one in the history of the United States before—or indeed, since—had ever achieved anything like the personal triumph accorded William Jennings Bryan. "Never before had a national campaign seen the Democratic party so abandoned by men of substance or with so slender a purse," wrote Professor E. Benjamin Andrews. Yet even so, a shift of only 14,001 votes, distrib-

uted over five states, would have elected William Jennings
Bryan twenty-fifth President of the United States; and while
Major William McKinley, Jr., had given indisputable evidence of proper Presidential dignity by remaining on his
own front porch throughout the campaign, while trainloads
of the faithful were fetched, charges prepaid, to do him
homage, his virile young rival had improved the occasion to
see America first.

Bryan had faced five million of his countrymen and
shaken hands with most of them. They felt that they knew
him as they had never known a Presidential candidate before, and at the end of the campaign William Jennings Bryan
had 186,000 letters and telegrams on his hands to prove how
intimately they felt it.[14] He had covered 18,009 miles and
had delivered some 600 speeches. By and large, if any man
knew these United States and the inhabitants thereof William Jennings Bryan was he. Merely wishing him out of the
way was not going to get rid of him.

No one appreciated this more keenly than the Republican
leaders. They recognized that nothing short of a political
convulsion, a cataclysm, an act of God, would rid the country of William Jennings Bryan and all he stood for. The nearest thing to an act of God that the Republican leaders could
conceive was war; providentially here was war at their very
doors. In the event of war, of course, every citizen with political aspirations would have to support the government or
suffer the fate of Daniel Webster and Henry Clay. William
Jennings Bryan would be trapped.

Unfortunately the Democrats too could play at that game.
By clamouring for a crusade in the interests of civilization, a
war without thought of conquest or aggrandizement, an
altruistic war, a war for the benefit of humanity—in short, a
war—the Democrats could throw into high relief the gross
materialism ruling Republican counsels. No ideals! Cynically
weighing the dollars of the sugar planters and tobacco
growers against the lives of women and children dying on the
nation's doorsill! Or, by the same token, in case the Administration should decide to go to war, they could raise an even

louder outcry against the fruitless sacrifice of precious American lives for a lot of good-for-nothing half-breeds.

Under the circumstances it was small wonder that President McKinley did not know which way to turn, or that William Jennings Bryan knew even less what stand to take toward the Cuban rebellion. Bryan's horizons had been pushed back a long way since that fateful July day when, with $100 in his pocket, he had invested in a $2-a-day room without bath at the Clifton House, Chicago[15]—two cheap wooden bedsteads, a plush lounge, and a few chairs[16]—and hoped for the best. He had met a vast number of his fellow citizens in fourteen weeks campaigning, and captured most of those he met, body, boots and breeches. He had met Robert Treat Payne, Jr., Brooks and John Quincy Adams, Julian Hawthorne, James Creelman, Clarence Darrow, Dr. Albert Shaw, Professors John Clark Ridpath, E. Benjamin Andrews, and Edward A. Ross, Tom Johnson of Cleveland, William J. Gaynor of New York, Colonel Edward M. House of Texas, and a young newspaper man from California, recently come East, William Randolph Hearst. He told Boss Croker of Tammany Hall the story of how Governor Boyd of Nebraska, for whom Bryan had campaigned all one summer, turned to Bryan at the banquet of the celebration and said: "I understand you are on the programme. What do you do—sing or speak?" Croker slapped his thigh in delight and cried: "Tammany's going to back that man—or else he's going to run off with Tammany."[17] Everyone who came into contact with Bryan found him refreshing and genuine, if naïve. All were eager to help him.

They could do nothing. They could not live with William Jennings Bryan out in Lincoln, Nebraska, and supply the gaps in his knowledge of public affairs that he was now far too busy ever to supply himself by reading and study. They could not even ease this young man of the burden that pressed most heavily upon him at the moment the campaign ended— the Herculean task of paying the butcher, the baker, and the tax collector, and of sending his children to school. The silver-mine owners were through with Bryan. His engagement with the Omaha *World-Herald* had been solely a means of securing the nomination for the Presidency. It was at an end. William Jennings Bryan was out of a job with a wife and three children to keep, 186,000 letters to answer, and the dignity of a Presidential candidate to maintain. The outlook was hardly brilliant.

When Bryan returned to Nebraska at the close of his second term in Congress he brought with him the nephew of Cotter Bride, in whose house the Bryans lived in Washington—Dan Bride, fresh from the Emerald Isle. Now Dan Bride chipped in what savings he had and even wrote his uncle in Washington for a loan to tide Bryan over. Philo S. Bennett, a New Haven grocer, had met Bryan during Bryan's invasion of "the enemy's country." He too came to the rescue with an offer of $3,000. A bit here and a bit there, the emergency was met, not without desperate expedients.

Mrs. Bryan worked furiously, writing a word or two on the corner of each letter to be answered summarizing its contents—"boy baby," "triplets all named after W. J. B." In time a dozen form letters were developed to take care of the bulk of the correspondence. In time, too, William Jennings Bryan's brother Charles learned to sign Bryan's name so expertly that even the banks could not tell the difference.[18]

Together William Jennings Bryan and his wife compiled a voluminous account of the campaign to which they gave the inspired title: *The First Battle*. They offered the book for sale by subscription at $3.75 a copy. It proved an instant success.[19] In thousands of homes throughout the Middle West where previously only the Bible found lodgment this "weird hodgepodge of autobiography, Bryanesque philosophy and propaganda"[20] was given an honoured place on the marble-topped centre table. The profits on the book were $26,000.[21] Slowly, painfully, the corner had been turned. Mrs. Bryan invested this, their first considerable earning, in government bonds—bonds that paid interest in gold.

It was not poverty alone, however, that had William Jennings Bryan by the throat in those days of enforced readjust-

ment following defeat. Something more momentous threatened the very air of supreme confidence that had always been
Bryan's chief source of power over men. When, during the
campaign, the press of the East had depicted him as a barn-
storming actor and called him "assassin" and "anarchist,"
nominated by a convention of "Satan-inspired traitors seeking to overthrow American institutions,"[22] Bryan merely
smiled. He knew himself so much more essentially conservative[23] than these imitation Marie Antoinettes too newly
arrived at wealth to admit knowledge of the needs of the
masses. The Republican newspapers charged him with being
a penniless *arriviste* who had never made a living and never
could. Had he won, that also would have made no difference.

But back in 1894, when he had failed of election to the
Senate, he and Mary had stumbled into the down-at-heels
little house in Lincoln the night that the result of the canvass
was known, and there in the darkness of their front parlour
she had put her arms about him and begged him to give up
politics.[24] He had not done it. He had risked everything they
had on this fantastic try for the Presidency. He had lost.
Now he must face the fact that by current American standards he really was a failure. He no longer had either profession
or trade. He could not step into a bank and borrow a nickel
without asking some substantial citizen who had stayed at
home and attended strictly to business to go his bond.[25]

If William Jennings Bryan would amount to anything in
the community, or in his own eyes either, he must make
money. It was the law of American life. "The voice of Mr.
Bryan" might be, as a distinguished Senator said, "the command of six million Democrats who had voted for him."[26]
It could not command the grocer.

In this dilemma two roads opened before William Jennings
Bryan. He could return to the law. It would mean giving up
politics and be a long row to hoe, and a hard one besides.
His was not a legal mind.

His chain of argument once completed, his theory becomes to
him an almost sacred thing [wrote his friend Willis John Abbot].
If confronted by a condition which throws doubt on the theory,

the condition must be explained away, for the theory to him is the superior.[27]

In a lawyer such inelasticity would obviously be fatal. On the other hand the lecture platform beckoned.

Even as late as the 'nineties the Chautauqua circuit was of the very first respectability. "Distinguished foreigners, military heroes, great travellers and explorers, politicians and statesmen—all are heard at Chautauqua," wrote Mrs. Bryan.[28] It was true. Nothing was more characteristic of the America of that day. William Jennings Bryan would be fortunate to find a place on the Chautauqua programmes. "By lecturing," he explained, "I am able to visit the different parts of the country and discuss various questions concerned with the government without being a burden to anyone and can at the same time earn a living."[29] He was able to do a great deal more than that. He could, and he did, keep alive the personal touch he had gained during the campaign with millions of his fellow citizens. What he lectured on was of minor consequence.

For, after all, William Jennings Bryan was his own best political platform. He was a "good man" whom millions trusted implicitly because he so patently believed what he preached.[30] Never before in the history of the country had a man stood in the presence of the electorate in quite the same garb of righteousness as William Jennings Bryan in 1896. The fact that he had in himself no such belief as he inspired in others was his chief handicap. Human weakness, sinfulness, errancy, were of his creed, ingrained. He begged his followers to believe in the causes he advocated. They believed, instead, in him.

In the East Bryan's début as a lecturerer was inauspicious. His receipts were attached at New Haven,[31] and only forty-one attended a luncheon at the Hotel Bartholdi, in New York. But among those forty-one were Richard Croker, Senator Gorman, and Henry George. At Carnegie Hall Bryan addressed a mere handful. "Our adversaries at first accused me of being in the pay of the silver-mine owners," he complained. "Now they censure me for charging people to

hear me lecture."[32] Asked point-blank if the Silver League
paid his bills, "Not at all," Bryan protested. "There is
nothing at all in those stories."[33] He called on McKinley, too,
and when the President explained that he had not yet read
the autographed copy of *The First Battle* Bryan had sent him
Bryan merely smiled. "There is no law which compels you
to read it," he said.

But out in the great open spaces William Jennings Bryan
the lecturer "proved to be one of the greatest, if not the
greatest, success of the season."[34] Men, women, and children
flocked to hear him on bimetallism or government control
of the Union Pacific and Central Pacific railways[35] or "Our
Immortals" or any other subject he chose. To these simple
folk Bryan was "just one of them."[36] He said what they
thought and in precisely the way they thought it. He gave
plausible verbal clothing to sentiments that were emotional,
not reasoned—their frustrations, their discontents, their
nebulous aspirations. William Jennings Bryan was more to
his hearers than any of the numerous evangelists of the day,
preaching salvation by hope. For what Bryan counselled
was not patience but political action; what he offered was
not an uncertain recompense after death but immediate help
for the infirmities of them that followed him.

With war with Spain the outstanding cloud on the political
horizon of the country Major William McKinley, Jr., appointed John Sherman, already in his dotage, to conduct the
foreign relations of the United States, thus making a place for
Mark Hanna as Sherman's successor in the Senate. If ever
the leader of an opposition party was presented with an opportunity to attack his successful rival, this "disregard of
common decency no less than the safety of the nation," as
John Hay characterized the President's action,[37] furnished
William Jennings Bryan a rare opening. He forebore.

We want no wars of conquest; we must avoid the temptation
of territorial aggression [McKinley declared]. War should never be
entered upon until every agency of peace has failed.[38]

Bryan took the President at his word.

There were those, however, in whose ears McKinley's eternal platitudes had a tinny sound, and in none more so than William Randolph Hearst's. He sent Murat Halstead and Richard Harding Davis and Frederick Remington to Cuba to play up the atrocities of the Spaniard in print and picture. Shortly the country was aflame with hatred and war spirit. It may be that Hearst did not reply to Frederick Remington's complaint that "There is no trouble here. There will be no war," with the famous telegram: "PLEASE REMAIN, YOU FURNISH THE PICTURES AND I'LL FURNISH THE WAR."[39] He should have. For William Randolph Hearst and Major William McKinley, Jr., between them, did furnish the war.

Hearst's share was the publication of a private letter from the Spanish Minister in Washington in which the President of the United States was described as "weak and a bidder for the admiration of the crowd, besides being a would-be politician who tries to leave a door open behind himself while keeping on good terms with the jingoes of his party."[40] The characterization possessed the unforgivable quality of truth. When a week later, the United States battleship *Maine* was blown up in the harbour of Havana, "war," according to Theodore Roosevelt, "became inevitable."[41]

To one of Theodore Roosevelt's sanguine temperament war was usually inevitable. But in this instance it was nothing of the sort. On March 29, 1898, the President of the United States sent the Spanish government what was virtually an ultimatum regarding Spain's conduct of her Cuban affairs. Two days later General Woodford, the American Minister at Madrid, cabled:

I believe the ministry are ready to go as far and as fast as they can and still save the dynasty here in Spain. They know that Cuba is lost. Public opinion in Spain has moved steadily towards peace.[42]

The door to peace stood open, McKinley hesitating as usual on the threshold. His own party was torn over the question of war or peace. "He is in danger of ruining himself and the Republican party by standing in the way of the people's wishes," was the lofty sentiment of the Hon. Russell A. Alger, Secretary of War.[43] "McKinley has no more backbone than a chocolate éclair," sneered Theodore Roosevelt.[44] The moment for William Jennings Bryan to say his say, too, appeared to have come.

The time for intervention has arrived. Humanity demands that we should act [declared Bryan]. War is a terrible thing and cannot be defended except as a means to an end, and yet it is sometimes the only means by which a necessary end can be secured. War is the final arbiter between nations, when reason and diplomacy are of no avail.

But reason and diplomacy were still of avail. Three days after Bryan had given out his pronouncement, General Woodford cabled:

I am sure that before next October I will get peace in Cuba, with justice to Cuba and protection to our great American interests.[45]

And a week later, with a speed surprising in Spaniards, the Spanish government accepted *in toto* President McKinley's terms:

Before August first, on one of the following bases: either such autonomy as the insurgents may agree to accept, or recognition by Spain of the independence of the island, or cession of the island to the United States [cabled General Woodford]. I am satisfied that the present government is going, and is loyally ready to go as fast and as far as it can.[46]

With this highly gratifying cable in his pocket President McKinley the following day sent a message to Congress demanding in substance that war be declared.

A fortnight later William Jennings Bryan volunteered his services in the defence of his country.

CHAPTER XIX

KANSAS CITY

IF THERE was one thing that Major William McKinley, Jr., found more difficult than another it was making up his mind. He never did really come to any conclusion one could put one's finger upon about free silver. And now that war with Spain was at last decided, he seemed to have no idea what its purpose was.

But if the President was dark in his mind as to where the country was going under his leadership his truculent young Assistant Secretary of the Navy suffered from no such misgivings. Six months before war was declared Theodore Roosevelt was planning for "our Asiatic squadron" to "blockade and, if possible, take Manila."[1] And while the Senate of the United States was solemnly engaged in declaring to all the world, in respect of Cuba

That the United States hereby disclaims any disposition or intention to exercise sovereignty, jurisdiction or control over said Island except for the pacification thereof and asserts its determination, when that is accomplished, to leave the government and control of the Island to its people,[2]

Roosevelt's *alter ego*, "Massachusetts's sweet-scented 'scholar in politics,'"[3] was writing him that

Porto Rico is not forgotten, and we mean to have it. Unless I am utterly and profoundly mistaken, the Administration is now fully committed to the large policy that we both desire.[4]

Henry Cabot Lodge was not apt to be utterly and profoundly mistaken in such matters. Nor was he.

The Spanish force in Cuba was anything but formidable,

as even the Spaniards realized. The last batch of reinforcements sent out from Spain numbered only 16,000, "most of them raw recruits, a large proportion boys not seventeen years old."[5] However, it was well to be on the safe side. So President McKinley called for 200,000 volunteers and in time accumulated an army of some 275,000 in round numbers,[6] or two for every Spanish soldier on the face of the earth. For the honour of American arms it should be recorded that 136,000 of these never stepped foot off their native soil—the Spaniards were in due season beaten in battle, not smothered to death by sheer numbers.

To William Jennings Bryan the processes of war appeared baffling from the outset. The offer of his warrior's might was made in good faith.

I believe that every citizen should support the government when final action is taken, whether he approves of the action or not,

he declared.[7] He at least had done so. Yet his gesture was not even vouchsafed the courtesy of acknowledgment. Theodore Roosevelt, on the other hand, whose political fame rested on having run third in a campaign for Mayor of New York, was given every facility to help organize a regiment of "cowboy soldiers," while Bryan, for whom six and a half million Americans had voted to be commander in chief of the Army and Navy of the United States, cooled his heels as a mere recruit[8] awaiting assignment. Indeed, Roosevelt throughout played his cards with striking adroitness. It was his war. He had worked hard to bring it about, and he proposed to extract the maximum advantage from it. What bothered him was just where his best chance would lie. At first blush it looked like a naval war, and as Assistant Secretary of the Navy, Roosevelt was admirably placed. But shortly Admiral Dewey steamed into Manila Bay and skimmed the cream off the crock of naval glory. Five days later Theodore Roosevelt was sworn in, with impressive ceremonies, as a lieutenant colonel of cavalry.[9] Within a month he was on his way to Cuba, fully trained in the arts of war.[10]

Elected captain of the first company of the Third Regiment of Nebraska's Volunteers, Bryan declined the honour.

"I know nothing about military matters," he said. Quietly he and the faithful Dan Bride prepared to transfer, as privates, to the First Nebraska Volunteers, bound for the Philippines.

But to thousands of loyal and patriotic Americans of the Middle West the shabby treatment accorded their idol was more monstrous than anything that had taken place in Cuba. With or without authorization from Washington, Governor Holcomb empowered Bryan to recruit a regiment,[11] and before one could say "Jack Robinson" a regiment was ready. From Newport News to Oklahoma companies offered themselves, full strength and "drilling three weeks."[12] In the hundreds of letters pouring in upon Bryan nothing was more conspicuous than the blood lust of the men of God. From every corner of the land and every variety of pulpit the humble followers of the Prince of Peace attested their qualifications for slaughter with imagination and enthusiasm.[13] It was at once a revelation and a comfort to William Jennings Bryan. He had had his doubts on the head of the Sixth Commandment, but they appeared to be officially resolved.

Universal peace cannot come until justice is enthroned throughout the world [he declared]. Until the right has triumphed in every land and love reigns in every heart, government must, as a last resort, appeal to force.[14]

The millennium plainly was a long way off; and the part of wisdom was to get the most one could in an imperfect world.

So far as Bryan was concerned, this was much more easily said than done. The Administration of Major William McKinley, Jr., looked with a sour eye upon his assertion that "history will vindicate the position taken by the United States in the war with Spain."[15] Nobody asked for Bryan's approval, and no stone was left unturned to dispense with his coöperation. When Bryan's regiment was ready for service, Secretary of War Alger curtly ordered the Governor of Nebraska to send him 600 men immediately to be used as replacements—which would have shattered Colonel Bryan's command overnight,[16] and left him a mere recruiting sergeant. Instantly Major General Joe Wheeler offered Colonel Bryan a place on his staff,[17] and the Governor of Missouri tendered him by telegraph the command of a regiment of Missouri volunteers.[18] Reluctantly the War Department receded, and Colonel William Jennings Bryan went to war.[19]

He did not, however, proceed very far along the road to military glory. If the Administration had been mistrustful regarding the political advantages which might accrue to Colonel Bryan from establishing beyond peradventure that he was not "only a patriot with his jaw,"[20] its doubts were resolved by the triumphal progress of the Third Nebraska Volunteers across the country. It was like nothing so much as the campaign of 1896 over again—thousands fighting to shake the hero's hand, eloquent words delivered from the back platform with appropriate military reticence, bands playing "El Capitán" and "There'll be a Hot Time in the Old Town To-night," mingled cheers and tears in that welter of emotion so dear to the American heart.

"The Civil War is over, never to be resurrected," thundered the son of the late Silas Bryan. "In time of danger the men who wore the Gray would be as loyal as those who wore the Blue."[21] The ladies of Nashville with their own lily-white hands prepared two thousand sandwiches, a thousand lunch boxes, and a thousand gallons of hot coffee for Bryan's 1,328 Nebraska Boys.[22]

"War is harsh," said William Jennings Bryan. "It is attended by hardship and suffering."[23]

In truth the army was a blind alley to Bryan. "He amassed innumerable experiences, but no experience," wrote Sydney Brooks in after years. "He knew everything and understood nothing."[24] Of no phase of his life was this truer than of Bryan's military service. He appeared unable to grasp that the sole business of a soldier is to kill. To Bryan the function of a soldier was to be killed—he saw war a game to be won by sacrifice hits.

The essence of patriotism lies in a willingness to sacrifice for one's country [he had said at Arlington Cemetery on Memorial Day four years before]. A life or life's most precious blood he yielded up for the welfare of his fellows—this is the simple story which proves that it is now, and ever has been, more blessed to give than to receive.[25]

It was William Jennings Bryan's concept of life: the meek should inherit the earth and the kingdom of heaven belong to the poor in spirit. The only path to any enduring glory led straight to the grave. Fulfilment, heroism, were inseparable from defeat. So he had been taught at the knee of Mariah Elizabeth Jennings. So he had learned among the women of his childhood, huddled in the shadow of a war from which death alone had emerged glorious. And so, too, in church and Sabbath school, a faith erected upon a foundation of surrender—"not as I will but as Thou wilt"—had become the prison of his spirit. His was the supreme sentimentality of his countrymen, to whom a lump in the throat makes the whole world kin.

In all of this William Jennings Bryan was the antithesis of Theodore Roosevelt who, as Grover Cleveland had predicted, was having "his share of strut and sensation,"[26]—perhaps a bit more than his share. Everyone, and indeed everything, conspired to give the young "Rough Rider" the opportunity of which he was so avid. Certainly never in the previous history even of so martial a land as the United States had anyone contrived to garner so many foot pounds of political advantage out of a minimum of military service. Yet nothing about the conduct of the war pleased Roosevelt; he was prodigal with his criticisms.

The day the Rough Riders reached Tampa, Roosevelt pronounced the "railroad system in the wildest confusion"[27] and entered in his diary:

No words can paint the confusion. No head, a breakdown of both the railroad and military systems of the country. . . . No plans; no staff officers; no instructions to us. . . . Worst confusion yet; no plans; utter confusion.

He wrote his sister:

> It seems to me that the people at Washington are inexcusable for putting us aboard ship and keeping us crowded to suffocation on these transports in Tampa harbour in a semi-tropical sun.[28]

Colonel Bryan had his own troubles, and under conditions which embraced no glory. His Nebraska Boys sickened and died in the fever-ridden hell-hole where he was encamped, near Jacksonville, Florida.

> The next war I shall certainly go if Will does [Mrs. Bryan wrote Dan Bride, who was Bryan's orderly]. If Will decides to stay in longer, I am thinking of changing places with you. . . . It seems to me I get more anxious all the time. . . . This is not a pleasant life [she added, wistfully].[29]

The Administration newspapers dealt savagely with Bryan whatever he did.[30] He, too, fell ill and straightway was accused of "fighting campaign fever at a good hotel" and mercilessly lampooned in consequence.[31] Yet when Bryan was urged to applaud an editorial written by William Randolph Hearst attacking the Administration, he replied:

> I do not think it would be proper for me to put myself in the attitude of either criticizing what has been done or advising what should be done in regard to the ordinary conduct of the war.[32]

He was, he said facetiously, suffering from "military lockjaw."[33] It was a malady against which Roosevelt appeared to have been inoculated early in the hostilities.

Theodore Roosevelt served 132 days[34] and within a fortnight of his demobilization was campaigning for the governorship of New York on the strength of his military record. William Jennings Bryan served 208 days, as perilous from Secretary Alger's "embalmed beef" as from Spanish bullets. But the day he put off his uniform, Bryan had something on his mind besides public office.

For when Admiral Cervera sailed out of Santiago harbour "to suicide, dragging along with me those 2,000 sons of

Spain,"[35] as he put it, he left McKinley in as bad a hole as
the President's worst enemy could have wished for him.
With the destruction of Cervera's fleet the war was over,
and war plays curious tricks upon the minds of men.

Forcible annexation [declared McKinley in December, 1897]
cannot be thought of; that, by our code of morality, would be
criminal aggression.[36]

Beyond a doubt he voiced the conviction of ninety-nine out
of a hundred of his countrymen at the time he spoke. But
seven months later, with the blood of an easy victory in their
eyes, the great American public saw matters in another light,
and what McKinley had to do was to find a pious reason to
change his stand on the aggrandizement of the United States
as rapidly and as completely as he had changed his stand on
bimetallism.

According to Richard Olney, "the Methodists of the land
laboured with him in the line of the policy to which he seems
inclined"[37]—the benighted Filipinos had never been exposed
to the civilizing doctrine of John Wesley and would be a
fertile field for missionary cultivation. McKinley, however,
refused to admit the intervention of any intermediaries.

The truth is I did not want the Philippines and when they came
to us as a gift from the gods, I did not know what to do with them
[he explained]. I walked the floor of the White House night after
night until midnight; and I am not ashamed to tell you, gentlemen,
that I went down on my knees and prayed Almighty God for light
and guidance more than one night. And one night late it came to me
... that there was nothing left for us to do but take them all, and
to educate the Filipinos, and uplift and civilize and Christianize
them, and by God's grace do the very best we could by them as
our fellow-men for whom Christ also died. And then I went to bed,
and went to sleep and slept soundly.[38]

Whether it was on this occasion that he received the
slogan: "Shall we haul down the flag that floats over our
dead in the Philippines?" McKinley did not reveal.

Bryan also prayed for guidance, and curiously enough received an entirely different message from on high:

It is the voice of the serpent, not the voice of God, that bids us eat[39] [he said]. . . . The hour of temptation has come. . . .[40] If a contest undertaken for the sake of humanity degenerates into a war of conquest, we shall find it difficult to meet the charge of having added hypocrisy to greed. . . .[41] Avarice paints destiny with a dollar mark before it; militarism equips it with a sword. . . .[42] Be not deceived. If we expect to maintain a colonial policy, we shall not find it to our advantage to educate the people . . . lest they learn to read the Declaration of Independence and Constitution of the United States and mock us for our inconsistency.[43]

As for hauling down the flag, Bryan was as ready to do that as Zachary Taylor had been[44] in Mexico City.

William Jennings Bryan felt that he could see as far through a millstone as the next man. And when he perceived, even from no loftier observation point than Lincoln, Nebraska, the British subjugating the Boers, the Germans reaching out to South America, the Russians taking possession of Port Arthur, the French seizing Fashoda, the Japanese despoiling China, and now his own country about to depart from the ancient ways like Rehoboam, the foolish son of a wise father, the danger was clear and very real to him.

The nation [he said] is of age and it can do what it pleases; it can spurn the traditions of the past; it can repudiate the principles upon which the nation rests; it can employ force instead of reason; it can substitute might for right; it can conquer weaker people; it can exploit their lands, appropriate their property and kill their people; but it cannot repeal the moral law or escape the punishment decreed for the violation of human rights.[45]

On the whole Bryan had the best of the argument any way one looked at it. It availed him nothing. His countrymen had suffered so long from an inferiority complex in the presence of older and more patronizing nations that they hugged to their bosoms the opportunity to lord it over a lesser race. It might be true, as Bryan said, that "a republic can have no subjects."[46] But Republicans could.

That was what William Jennings Bryan saw, to the
exclusion of everything else, in the drift of America toward
imperialism following the Spanish-American War. He was
the only man who did see it. Many opposed turning the
United States into a shoddy imitation of the British Empire
—Senators Hoar and Pettigrew, Moorfield Storey and Andrew Carnegie, Carl Schurz and Grover Cleveland. They
would "save the people from themselves"; but their way
was not the way of democracy. They would organize a compact minority in the Senate to refuse ratification of any
treaty of peace with Spain until one could be secured that
would keep the United States forever clear of a colonial empire.

To Bryan this was surrender. The employment of a
minority to effect any end, however desirable, was the beginning of tyranny, he held. How could a great question affecting the whole future of the nation be decided by a handful of
Senators? What sort of democracy would that be? Henry
Clay had made one adroit compromise with slavery after
another; where did they lead? One source of authority and
one alone could decide—the people of the United States.

But before the question of imperialism could become a
political issue the war would have to end. If Bryan had
learned no other thing from his military service he had
learned that the people of a nation at war neither think nor
talk nor act like the people of a nation at peace. There must
be a treaty of peace with Spain, and that speedily. If it included the cession of the Philippines, the Ladrones, and
Porto Rico to the United States as colonies, possessions,
wards, or whatever other appropriate terms might be revealed to President McKinley at midnight, so much the better. The issue would then be clear-cut.[47]

So Bryan argued, to the consternation of the opponents
of the Spanish treaty. They had counted on him and in their
eyes he betrayed them.

I was so incensed by his effort to induce me on the score of expediency to change front [Senator Pettigrew said] that I finally

told him that he had no business in Washington on such an errand; that his stand reflected on his character and reputation as
a man and indicated a lack of knowledge of human affairs which
must make his friends feel that he was not a suitable person to be
President of the United States. Despite the vigour of my statement, I doubt if Bryan understood what I was driving at.[48]

It is quite certain that Bryan did not understand what the
opponents of the Spanish treaty were driving at, nor they
what he was driving at, either. As Bryan saw the matter it
was the Republican party that was seeking to fling over the
shoulders of Major William McKinley, Jr., the imperial
mantle of Philip of Spain. Let them take the responsibility,
then, and he would fasten upon the Republican party the
stigma of ruling over subject peoples as Lincoln had fastened
the defence of slavery upon the Democratic party.

With the fire of this lofty purpose in his eye Bryan went to
Washington and cajoled and dragooned seventeen Democrats
and Populists in the Senate into approving the Spanish
treaty

with its program of annexation, by the narrow margin of one vote,
thus saving William McKinley from a defeat akin to that which
befell Woodrow Wilson two decades later.[49]

Had William Jennings Bryan read some other history of
the United States besides Bancroft's he might have had an
inkling of what would happen the moment the United
States fell heir to the Philippines and Porto Rico. For
suddenly it was all over. "The Philippines are ours and
American authority must be supreme throughout the archi-
pelago," declared McKinley.[50] "Of course!" said the man
in the street. "What is the fuss about?"

By the time the National Democratic Convention rolled
around, the annexation of the Philippines by the Republican
party was about as stirring a campaign issue as the annexation of Texas by the Democratic party half a century before.
If ever a man had misjudged his fellow citizens, Bryan had.

He did not know it. In a vague way Bryan had the feeling
that the great moral question of the future of the Filipinos

was not going to be quite the great political question he had hoped. He clung to it, however. He clung to free silver, too. David B. Hill put pride aside and journeyed all the way to Lincoln to beseech Bryan to forswear the silver heresy, especially now that it made no difference, anyhow. Bryan would not budge.

His argument had been vindicated that want of money had been the cause of universal distress and more money was the remedy [said William M. Stewart]. When the remedy came from the output of gold, he should have claimed vindication of his theory. One of two things must be said of him—he either did not understand the money question or he was willing to deceive the people.[51]

Few thought Bryan insincere. But he did desperately need an issue. One was presented to him in 1899, but he brushed it aside:

An old man whose son had gone to the bad from the saloon took Bryan by the hand and in a plaintive voice inquired:
"Mr. Bryan, why don't you come out against the saloon?"
Mr. Bryan's reply was: "The saloon is a local question."[52]

A month before the Democrats assembled at Kansas City, William Jennings Bryan felt that he had to proclaim something as the issues of tne coming electoral struggle. He did the best he could.

Three questions contest for primacy—the money question, the trust question and imperialism [he wrote]. The issue . . . is the issue between plutocracy and democracy. All the questions under discussion will, in their last analysis, disclose the conflict between the dollar and the man.[53]

In order that there might be no mistake about this the management of McKinley's campaign was again intrusted to the Hon. Marcus Alonzo Hanna.

CHAPTER XX

FALTER

BRYAN is, I believe, a good deal stronger than he was three years ago and it looks as though it was going to be a serious struggle in 1900 [Roosevelt wrote Lodge a year before the election]. Around the State of New York I am surprised to find how many of the working men who were with us three years ago, are now sullenly grumbling that McKinley is under Hanna's dictation; that Bryan is the only man who can control the trusts; and that the trusts are crushing the life out of the small man.[1]

With 39 per cent. of the male workers of the country out of work from four to six months a year and the average wage $1.29 a day—less than it had been ten years previous[2]—it was small wonder that the toiling masses regarded the Advance Agent of Prosperity with a jaundiced eye.

In those days after the war Bryan had other things on his mind for the moment. His youngest daughter was ill, and he wrote his old friend Governor Hogg of Texas to find him a place to spend the winter. It was Colonel Edward M. House who, with an eye to the future, found "a home for the Bryans practically within the same grounds as ours," he says. "I found Mrs. Bryan very amenable to advice and suggestion but Mr. Bryan was as wildly impracticable as ever." To a gentleman of Colonel House's peculiar cast of mind amenability to suggestion was the one test of intelligence. So far as Bryan was concerned: "I believe he feels that his ideas are God-given and are not susceptible to the mutability of those of the ordinary human being,"[3] Colonel House records.

Others there were who knew Bryan better. To Louis Post and Tom Johnson, Bryan unbosomed himself at about the same period:

My friends who suppose that I have any personal ambition for the presidency are mistaken [he said]. I regard myself as a Moses rather than an Aaron.[4]

It was well that he did. For in the campaign of 1900 there was no question who was captain of the good ship Democracy. Bryan dictated platforms, candidates, and campaign strategy—even Boss Croker of Tammany Hall backed him with an enthusiasm which may really have been as unfeigned as the exigencies of politics in the Empire State would allow.

Yet when the electoral struggle came no one seemed very clear what it was all about, least of all William Jennings Bryan.[5] Millions of voters, whose sole conception of the issues at stake was gained from their daily papers, had not the vaguest idea what was meant by a "trust." Bryan himself was muddy on the subject[6]—there had been nothing about "trusts" in good old Dr. Sturtevant's Christian view of economics as taught at Illinois College. What Bryan needed, and needed badly in the campaign of 1900, was a little volume, with pictures if possible, dealing with monopoly in the offhand way that *Coin's Financial School* had covered the currency question. From such a work he might have learned to reduce the trust question to words of one syllable for the consumption of the great American public.

At first Bryan "fairly startled the reflecting portion of the community" with his speech of acceptance. "It seemed for a moment as if the party in power would be forced to reckon seriously with the opposition throughout a sustained debate," said Carles Francis Adams.[7] He added, however:

The canvass deteriorated as it progressed . . . and finally degenerated into a mere trial of endurance between himself and the talking candidate on the other side.* . . . A less inspiring competition could hardly be imagined.[8]

Alfred Henry Lewis, who had known Bryan since his earliest days in Congress, and liked him, thought he had the secret.

---

*Roosevelt.

Bryan's error was grown of a multiplied experience of cheap men [he wrote]. He had met many men, but not the right men. Bryan for four years had met only those who came to him.[9]

Bryan's failure to meet the exigency lay in causes that stretched farther back. It was not so much that he had not met the right men in the years between 1896 and 1900 as that he did not know them when he met them. His standards of judgment, rooted in the religious atmosphere of his childhood, were ethical, not practical. To Bryan a good man must be good for something, and a good argument convincing whether based on sound premises or not. McKinley might have, as John Hay said, "a genuine ecclesiastical face of the XV Century";[10] William Jennings Bryan had that kind of mind.

That Bryan should turn a deaf ear to the pleadings of David B. Hill for "moderation in regard to the silver issue" in 1900[11] was natural enough. David B. Hill was of the crude, old-fashioned type of self-seeking politician whose motives were transparent even to Bryan. But others, devoted to Bryan and all he stood for, furnished him with the economic not the political reasons why the discovery of new supplies and new methods of refining gold disposed of the silver issue forever. To Bryan at this crucial juncture, these considerations were meaningless.

He would not consider these new gold supplies as serious factors in shaping monetary policy [says Professor E. A. Ross], but merely suggested how to parry arguments based upon them brought up by our opponents. He would say: "Tell them this" or "Meet that point this way."

"I saw that Mr. Bryan was no realist," Professor Ross added sadly.[12] Others saw it, too.

He does not reason for principles [Louis Post wrote Tom Johnson]. When you and I see an evil, our impulse is to learn the cause and remove it. When Bryan sees an evil, his impulse is to invent some scheme for circumventing it.[13]

More than anything else this quality endeared William Jennings Bryan to his fellow countrymen. So they also reasoned.

Midway the campaign practically collapsed for want of funds.[14] In desperation, Bryan sent a trusted agent to the silver-mine owners of the West with an urgent appeal for help. He had been square with them. What would they do for him now in his hour of need? Fortunately the silver-mine owners were cut of other cloth than Wall Street operators. Senator Clark of Montana contributed $50,000 to the campaign fund. Marcus Daly, who hated Clark, was on the opposite side of the political fence; but what were politics between friends? He told Bryan's agent of some $23,000 in bank, left over from the previous campaign, but Bryan could have it now if he wished. In due season Millard Fillmore Dunlap, Bryan's treasurer, received a check for the amount. These two sums were the only contributions of consequence made to Bryan's fight in 1900[15]. If William Jennings Bryan learned no other lesson from the experience, he learned that the champion of the poor must depend upon the humble dimes and nickels of the disinherited.

There had been something wholly admirable about the energy and fervour with which Bryan had stumped the country in 1896, doing his one-night stands in jerk-water towns, without complaint or pretentiousness—the Tribune of the People, for whom Henry George and Eugene Debs alike voted. This quality was gone. William Jennings Bryan was no longer a poor young man who had staked everything he had in the world on one ambitious fling at the highest prize. There was coming to be about him the flavour of one to whom politics were a trade.

Roosevelt did his best to revive the fears of four years back by rattling the skeleton of free silver, which none better than he knew was a dead issue. "The wage earner," he confided to Henry Cabot Lodge, "is no longer interested in free silver and cannot be frightened by the discussion of it,"[16] which was plainly a pity. There was, he said, "no enthusiasm for us and there seems to be no fear of Bryan."[17] However, the outlook was not altogether bleak: "I have waded into brother

Bryan pretty heavily and he is beginning to feel sore," Roosevelt wrote his political mentor, in high glee. "What a thorough hypocrite and demagogue he is and what a small man!"[18]

Edgar Lee Masters described Bryan in Chicago, escorted by policemen through the vast crowd which blocked Michigan Avenue:

> He was still young and there was a dramatic charm to him as he flapped a black silk handkerchief around his neck, sailed into the trusts for threatening the workers with starvation if they voted for him, declared he would close every trust in America if he became President. . . .[19]

> Hanna got considerable of a panic early in the canvass [John Hay wrote to General Horace Porter], but I imagine it was nothing but a money panic, and if, after Bryan's letter of acceptance, the men who have money refuse to do anything in their own defense, they will deserve to be robbed of the enamel of their teeth.[20]

They did not refuse. The horny-handed sons of toil might be bewildered where their interest lay, but "the men who have money" were not. They put up two and a half millions as cheerily as crickets, and glad to get off so easily. The Democratic party had not one fifth that amount.[21] When the ballots were counted William Jennings Bryan ran 100,000 votes behind his record of 1896. He lost Populist Kansas and his own state into the bargain. In the agrarian West between the Mississippi and the Pacific, where his greatest strength had lain, the ranks of the faithful wavered and broke. It might not prove a Waterloo, but it had all the symptoms of a Moscow.

Nevertheless, William Jennings Bryan still had to his credit some 800,000 more votes than had ever been cast for a Democrat for the Presidency of the United States in the history of the country. He was a badly beaten man: there were no two ways about that. But he was still the legitimate leader of his party, and whoever sought to oust him must move in the dark as a conspirator.

For Bryan the experience was epochal. He had felt in 1894

that a revolution was in progress and that a man of courage
and a certain ability to capture the hearts of his fellow men
had only to offer himself to lead the revolution to triumph.
He knew, now, that this was not true. The Lincoln tradition
had betrayed him. The processes of change in a democracy
were gradual. He must begin again, and begin at the beginning. Two things he needed—or indeed any other man who
would essay the task that lay before William Jennings
Bryan, after the election of 1900. He must have money.
Twice he had been beaten by the sheer weight of dollars.
He must now so organize his followers that they should themselves contribute the costs of their own defence without
feeling it. He must also have a sure way of reaching the six
and a half million voters who constituted his political stock
in trade. He must be able to tell them what he thought; but,
far more important, he must be able to keep abreast of
what they thought. Otherwise he was neither a Democrat
nor a leader, for a Democrat plainly was one who found out
what the people wanted before they were themselves conscious of it, and a leader one who gave those wants appropriate expression.

The election was hardly over before Bryan was offered an
editorial position on a Denver evening paper at $10,000 a
year.[22] But Bryan cordially disliked working for others. He
had tried it under Gilbert Hitchcock, on the Omaha *World-
Herald*, and even the Bryan children came to reflect his
feeling about that job. "God is above us and the devil and
Hitchcock below," they would say. What Bryan wanted
was something of his own. He had amassed a little money;
now he risked it in the venture of a weekly newspaper.

Intending to devote my life to the study and discussion of public
questions, I have chosen this method because it will best accomplish the purpose which I have in view. Through such a paper I
shall be able to keep in touch with social, economic and political
problems. The paper will at the same time, if successful, provide
an income sufficient for my pecuniary needs, and this kind of work
will allow me more time with my family than I have been able to
enjoy for several years past [his announcement read with engag-

ing candour]. The paper will be called *The Commoner* and will defend the principles set forth in the Kansas City platform. I shall be the editor and publisher.

Bryan had no need to worry for the future. Before a stick had been set the books of *The Commoner* showed that 17,000 had paid $1.00 each for the new publication. The paper was, said Bryan in his first editorial, "to aid the common people in the protection of their rights, the advancement of their interests, and the realization of their aspirations." Dr. Hiram K. Jones himself could hardly have done better. Among the common people were included by special dispensation the "rich man who has honestly acquired his wealth and is not afraid to intrust its care to laws made for their fellows." Of these, however, there was never any emembarrassing number on the subscription list of *The Commoner*.

Bryan's political pastorate appeared at an end. *Judge*, which in 1896 had depicted the Boy Orator of the Platte as an assassin and an anarchist, printed a flattering cartoon with the caption:

THE END

Judge: "Good-bye, Bryan! Sorry to see you go; for while we have differed in *politics*, yet as a *man* I hold you in great esteem. Ta-ta!"

On Jackson Day, in Chicago, Bryan, according to the New York *Tribune*,[23]

in a speech pathetic to the last degree laid down the sceptre of the leadership of the Democratic party and retired to private life. With his eyes wet with tears he declared that he had never for a moment . . . placed self-aggrandizement above the principles that he advocated.

"I hope to God that when I die men may say of me that I was honest with myself and honest with the great trust that has been reposed in me," he said.

That day was the biggest day the stock market had ever known—for the first time in history transactions crossed the $2,000,000 mark.[24]

But William Jennings Bryan was only forty, and death was a long way off. Nevertheless, his abdication was not a feint. He felt that he had had his chance, and, besides, his eye discerned no issue on the political horizon that held promise of victory. Not that he was not constantly alert to seize one, if it presented itself—Bryan was always looking for issues, his friend Millard Fillmore Dunlap says. He had need to be, for others were always appropriating his[25]—the income tax, direct election of Senators, currency reform, the establishment of a Department of Labour, the building of a transisthmian canal from Atlantic to Pacific, democratic control of courts, a comprehensive plan to reclaim the arid lands of the West—and, above all, a political programme of social justice—"the Man against the Dollar."[26] For all of these William Jennings Bryan had for a while been as a voice crying in the wilderness. Then, one by one, what he sponsored became the common demand of millions.

While Bryan was pondering these things there came to mind that scene two years before when the old man with a wayward son had pleaded so pathetically: "Mr. Bryan, why don't you come out against the saloon?" It was an idea. To Louis Post, Bryan wrote tentatively, on April 20, 1901:

> I am in favor of the local option plan and am very glad to endorse the experiment. I believe that a new system should be experimented with before it is generally adopted in order that the theory may be tested by practice, and it is entirely in harmony with the idea of local self-government.[27]

He had Mayor Tom Johnson of Cleveland in mind for the Presidential nomination in 1904. "It is all right to have him discussed," he wrote at the same time, "but too early to select candidates. I have great confidence in him."

Concerning his own intentions, Bryan was candour itself.

"I am not a candidate for any office," he declared repeatedly. "However, I would not enter into a bond never to become a candidate."[28]

Meanwhile the world moved into the new century at accelerated speed. . . . The organization of the United States

Steel Corporation, with a capitalization of $1,403,450,000 was announced. . . .[29] All over the land men went to work swinging their full dinner pails and whistling "Tell me, pretty maiden." . . . By an amendment to the bill appropriating still vaster sums for the army, Congress wed Cuba to the United States forever in a morganatic marriage. . . . The Supreme Court, with Solomon-like sagacity, reached the decision that Porto Rico and the Philippines were not part of the United States, but not foreign, either.[30]

"No matter whether the Constitution follows the flag or not," said Mr. Dooley, "the Supreme Court follows the illiction returns."

It was clear at last that imperialism was neither cause nor effect, but a symptom. . . . The flowing moustache of the romantic 'eighties gave way to close-clipped, businesslike little nail brushes on the upper lip, more appropriate to those who had taken up the White Man's Burden in solemn earnest. . . . William Howard Taft was appointed Governor of the Philippines. . . .

The manhood of America hunted and fished less and began to play golf, instead, or to take exercise vicariously, watching football games. . . . The women did their chastity into the impregnable armour of straight fronts, and male and female alike choked their emotions with high collars. . . . Rainy day skirts that fell to the shoe tops provoked many a sermon, and bicycle riding and cigarettes menaced the morals of the nation. . . . Queen Victoria died, fat and full of years, and Carrie Nation became a heroine. . . . A few adventurous spirits purchased and even drove what were known as horseless carriages, to the merriment of the yokels. . . . A Brazilian flew a dirigible balloon around the Eiffel Tower, but two Americans by the name of Wright, experimenting with flying machines, were looked upon as mildly insane. . . . Work began on the first subway in America. The New York Appellate Court decided that, in all probability, "the enterprise would be abandoned."[31] . . . Drs. Walter Reed, Aristides Agramonte, Jesse W. Lazcar, and James Carroll announced that yellow fever was carried by mosquitoes,[32] but no one thought much of the discovery. . . . William Jennings Bryan planned a trip abroad to study the effete nations of the Old World[33] . . . He purchased a complete set of *Stoddard's Lectures on Travel Abroad* in preparation. . . .

But William Jennings Bryan lacked that dash of luck that played so capital a rôle in the career of Abraham Lincoln.[34] On September 6, 1901, McKinley was shot. If ever a man prayed fervently that the life of another be spared, Bryan prayed for McKinley's recovery. But an inscrutable Providence appeared to have other designs. Eight days later McKinley died.

And the strenuous Theodore became twenty-sixth President of the United States.

PART V
CLIMAX

"Get thee up . . . and lift up thine eyes westward, and northward, and southward, and eastward, and behold it with thine eyes; for thou shalt not go over this Jordan.

"But charge Joshua and encourage him, and strengthen him; for he shall go over before this people, and he shall cause them to inherit the land which thou shalt see."

CHAPTER XXI

1904

IT WAS a great pity that William Jennings Bryan could not have been sent to jail for a while, as Eugene Debs was. For Bryan had no leisure to read, study, and reflect upon the rapidly increasing number of subjects his followers expected him to pass in judgment. Even had Bryan been as omnivorous a reader as Roosevelt, it would have profited him little.

His bookshelves [writes Prof. E. A. Ross] abounded in crank books presented by the authors themselves, while the great contemporary authorities on economics, money, etc., were conspicuous by their absence. I doubt if Mr. Bryan ever realized that economics is a developing subject and that the great authorities that stood out when he was in college fifty years ago were being supplanted by later authorities.[1]

The truth was that William Jennings Bryan did not live in a developing universe. Quite literally in his view "God saw everything that He had made, and, behold, it was very good."

It was not altogether Bryan's fault that he failed to keep abreast of advancing knowledge. "He has had less time to himself than any mature man I have ever known," said his friend, the Rev. Martin D. Hardin.[2] It was true. There was, first of all, *The Commoner* to be got out weekly, no mean task in itself. Then there were hundreds of letters to answer on every conceivable subject. Between 1896 and 1900 Bryan's correspondence cost him $2,000 a year. There were demands for addresses on public occasions, lectures, Chautauquas, county fairs—heaven knows what all. Even when he remained at home, Bryan was besieged by a constant stream of callers. He would be up betimes in the mornings and hard at work on his mail, collarless and in his shirt sleeves, when the door bell would ring. It might be anybody from a Japanese schoolboy to the president of a Baptist college. Bryan was a sore trial to Mother, answering the door himself, without coat or collar. But he did not care.

Then in addition to these preoccupations, there was the Bryans' new home, Fairview, to be erected on a hilltop a short distance from town, where he and Dan Bride lived together in the barn while they oversaw the building of the house. Bryan was as proud of his country place as ever Silas Bryan had been of the deer park at Salem. Already in his mind's eye he could see it another Monticello to future generations of Democrats. . . .

In truth, William Jennings Bryan had come a long road. He was not boasting when he said that he could have made $50,000 a year at lecturing had he wished to devote himself entirely to it. Even now, in the five years since the disastrous campaign of 1896 had left him without a broad copper to bless himself with, Bryan had accumulated over $30,000 in the bank and owned bits of property here and there,[3] which he was constantly purchasing with an incurable if mistaken optimism.[4] Only five years before, those of his fellow citizens who in their own eyes represented the true Americanism, had been contemptuous of William Jennings Bryan. He was not solid, well-to-do, prosperous. Their scorn with its implication of failure, penetrated Bryan's skin as no other animadversion ever did in all his life.

Yet to Bryan, as to the majority of his countrymen, wealth of itself was not as yet significant. The captains and kings of the New World—the Jay Goulds, the Vanderbilts, the James J. Hills, the Collis P. Huntingtons, the Harrimans, the J. P. Morgans—were not eminent because they had amassed great fortunes, but because they had fought a winning fight. Success, not mere security, was the American ideal.

In the humbler ranks of those who had thus succeeded, Bryan felt that he had taken his place. He had not, it is true, been elected President of the United States. But he had won acknowledged leadership. If George M. Pullman and Andrew Carnegie were captains of industry, what was William Jennings Bryan, under whose political banner both had been content to serve as privates? Did Bryan not create his own income? Was he not indifferent to his capital, as they were? Rarely did Bryan know how much he was worth, or care. More: did not Bryan dispose of resources that the successful of the world could never command in democratic America—the devotion of millions of men and women? Those who measured their power by their money must buy their political representatives—their lawmakers, their judges, their lobby-ists—low-grade human ore at best. But the struts of Bryan's power were of pure metal, tempered in the fire of faith.

It vexed Bryan that the financial and industrial leaders of the East persisted in ignoring this, that they still held him in light esteem. His feeling was not personal. But to Bryan's mind indifference to the expressed will of a compact and uni-fied group of six and a half million voters was a denial of the very principle of democracy. The son of Silas Bryan could tolerate nothing of the sort.

Beware of the radicals who come after us [he warned]; the men who will not be content to stop the wrong, but who will demand that you go back and restore the wrong.[5]

It was perhaps this feeling of bafflement more than any-thing else that nurtured the friendship of Bryan and Philo Sherman Bennett, the New Haven wholesale grocer. Bennett was no Wall Street magnate; he was not even a millionaire. But he was the nearest to it that Bryan knew in any intimate way. He had come to Bryan's rescue, financially, in 1896, and on several occasions since. He had underwritten the launching of *The Commoner* and taken charge of Bryan's investments for him. A vague, kindly old man, was Philo Sherman Bennett, self-made, with sentimental ideas of bene-fiting mankind with his modest fortune of $300,000. He looked upon Bryan as a sort of Joshua, ready to bid economic laws stand still if only he were President of the United States.

They talked together frequently of what a real philanthro-pist might do toward remaking the world in a spirit of human brotherhood. It was a new angle of vision for William Jennings Bryan. From childhood, he had known two methods by which the world might be made better, and only two: religion and politics. He had had both of his father, together with a certain almost superstitious faith in the efficacy of Christian education. Consulted by Bennett as to how the grocer might accomplish the most with his money, it seemed to Bryan that some form of political education should be the solution. So he suggested prizes for essays on the science of government to be established in various colleges.[6] The prizes should not, of course, be so large as to turn the footsteps of the young men winning them into the paths of Plutocracy—the annual interest on $400 would be about right, Bryan thought. Then, too, there were deserving poor boys and poor girls to be sent to sound Christian institutions of learning. That would be another novel way of bettering the world.

With all of this Philo Sherman Bennett heartily agreed. But in Bennett's conception and perhaps in Bryan's, too, the one outstanding factor in the political education of the American people was William Jennings Bryan. He preached the true faith day in and day out to more people than any other single individual had ever reached. He had dedicated his life to that particular work and to no other. He did not at the moment need money, but he had before and he might again. To what better use could one who regarded Bryan as a political Messiah put his money than to endow the Peerless Leader with, say, $50,000?

There was one practical difficulty. It had not been so long since $50,000 would have seemed a very great deal of money to Bryan. It would still seem a very great deal of money to thousands of his followers, however familiar they might be with St. Paul's Epistle to Timothy. There was, of course, no earthly reason why Bennett should not leave Bryan $50,000 in his will—or even $100,000 if he liked. He had it. No one would be robbed. Mrs. Bennett was old enough to be Bryan's mother. With the $100,000 left her she could live the remainder of her days in luxury. It was, after all, Bennett's own money. On the other hand, there were excellent reasons of expediency why the bequest should remain confidential.

In the spring of 1900 in Bryan's den in the little house in Lincoln, Philo Sherman Bennett and Mr. and Mrs. Bryan drew up a will. $10,000 went to Bryan to establish prizes "for the best essay on free government."[7] $10,000 more went to Bryan for the education of poor boys and a like sum to Mrs. Bryan for the education of poor girls. $1,500 was set aside to turn Bryan's birthplace in Salem, Illinois, into a memorial library. And $50,000 was bequeathed to Grace Imogene Bennett in trust, for a purpose set forth in a sealed letter to be found with the will. The letter provided that $50,000 should go to William Jennings Bryan, who was to be the executor of the will. The will would be public, but the letter would not. Bryan would receive his $50,000 and no one but Mrs. Bennett be any the wiser. Mrs. Bryan typed the document, and Philo Sherman Bennett paid Bryan a fee of $300 for drawing his will and departed, well content. Of the terms of her husband's will Mrs. Bennett knew nothing until after his death.[8]

On August 10, 1903, Philo Sherman Bennett was killed in an accident; but his will was not immediately presented for probate. Bryan had other troubles on his hands. On October third, his eldest daughter, barely eighteen and still in college, was married to an artist almost her father's age whom Bryan had fetched to Fairview to paint his portrait.[9] Mrs. Bryan flatly refused to come downstairs to attend the ceremony.[10] Bryan, grim faced, saw it through before he left for New Haven to file Bennett's will

At New Haven more trouble awaited him. For there were unhappily other bequests in Bennett's will besides those to the dead man's family and to Bryan and Mrs. Bryan. One in particular had seemed innocuous enough to Bryan at the time he drew the will—his mind had been upon the matters he and Bennett had talked over in a spirit of altruism to which such mundane things as "other women" were foreign. The provision was not innocuous, however, to Mrs. Bennett. When she found that her late lamented husband had left $20,000 to a lady at whose home Bennett had been accustomed to live when on business trips to New York, she took the whole will to court, and the fat was in the fire.

Everything that Bryan had hoped would be privily arranged became a seven days' wonder. The very method Bryan had chosen to avoid publicity suddenly developed into a mystery, titillating the curiosity of a sensation-seeking public. The newspapers were full of the case. Yet it was characteristic of William Jennings Bryan that throughout the hearings he never once referred by word or innuendo to the real cause of Mrs. Bennett's action. He would not concede that there was or could be any question of the purity of Bennett's motive in leaving $20,000 to Mrs. Foster. He set his jaw and fought the case in the Connecticut Supreme Court, less to establish his right to his own legacy than to prove that his friend and benefactor's will included no provision that should not have been there in all propriety. And in this he was sustained, albeit he was denied the $50,000 Bennett had left him.

Bryan's experience with the Bennett will worked him both damage and benefit. Unquestionably it injured him politically, precisely as he had foreseen it would if Bennett's bequest became known. Skeptics laughed in ribald joy at the spectacle of the apostle of the disinherited fighting doggedly for a dead grocer's $50,000. Others who had made the painful sacrifices of the poor in Bryan's support in 1896 and 1900 were shocked and wounded. Bryan did not make a good witness for himself in court, and there were those who winced to see the Tribune of the People compelled to go back and correct testimony which had been misleading. Millions who had felt that William Jennings Bryan's strength was as the strength of ten because his heart was pure, were not so sure, now.

The experience came at a moment when Bryan was sorely in need of revelation of himself to himself. He had been unbelievably naïve in the matter of Philo Bennett's will. The tendency was undoubtedly growing upon him to see things as he saw them and to ignore every other possible angle of vision. The contacts he had made in his two campaigns, the

unaccustomed environments into which he found himself
projected, the supersession of the early, simpler Populist
programme by national and international issues involving
intricate economic factors and knowledge of foreign affairs,
revealed serious gaps in Bryan's equipment. Even Lincoln,
Nebraska, was no longer the bucolic town to which the
Bryans had moved fifteen years previous, because Jacksonville was too sophisticated for one bred in the constricted
atmosphere of Egypt. Lincoln was acquiring the same academic tone.[11] But Bryan was not. True, the Round Table of
Lincoln confined its intellectual activities to current events
while the Plato Club of Jacksonville had been somewhat more
catholic, perhaps even diffuse, in its field. But then, the
Bryans had never been comfortably at home in the rare
atmosphere of the Plato Club, either. In Lincoln no less
than Jacksonville, or for that matter the whole Middle West,
the touchstone of culture was travel and the accepted
method of acquiring knowledge was to listen to someone
talk.

So William Jennings Bryan decided to broaden his horizon
by travel.

He went to Cuba first. To his wife the perils and potential
heroism of Colonel Bryan's service as a soldier always remained a sharper memory than any other.[12] "I am feeling very
uneasy about Havana," she wrote while the war was still in
progress. "Take plenty of quinine and keep well."[13] Now
Bryan visited Havana in safety, and in triumph. . . . He went
to Mexico, too. . . . These were but preliminaries. It was
William Randolph Hearst who made the great adventure of
the European tour possible. Bryan was to write a series of
articles for Hearst's paper that would pay his expenses and
more besides. The moment the Bennett will case was out of
the way, Bryan, Stoddard in hand, sailed for foreign parts.

The trip was momentous. Bryan covered Ireland, England,
Holland, Germany, France, Italy, Switzerland, and even far-
away, inaccessible Russia, and was back under the skirts of
the Statue of Liberty in nine weeks. He asked hundreds of
people, from Pope to peasant, questions whose answers

were set down in black and white in the pages of the *Encyclopædia Britannica*. He gathered voluminous notes on the length, breadth, and thickness of the ship on which he sailed, how many first, second, and third class passengers it carried (not forgetting the crew), and how much each paid, all of which he incorporated in his articles for Hearst, printed in *The Commoner* later, and published in a book, besides. . . . He talked to the Czar of all the Russias about free speech. The Czar found the topic a bit quaint. No one had ever hampered his freedom of speech. Bryan also felicitated Nikolai Alexandrovich on the establishment of the International Court of Arbitration at The Hague. The idea of substituting "the reign of reason for the rule of brute force," as he expressed it,[14] struck a responsive chord in the heart of the Nebraskan.

He was delighted to find the newly elected Pope Pius X a gentle old man—Bryan was sure that "heart characteristics will dominate the present Pontiff's course," he wrote.[15] It was the heart characteristics in those he met that appealed most to William Jennings Bryan. Naturally, therefore, his visit to "Tolstoy, the Apostle of Love,"[16] was his most satisfying experience.

My object in visiting him was [he wrote] to see the man and ascertain if I could, from personal contact, the secret of the tremendous influence he exerted upon the thought of the world. I am satisfied that, notwithstanding his great intellect, his colossal strength lies in his heart more than in his mind. . . . Love is the dominant note in Count Tolstoy's philosophy. . . . It is his shield and sword. He is a deeply religious man.[17]

Bryan was not altogether clear, however, just what Tolstoy's religion was; so he asked. Tolstoy gently suggested that Bryan read his book on the subject.

Tolstoy's career shows how despotic is the sway of the heart and how, after all, it rules the world [wrote Bryan]. For while his literary achievements have been admired, the influence which they exert is as nothing compared with the influence exerted by his philosophy . . . his simple presenting of the doctrine of love, exemplified in his life as clearly as it is expressed by his pen.[18]

Bryan did not appear to be familiar with Tolstoy's simple presenting of the doctrine of love in the pages of *Anna Karenina*.

The Russian was astounded and bewildered by the American's outlook on life.

"Bryan certainly does talk a lot," he commented drily.[19] Tolstoy could not understand why anyone should travel seven thousand miles to ask him how many peasants in Yasnaya Polyana owned their own land and what proportion of them could read and write. He referred his visitor to the Russian Year Book.

In Moscow, Bryan was favourably impressed by the fact that most of the pictures in the art gallery were "devoted to home scenes and historic events." "In this gallery the nude[20] in art is noticeable by its absence," he added with approval. In Switzerland, a nutcracker in the shape of a head of President Roosevelt gave Bryan a thrill of national pride.[21]

The German scheme of state ownership of public utilities arrested Bryan's attention at once. Here might be an issue for the Democracy of America. In *The Commoner* he launched tentatively, the idea of state ownership as distinguished from existing and inadequate Federal control, and from the possibility of nationalization which appeared to be constantly drawing nearer in the United States.[22] The idea was not new to *The Commoner's* Populist subscribers, and as the paper had few readers in Wall Street it created no stir at all.

When William Jennings Bryan returned to the United States he returned in triumph. Charles F. Murphy, newly chosen head of Tammany Hall, Congressman William Randolph Hearst, Edward M. Shepard, Henry George, Bourke Cockran, Henry B. Maurer, and even James B. Weaver, once the idol of the Populists, were on hand to do him honour. None better than Bryan, however, knew how much of that was lip service. The Democratic party machinery was in the hands of Bryan's old enemy, David B. Hill, and August

Belmont, the seducer of Grover Cleveland from the path of Democratic virtue, dictated its policies. Between these and Theodore Roosevelt, Bryan was inclined to prefer Roosevelt, and expressed freely his approval of the President's progressiveness. If Bryan felt that the doughty Colonel had borrowed gluttonously from his own programme, he made no point of it. What Bryan did not approve in Roosevelt was the "taking" of Panama, of which the President seemed so inordinately proud, and the swaggering militarism which Roosevelt appeared to share with numerous great men of history, compelled to compensate for inadequate physical endowments by an exaggerated truculence. Bryan was big enough himself not to have to carry a Big Stick.

Mark Hanna was dead. Even Boss Croker of Tammany Hall had departed this political life. The politics of the country had fallen upon evil times. Save Bryan and Roosevelt, there were no giants in those days. As the time for the national conventions approached, it was clear that Roosevelt was his own candidate, while what Democratic Presidential timber there was would hardly make respectable saplings. Everywhere the cry among those who had appointed themselves to reorganize the Democratic party after its two defeats was not "Elect a Democrat President!" but "Bury Bryan!"

It was easier said than done.

He dies hard [complained *Lesile's Weekly*], for he realizes that the moment he drops out of sight his free advertising in the newspapers, which has given him a handsome fortune, will cease, and then he must go to work like any other man, to make his money with his wits and give his jaw a rest.[23]

Not without malice, Bryan reproduced this editorial in *The Commoner*. Such things disturbed him little. He went diligently about the business of saving what he could of the Kansas City platform which embodied his articles of faith. Bryan was interested in measures, not candidates; it was to the standard of William Randolph Hearst that the disinherited flocked in 1904, as they had to Bryan in 1896. To

the hosts of Hearst, many former Populists and more still of
that growing class of industrial workers, deprived of the advantage of being brought up in the gentlemanly tradition
of American party politics,[24] Bryan, with his eternal political
amenities and his insistence on party regularity, was as conservative as Alton B. Parker, more conservative than Roosevelt.[25] Nevertheless, Bryan raised no objection to his closest
henchman, Millard Fillmore Dunlap, becoming Hearst's
political manager in Illinois.

Hearst swept Illinois and suddenly the old line politicians
were beset by a horrid vision of another Chicago convention,
with the Illinois delegation starting a stampede to Hearst.
Something had to be done about it. So John P. Hopkins and
Roger Sullivan, twin bosses of Chicago, promptly black-
jacked a hand-picked set of Parker delegates through the
state convention and sat back content that a glorious victory
had been won by the more practical forces of Democracy.
Even Hearst abandoned the unequal fight.[26]

But Millard Fillmore Dunlap called upon Bryan for help,
and Bryan came.

He had no faith in Hearst or anything Hearst stood for. His
best friends pleaded with him to reserve himself for a fight
on the platform, and let the matter of the Hearst delegates
go; they pointed out that Hearst himself had given up.

We do not know whether there will be a chance to fight on the
platform [Bryan replied], and we have made it a rule through life
to do the thing that seems the right thing to do at the time, and
this is the right thing.

"No greater fight, single-handed, was ever made than the
one he made at the St. Louis convention of 1904," wrote
Charles Willis Thompson. "He was all alone and so he could
not miss a single fight; there was no lieutenant to whom to
turn the job over. He flashed from one room, where a fight
had been just completed, to another, there to carry on the
next one."[27] In the same hall where, eight years before, Bryan
had seen McKinley nominated.

... on the eighth anniversary of his Cross of Gold speech, he appeared in the huge amphitheatre with its hot, restless, jostling crowd, that was causing all kinds of confusion and disorder ... a mighty greeting like the simultaneous fire of a thousand guns made the air tremble and vibrate with the electricity of human feeling ... On Bryan's face was a handsome smile, in his full, dark eyes was a look of joy and triumph. No one else had been able to do anything with this mighty mob [wrote Louis Post]. Then the hero raised his hand. The vast volume of discordant sound died away like the sudden stoppage of all the machinery of a great factory. ... When Bryan lifted his matchless voice, a thrill of delight went through the audience.[28]

Bryan lost his battle for the Hearst delegates, but he left an uncomfortable feeling with those in control of the convention that the reports of his political demise had been greatly exaggerated. In fact, Bryan was just beginning to fight. For sixteen hours, alone and single-handed, he held the committee drafting the platform at bay until he won every point—the Democracy of the nation would make no sacrifice to the god of gold. ... Bryan was staggering with fatigue and illness.[29] His physician ordered him to bed. But William Jennings Bryan had not finished his job.

Under the strain of this titanic struggle the convention became a bedlam. Champ Clark, the chairman, could do nothing with the crowd;[30] he could not even complete his own speech nominating Gen. Francis Marion Cockrell, of Missouri, with which he had hoped to stampede the delegates.[31] It was four o'clock in the morning when Bryan mounted the platform.

"He opened his speech in a husky voice, and his gestures were those of a weak body. His eyes were dull at first, but they began to glow as his voice cleared out and the passion of his soul began to come out in very sharp gestures. The audience was hushed and still; he might have been speaking to an empty house. . . ."[32]

Eight years ago a Democratic national convention placed in my hand the standard of the party and commissioned me as its candidate. Four years later that commission was renewed. I come to-night to this Democratic convention to return the commission.

You may dispute whether I have fought a good fight, you may dispute whether I have finished my course, but you cannot deny that I have kept the faith.

"As he talked the purple shadows of the coming day were seen through the windows, and before he closed the dawn was gray about him."

I failed, you say. Yes, I failed. I received a million more votes than any Democrat had ever received before, and yet I failed. . . . The great issue in this country to-day is "Democracy versus Plutocracy" . . . whether this is a government of the people, and administered by officers chosen by the people, and administered in behalf of the people, or a government by the moneyed element of the country, in the interest of predatory wealth. . . . I ask you to help us meet this issue. You tell me that the Republican candidate stands for militarism. Yes, but he also stands for plutocracy. You tell me that he delights in war. Yes, but there is another objection to him, and that is that he does not enforce the law against a big criminal as he does against a little criminal. . . . The Government must be administered according to the maxim: "Equal rights to all and special privileges to none."[33]

"He had carried the banner of social democracy in America further than any other man had carried it. It is not free silver that Bryan stands for, and he knew it, in the breaking day, when his party told him to stand aside. Bryan has stood for as much of the idea of socialism as the American mind to-day will confess to," wrote William Allen White. And he added: "In all he did at St. Louis, he acted with a moral courage good to behold."[34]

CHAPTER XXII

DEMOCRACY GOES CONSERVATIVE

SICK and alone in his room at the Jefferson Hotel, Bryan was soon to know that he could not save everything for radical Democracy. A new force had arisen against him.

For years he had dogged the footsteps of Lincoln, dreaming of himself as the humble son of the people fighting in a righteous cause. But the footsteps of Lincoln were an open pathway for any man. Somewhere William Jennings had gone astray. Was it that emotions were more vital to him than convictions? Was it that his own eloquence emasculated his capacity for action? A man of action had arisen to capture Bryan's settings and properties.

Roosevelt was to take the centre of the stage.

Strikingly alike in ideas; superficially alike in manner; violently opposed in effect; Bryan, the orator, Roosevelt the actor. The Spanish War had defined their differences. In uniform Bryan was the dutiful suffering citizen. On San Juan Hill, Roosevelt, the citizen soldier, charged into jingoism. Bryan had espoused the cause of the common man. Roosevelt dramatized himself as a foe of trusts. Harsh-voiced, pugnacious, domineering Roosevelt! Mellifluous, emotional, long-suffering Bryan!

Bryan expected God to accomplish miracles in his interest. Roosevelt depended on himself. Do the meek really inherit the earth? Bryan must have asked himself.

T. R. was not meek.

These two were the logical opponents. Instead, stepped into the picture Judge Alton B. Parker, placid, colourless, mediocre, conservative. In convention assembled the delegates had "stolidly voted under orders from their bosses."[1]

Judge Parker had been selected in the hope that his name and the forces he represented would shout to the country, "The Democratic party is as respectable as the Republican!" Underlining it, ex-Senator Henry Gassaway Davis, octogenarian and millionaire, was named for Vice President. Bryan might write the platform; the bosses would name the candidates.

The fates were with Bryan for the moment. The Honourable Alton B. Parker, to avoid Bryan's economic motley, telegraphed the unequivocal statement that he stood for the gold standard; that if his position was unacceptable to the convention, he would decline the nomination.

The convention flew into an uproar.

Wild with rage scores of delegates ... tore their badges from their coats, threw them on the floor of the convention hall and stamped upon them. ... Senator Tillman rushed over to David B. Hill and shook his clenched fist in the New Yorker's face. Hill nervously wiped his perspiring forehead and suggested they "talk it over."[2]

Bryan's views immediately became of the utmost importance. Delegates rushed to the Jefferson Hotel to give vent to their fury. He tried to soothe them. "It is no more than you might have expected," he said. "From the tactics they pursued, you should have known it was not compromise they demanded, but surrender." Having allowed himself the minor satisfaction of omniscience, he pulled himself together and went to address the convention.

He entered the hall at ten-thirty. His voice was weak and shaken with illness as he rose to present his hastily considered solution: to send a message to Judge Parker, asking him to state his views on all aspects of the money question. There should be no dodging. If the Democratic party and its candidate favoured gold, that fact should be squarely presented to the voters. Politically shrewd, as always, he grasped the chance to give the bosses a black eye detectable even to the blindest of the rank and file. It was the death rattle of 16 to 1. It was the crucifixion of Democracy on the "Cross of Gold."

His proposal was, of course, overwhelmingly defeated. The convention replied to Parker:

. . . . The monetary standard . . . is not regarded by us as a possible issue in this campaign. . . . Therefore there is nothing in the views expressed by you in the telegram just received which would preclude a man entertaining them from accepting a nomination on said platform.

Bryan acknowledged defeat and withdrew with the ironic words: "We are not going to do one thing to mar the harmony of the convention."

Bryan was in a quandary. Parker alone was bad enough. Parker and gold was disaster. But with his high confidence in God, Bryan felt sure that light would be granted him. Perhaps it was both good politics and pious wisdom to accept the inevitable. He summed it up ringingly in *The Commoner* a few weeks later:

To those who think that a temporary victory of the conservative element ends progress in the Democratic party, let this reply be made: "O ye of little faith!" . . . He lacks faith in the purposes and plans of God who for a moment falters in the great struggle between truth and error.

The fact remained that in defeat Mr. Bryan still swayed well over 6,000,000 voters. What was he to say to them? The Democratic National Committee waited with something more than curiosity to hear that statement.

Bryan decided. He would support Mr. Parker for four reasons: because the Democracy opposed imperialism, because the Democratic platform declared for the reduction of the standing army, because Roosevelt stood for the race issue, and because Roosevelt stood for the spirit of war.

But [he went on] I shall not misrepresent the situation or appeal for votes for the ticket upon false grounds. . . . On the money question Mr. Parker is as thoroughly committed to the side of the financiers as Mr. Roosevelt. . . . Nothing good could be expected of him on the money question. . . . The nomination of Judge Parker virtually nullifies the anti-Trust plank. . . . The Labor plank

was . . . straddling, meaningless. . . . The triumph of the Wall
Street element of the party denies to the country any hope of
relief on economic questions. . . . I have nothing to withdraw of the
things that I have said against the methods pursued to advance
his candidacy. It was a plain and deliberate attempt to deceive the
party . . . by crooked and indefensible methods.[3]

What support was this?

He was not content with condemnation. His was a constructive programme:

After having stated that I shall support the ticket . . . I think it
due to the Democrats of the nation to say that the fight on economic
questions . . . is not abandoned. As soon as the election is over I
shall . . . undertake to organize for the campaign of 1908. . . . It
is only mentioned at this time that the readers of *The Commoner*
may know that the contest for economic reform will begin again
as soon as the polls close. . . .[4]

He could not wait for the campaign to end. On July
twenty-second he presented in *The Commoner* a programme for
radical Democracy. He apparently felt himself under no
obligation to the temporary commanders of his party beyond
the obligation not to interfere with their campaign. An
issue must be found for the future when, conservatives
routed, the party would again emerge under his leadership
as the champion of the man against the dollar. Hidden away
in his programme, now an aside, but later to be his most disastrous war cry, was this:

I have hitherto refused to take a position on the government
ownership of railways. . . . Recent events have convinced me that
the time is now ripe. I invite the Democrats, therefore, to consider
a plan for government ownership and operation of the railways.

It must have enraged the Parker men. It must have pleased
the G. O. P.

The managers of the Parker campaign felt that Bryan had
chosen a peculiar moment to proclaim his defection from their
standard. David B. Hill and the others who were engaged in
selling Democracy to Wall Street were finding that job

about all they could manage—and a little more. Why go to all the trouble of burying Bryan if the corpse insisted on remaining so lively? What was the good of announcing his passing in the press when from his grave he could produce such startling effects as this? Where did these respectable leaders find themselves? Safe in the arms of August Belmont and Thomas F. Ryan, to be sure. It was almost all that mattered to David B. Hill. But it wasn't enough.

Mr. Bryan was finding his compensations. He reprinted in his paper an article entitled "Finding Success in Failure," embroidered with laudatory comment. And he took his emotional vacation—a summer Chautauqua tour. Here was consolation. Hill and his cohorts might control a convention, but in the Chautauquas Bryan was king. The people followed him, for they knew his voice and a stranger they would not follow. "Success in Failure." He was reassured and comforted.

Those who credited him with greater facility for compromise than he possessed whispered that he would speak for Parker if he were asked. The rumour was without foundation. At the National Democratic headquarters everyone was uneasy and gloomy. The Democratic bid for respectability seemed to have been in vain, for after a brief hesitation the moneyed interests turned to Roosevelt and the Republicans. Roosevelt's election was almost a certainty.

Ryan and Belmont might contribute and induce their friends to do so; the Vice Presidential candidate might show confidence in himself by putting up $50,000 over the objections of his children; but it was impossible to compete with Republicans when it came to money. No Democrat was available with half the ingenuity of George Cortelyou, ex-Secretary of Commerce and Labour, who by methods never clearly explained induced the railways and insurance companies to contribute toward the election of their supposed mortal enemy, Theodore Roosevelt.[5] So ingenious was he that the policy holders of the New York Life Insurance Company contributed $148,000 to Roosevelt without knowing anything about it until after it was done.[6] E. H. Harri-

man, by request or out of spontaneous admiration, contributed $235,000.[7] The Democrats, whose campaign chest
eventually held $620,644, of which Belmont admitted giving
$250,000,[8] could not meet such extraordinary competition.

But money was not the only thing, as Mr. Hill was discovering to his dismay. Judge Parker might be pleasant,
charming, and reliable, but he didn't possess "the art of
winning popular applause, nor did he have the knack of
sounding clarion calls."[9] Opposed to a candidate whose chief
stock in trade was personality, this was a decided handicap
—so grave a handicap, indeed, that the most serious problem
of the moment was to find a speaker who *could* win popular
applause and who *did* have the knack of sounding clarion
calls.

The orator of the party was officially dead.

Suddenly Mr. Hill announced that he would retire from
politics on January 1, 1905.[10] Almost immediately Tom
Taggart, Mayor of Indianapolis and Chairman of the Democratic National Campaign, invited Charles A. Walsh, a
Bryan man of long standing, to come to New York and take
a desk at headquarters. Hardly had he been installed than a
wire came from William Jennings Bryan for Mr. Taggart.
"Let me know where you think I can help. Glad to devote
as much time to it as I can spare."[11] It looked as though the
fish might bite, but perhaps this was only a tantalizing
nibble and he would go swimming calmly out of their ken
once more. They must find rarer bait.

The New York papers printed the story of the next move,
and no one has ever seen fit to deny its authenticity. Chairman Taggart offered to send $50,000 to Nebraska to save the
legislature for Bryan (in case Bryan should be thinking of
the senatorship), if in return he would speak for Parker at
Madison Square Garden.[12] If the offer was ever made, it
was never accepted. Perhaps it savoured too much of straight
buying and selling. Instead of invading the stronghold of his
adversaries, Bryan spoke for Folk in Missouri and incidentally for Parker—the latter because of his professed desire to
maintain party harmony.

But hope must have revived in the breasts of the gentlemen in New York when, with strange precipitancy following the recent rebuff, Mr. T. S. Allen, Bryan's brother-in-law and Chairman of the Nebraska State Central Committee, appeared in their city to solicit a sum of money for the state campaign.[13] The money (said to be $15,000) was dispatched by Thomas Fortune Ryan and August Belmont through the Democratic National Committee. In 1908 when the story broke the New York *World* interpreted the event thus: "There was a belief that if the state elected a Democratic legislature, Mr. Bryan would be chosen United States Senator." At that time only Mr. Allen, of those who were said to have taken part in the transaction, could be immediately reached. He admitted that the money had come to him from the National Committee and indeed that he had solicited it.[14] He said further that he had turned it over to James C. Dahlman, who was in control of the funds for the state campaign. That he had ever considered the contribution a bribe to gain Bryan's whole-hearted support of Judge Parker, or to help elect Bryan to the Senate, he vigorously denied. He pointed out that Bryan was already supporting Parker, so what would be the object in buying him? What he neglected to point out was the negative and almost valueless nature of Bryan's support up to that time.

As for Bryan, it developed that in 1904 he had known nothing of the receipt of the money, and when he learned of it in 1908 he denied flatly that it had been used directly or indirectly to further his interests. The subject of his aspirations toward the senatorship he ignored, but he offered to return the money to the donors if the charge could be proven. Yet the Nebraska law demanded a full and public accounting of all campaign funds, and though for days the *World* bombarded Bryan with questions as to why that law had not been complied with in 1904, and why the lapse should not be sifted in 1908, Bryan ignored the whole issue.

Whatever the exact facts—and while it has been established that money was sent from New York to Nebraska,

its disposition has never been determined—it is indisputable
that Bryan's support of Parker immediately became more
vigorous. Perhaps Mr. Dahlman, into whose hands the
$15,000 eventually came, brought gentle pressure to bear
upon him. At any rate, though he never retired from his
original position, he presented it with more enthusiasm and
persistence.[15]

Indeed it would have been a shortsighted policy that
would have led him to retire from that position. He had his
enemies and the enemies of Democracy to consider.[16] The
Populists had threatened, if he should come out flat-footed
for Parker, to flood the country with handbills quoting his
earlier attacks on the Democratic candidate. The Republican press would have gleefully made huge capital of any
reversal of position. So he played variations on the theme
that "on every question upon which Judge Parker's position
is open to criticism, President Roosevelt's position is worse;
where they differ, Parker is right and Roosevelt is wrong."[17]
Perhaps his denial of Tom Watson's allegation that consist-
ency demanded his championship of the Populist cause was
an equally valuable contribution to the Parker cause.

"Every vote for Watson (Populist candidate for President)
is a vote for Roosevelt," he told his followers.

It was not an ideal situation. To be a practical politician
and at the same time a political moralist was no easy job.
His present course was open to captious criticism. But what
would be said if he refused to support Parker?

His conscience was at rest. He had done the right thing.
And he could console himself with the thought that he had
virtually written the platform, which was more important
than the candidate. Besides, there was always the lurking
possibility, lost if he withdrew from the campaign, that the
Senate might seek him. In the Senate there was much to be
done for the common man.

So in the final issue of *The Commoner* before election he
fired one more shot out of the same old gun and sat down to
await the results: "No Democrat who is interested in Mr.
Bryan personally or in Mr. Bryan politically, or in the re-

forms for which Mr. Bryan has been fighting, can afford to assume responsibility for four years more of Rooseveltism."

The results justified his political insight. Judge Parker polled nearly a million and a half votes less than Bryan had received in 1900. It was the worst Democratic defeat in years. It was due not to a large Republican vote but simply and solely to a small Democratic vote. The common man gave evidence of his disapproval of the Democratic party by casting 400,000 votes for Debs and Socialism as against 90,000 in 1900. The conservatives were confounded.

Bryan did not rest. Immediately after the election he began to drive home his point. *The Commoner* came out with the headlines:[18] PREPARE FOR 1908—DEMOCRACY VERSUS PLUTOCRACY—THE ELECTION'S LESSON. He offered his explanation for the defeat of the party:

The result was due to the fact that the Democratic party attempted to be conservative in the presence of conditions which demanded radical remedies. It sounded a partial retreat when it should have ordered a charge all along the line. . . . The Democratic party has nothing to gain by catering to organized and predatory wealth. . . . The Democratic party . . . must take the side of the plain, common people. . . . To doubt the success of our cause is to doubt the triumph of right, for ours is and must be the cause of the masses. . . . "With malice toward none and charity for all" let us begin the campaign of 1908.

And then he began to prepare!

CHAPTER XXIII

AROUND THE WORLD TO
MADISON SQUARE GARDEN

THE leader was again in command. Bryan's position had been vindicated. He immediately started to regiment the radical Democrats. On Jackson's birthday he began a whirlwind campaign, as though the hours were the last rather than the first of a four years' battle. His plan was to fire the faithful in the Mississippi Valley, then sweep eastward by Jefferson's birthday.[1] With a victor's gesture of forgiveness, he called on "Men of all elements"[2] to follow him.

For once he decided that oratory was not enough, and sought to give his enthusiasm an almost statistical foundation. He used the time-worn device of pledge cards. They were printed in *The Commoner* and the faithful were asked to record upon them their promise to take part in the local primaries. The flood of returning cards encouraged him to quicken his activity. For a time he visualized election day as a week off, and in his own mind, the Presidential candidate was a known quantity.

Presently he realized that a four-year fight was an impossibility. Only political zealots are really interested in such matters except between June and November of a Presidential Year. Furthermore, the Peerless Leader was without an issue. He was again indulging in activity without ideas. The popularity of The Man in the White House was stifling him, and it is ironic that when he looked around for something else to do he reached out to grasp that man's hand.

Early in January, with fine magnanimity, he called on President Roosevelt. After a round of handshaking in the anteroom he was ushered into the President's private office.

"Some people think I am a terrible radical," he began, "but really I'm not so very dangerous after all."

The joke in this was not now apparent to Mr. Bryan. Was it to T. R.?

Emerging, Bryan confronted the reporters and said: "I told the President that I heartily endorsed many of his policies and that I would support him every time I thought he was right." It was a generous gesture. But on being asked if he were going to take luncheon with Mr. Roosevelt, he spoke regretfully: "No, Bourke Cockran has invited me to eat with him."[3]

In Bryan's promise to support the measures of a Republican President there was no inconsistency. The truth was that Roosevelt was cleverly adopting and promoting measures originally blazoned on Bryan banners. Roosevelt was taking the road along which Bryan had, for twelve years, been trying to guide the Democratic party. Political observers knew it. Sydney Brooks pointed out that "Bryan's words and Roosevelt's deeds bear comparison."[4] And the New York *Sun* asked querulously whether Mr. Bryan had flopped to Mr. Roosevelt or Mr. Roosevelt to Mr. Bryan.[5]

Bryan kept his word scrupulously, for not only did he endorse many of Roosevelt's policies but he backed them with genuine enthusiasm. When the Hepburn Railway Bill, empowering the Interstate Commerce Commission to regulate rates, came before Congress, Bryan urged the Democratic representatives to vote with Roosevelt. "The feeling of helpless rage," wrote Prof. H. T. Peck in *Twenty Years of the Republic*, which the people felt at seeing ignored the laws they had made in several states for the control of corporation greed and corruption, "had permeated the entire country in 1905 and prepared the minds of the people for measures far more drastic than any which had hitherto been known."[6] The Hepburn Bill was one of these and eventually passed by a vote of 346 to 7.

Meanwhile, under the spell of Roosevelt the muck-rakers captured the public mind. The circulation of *Everybody's Magazine* fattened on Thomas Lawson and his *Frenzied*

Finance. Ida Tarbell hung out John D.'s dirty l nen. Lincoln Steffens and Upton Sinclair rooted in sties filled with dirty politics and dirty beef. And William Jennings, always with his ear to the ground, added his shout to the "tainted money" chorus.

His opportunity came when, in January, his Alma Mater extended to him an invitation to serve on the Board of Trustees. There was a nigger in the woodpile. The college had a deficit of $36,000 and was going from bad to worse. In this crisis Bryan wrote to his friend, Millard Fillmore Dunlap, already a trustee, that he was willing to help out, not by any great gift, but by doing what he could.[7] The Board of Trustees asked him to come and talk matters over with them, so he stopped off on his way East.

He refused to enter into any detailed discussion unless the college agreed to sever certain questionable affiliations, notably that with the University of Chicago. The basis of his objection to that university was that it had been built with John D. Rockefeller's "tainted money." Nothing could have better pleased the man in the street than this stand of Bryan's. Even college professors, symbols of meekness, resigned when their institutions accepted money from questionable sources. The Congregationalists, in a spasm of righteousness, returned a gift of $100,000 that Rockefeller had tendered them for use in foreign missions.

Could Bryan, the enemy of "big money," neglect to stand beside them? Bryan's dialectic on this subject must have bewildered the less elastic-minded among his followers. Apparently tainted money could be cleansed. He argued: (1) repentance cleanses money as it cleanses the soul; therefore money might be taken from a *repentant* rich man;[8] (2) death was apparently an even more effective scouring soap than repentance; the fortune of a rich man, dead, was pure; (3) the gold of a live unrepentant Croesus could be used in good works, if no obligation was implied.

The money solicited from Carnegie by Mrs. Bryan and William Jennings for the building of a Carnegie Public Library at Lincoln[9] must have come within this last category.

The gift of Rockefeller's money, Bryan felt, *did* imply other obligations and was therefore burdened with pitch that defiled. Let not Mr. Rockefeller despair, however. Even he was not beyond redemption, and Mr. Bryan benevolently hoped that he would come to "see the wickedness of his trust methods" and by reforming prove to be a "powerful factor in the overthrow of trusts." Charity for all! Meantime, he had not repented and his money was unclean to the touch. Therefore Illinois College must break with the University of Chicago.[10] The gesture was to the whole nation.

It was natural, following the recent dramatic events, that Bryan should have been asked to deliver the commencement address at Illinois College. He insisted that a simplicity befitting a man of the people should characterize the occasion. "I do not care to wear the gown and cap," he wrote to President Rammelkamp. "I suppose that it is not compulsory, and I have some prejudice against it—when suggested for myself not when worn by others," he added graciously.[11] So the Great Commoner appeared in the conventional black suit and gave the graduates of the Class of 1905 his blessing and some valuable advice. "Better loving companionship," he told them, "than intellectual solitude."[12] Was not this a neat summary of the results of his lifelong meditation on the subject?

Later, the college, backsliding in the acceptance of Carnegie money, was to lose its William Jennings Bryan. The famous old grad resigned as trustee, and had his name erased from the roll of the alumni, but remained loyal to the literary society where his golden voice first sounded clear.[13]

His thoughts now returned to the 1908 campaign. Still no issue seemed adequate strategically. It was painfully obvious now that Roosevelt was soaking up Bryanism. The public was forgetful. The policies for which Bryan had struggled to the sound of hoots and hisses were now greeted with cheers and enthusiasm, but his name was no longer associated with them. Roosevelt was acclaimed for the treaty he had engineered between Japan and Russia, but no one seemed to remember—or, if they did, they weren't shouting it from the housetops—that as early as February 17, 1905, William Jennings Bryan had suggested, for the betterment of mankind, that the United States compose the differences between these two peoples.

By a twist of irony it was a speech made by Roosevelt at Wilkes-Barre that planted the germ of an idea. T. R. spoke on temperance.[14]

From this, Bryan took the next step, and toyed with the idea of national prohibition. On his way from one speaking date to another, he stopped off in Chicago to talk it over with his old friend, George Shilling.[15] They argued all night and arrived at the disappointing conclusion that the time was not ripe for so radical a departure. Reluctantly he laid it aside. The moralist was not triumphant— yet!

He found himself at loose ends. Instead of opening a book, or concentrating on the problems of modern life, he decided to satisfy his craving for movement by a trip around the world. He did not stop to realize that America was slowly coming of age; instead, he indulged his schoolboy fancy.

But first he made a political gesture or two. He wanted to pose as the constructive citizen, approving the present course, and indicating the desirable future. In the columns of *The Commoner* he wrote:

You performed your duty in a manner creditable to yourself and to your country. You have been hailed as a peacemaker and you realize how the peaceful victory thus achieved by you outshines your military exploits. Why not use the present opportunity to put on foot a movement for the establishment of a permanent peace? . . . Why not ask Congress for the authority to submit all international questions . . . to an impartial board for investigation and report? . . .

The moral prestige which our nation now enjoys would . . . enable it to lead a successful peace movement.

. . . Few men have yet had it in their power to do so much for humanity—will you improve the opportunity?[16]

Mr. Roosevelt made no reply either to the compliments or the suggestions. Some editorial writers, like the one in the

Omaha *Bee* for September twenty-ninth, thought it "a little presumptuous for Colonel Bryan to offer advice continually to Mr. Roosevelt on the subject of running the government."

But whether or not the derisive use of his title was lost on Colonel Bryan, he was not a bit abashed or perturbed. In September he released a genial farewell letter to the President:

> Permit a parting word. You have the contest of your life before you and I desire to render you all the assistance in my power. You have asked Congress to enact a law so enlarging the powers of the Interstate Commerce Commission as to permit it to fix and enforce a reasonable freight rate. . . . The railroads will try to persuade you; if they fail in this they will try to scare you: if they fail in this also they will try to defeat your recommendation. It will embarrass you to have strong party leaders against you; you may have been embarrassed by having so many Democrats coöperate with you, but you must reconcile yourself to both. . . .
>
> Pass over the railroads and appeal to the people. . . . It is inconceivable that the people should create a corporation without reserving the rights to so control it as to make it subserve the public interest. . . .
>
> The Democrats, if they had no higher purpose than to secure control of the offices, might wish you to lead the railroad element in your party, but they are citizens first and Democrats afterward. . . .

Then, with a few helpful hints for reducing the tariff and establishing a permanent board of arbitration for labour disputes, he concluded:

> Stand by your guns! You have developed a reform element in the Republican party; you must lead it or suffer the humiliation of seeing the leadership pass to someone else.
>
> . . . Go forward! You owe it to yourself, you owe it to your party, and more than all, you owe it to your country.[17]

With these words ringing, or so he hoped, in the ears of his countrymen, William Jennings Bryan, with Mrs. Bryan, William Jennings, Jr., and Grace, started for San Francisco, on their trip around the world.

Bryan was the real innocent abroad. He was the great man

from the small towns, "a peculiar product of your country,"[18] said Asquith. He found the world pleasing as he found it American. He had no idea that social morals could be relative and believed that principles were universally true or not true at all. A worm in his cabbage in India, or the lack of free speech in Russia, upset him equally, when he was on tour. But he could and did, with brilliant insight, grasp the politics of any situation.

Eating and preaching were his two great intemperances. He was now gratifying both. At table he experimented with cocoanut milk in Hawaii, with buttered radishes two feet long and two and a half inches thick in Japan—native dishes wherever he went. Preaching Christian principles en route, his evangelical soul bubbled over when he and Mrs. Bryan gathered pebbles on the shores of Galilee, one grain of inspiration for each member of the Normal M. E. Church.[19]

Bryan liked Japan. The people were "Frenchmen done in bronze."[20] The social system betrayed satisfying occidental traits. He enjoyed the official receptions. At the one for Admiral Togo, hero of Port Arthur, Bryan rose from his seat in the front row to toast the admiral. He drank it in water because the admiral's victory had been on water, but said that he would gladly drink one in champagne when the admiral won a victory on champagne. Equally suave was his remark on the same occasion: "Steam has narrowed the Pacific and made us neighbours; let Justice make us friends."[21] He was less apt at Waseda University, with "I have never felt that I could hold anyone in contempt because he was not so large as another." But the Japanese liked Bryan. They forgave him even this, and he was his old self speaking before the Y. M. C. A.

Let a man keep his mind on the things he can understand, and live up to them, and he will be kept so busy that there will be no time left him to trouble his head about what he does not understand.

But William Jennings did not follow his own advice in later years.

In private audience with the Mikado, "fifty-three years old, about five feet six inches high and wears a beard," Bryan was quelled. Japanese etiquette forbade the man to ask questions who had never before been hindered from speaking his mind. But he was consoled before he left Japan.

He was presented with the badge of the National Temperance Society.

Korea presented him with two stone lions and a figure of speech. One lion's mouth was open; the other's closed. The first was radical; the second conservative. Said Bryan, "the two are inseparable, and for social prosperity we need them both."

In China, the coolie shook his democratic dogma. For William Jennings was forced to contract his all-embracing democracy to exclude this inadequate image of God—too inadequate to be admitted into the United States without "injustice to our social ideals." The ardent Christian found Confucius also inadequate—he lacked any "suggestion of a heart overflowing with love"—but his spirit was again elevated by his experiences among the Christians of the Philippine Islands.

The Sultan of Sulu, arrayed in a "swallowtail of blue broadcloth trimmed in brass buttons, a red fez, and tan shoes and followed by a retinue of forty datos and a band of native tomtoms, came riding on a pony" to pay him homage. He took the Bryan family to see the native spear dances and presented them to his family of four wives and "three or four concubines, he does not know which."[22] If Bryan was disconcerted, he maintained his poise, and at a reception tendered him by the Elks of the Islands said:

Whatever may be said of the government methods of Spain and of the political corruption of her colonial representatives, she established the Christian faith in the Islands.

The Christian faith was represented in the north by the Sultan of Sulu and his wives and concubines. But one observation he did make that cut to the quick of the Philippine problem, when he pointed out that most of its evils sprang from the fact that "the colony is governed by laws made for it, but not binding upon the country which makes the laws."

Man's works in India amazed him, but Mt. Everest attested to the greatness, goodness, and wisdom of God. He rebuked England resoundingly:

> . . . the trouble is that England acquired India for England's advantage, not for India's, and that she holds India for England's benefit, not for India's. She administers India with an eye to England's interests, not India's.[23]

In Egypt, the Sphinx proved disappointingly small, but he made good use of her at a later crisis of his life. He found a sermon in every stone in the Holy Land, and in the waters thereof as well; but he did not forget the authentic source of eloquence when he gathered pebbles on the shore of the Ægean to remind himself of the struggles of Demosthenes before his name was "known to fame."

He glimpsed the Sultan of Turkey on his way to the mosque, delighted in the Austro-Hungarian state-owned railways, was guest of honour at a banquet given for him by Louis Kossuth's son, attended the opera in Vienna, and bought clothes. All were happy events except the clothes. For when the trade journal of the London tailors reviewed Mr. Bryan it complained that his "frock coat [was] heavy and shapeless, with a sombreness quite hurtful."[24]

Things more important than clothes soon engaged his attention. News from home proved that the stage was being set for the triumphal entry of the world-touring hero shortly to return with a message to his cohorts.

That message would be the turning point in the hero's political career. What would it be?

His departure from the American scene was proving to be a wise move. The complete rout of the conservative element in the Democratic party in 1904 had strengthened and encouraged the more radical elements, who had been gaining so rapidly during Bryan's absence that they now dominated the situation. Indeed, one wing of the party was far outstripping Bryan on the radical road, and in order to destroy at a blow the dangerously mounting influence of William Randolph Hearst, the leaders of the National Democratic Club of New York announced in April that Mr. Bryan might easily qualify as standard bearer of the regular Democracy, if he were ready to acknowledge other issues as of greater importance than 16 to 1.

In Indiana things were stirring also. The State Convention cabled greetings, apostrophizing Bryan as "that wise and conservative statesman, unfaltering patriot and superb leader."[25] Colonel Watterson, once an unbridled detractor, wrote an enthusiastic editorial under the headline: HURRAH FOR BRYAN! He had, Marse Henry thought, "served his probation and earned his reward; with increasing years and study and travel has come increasing wisdom."

Certainly the trip around the world was proving a stroke of genius. Colonel Watterson would soon realize that travel for Bryan was, as Emerson called it, "A Fool's Paradise."

Bryan's answer was prompt, and his jubilation may have been responsible for its somewhat startling character. "It is time to call a halt on Socialism in the United States," he wrote. "The movement is going too far." Curiously enough, the same issue of the *Tribune* that carried this statement said that the names of Tim Sullivan and O. H. P. Belmont had been added to the reception committee.[26] "Politicians learn to come in out of the rain," commented the *Tribune* editorially.

Socialism was going too far. But where was William Jennings going?

Meanwhile, Bryan was solving the Russian problem. He attended the first meeting of the Duma, which was existing from day to day under the threat of being dispersed by the Czar. Mr. Bryan advised strengthening the Duma, the establishment of agricultural banks, recalling the exiles, and permitting the Duma to confer with the ministry on the land questions. This accomplished, the Czar would "have no reason to fear bomb throwers or hostile criticism." Curiously enough, the man with whom Bryan talked at greatest length about these matters was A. P. Isvolski, who later turned his attention to the international situation and was able to declare in 1914: "*C'est ma guerre.*" Chiding the Russians for their easy-going habits, Bryan insisted that the American Embassy open each morning at nine, even though nobody in St. Petersburg was ready to do business before eleven. But Mr. Bryan was up and about!

Borrowing the equivalent of about thirty cents from one of the secretaries of the embassy (Paxton Hibben) for some unknown purpose, he left Russia for Norway, where he attended the coronation of King Haakon VII.

Now messages hinting at 1908 came in with increasing frequency. But Bryan was still hedging. In reply to a letter from Senator Jones offering an obvious opportunity for a declaration, Bryan wrote:

I shall do no more to secure another nomination, and do not want one unless conditions seem to demand it. . . . There are, however, certain reforms which I would like very much to see accepted, and to assist in the acceptance of these reforms I am willing to become the party candidate again.[27]

From Norway the Bryans went to London through Sweden and were glad to be among English-speaking people again. Three sacks of mail awaited them at the London Embassy. At the Fourth of July dinner Ambassador Whitelaw Reid introduced the visitor to an overwhelmingly enthusiastic audience of Britons and Americans, as "a typical American whose whole life has been lived in the sunlight."

It was an inspiring occasion. In a glow of Anglo-American good-fellowship, Bryan responded by hailing the two great English-speaking countries of the world as forces in spreading education, brotherhood, and the English language among the benighted millions of India and the Philippines. If America had forged somewhat ahead of England in the movement for righteousness, all the greater reason for humility.

If it has been allured by Providence to a higher ground, may it lead the way in winning the confidence of those who follow it, in exerting the spirit of Him who said: "And if I am lifted up, I shall draw all men unto me."[28]

The triumphant hour was dimmed. The golden voice of Bryan boomed. The distinguished Americans and Britons cheered. Alice Roosevelt Longworth, sitting "beautifully dressed in white" in the centre of the gallery whence the ladies were permitted to look down upon their Anglo-American lords (including Adolph Ochs), received marked attention. When the band played "The Star-Spangled Banner," she stood up and everyone's glass was raised to her, as though she were Columbia.[29] The shadow of T. R. fell even here.

However, Bryan had no real reason to complain. At the hotel he was besieged by callers. He and Mrs. Bryan spent the "week's end" at Wrest Park with the Whitelaw Reids and visited the peers of the realm. The custom of dining at eight-fifteen astonished them, but they were naïvely delighted at such high-toned conduct. It was curious to see Bryan, the Great Commoner, in such an atmosphere. As J. A. Spender observed, "he was not at all quenched by it."[30]

Not even J. P. Morgan himself could destroy this equanimity. When the two men were introduced at one of Ambassador Reid's receptions, Morgan said: "Bryan? Bryan? The name sounds familiar. But I have not had the pleasure of meeting you before." They looked at each other narrowly as their hands met, then drifted quickly apart.

Reporters were growing insistent that Bryan make some declaration regarding his political future but, though there is ample evidence that he was giving the matter deep and constant thought, he was not yet ready to make public the results of his thinking. One statement he did make. "I am more radical than ever," he said, "while the platform of the Democratic party is essentially conservative," and went on to explain that "what used to be called radical is now called conservative. The doctrine has not changed, but public sentiment is making progress."

He found himself somewhat disturbed by the unanimity of Democratic approval. It was the dissident note that stirred Bryan to action. He was suspicious of the new-found allegiance of men of wealth and tried to show where his heart really lay by writing home asking that donations to his reception of welcome be limited to $50 per person.

He was soon given a more striking opportunity to define his position toward the questionable elements within the party. When he learned that Roger Sullivan, the Chicago boss who had railroaded a Parker delegation through a state convention to defeat Hearst, had been named Democratic committeeman from Illinois, with every prospect of controlling future state conventions, he immediately wrote Judge Thompson to demand Mr. Sullivan's resignation, on the ground that he was too closely allied with the big corporations and had won his place through fraud.

The request created a furor but went unheeded. Sullivan remarked that the Czarism implicit in Bryan's action was no part of the Democratic philosophy, and retained his place. But Bryan was comforted by Louis Post's assurance that though the move had been a mistake from the viewpoint of practical politics, in the eyes of his "genuinely Democratic friends it was an admirable thing"[31] to have done.

With his unfailing sense of the dramatic, Bryan played his most sensational card on the eve of his departure from London on July twenty-fourth. Before the Inter-Parliamentary Peace Conference he delivered a speech wherein he presented a plan for the establishment of a tribunal of impartial Powers which, after arbitration had been tried and before war could be declared, should pass upon the question of national honour under dispute. If President Roosevelt considered his suggestions beneath comment, there were others who might feel differently. He was right. The Peace Conference incorporated his plan in a resolution to be presented before the Conference at The Hague. All the London papers printed his speech in full, and the London *Times* reviewed it in a lengthy and, for the *Times*, enthusiastic editorial, even while pointing out that Mr. Bryan had borrowed freely from the Anglo-American Arbitration Treaty and emphasizing the fact that while such exalted understandings might exist between friendly and enlightened nations like the United States and

Great Britain, "for the generality of Powers we can hardly regard Mr. Bryan's resolution as anything but a counsel of perfection."[32]

Next day Bryan was presented in private audience to His Majesty King Edward VII. It was evidently a gayer occasion than his audience with the Mikado. From all that is known, the King and Bryan seem to have had a good time together. Bryan was himself and so was Edward. Nor in his own account of the interview, did William Jennings make capital of the fact that the audience was not sought by him, but suggested by the King.[33]

Perhaps he considered it no more than his due.

The Bryans left England, accompanied by Millard Fillmore Dunlap and Colonel Weertman of St. Louis, to journey hurriedly through Holland, up the Rhine to Switzerland, through Italy and across to Spain. By the time they reached Granada, what with banquets and travel and heat, William Jennings found himself out of underwear. He could have bought himself a new suit, but the habit of years is hard to overcome, and no honours could turn the head of Mary Bryan.

In the palatial suite of the Washington Irving Hotel she washed his underwear in a basin.[34]

They boarded the *Princess Irene* at Gibraltar, which, unlike the Sphinx, was not a disappointment. Bryan was the centre of interest among the passengers. He entered with wholehearted enthusiasm into the deck sports and talked to everyone.[35]

But for long hours he was closeted with Mrs. Bryan in their stateroom, carefully going over each word of his Madison Square Garden speech. He must be letter perfect. The chances of victory seemed greater than ever before. The speech would be his platform and determine his political future. The stakes were high.

Every important Democrat was on hand for the Garden meeting. The home folks, led by James Dahlman, the "cowboy mayor" of Omaha, had chartered a special train and come East a hundred strong. Even the railroads had caught the fire of enthusiasm and made special rates for the trip[36]—a concession to a private citizen not known since the days of Admiral Dewey's popularity. Pictures of Bryan were being sold on the streets. On the night before his arrival, fifteen senators and eighteen governors were in the City of New York. Next day it would have been hard to find a prominent Democrat outside of it.

The Nebraskans chartered a tug and sailed down the harbour to meet the *Princess Irene*. Jim Dahlman brought his lasso down over the shoulders of the Peerless Leader, who was lifted into the arms of clamorous friends.

"The sight of you," said Bryan happily, "is good for sore eyes."[37]

That night he slept on board the houseboat of L. F. Nixon, and when the party stepped off Mr. Nixon's private yacht landing the next day it was Tom Taggart who first shook Bryan's hand. Roger Sullivan was there, too, bearing no apparent grudge against "Czar" Bryan.

It was a glorious home-coming. "Has ever an American citizen," asked Frank Cobb in the *World*, "returned to such a delirious free-will greeting?"

Madison Square Garden was sweltering hot that night. It must have reminded Bryan of 1896, as he pushed his way through the throngs that blocked the streets. Inside the Garden he surveyed

Democracy in all its modern forms—in the Bryan form of free silver, in the Hearst form of public ownership, and in the Johnson form of populism. . . . Beneath the passion, beneath the rage of opinions and beneath the rabid uproar of the Bryan devotees could be observed the quiet, orderly crowd of the anonymous, whose political beliefs were nebulous—the thousands who doubt and hesitate and recoil from creed to creed, and who had come to be convinced. . . . What they wanted most was Bryan—always Bryan.[38]

Bryan stood before them. He was "like an idol hewn from a block of stone," and the idol pressed its lips tightly together and blinked its eyes to keep back the tears, but could not. The crowd cheered and cheered.

He began to speak. His eloquent plea for Democracy, his forensics against plutocracy were familiar enough. Direct election of senators, income tax, the trust question—out they came, the good old issues that he had cherished and sustained in the days of their adversity but that now, alas, in their prosperity could serve him no longer. He even made a polite and hearty reference to their adoption by the Republican party under Roosevelt.

And then the bombshell burst. His statement to the reporters in London had been no idle chatter. He was indeed more radical than his party. For he said:

I have already reached the conclusion that railroads partake so much of the nature of a monopoly that they must *ultimately* become public property and be managed by public officials in the interests of the whole country in accordance with the well defined theory that public ownership is necessary where competition becomes impossible. I do not know that the country is ready for this change; I do not know that a majority of my own party favor it, but I believe that an increasing number of the members of all parties see in public ownership the only sure remedy for discrimination between persons and places, for extortionate rates for the carrying of freight and passengers.

The rest went for nothing! The undisputed leader of the Democratic party, the personification of Democracy itself, had defined the issue of the 1908 campaign—government ownership of trunk-line railways. He had forced the issue into the open with a magnificent sweeping gesture.

Hearst, the old enemy, was jubilant. Had Bryan actually entered his camp? He slipped out of his box before the end of the speech to arrange an immediate private conference with Bryan.

The Republicans were jubilant.

I drew a sigh of relief after reading Bryan's speech [wrote Roosevelt to Lodge four days later]. I think he has helped us immensely. Down at bottom Bryan is a cheap soul. He felt that he had to take an attitude that would show he was really a great deal more radical than he was.

Roosevelt was wrong, Bryan had spoken with passionate conviction. His motives for advocating government ownership at this time were complex and no more purely altruistic than are the motives of most politicians. Yet of his belief in the policy there can be no doubt to the unpartisan mind. He had been harping on it in *The Commoner* for two years, despite the lack of any answering enthusiasm. He had disregarded the warning of John Sharp Williams,[39] who, as official ambassador of the National Democratic Committee, had assured him in London that its introduction into the campaign at this stage would be bad politics.

If he hedged later, it was not because he had ceased to believe, but because he wanted the nomination even more than he wanted government ownership. He believed, but he was not willing to go to the stake for his belief.

William Jennings Bryan was not of the stuff of which martyrs are made.

Out in Normal the Methodist Episcopal Church gave the last of a series of receptions that marked Bryan's progress across the country. After suitable speeches of welcome, Mrs. Bryan presented the church with two olive wood collection plates from Jerusalem, and William Jennings listened with a full heart to the singing of his favourite hymn:

> I'll go where you want me to go, dear Lord,
> I'll be what you want me to be.

CHAPTER XXIV

1908

BRYAN had always listened for the voice of the people before speaking. "The voice of the people shall be recognized," he had said, "if not as the voice of God, at least as Bancroft defines it, as the best expression of the divine will to be found upon the earth." If he had listened before Madison Square Garden, he had not heard aright; for now the voice spoke in accents harsh and denunciatory. It did not want government ownership of railroads.

The moralist might speak bravely of fighting to convert the mistaken majority, but what course was left open to the practical politician? None, it seemed, but strategic retreat. It must have been an agonizing decision to make. If he abandoned the issue—or even laid it gently aside for future reference—where would he find another to mark the line of cleavage between Democrat and Republican?

No sooner were the words out of his mouth at Madison Square Garden than Roosevelt had taken all the safe ideas to himself. Now in early December he launched a special message to Congress, suggesting income and inheritance taxes, publicity on campaign contributions, and opposing the use of the navy for the collection of private debts. Bryan's ideas; and Bryan did what he could to keep his head above water by printing the message together with the parallel passages from his own earlier speech![1]

This technique brought out the essential identity of the two party leaders. The crying need was for a definition of their differences. Again and again Roosevelt was stealing the Bryan thunder, and the situation was so apparent to the public that a few months later Bryan was introduced as "a great American whose policies now nominate the White House."[2]

Only to a mentality like Bryan's could the social forces responsible for this phenomenon have remained obscure. In the years since 1896 he had seen Roosevelt rise to power through the exploitation of measures he knew to be his own, and it was natural to him to suppose that his agitation of those measures had so thoroughly aroused the conscience of the nation that the Republicans had been forced in self-defence to adopt them. The true explanation would never have occurred to him, nor would he have readily accepted it, had it been pointed out.

As early as 1896 the aleatory capitalism that had been prevalent in the United States since 1870 was beginning to yield to a more beneficent conception of social life, defined by Dr. Charles Beard as social democracy. After 1896 its progress was rapid and the peak of its development was reached in the early years of Wilson's administration. Inevitably the reforms characteristic of the movement were absorbed by the party in power, and it was for those very reforms that Bryan had been first to fight, prompted by that instinct that made him the people's leader. Therefore he mistook what was a natural social development for the work of his own hand, and though it was gratifying to have been proven right, it was less gratifying to be ousted as leader of the righteous cause.

He stood between the devil of government ownership of railroads and the deep sea of an issueless campaign. To fight for the former courted disaster. There was always the chance that in the deep sea he might happen on a bright and glittering fish.

So softly the drums began to beat the retreat:

> Until the people are ready for ownership, it [*The Commoner*] will urge regulation of the strictest kind under the most favorable circumstances.[3]

The people (and the politicians) were unanimously in favour of a campaign along the lines of 1896 and 1900. So early in February 1907 Bryan, accompanied by Mrs. Bryan, started on a three months' speaking tour of the West. His first concern was to undo the mischief he had done, to soothe, to reassure, to make perfectly clear his true stand on the question of government ownership, which seemed somehow in danger of misinterpretation.

It was the word "ultimately" that saved him. He pointed out that he had been

careful to say that he did not know that the country was ready for it, or that a majority of the Democrats favoured it. Mr. Bryan [editorial third person] has no desire to force government ownership upon the country, and he would be powerless to force government ownership upon the country against the will of the people, even if he desired to do so. . . . It is not necessary—[4]

And one can almost see him climbing up the rescuing rope

—to abandon one's views of things ultimately, in order to act upon things immediate.

Had he wavered from the beginning, or was it an act of God that led him to introduce that saving word into his speech? The only trouble was that the "things immediate" lingered coyly beyond the horizon and refused to be coaxed out. To cap the climax, whether as a piece of bold strategy or characteristic obtuseness, he actually went so far as to write to the *Wall Street Journal*,[5] the Capitalists' Own, that in his opinion there was "no hurry about government ownership."

Certainly this position found no opposition in that quarter.

The *Wall Street Journal* was not the only newspaper that needed conciliating. Mr. Hearst, after his talk with Bryan on the occasion of the Madison Square Garden speech, had undoubtedly resolved to support him to the last ditch on the government ownership issue. With Mr. Bryan deserting the issue, what was Mr. Hearst to do? He decided to form a new party, the Independence League, and announced its birth May 3, 1907. His erstwhile ally, somewhat nonplussed, magnanimously welcomed the new party and expressed his

"DE—LIGHT—ED!"

THE DEMOCRATIC DONKEY IS BEGINNING TO LOOK LIKE SOMEBODY.

The Political Situation of 1908 as Cartooned by Joseph
Keppler in *Puck*

THE NATIONAL DEMOCRATIC CASH REGISTER.

Now Fat and Opulent, is Becoming Less and Less
the Crusader—1908

conviction that it would rally to the support of Democracy in the end, as the Populists had done in 1896.

Satisfied that the West was bursting with promise of an abundant harvest of votes, Bryan turned to New England, where he also found himself popular. Compromise had its compensations. Even in New York City, stronghold of his enemies, the evidences of good will on all sides warmed his heart as a foretaste of what was to come. There he struck his first real blow for one of the fish he found in the sea—publicity on campaign contributions.

The objection to the campaign funds that are contributed secretly, and spent secretly, is that they are contributed for a purpose that the public does not understand, and to carry out a policy against the public.

He made it clear that his battle was against the corporations. He realized, he said, that the individual could be moved to the contribution of large sums only through motives of patriotism, but corporations were not so altruistic. He urged that all large corporation contributions be made public *before* election day, and that failure to comply be made a penal offence.

As an interlude to political campaigning he served as commencement orator in many sections of the country, and wherever he spoke his topic was Faith—faith in one's self, faith in mankind, faith in God, and faith in our form of government. But neither by faith nor any other healing miracle could he quite exorcise the devil he had raised in government ownership, until on July twenty-sixth he made the following emphatic statement in *The Commoner*:

Government ownership is not an immediate issue. The large majority of the people still hope for effective regulation, and while they so hope, they will not consider ownership. While many Democrats believe—and Mr. Bryan is one of the number—that public ownership offers the ultimate solution of the problem, still, those who believe that the public will finally in self defence be driven to ownership recognize that regulation must be tried under the most favorable circumstances, before the masses will be ready to try a more radical remedy.

Regulation cannot be sufficiently tried within the next year, and there is no desire anywhere to make government ownership an issue in 1908. . . . To inject government ownership into the next campaign would simply give representatives of the railroads a chance to dodge the issue of regulation and deceive the public.

Having settled that business to his own satisfaction, he was free to turn his attention elsewhere.

In September Oklahoma had its first elections. Bryan had exercised an important influence on the writing of the new state's constitution, and he was present to support it and to help Democracy elect a governor. The candidate was C. N. Haskell.

He was a friend when I needed friends [Bryan told the people]. I am glad to be able to pay back in this campaign a part of the debt that I owe Mr. Haskell for his services . . . so strong, so able, so faithful a Democrat.

The constitution was adopted and Haskell elected, but Bryan was later to regret his championship.

In Nebraska, where this period marked the height of his power, he wrote the platform and named the candidate for the state ticket. It was growing evident that publicity on campaign funds was to be for him the outstanding issue of the campaign, and in Nebraska he concentrated on it to the complete disregard of government ownership. The convention was persuaded to come out against corporation contributions and in favour of adequate publicity for large donations.

It was not only in Nebraska that things were going his way. His stock in the Democratic party was high and steadily mounting. In New York he received a tremendous ovation, and, though he spoke three times, there were still crowds turned away.

In Mr. Sullivan's State of Illinois a monster rally was held to honour him. The real indications of his approaching victory at the convention lay deeper than these surface demonstrations. They lay in an indefinable atmosphere of success, in a consciousness, all-pervading, though it rose from undefinable sources, that Bryan was the man of the hour.

To oppose Bryan in those days [1907-8] [wrote Arthur Wallace Dunn] was almost Democratic treason . . . to be suspected of disloyalty was almost like buying a ticket to private life.[6]

And Frank Kent's comment is:

There were some bitter protests and much talk of a fight with him, but there was no one to make it. The Bryan sentiment was a concrete political fact that caused most of the Democrats in Congress to accept his leadership without question. Among certain conservative senators a movement started looking to the rejection of Bryan as a candidate . . . but the movement got nowhere. . . . From the beginning of 1907 [there was] no doubt at all about his nomination.[7]

It was this "Bryan sentiment" that rendered harmless the attacks made against him. People might talk ironically of his "divine right"[8] to the nomination. Watterson, alienated by government ownership, might thunder that "hope lessens of Democracy until William Jennings Bryan is politically dead." The New York *Sun* might scoff at party issues by defining a Republican "at the present time . . . as a descendant of the followers of Lincoln who has appropriated all the doctrines of William Jennings Bryan";[9] and Joseph Pulitzer might suggest to his editors that they play variations on the theme, "What is the *real difference* between the Democratic and Republican parties?"[10] Pulitzer might, in fact he did, do worse, for he dragged out the story of the Belmont-Ryan contribution in 1904. But all to no avail.

Even the rumour that James Guffey of Pennsylvania, who had presented Bryan with a stained-glass window for Fairview in 1905, was planning to send an anti-Bryan delegation to the convention, and the New York *World's* question that New York do likewise, had not the desired effect. Bryan was too firmly entrenched. Nothing could shake him.

His sense of security seemed to be producing an unfortunate effect upon his conduct. More than a hint of arrogance appeared.

You people complain [he said] because I have declared for initiative and referendum. That ought to be an issue. I will drive every man out of the Democratic party who does not support it.[11]

And when Senator Daniel suggested to him that some of the issues for which he had stood in the past had proved to be wrong, and that he might be wrong again, he answered: "I have always been right."

The righteous man was forgetting the inheritance of the meek and gave further evidence of the fact when, after having accepted an invitation to speak at the New York Democratic banquet in April he learned that Woodrow Wilson and not himself was to be the speaker of the day, and cancelled his acceptance. A strange prelude to a remarkable adventure in coöperation and discord.

At intervals he attacked the trusts, and tried to kill two birds with one stone by badgering Joseph Pulitzer to reveal his connection with them. Pulitzer refused to be provoked, even when *The Commoner* bloomed with the headlines

A FULL GROWN QUESTION

What is the Extent of the Financial Interest
Held by Joseph Pulitzer, Owner of the New
York World, in Railroad Companies and
Great Corporations Commonly Known
As Trusts?

Pulitzer refused to answer, but William Howard Taft, already known as the Republican choice for the nomination, issued a statement on the general question of trusts, that Bryan regarded as inadequate. For Bryan there was only one adequate solution of the trust problem—to exterminate the trusts. Black was black, not gray.

The Conference of Natural Resources at the White House
in May, a gathering of the great from the President down
and including Andrew Carnegie, James J. Hill, John Mitchell,
the labour leader, and Tom Johnson, was chosen as occasion
for another anti-trust blast. In a picture Bryan is shown
seated between Carnegie and James J. Hill.[12] As a magnanimous opening gesture and with perhaps a sidelong glance at
"party harmony," he offered a resolution "that the conference express its deep regret that ex-President Cleveland
is prevented by sickness from participating in this historical
meeting and express its sincere hope for a speedy recovery."
The resolution was passed. Then he rose to give utterance
to one of those felicitous phrases that have passed into the
very texture of our public life:

There is no twilight zone [he said] between the nation and the
state . . . in which exploiting interests can take refuge from both,
and my observation is that most—not all, but most—of the con-
tentions over the line between nation and state are traceable to
predatory corporations which are trying to shield themselves from
deserved restraining regulation.

The trusts, apparently, were supposed to be shorn of their
last refuge by this speech.

There was little more to be done politically, and Bryan
was content to await the results at Fairview. Against his
domestic background he was an amiable figure. Although his
property had just been evaluated at $84,500,[13] he opened the
door to callers himself, while the Negro servant read a novel
in an easy chair.[14] Bryan was notoriously easy with his servants, and they sometimes took advantage of his generosity.
He found time to attend three weddings in ten days and to
buy gifts for each of the brides.

There seemed to be no ill will in him, even against Joseph
Pulitzer. When a *World* reporter called for an interview, he
was received with the utmost friendliness, even taken into
the bosom of the family. For William Jennings was about to
accompany Mrs. Bryan into town to buy some chairs, and
he invited the reporter into the two-seated rig with them,

behind the horses, Silas and John. And while the candidat
made his purchases the reporter held the reins.[15]

All was now in readiness for the convention, which Bryar
did not propose to attend himself. He sent his brothe
Charley. A tent was pitched in the yard at Fairview with
telegraph and telephone connection to Denver.

On July seventh that city was in a tumult. The Nebras
kans entered the Convention Hall, bearing a red, white, anc
blue banner with Bryan's picture painted on it. The demon
stration that greeted them, says William Allen White, wa;
"the greatest ever made in history."[16] Only one discordan
note was struck. From Pennsylvania there arrived two dele
gations—one, headed by James Guffey, definitely opposec
to Bryan. For a time it looked so much as though the Guffey
delegation might be seated, that Charley Bryan went so
far as to propose a compromise with them;[17] but in vain
The day was saved, however, when the Committee on Cre
dentials threw the delegation out, on the ground that thei
credentials were not in order and that proof was available
showing that they had used seventeen hundred Republican votes at the primaries, to insure their election.

At Fairview Bryan made a short speech on the subject
"Mr. Guffey, national committeeman, deliberately and wilfully sought to defeat what he knew to be the expressed will
of the Democrats of Pennsylvania. . . . I have notified Mr.
Guffey that wherever my opinion has been asked, I have
stated that I would regard his selection as unfortunate."

Eight hundred telegrams passed between Charley Bryan
and his brother, and finally William Jennings was nominated
Democratic candidate for the Presidency for the third time,
having received $888\frac{1}{2}$ votes out of a possible 994 on the first
ballot. The platform on which he proposed to run defied the
trusts, demanded a revision of the tariff and publicity on
campaign contributions before election.

Government ownership was not an issue of the campaign.

The man to oppose Bryan had been selected at Theodore
Roosevelt's dictation. William Howard Taft was no more
than a competent administrator, whom Roosevelt's endorse-

ment had given enormous prestige among the progressive
Republicans, while the conservatives rallied to him in
the hope that he would prove less aggressive than his spon-
sor. He did not seem an irresistible adversary. Everything
was shaping up for an issueless campaign with Bryan fighting
a weak antagonist.

On July twenty-fourth the Democratic National Committee met at Fairview, with Mr. Sullivan of Chicago still
a member. It was voted that the utmost publicity be given
campaign contributions. No single contribution might ex-
ceed $10,000. All contributions over $100 were to be plainly
recorded. None over $100 would be accepted within the last
three days of the campaign. A month later Bryan delivered
his speech of acceptance. The railroads that had made
special rates for those wishing to hear Taft (surely a significant indication of the true aspect of affairs) failed to extend
a similar courtesy to Bryan.[18]

Recognizing [said William Jennings Bryan] that I am indebted
for my nomination to the rank and file of our party, and that my
election must come, if it comes at all, from the unpurchased and
unpurchasable suffrages of the American people, I promise, if
entrusted with the responsibilities of this high office, to consecrate
whatever ability I have to the one purpose of making this, in fact,
a government in which the people rule—a government which
will do justice to all, and offer to everyone the highest possible
stimulus to great and persistent effort, by assuring to each the
enjoyment of his just share of the proceeds of his toil, no matter in
what part of the vineyard he labors, or to what occupation, profession or calling he devotes himself.

He was still bearing the crusader's banner high on the open
road, but it is difficult to reconcile with the crusading spirit
what was going on behind closed doors.

William Jennings Bryan had apparently made up his mind
that to collect votes, whatever their source might be, was
more important than to stick to principles. Senator Pettigrew of North Dakota had spent a week with him at Fairview before the convention and at Bryan's invitation

stopped there again on his return. And Bryan made what might have seemed a singular request in view of his brave words of an earlier day. Knowing of his intimacy with Boss Sullivan of Chicago, he asked Pettigrew to bear him a message from the Democratic nominee—to say that Sullivan would receive "due and proper consideration" if Bryan were elected; that he would be "consulted about affairs" in his locality; and that his "political importance would be recognized."[19] The same message was to be delivered to Boss Murphy of New York and to Arthur Brisbane.

What had become of Bryan's repudiation of an unworthy political associate, his denial that any candidate had a right to make his "action depend upon expediency"? Perhaps it was again a question of ultimate good.

Pettigrew had no trouble with Sullivan or Murphy; but Brisbane was another story. "Bryan doesn't know enough to be President," he told the messenger. "He is a provincial fellow, prejudiced by his training." Pettigrew had his answer ready. He asked Mr Brisbane how much money he had made during the preceding year through his writings.

"About $70,000," was the reply.

"That's nothing. Bryan made $100,000 from the sale of his books and through his lectures, and yet you say Bryan doesn't know enough to be President."[20]

Unfortunately, Mr. Brisbane refused to be shaken even by this peculiarly American argument.

The campaign was dull. Hearst from Paris cabled a refusal to support Bryan, coupling it with the information that his support had been sought by Gompers. Gompers denied it.[21] Bryan said Hearst's platform was practically identical with his.[22] But Clarence Darrow, disgusted by Bryan's many retreats, went over to Hearst. The National Manufacturers' Association sent out a four-page leaflet advocating that business men unite, regardless of party, to defeat Bryan. Bryan said he was sure of election because Americans would not vote for a man who did not believe in the divinity of Christ![23]

Haskell of Oklahoma was made treasurer of the National Committee, and became the source of the principal excite-

nent of the campaign. For Hearst made the charge that
Haskell in 1888 used his influence to secure favour for the
Standard Oil Company; and Roosevelt hinted that his appointment indicated an insincerity in Bryan's attitude
oward trusts. But Bryan replied that he for one had been
gnorant of Haskell's oil connections, nor did he believe
hem to be common knowledge. If they were, why had Taft
llowed him to become Governor of Oklahoma? At any rate,
aid Bryan, his resignation had been offered and accepted
t once. That the resignation was offered at Bryan's request,
a fact vouched for by Claude G. Bowers,[24] was not revealed.

The *Sun* found "no one excited" by the campaign "but
he performers."[25]

The *Times* and *Herald* agreed that Roosevelt could run
n Bryan's platform without discomfort. Despite all the good
work Bryan had put in for publicity on campaign funds, it
had not proved to be the impressive issue he needed, and
when Taft came out in agreement with him, specifying only
hat publicity need not be before election, most of its tenu-
us worth evaporated. As a final blow, Taft announced, with
Roosevelt's approbation but without regard to his platform,
hat he favoured income taxes. No wonder the Washington
Post commented that "people refuse to go into hysteria in
908 over the puny little questions that divide the two
arties"!

At Fairview on election night Bryan went upstairs at ten
'clock to be alone. At eleven he sent a message of thanks to
is neighbours for carrying his own precinct. He was confi-
ent to the last and conceded victory only when his cause
ad been hopelessly and obviously lost.

"If I could regard the defeat as a purely personal one,"
e wrote a few days later in *The Commoner*, "I would con-
der it a blessing rather than a misfortune, for I am relieved
f the burdens and responsibilities of an office, that is at-
active only in proportion as it gives opportunity to render
 larger public service." But for the party the message is
A BATTLE LOST—A WAR BUT BEGUN!"

In his bafflement at his crushing defeat, Bryan asked the

readers of *The Commoner* to write letters giving their versio
of the reasons for his failure.

He ran them for weeks under the heading:

SOLVING THE MYSTERY OF 1908

But for William Jennings Bryan it was a mystery nev
to be solved.

CHAPTER XXV

TOWARD PROHIBITION

`HE friend of the people had again been rejected by the
eople. Few men can become habituated to defeat. William
ennings Bryan was one of them. Did he believe that victory
as still a possibility; or was there some inner prompting
aat told him that his was a voice too important to be
illed? Between the triumph of righteousness, he came to
`gue, and political success, there was no necessary connec-
on.

What was righteousness in 1908?

1908 . . . Cleveland, the last living Democrat who had oc-
pied the White House, died. . . . The march of science had
nnelled the East River from Manhattan to Brooklyn. . . .
resident Eliot resigned from Harvard. . . . Harry Thaw
as committed to Matteawan, acquitted of the murder of
anford White. . . . The future "Saviour of the World,"
oodrow Wilson, was making himself into Presidential
mber. . . . The prelude to the World War, unrecognized by
ose who listened, was being played: H. H. Asquith be-
me Prime Minister of England. . . . France and Germany
rangled over Morocco. . . . Austro-Serbian antagonism
red.

Bryan turned his eyes toward South America. It was
ere that he carried his message of good will. In Peru he
ld his listeners: "There is more idealism in the United
ates than anywhere else in the world. The people of the
nited States are doing more in an unselfish way for the
nefit of the human race."[1] Idealism, not guns and capital,
the conquering force.

Idealism was all very well. But his discussion of the
nama Canal became an exercise in economics. "The

canal should be open to the commerce of the world," h
wrote in the New York *World*, "without other charge tha
that necessary for expense of operation and maintenance
This policy is demanded in the interests of our own people
Every dollar collected in tolls increases the rates charge
for transcontinental lines."

Again, the conflict of idealism and practice would aris
to plague him, when his task became actual statecraft an
not the delivery of oratorical good will!

The South American tour was an unqualified success
"Even the bitterest critics of William Jennings Bryan," sai
a New Orleans daily, "should feel kindly to him becaus
of the good work he is now doing for his own country i
South America."

However his speeches in foreign countries may have ad
vanced his moral prestige, however much it may hav
proved pleasurable to him to travel, his first significant polit
ical act following 1908 was his entrance into the prohibitio
controversy—and yet was it not as moralist rather tha
politician that he approached the question?

From now on William Jennings was the moralist. Prohi
bition! Peace! God!

Although he had been a teetotaler all his life, although hi
lips had never touched liquor, he must have forgotten tha
in 1890 he had been sent to Congress by the saloon. Pri
vately he had opposed liquor, and especially the saloon. H
had talked temperance on Chautauqua circuits, but politi
cally he had found it convenient to be non-partisan. In 189
he had said: "The prohibitionists and anti-prohibitionist
are in two classes. The people who, in exercising their pe
sonal rights, use liquor, do not interfere with those who d
not. The other side should be as honourable. It is unjust fc
one man to say that another must 'like like I.'"

In 1890 he had argued with Pussyfoot Johnson agains
prohibition.

But in twenty years a man may change his mind.

He now felt that his hesitation had justifiably earne
for him the blame of the parents of the land. Yet even no

he could not bring himself to make an immediate declaration for national prohibition. He approached that position gingerly, through the issue of county option.

The opportunity for him to make his declaration came through an impasse in Nebraska state politics. Nebraska had tried local option and found it a failure. The saloon keepers of a town that declared itself dry removed themselves across the town line and set up business there. This might be an inconvenience for both drinkers and dealers, but it was hardly prohibition. Local option having failed, the question of county option now rose to take its place, and Bryan declared himself in favour of county option.

The arena for the battle was the State Convention at Grand Island, Nebraska, on July 26, 1910. Three parties were represented. One was led by Dahlman, who had backed Bryan for Congress in 1890, who had received the Ryan-Belmont money in 1904 and in 1906 had joyously lassoed his friend on his return from Europe. Dahlman was definitely opposed to county option. The second party was led by Governor Shallenberger, who tried to straddle the issue by announcing that while neither he nor his party advocated the county option bill, yet he would not veto it if it were passed. The third, a decided minority, was led by Bryan and demanded that a plank be inserted in the platform declaring for county option as the best method of dealing with the liquor question.

From the moment that Bryan entered the convention tent, the hostility was apparent. Hardly had he seated himself when a resolution was presented, the sole aim of which was to prevent Bryan from speaking on county option until the convictions of the delegates had been recorded. Bryan was on his feet in an instant to oppose the move and, as though to indicate what was coming, he lost. When he finally rose to speak in favour of county option, he was greeted by as many boos as cheers.

It must have pained him to listen to the hoots of those whose friend he had been for so long. He spoke to them pleadingly. Let them not accuse him of indifference to party harmony. Had not harmony reigned in Nebraska for sixteen years? Whose doing was that, if not William Jennings Bryan's? "Can you believe that anything less than an imperative sense of duty would lead me to differ from you? Never in my life have I performed a duty that I less desired to perform; and never have I felt more sure that I was performing a duty."

His eloquent plea did not avail. Sentiment was pitted against the political control of the liquor interests, and sentiment was an inadequate weapon. When the balloting ended Bryan found himself hopelessly defeated and repudiated by the party in which he had been a dominant influence for fourteen years. Was it a sign that his leadership was weakening?

He had undoubtedly shown great moral courage in taking and maintaining his stand, and that he was sustained in defeat by a belief in its righteousness can hardly be disputed. "I dreaded, as I have never dreaded anything before, entering a discussion where I might find myself out of harmony with those men whom I have loved and with whom I have worked for years." But "we never espoused a more righteous cause; we never faced an enemy more deserving of attack. If a retreat is to be sounded, it must be sounded by another. I shall never do it, never, never, never!"

These are not the words of political expediency but of passionate faith.

It is equally apparent, however, that other elements entered into the situation. Bryan's own explanation was that he was forced into active resistance by the liquor men when, by lobbying, they made county option an issue. But a certain vindictiveness seems to have played its part. After all, it is difficult to go down three times to defeat, retaining one's charity for all, and when Bryan arose for the third time there was evident in his temper a strain of rigidity, a note of intolerance that had not been marked before.

Again and again he made reference to the fact that the liquor interests, despite his own deliberate non-resistance, had given material aid to his enemies in 1908.[2] He held them responsible for the fact that initiative and referendum had not been made an issue; he accused them of having traded him off in Nebraska and Missouri, in Ohio and Indiana, in Illinois and New York, insisting, meantime, that personal rancour found no place in his heart. Yet at Grand Island he had called them heatedly a "band of political assassins"; which implies more than moral distaste.

The convention nominated Dahlman for Governor, and Bryan fought the election of his old friend fiercely, even going so far as to announce that he had prayed for his defeat and the election of the Republican candidate, who had declared for county option.

"In speaking for the State ticket," Bryan said, "I shall not be able to present any arguments in favour of Mr. Dahlman. His position on the liquor question makes that impossible. . . . [It] would embarrass me in the fight that I expect to make hereafter to save our party from the odium of being the representative of the liquor interests." Dahlman was defeated and Bryan declared his intention of crusading, both at political meetings and on the Chautauqua circuit, against the liquor interests.[3] But he would confine himself to the question of county option. If the issue were to be made a national one, then the liquor people had made it so, as they had made it a state issue.

Bryan had been badly beaten. County option had carried the state, but not through his agency. The fact that the Democrats had been defeated in Nebraska, in this year of Democratic victories in other states, was of itself significant. His political position was most insecure at this moment, and he was never to recover security. Yet his decline was neither precipitous nor immediate. He was to make remarkable recoveries and his influence over that element, represented by the six and a half millions who had voted for him in 1896, remained long a powerful factor in the councils of the Democratic party. He still occupied an enviable eminence but it was no longer preëminence; and his increasing insistence on his own prestige, his growing rigidity and intolerance, his assumptions of dictatorship, were symptomatic of the fact that he needed carefully to manage his power, to make it effective at all.

That the weakening of his own position should have come at a time when his party was gaining in strength all along the line added irony to the situation and did nothing to alleviate whatever bitterness now tinged his outlook.

Daily the prospects for the Democrats grew brighter. It grew increasingly clear that they were going to be able, barring accidents, to elect their man President in 1912.

Liberalism was the watchword of the hour[4] and the Republicans under Taft were showing no disposition to adopt it. The tariff revision, pledged by Taft's platform, had resulted in the Payne-Aldrich Bill that revised the tariff upward, and not down as had been expected. The President's speech at Winona, Minnesota, defending it as "the best tariff bill that the Republican party had ever framed and . . . the best the country had ever had" aroused a storm of protest and aligned the liberal Republicans against the administration. Taft was in favour of conservation of natural resources; but he had been unfortunate enough to create exactly the opposite impression. This so widened the breach that not even the enactment into law of a number of liberal policies—notably the parcel post and postal savings systems—could serve to heal it. As for the Federal campaign publicity act passed at this time, none but the wilfully partisan would have denied that the credit and honour for its passage were chiefly due to William Jennings Bryan.

This prevailing dissatisfaction with Taft found voice in the elections of 1910. In New Jersey Woodrow Wilson defeated the Republican candidate for Governor, who was up for reëlection. Maine and Massachusetts went Democratic. Judson Harmon, Democratic Governor of Ohio, was re-elected by many more votes than had originally gone to elect him. In New York State the Republican candidate for Governor, even with the support of Theodore Roosevelt, went down to defeat before the Democratic candidate. In the national elections the Democrats gained control of the Senate and the House, overthrowing Uncle Joe Cannon, and made an end of Cannonism. And worst of all, from the standpoint of Republican prospects, Theodore Roosevelt began to make it very clear that he was displeased with his heir and a parting of the ways was imminent.

Bryan entered the 1912 campaign with the defeat at Grand Island weighing upon him. Far from being subdued, he seemed surer of himself than ever before. His tendency toward dogmatism, which in 1909 had moved Senator Bailey to remark, drily, that there had been a time "when Mr. Bryan did not regard a Democratic platform exactly as a Christian regards the Ten Commandments," was apparently intensified. He had travelled a long way from the man who had been willing to give support of a kind to Judge Parker and even from the Bryan of two short years before, who had reversed himself and accepted the judgment of the rank and file, that government ownership of railways was not a suitable issue for a national campaign.

The Democratic platform was now to be regarded in the light of a political revelation, and he who departed therefrom was a heretic.[5] Firmly clutching his yardstick, Bryan prepared to measure aspiring candidates for the Democratic nomination in 1912.

Three seemed to Bryan most worthy of serious consideration: Champ Clark, Speaker of the House; Judson Harmon, Governor of Ohio; and Woodrow Wilson, Governor of New Jersey. Occasionally he would characteristically befog the issue by mentioning with seeming favour men like Governor Folk of Missouri or Senator Culberson of Texas.

To these and others he sent a questionnaire, designed to ascertain their orthodoxy and laying great stress on the positions they had taken in earlier campaigns, "for a man who went wrong in any of these campaigns is still wrong, unless he has undergone a revolutionary change of sentiment."[6] With the exception of Folk and Marshall, who never reached more than the status of favourite sons, the candidates refused to attend "Mr. Bryan's school session";[7] but he was swerved in no wise from his course, and continued to wield the pedagogue's pointer whenever he got the chance.

Despite his less commanding position, however, and the blunders into which his dogmatism led him, his influence was acknowledged and sought by every faction within the party that had any hope of getting it. And when in a speech delivered August 14, 1911, at Columbus, Ohio, he turned his thumbs down on Judson Harmon as a suspected friend of Wall Street and the saloons, the backers of Champ Clark and Woodrow Wilson began vying with one another for his favour, each feeling that the other was his only formidable rival, except for the ever-present possibility that William Jennings still considered himself a candidate.

Whatever his secret thoughts may have been, it was a possibility that Bryan consistently denied. All through 1911 and the early months of 1912 he published letters from his readers, urging him to run, together with emphatic assurances that he had no intention of running. By this device he underlined his own power and prevented the political situation from jelling prematurely. Three times Champ Clark, who declared himself unwilling to compete against Bryan, since they drew their support from the same sections of the country, asked him whether he meant to run, and three times Bryan answered in the negative.[8]

But with his interest unengaged elsewhere, he showed himself strangely reluctant to come out emphatically for either of the leading candidates. He was perfectly willing to hear all that might be said in their favour, but he would not actively advocate the cause of one or the other. In *The Commoner* he devoted as much space to Wilson, the stranger, as to Clark, his friend, though the latter felt that that friendship should have given him the edge. Had he not enthusiastically supported Bryan during his own campaigns, and—in 1896—at considerable financial sacrifice?

But William Jennings refused to be stampeded. He invited Champ Clark to his birthday party on March 20, 1911, in order, so he said, to give notice that he regarded him as an "available man for the nomination." He commended him highly on April fourteenth for his speech at the opening of Congress.

IT'S BACK!

Drawn by E. Flohri for Leslie's Weekly.

Bryan's Return from Europe, from a Drawing by
E. Flohri in *Leslie's Weekly*

Bryan in 1908, Standing Before the Office of the
Commoner at Lincoln

But at the Jefferson Club of Iowa on May first, "he paid particularly strong tribute to Governor Wilson of New Jersey" and "spoke a little of Speaker Clark of the House."

On September first he graciously admitted Clark to be a great improvement over Cannon; but on November twenty-fourth he showed the direction of his thoughts by accusing the Speaker of sacrificing his gifts for leadership in order to preserve harmony between all groups within the party.

Who will lead [wrote Bryan]? Mr. Clark is ... right on all public questions. Will he step forward and order a charge? Or will he act as umpire and watch the fight? He won his spurs as a fighter; and he cannot hope to retain the confidence of his friends, if he turns the leadership over to another.

If Mr. Clark had exhibited as Speaker the qualities of leadership that made him Speaker, he would now be without a rival in the race for the presidential nomination. He has time yet to make himself a formidable candidate, but to do so he must LEAD.

But if he refused to throw his support whole-heartedly for his friend, he withheld it with equal deliberation from the stranger, and weighing one against the other, he found for neither.

Woodrow Wilson had not fought with the Democrats in 1896, and he had made some exceedingly disparaging remarks about their candidate. Since Bryan's political information was exhaustive, he perhaps knew that Wilson had absolutely refused to have his name discussed for the Vice Presidential nomination in 1908, if Bryan were the candidate.[9] These were black marks against him.

But his startling, and dramatic defiance of the state bosses of New Jersey in February 1911, when he was only Governor-elect, had gone far to redeem him in Bryan's eyes. In according Wilson's conduct full praise on this occasion, Bryan suggested that his misstep in 1896 might have been due to ignorance of the factions with which he, Bryan, had been contending, and went on to say:

The first contest will come in the effort of the special interests to control the Democratic national convention of 1912. . . . Let us

hope that in that great contest Governor Wilson will be found
speaking the same language he spoke during the New Jersey senatorial contest, fighting the same battle for the upbuilding of a
Democratic party that shall be free from the domination of
special interests.

Still William Jennings would go no farther than to "hope,"
not even at the urgency of Colonel E. M. House, who had
been good enough in 1898 to find him a place in Texas where
he might take his daughter Grace for her health. The Colonel
had always, as a Democrat, been interested in national
politics, but had held aloof while Bryan was all-powerful.

In 1911, convinced that Bryan's chances for securing the
nomination were slim, House cast about for a star to which
he might hitch his wagon, and finally picked on Wilson as
the brightest. Taking advantage of his long acquaintance
with Bryan, he sounded him on the prospects of his support.[10]
House found in him an agreeable and willing listener who
would not commit himself.

In November 1911 Bryan went with his wife to Jamaica,
after having promised politely to read with interest any
press clippings or other bits of information relating to Governor Wilson that Colonel House might choose to send him.
For his own part, he proposed to read regularly only the
New York *World* and the Washington *Post*, papers that were
hostile to him.

En route to Jamaica the Bryans were shipwrecked, but
with no ill effect. On the contrary. Good sprang from evil,
for it resulted in the enactment into law of a bill framed
by Bryan, providing that all vessels should carry two wireless
operators, that the key might be manned day and night.[11]

He never had difficulty in seeing the obvious.

PART VI
NEW LIFE

"Faith in God, belief in Christ and confidence in the people, these three explain such success as I have achieved. To lead one must believe in the triumph of the truth and he cannot do this unless he believes in God. To lead one must also know the truth—and 'Christ is the way, the truth and the life.' To lead one must be going in the same direction as the people and to do this he must not only sympathize with them, but trust them."

William Jennings Bryan.

CHAPTER XXVI

BALTIMORE

COLONEL HOUSE let no grass grow beneath his feet.
Bryan had hardly arrived in Jamaica before the promised
letters began to follow him. House's task, was clear. He had
to convince Bryan that, whatever had been the cause of
Wilson's unorthodoxy in 1896, he was now a thoroughgoing
radical Democrat. Before the latter's departure for Jamaica,
Bryan and House had discussed both the Supreme Court
ruling on the case of the Standard Oil Company and the
Aldrich plan for a national central bank, and Bryan had
expressed his strong disapproval of both. He regarded the
former as a move designed to emasculate anti-trust legislation. "We may as well recognize that we now have no criminal law against the trusts," he had written in the *North
American Review* for July; and he considered that the
Aldrich plan would tend rather to tighten than loosen the
hold of the "money trust." House must have rapidly made
it his business to get Wilson's viewpoint on both these issues, for under date of November twenty-fifth he wrote to
Bryan:*

. . . Governor Wilson called yesterday afternoon and was with
me for an hour and a half.

I am pleased to tell you that when I asked him what he thought
of the Supreme Court ruling about which we talked when you
were here, he replied in almost the exact terms you used to me. As
far as I can see, your positions are identical.

He is also opposed to the Aldrich plan. . . .[1]

---

*This quotation and the two following are reprinted from *The Inti-
mate Papers of Colonel E. M. House*, arranged as a narrative by Charles
Seymour, used by permission of Houghton Mifflin Company, Publishers.

Then the Colonel went on with what he probably thought was a subtle bit of strategy:

There is some evidence that Mr. Oscar Underwood and his friends intend to make a direct issue with you for control of the next convention, and it looks a little as if they were receiving some aid from Champ Clark and his friends.

My feeling is that we can lay them low, but we must not lag in the doing of it.

But House's information about the Clark moves which he undoubtedly thought very new, and shrewdly conveyed, was already in Bryan's possession. For all the Colonel's delight in political subtlety, he apparently never did read *The Commoner!*

On December sixth a second letter arrived, obviously written to lay out for burial the Wall Street alliance bogey:

I took lunch with Colonel Harvey yesterday. It is the first time I have met him. I wanted to determine what his real attitude was towards Governor Wilson, but I think I left, as much in the dark as ever.

He told me that everybody south of Canal Street was in a frenzy against Governor Wilson and said that they were bringing all sorts of pressure upon him to oppose him. He said he told them he had an open mind, and that if they could convince him he was a dangerous man, he would do so.

He said that Morgan was particularly virulent in his opposition to Governor Wilson. I asked him what this was based upon, and he said upon some remark Governor Wilson had made in Morgan's presence concerning the methods of bankers, and which Morgan took as a personal reference. . . .

We are going to try to devise some plan by which we can use this Wall Street opposition to Governor Wilson to his advantage.[2]

From Bryan's reply, written December twenty-eighth, House could have derived little satisfaction.

. . . Am anxious to get back and find out more of the political situation. I shall attend the Washington banquet on the eighth of January, and will have a chance to learn how things are shaping up.

I am glad Governor Wilson recognizes that he has the opposition of Morgan and the rest of Wall Street. If he is nominated it must be by the Progressive Democrats, and the more progressive he is, the better.

The Washington banquet will give him a good chance to speak out against the trusts and the Aldrich currency scheme.[3]

Nevertheless, the antiphony of "Wilson or Clark, Wilson or Clark" must have been running pretty steadily through Bryan's head.

Was there, perhaps, an undercurrent of "William Jennings Bryan"?

The annual Jackson Day dinner at Washington, attended by every Democrat of importance, was the first big political event of the year, and Bryan came home for it. Two days before the dinner, Wilson's enemies flung into the Democratic camp a bomb, the purpose of which was to make mincemeat of the Governor of New Jersey. They released a letter written five years earlier by Wilson to Adrian Joline, expressing the wish that "something at once dignified and effective" might be done to "knock Bryan once and for all into a cocked hat."[4]

Surely here was something that would move Bryan out of his seat of judicious impartiality and set him against Wilson.

But Bryan refused to get excited. The more he was badgered for a statement, seemingly, the more stubborn became his determination not to give one.

"If Mr. Wilson wants to knock me into a cocked hat," he told a New York *Sun* reporter, "he and the *Sun* are on the same platform."

His calm was admirable, which was more than could be said for the group gathering at Washington. To arouse Bryan's active hostility was to lose every chance of the nomination, and the Wilson men gathered in excited conclave to determine how that calamity might best be averted. It was finally decided that no direct reference should be made to the letter but that, at the dinner itself, Wilson should pay handsome tribute to Bryan's leadership of the Democratic party.[5]

The great day arrived. To a group of newspaper men before whom he spoke in the afternoon, Governor Wilson gave an inkling of what was to come. "Even if a man has written letters it ought not to embarrass him. . . . Even if a man changes his mind it ought not to embarrass him."

How was he going to convince Bryan that he had changed his mind about what had seemed so desirable five short years ago?

Bryan for his part seemed intent on creating an impression of good will. When the party leaders gathered for dinner at the Raleigh Hotel, he exchanged, according to his own account, "cordial greetings"[6] with Champ Clark; then went straight to Governor Wilson, and with his hand on his shoulder talked with him for several moments.[7]

Hearst, Clark, and ex-Governor Folk of Missouri all spoke, pleading for party harmony, and Wilson took his cue from them. While there had been, he said, and might be again, legitimate differences of opinion on specific measures and proposals, there was one "fixed point in the history of the Democratic party, and that fixed point has been the character and the devotion and the preachings of William Jennings Bryan. . . . He has not, any more than Andrew Jackson did, based his career upon calculation, but has based it upon principle . . . when others were faint-hearted, Colonel Bryan carried the Democratic standard. He kept the fires burning which have heartened and encouraged the Democracy of the country."[8]

When Wilson had finished Bryan leaned toward him and said, "That was splendid!"[9] The Wilson contingent beamed their approval, and the Governor, completely reassured, returned to Trenton. He told Tumulty that Bryan had bidden him not to worry over the Joline letter.[10] He had graciously interpreted it as a reference to the currency question in 1896, and of course it was not news to him that Wilson had not been with him at that time. He was disposed to forgive a man who had learned so much in recent years and was now so eminently right on the trust question. Bryan clung to his position of neutrality as between Wilson and Clarke, but certainly the friendliness of his attitude toward the former was in no whit diminished as a result of this episode.

He was hearty in his approval of the break with Harvey, which occurred at about the same time. Colonel George Harvey had been a Wilson partisan in the midst of the Wall Street hosts, having appraised him through his writings as a conservative Democrat in command of a somewhat Jeffersonian rhetoric, ignoring the significance of his later radicalism and his record as Governor of New Jersey, wherein lay his appeal to the liberals.

But in the eyes of many others besides Bryan, Harvey's backing was doing Wilson more harm than good. When Harvey asked Wilson bluntly whether his advocacy embarrassed him and Wilson as bluntly answered that it did, those suspicious of Harvey could not but be pleased. Wilson, said William Jennings, had done well. If he would cut off all his questionable friends, he would do still better. Furthermore, he added piously, "it should matter little to him whether he reaches the White House. Rendering service counts."[11]

Relations between Bryan and the Clark forces were less happy. Despite Bryan's "cordial greetings," Clark felt that he had been treated with "scant courtesy" at the Jackson Day dinner.[12] Neither did he relish the fact that Bryan was advising many states in which he spoke to split their delegations, with the idea, perhaps, that a division of strength might more readily bring about the deadlock that gives the dark horse his chance. He even suggested that Clark split the Missouri delegation with Folk, a suggestion that was received without enthusiasm.

Bryan felt himself aggrieved when Clark opposed the measure, then agitating Congress, for an investigation of the "money trust." "There had not been a campaign in which I was a candidate," said Bryan, "that I would not have been elected, but for the money trust." Yet Champ Clark had voted against the investigation. How could Bryan help but regard this course with suspicion?

Neither did the Missouri platform meet with his approval.

"It is painfully incomplete," he wrote in *The Commoner*. "Speaker Clark owes it to the Democracy of the nation to supplement it and bring it up-to-date."[13] But when Hearst asserted that Bryan and the Speaker of the House held opposing views on most political issues, Bryan replied by reviewing the work of Congress, noting how much of it he approved. Curiously enough, he did not mention Clark at all.[14] And Arthur Mullen, Clark's campaign manager, is responsible for the statement that at Bryan's birthday party in 1912 it was made apparent that "the whole game was to knife Clark."[15] However that may be, it is certain that never once after his return from Jamaica did Bryan come forth in unreserved praise of any act or word of the Speaker of the House; and when the Nebraska delegates were instructed for Clark the notice in *The Commoner* took the form of an inconspicuous paragraph on page two.[16]

In the Republican party division, not harmony, was the watchword. Roosevelt had flung his hat into the ring in February and was wrestling with LaFollette for leadership of the Progressives, while they vied in their efforts to butcher the amiable Taft. Bryan attended the Chicago convention as a newspaper correspondent. The Coliseum was filled with "red-faced, perspiring men . . . coats off and flashing fists . . . pummeling each other. The sultry air was charged with dynamite."[17] Bryan looked on as the Roosevelt delegates were jockeyed out of the convention on technicalities, while the few who were allowed to remain refused to vote. His orator's soul must have thrilled to Roosevelt's war cry: "We stand at Armageddon and we battle for the Lord!" —and he wondered, perhaps, why he hadn't thought of it first.

Never before in American politics [he wrote] has a committee witnessed such a scene: a man, one of the most forceful figures of his time, twice a President . . . contending against an administration that he created, for the honor of a Republican nomination.[18]

But the party organization, controlled by the conservative interests, was too strong even for that strong fighter, and before the end Bryan saw how things would go. Taft was going to be nominated and Roosevelt would run on an independent ticket; and with a split in the Republican ranks the Presidency was within the grasp of the Democrats, provided they had the wisdom to choose a progressive. His consternation may therefore be imagined when Josephus Daniels telephoned him from Baltimore that Alton B. Parker, that darling of the conservatives, had been recommended as temporary chairman of the Democratic convention.

He promptly sent a telegram of protest to the Democratic National Committee, which was ignored. But it took more than the Democratic National Committee to stop Bryan once he got started. His next move was to ascertain which of the Presidential aspirants stood with him on this issue and to what extent. To find out, he sent the following telegram to Governor Foss of Massachusetts, Governor Marshall of Indiana, Governor Baldwin of Connecticut, Governor Wilson of New Jersey, Governor Burke of North Dakota and Champ Clark:

In the interest of harmony I suggested to the sub-committee of the Democratic National Committee the advisability of recommending as temporary chairman some progressive acceptable to the leading progressive candidates for the presidential nomination. . . . Eight members of the sub-committee, however, agreed upon not only a reactionary but upon the one Democrat who, among those not candidates for the presidential nomination, is in the eyes of the public most conspicuously identified with the reactionary element of the party. I shall be pleased to join with you and your friends in opposing this selection by the full committee or by the Convention. Kindly answer here.

"Burke of North Dakota," Bryan wrote later, "sent the only explicit acceptance of the challenge offered by the Wall Street crowd. . . . Clark's answer was a straddle. . . . Governor Wilson's telegram, while not as direct as I would have liked, began with a sentence that led the delegates to accept it as a promise to oppose the Parker candidacy; which his delegates did."[19]

The sentence was: "You are quite right."

Armed with these replies and too impatient to wait for the final vote on Taft at Chicago, William Jennings left for Baltimore. With him were his daughter Ruth, his brother Charley, and his wife, fine looking and dignified, shedding on all "her motherly, encompassing smile, as serene as the prairie on a fine spring morning."[20]

The ride from the station to the Belvedere Hotel was punctuated by ovations from the crowd, in holiday mood. Baltimore was gay as Donnybrook Fair.[21] The Clark men had brought with them the appealing ditty:

> I don' keer if he is a houn'—
> You gotta quit kickin' my dawg aroun'.

The Wilson cry was appropriately a college yell: "We want Wilson! We want Wilson!"

But the man in the alpaca coat was not concerned with the byplay. He was scanning the field for the best progressive chairman to lead this progressive convention, and the final choice was Senator John Kern, Bryan's running mate in 1908.

The sessions began on Tuesday, June twenty-fifth. In the flag-draped armoury the delegates gathered, tense, expectant, and warm. Cardinal Gibbons called down the blessing of God upon the gathering, and on the platform behind him Bryan stood, "with closed eyes. He swayed noticeably, almost alarmingly, from side to side, and from time to time his lips were seen to move as the Cardinal's prayer went on. . . . The sympathy of many who watched went out to him, even those who were not in accord with his purposes. It was a scarred and heroic warrior who was about to go on the field of battle."[22]

He had not long to wait. The first business of the convention was the selection of its temporary chairman. The committee had the honour to present the name of Judge Parker. William Jennings Bryan arose to speak:

Mr. Chairman and gentlemen of the Convention: I rise to place in nomination for the office of temporary chairman of this

Convention the name of the Hon. John W. Kern of Indiana. . . . If any of you ask me for my credentials, if any of you inquire why I, a mere delegate to this Convention from one of the smaller states, should presume to present a name and ask you to accept it in place of the name . . . presented, I beg to tell you, if it needs to be told, that in three campaigns I have been the champion of the Democratic party's principles, and in three campaigns I have received the vote of six millions and a half of Democrats. . . . This is an epoch-making Convention. . . . John W. Kern has been faithful. . . . My friends . . . I appeal to you. Let the commencement of this Convention be such a commencement that the Democrats of this country may raise their heads among their fellows and say: "The Democratic party is true to the people. You cannot frighten it with your Ryans nor buy it with your Belmonts. . . ." We have been traveling in the wilderness. We have now come in sight of the promised land. During all the weary hours of darkness, progressive Democracy has been the people's pillar of fire by night. I pray you, delegates, now the dawn has come, do not rob our party of the right so well earned to be the people's pillar of cloud by day.

Having loosed his fiery shaft among the embattled plutocrats, he sat down to watch the conflagration

Kern was instantly on his feet, proposing that both he and Parker withdraw their names in the interests of harmony and leave the way free for a compromise candidate. He, John W. Kern, will withdraw, leaving the way open for a progressive candidate. He pauses dramatically to wait for Parker's reply—the hall is in a dead, expectant hush—but no reply comes. There is a slight buzz as one or two appeal to Parker. But Parker sits adamant. "You cannot expect victory if you humiliate the man who led your forces four years ago . . . you may kill him, but you do not commit homicide when you kill him—you commit suicide." If the fight is to go on, says Kern, there is but one man to lead it: William Jennings Bryan.

Bryan leaves his name in nomination.

The vote is: Parker 578, Bryan 509.

Have the Democrats committed homicide or suicide or what?

Whatever they have done, William Jennings is quite satisfied with his "defeat." For, winning or losing, he has given notice to the whole country that a fight is on in the convention and the issue is the people versus Wall Street.

In the hall the uproar is so great that Parker cannot make his speech. The crowd walks out on him. The convention adjourns until next day.

The early morning papers are on the streets announcing once more that William Jennings Bryan is dead. Back in his hotel William Jennings is not sure about that. The telegrams are beginning to come in. The people are speaking. "The fear of the people is the beginning of wisdom," William Jennings is to say soon now. And who should know better than he?

The influence he was exerting threatened to be more powerful than was expected, and the Clark men decided that a gesture of good will from them would do no harm. Will Mr. Bryan accept the permanent chairmanship? Mr. Bryan declined with thanks. That job was destined for Ollie James, a Clark man and a friend of Bryan's, whom Wilson, in a telephone conversation with Bryan from Sea Girt, had also endorsed.

At three o'clock next morning, while an exhausted William Jennings was preparing for bed, brother Charley, liaison officer, scout, and messenger boy extraordinary, brought in disagreeable news. William Jennings listens to brother Charley, but he does not stop getting ready for bed. Charley tells him that he has heard on good authority that there has been a deal between the Clark forces and the New York delegation, whereby the New Yorkers will go to Clark on the second ballot. The first is to go to Harmon, for whom they are instructed. All along the assumption has been that their second choice was Underwood of Alabama.[23] But the two important candidates have been badgering the New Yorkers for their votes. McCombs, Wilson's campaign manager, is obsessed with the idea that he cannot succeed until he arranges that Wilson get those valuable votes. But Wilson won't trade. Clark has done it. The New Yorkers are going to Clark.

William Jennings takes it all in, but doesn't stop preparing for bed. He has heard most of it from friendly delegates
in private conferences.[24] Charley rattles on. He says that if
such a deal is pulled off the public will abandon Democracy
and elect Roosevelt. He has a scheme. "Introduce," he says,
"a resolution to throw out of the Convention Morgan, Ryan
and Belmont and all their henchmen."[25] That will put the
Clark men in a box, for if they resent it they stand convicted.
If they don't resent it, out the objectionable delegates go
and Clark will be deprived of their votes. A neat scheme,
what? "I will call a conference of the progressive leaders at
seven A.M.," says Charley. To do this sort of thing one must
have support. There may be a riot.

"Go ahead!" says W. J., untying his shoes.

All next day Bryan was in committee, working on the
platform. Returning to the hotel in the evening, he found
brother Charley disheartened. He was unable to drum
up active support for his resolutions. The progressive leaders strongly doubted its wisdom. But brother Will was not
so easily frustrated. A version of the proposed resolution is
already in his pocket. He has become firmly convinced that
its introduction will further clarify the issue. Since others are
unwilling to commit themselves he must introduce it himself.

On his way back to the convention for the night session
William Jennings Bryan makes his final decision. He will
introduce it whether his friends think it wise or not. The die
must be cast. The blow must be struck.

But he is still hedged about by uncertainty. As he goes on
the platform someone pulls him by the coat tail and intro-
duces him to Mrs. Taft. He decides that there is no point
in hurting her feelings; so he strikes out a veiled reference
to her husband.[26] Mr. Taft later sent W. J. a letter of thanks
for this characteristic courtesy. And then, after being recognized by Ollie James, he began, "trembling and excited,"[27]
to read:

Resolved, That in this crisis in her party's career and in our
country's history, this Convention sends greetings to the people
of the United States and assures them that the party of Jefferson

and of Jackson is still the champion of popular government and equality before the law. As proof of our fidelity to the people we hereby declare ourselves opposed to the nomination of any candidate for President who is the representative of or under any obligation to J. Pierpont Morgan, Thomas F. Ryan, August Belmont, or any other member of the privilege-hunting and favor-seeking class.

Be It Further Resolved, That we demand the withdrawal from this Convention of any delegates constituting or representing the above-named interests.

The uproar that followed was without parallel. The hall was a bedlam of confusion, of thrusting arms and blazing eyes and shouting voices. Ryan moved to leave, but was restrained by his friends. William Jennings sat like a rock in a gale. Congressman Flood advanced to the foot of the platform. For some reason clear only to himself, Bryan extended his hand in amiable greeting to the gentleman from Virginia.

Flood refused to take the hand. William Jennings Bryan flushed red.

When he succeeded in making himself heard, the Congressman protested against the insult to Virginia in the person of her delegate, Thomas Fortune Ryan, and demanded that the second part of the resolution be withdrawn. As soon as some semblance of order had been restored, the question was debated and Bryan finally agreed to its withdrawal. But the confusion was so extreme that it is doubtful whether many delegates knew that the resolution had been emasculated.

The two thirds rule was suspended, and the voting on the amended resolution began. It got sound support. Even Charlie Murphy's gang, cynically smiling,[28] voted for it, and when the ballots were counted there were 883 for and $201\frac{1}{2}$ against it. Once more Bryan had outmanoeuvered his opponents. He had underscored the point he had made in the struggle over the temporary chairmanship. Nothing could have given him greater pleasure.

On Friday the balloting for the nomination began, with

Champ Clark leading Wilson by over a hundred votes. Harmon and Underwood were the runners-up. No dark horse was apparent, nor had either outstanding candidate a clear advantage as yet. For nine ballots there was little in the way of significant change, but on the tenth New York shifted to Clark—a not unexpected move—and at that signal Bryan entered the convention hall. Committee work was put aside and he settled down to fight the issue to a conclusion. The two blows he had struck had not served to put his opponents out of the running, so he prepared a third and, as it eventually proved, final one.

Bryan started out to defeat Clark—of that there is no question. But when he was disaffected from his old friend is hard to say. His gradual retreat had gone on for months, but had always been conducted behind a screen of generalities that could be interpreted as objective criticisms or warnings or what not. Even in convention he did not directly attack Clark—which embittered Clark to an excessive degree, for he could have rebutted direct attack but could say nothing effective against Bryan's innuendoes. Bryan's line was to attack Clark's friends and supporters. To this task he now addressed himself in earnest.

When he emerged from the committee room to find out what all the shouting was about, Bryan found the Clark enthusiasts doing a "snake dance around the room that lasted fifty minutes. They were mad with excitement and delight."

And no wonder. For when at one A. M. the results of the tenth ballot were announced, their candidate had achieved a majority with eleven votes to spare. Never since the days of Van Buren had a Democratic nominee polled a majority and failed to win the nomination. In the reckoning of the Clark forces their man had the prize in his pocket.

But William Jennings, taking his seat for the first time with Nebraska delegates, was not so sure. He had accepted instructions for Clark with the mental reservation that a shift could be made if circumstances dictated. Nebraska's second choice he considered to be Woodrow Wilson. Above

all he did not intend to vote for a candidate who commanded
the votes of the New York delegation. It was against the
New York group that he intended to make his fight. Clark
became, therefore, but a pawn in his game. Once he started
his final fight he stuck to his post with dogged tenacity.
Brother Charley fed him sandwiches and a friendly door-
man provided water.

On Saturday there seemed small prospect of an immediate
change. McCombs took fright and attempted to get Wilson's
permission to release his delegates and instruct them for
another man. But while Wilson was willing enough to concede defeat if need be, he was not willing to compromise his
supporters with instructions. But before McCombs could
act, less-agitated Wilson men frustrated him. William Gibbs
McAdoo took a hand at keeping McCombs out of the way.

Bryan made his decision during the thirteenth ballot. He
knew that Wilson was only to be kept in the running by
the inquiry of his trusted advisers, and that one of them
was already in a mood to throw up the sponge. As things
stood, the next logical step was to deadlock the convention and then decide what was to be done.

When Nebraska is called on the fourteenth ballot, Bryan
rises and asks permission to explain his vote. Permission
is granted.

"As long as New York's ninety votes are recorded for Mr.
Clark, I withhold my vote from him," he begins. That is as
far as he gets with his first effort. The direction of his thinking is sufficiently obvious. The convention goes into an uproar, but Bryan is a good waiter and eventually he gains the
attention of the unwilling mob and completes his statement:

... The vote of the State of New York in this Convention rep-
resents the will of one man—Charles F. Murphy—and he repre-
sents the influences that dominated the Republican Convention
at Chicago and are trying to dominate this Convention. I shall
withhold my vote from Mr. Clark as long as New York's vote is
recorded for him. And the position that I take in regard to Mr.
Clark I will take in regard to any other candidate whose name is
now or may be before the Convention....

With the understanding that I shall stand ready to withdraw my vote from the one for whom I am going to cast it whenever New York casts her vote for him, I cast my vote for Nebraska's second choice, Governor Wilson.

Barely had he finished when hisses and catcalls assailed him. He betrayed not the slightest emotion. His calm was tremendously impressive. Had he not in recent weeks told an inquisitive reporter that he had closely studied the technique of the Sphinx? There he sat, "in the seat of a delegate with his palm-leaf fan, without a tremor in his finger . . . with a little of the consciousness of power playing at the corners of his mouth and with the light springing in his eyes as the few who came to greet him touched his shoulder, [he] was the figure of a master. . . . Those who reviled him reviled a figure of stone. . . . Mr. Bryan had beaten the 'gang' to a frazzle and he still wore a smile."[29]

But in spite of the intense emotional outburst neither side scored a very obvious victory for the moment. Wilson gained five votes and Clark dropped one and a half. The reverberations, however, were what counted. Bryan was always skilful in manipulating events with an eye on the future.

However stern and secretive, this sphinx had never been known as a man of stone. And when the Clark men took their revenge for this terrific affront to their leader they touched him, by design, in a tender spot. Just as the thirty-third ballot was recorded they brought a banner into the hall inscribed: "I have known Mr. Clark eighteen years. He is absolutely incorruptible and his life is above reproach. Never in all these years have I known him to be on any side of a question that was not the side of the people. William Jennings Bryan in 1910."

This banner flaunted in his face and turned about so all might see provoked him to rage. He attempted to get permission to speak, but was denied a hearing. The Missouri delegates shook their fists at him and ill concealed their desire to finish him once and for all. The police surrounded him and the Texas delegation rushed to his defence. So violent was his excitement that he began to bleed from the nose. And then, to heap insult on injury, Stanchfield of New York chose this moment to denounce him as a "money-grubbing, selfish, office-seeking, favor-hunting, publicity-hunting marplot from Nebraska."[30]

The offending banner was ordered from the hall.

The victim, of course, was Clark. He was Bryan's enemy from now on. The gauge of battle was shortly to be thrown. When Clark came up from Washington that Saturday night he called in William Randolph Hearst and together they prepared a statement and a challenge:

Any man who would enter an alliance with any selfish interest or privileged class of this country to gain the nomination for the presidency is unworthy of the presidency and of the speakership of the House. If I have not entered into such an alliance, then the Democrat, however distinguished, who wantonly charges me with this act is a traitor to the Democratic party and to his professed friendship to me.

... With William J. Bryan and his charge made in the Convention to-day, the issue is proof or retraction. I shall expect him to meet the issue.

In their excitement neither of these tacticians recognized that Bryan had made a masked attack on Clark. He could easily deny that his shafts were aimed at the man who now announced himself to be the victim. Had not Bryan distinctly stated that he withdrew his support from Clark because he had accepted the votes of the New York delegation? Bryan took the obvious course, and ignored Clark's challenge. Nothing could upset his political sagacity.

But what was to be the next move? A Sunday recess afforded the gossipers a wonderful opportunity. Telegrams poured in and showed beyond a doubt that the rank and file of the Democrats had taken Bryan's word for it, that the fight was against plutocracy. Yet, while this poll of sentiment was useful, it hardly gave indication of how the deadlock was to be broken.

Mrs. Bryan has since written that she constantly urged

her husband to take the nomination himself. Such a course was undoubtedly a great temptation to Bryan. But beyond the dubious evidence of McCombs, we have nothing to show that he ever gave indication that he had himself in mind when he faced the Associated Press representatives to discuss the deadlock. It was, he admitted, a situation that seemed to demand the springing of a dark horse. With his usual facility he named off a few who might be groomed for the position: Ollie James, O'Gorman of New York, Culberson of Texas, and Kern. He dwelt on the fact that Kern had a good chance of getting the six and one half million votes that were nominally Bryan's. But beyond that he gave no indication of what was in his mind.

McCombs, however, felt that he knew what was in Bryan's mind. He felt sure that Bryan was after the nomination himself. Subsequently he developed his suspicions into a sizeable myth. At any rate his suspicions were the spur to a final appeal to Wilson to trade and win.

He proposed that Wilson should agree that, whoever did go into the Cabinet, Bryan should not be one of the number. If he could make that promise known, McCombs was sure he could get the necessary votes to put Wilson across. But Wilson refused to give any such assurance. He was not thinking of Cabinets at the moment, and certainly wasn't going to tie his hands so far in advance.

No trading was necessary. As the balloting dragged on Wilson made a slow but steady gain. The final blow to Clark's hopes was given by a man who apparently acted with a view of defeating Bryan's ambitions. Roger Sullivan of Illinois shared with McCombs the feeling that Bryan was seeking to manipulate the convention for his personal advantage. To make such a conclusion impossible he threw the Illinois delegation to Wilson.

On the forty-sixth ballot Woodrow Wilson was nominated.

No one is warmer in his felicitations or more heartfelt in his expression of delight than William Jennings Bryan. "To-night I come with joy to surrender into the hands of one chosen by this convention a standard which I have carried in three campaigns, and I challenge my enemies to declare that it has ever been lowered."

Bryan had defeated the New York delegation hands down. He had so manipulated the convention that he had changed the prevailing sentiment from conservatism to progressivism. He had done so by a series of dramatic moves that necessitated the sacrificing of an old-time friend who, henceforth, was a bitter enemy. But he had accomplished his end, and he went home satisfied.

CHAPTER XXVII

IN THE CABINET

IN SPITE of the fact that Mrs. Bryan's health was a cause for anxiety, her husband devoted his full energies to Wilson's campaign when it was launched. Mrs. Bryan did not accompany her husband on tour—a course traditional with her—but sought to regain her strength. She fought a losing battle, and before the campaign was over underwent an operation in a Washington hospital, which she did not allow William Jennings to know about.

It was obvious to all who took part in it, that the contest was between Wilson and Roosevelt, and Wilson's method of attack must have seemed strange to Bryan. Wilson dealt almost exclusively in abstractions and generalities. He did not attempt a popular appeal. Moreover, when Roosevelt was shot in October, Wilson cancelled all his speaking dates until his adversary should recover. Bryan could not see why Roosevelt's injury should protect him from criticism, and went right on criticizing—not the policies of the ex-President which were so largely his own, but his sincerity—on the ground that his conversion to the true belief had come too late in the day to be really convincing.

Bryan averaged ten speeches a day for seven weeks and was rewarded by the triumph of his party for the first time in twenty-odd years. Bursting with happiness and pride, he made a speech to his fellow townsmen.

"I am happier than Governor Wilson," he said, "for his joy is repressed by a sense of responsibility, while I am happy and free."[1]

His happy freedom was not for long. Wilson, despite his opinion of Bryan as "impractical and notoriously mistaken in his personal judgments,"[2] realized that he could hardly

form a Democratic Cabinet without including the man whose
support had done so much to put him where he was. With
House he first debated the possibility of giving Bryan a
foreign post, but the final decision fell on the position of
Secretary of State, "in order to have him at Washington
and in harmony with the Administration, rather than outside and possibly in a critical attitude."

The post was offered to Bryan in December and tentatively accepted.[3] It was characteristic that a moral concern
was the one thing that troubled him. Did Mr. Wilson think
that his inability to sanction the serving of intoxicating
liquors at diplomatic functions would interfere with his usefulness? Mr. Wilson believed it to be a matter that Mr.
Bryan must decide for himself. William Jennings decided
that his usefulness would not be destroyed by his being a
Prohibitionist. The question of office settled, he left for
Florida to rest.

The only flaw in his happiness was his broken friendship
with Champ Clark, which he would have liked to mend
but couldn't. "I have not accused Mr. Clark of wrongful
acts," he said, "but merely of failure to act," and he strongly
advocated his reëlection as Speaker of the House. Clark
would have nothing to do with the olive branch.

"He lied me out of the presidency," was his bitter rejoinder
to all efforts at conciliation, and at a dinner given to them
both, after Bryan was established at Washington, Thomas
Marshall describes how "Clark would address himself to
the host, who in return would translate for Mr. Bryan;
and Mr. Bryan would respond to the host, who in turn would
translate for Mr. Clark."[4]

Colonel House made a trip to Florida to consult with
Bryan about the personnel of the Cabinet and other appointments. The President-elect must have been glad to
hear that his Secretary of State showed "no disposition to
interfere even with his own Department," though he expressed a modest wish that he might name his first assistant and emphasized the wisdom of including a Catholic
and perhaps a Jew in the official family.

Again it was a moral point on which he felt strongly: the unfitness of Charles W. Eliot as Ambassador to China, "for Eliot was a Unitarian and did not believe in the divinity of Christ, and the new Chinese civilization was founded upon a Christ."[5]

These were minor matters. On the whole, House found him "as pleased as a child with a new toy. He is really a fine man, full of democratic simplicity, earnest, patriotic and of a fervently religious nature." And he hoped that much good would come from the influence of Mrs. Bryan.[6] House believed she had worked on her husband in favour of Wilson for some time before the convention.

It was a significant trio that stood before the Senate at the Inauguration: "Taft, standard-bearer of a vanquished party after sixteen years of power; Bryan, persistant plodder of progressive Democracy, thrice defeated, accepting a commission from a new chieftain; and Wilson, the man of the hour, victorious."[7] The persistent plodder must have whispered "Amen," as Wilson said: "I summon all honest men, all patriotic, all forward-looking men to my side. God helping me, I will not fail them, if they but counsel and sustain me."

But Bryan, who as a schoolboy had been elected vice president of his class, was still in second place!

From the Senate to the White House the car of Mr. and Mrs. Bryan followed closely behind the President's car, and the effect was tremendous. ". . . The people would recognize Will," wrote Mrs. Bryan, "and an . . . outburst would arise; women shouting and waving, men waving their hats and shouting, hundreds clapping their hands. I never expect to see such an ovation again."

The first Cabinet meeting on March fifth was informal, since the secretaries had not been sworn into office. It gathered at eleven o'clock in the morning. Bryan was full to the brim with enthusiasm and wit. After Wilson, he was the centre of all eyes. Little did he realize that there were those of his associates who regarded him with suspicion and even hostility. In the Cabinet there were Houston and

Garrison, with whom he would find himself at odds. And outside the Cabinet two of Wilson's closest friends would do
their best to discredit him—House and Page. But now
William Jennings asked for nothing better than an opportunity to bring to Democracy overwhelming successes in
governing the country. "It is apparent that Mr. Bryan
is setting out to follow the President's lead. He is obviously
gentle-natured, unsophisticated and deferential to the office
—unless he is playing a game," observed suspicious Mr.
Houston.[8]

Next day at the regular Cabinet meeting the question of
patronage came up. In reply to an observation of Postmaster
General Burleson, President Wilson said: "It makes no
difference whether a man stood for me or not. All I want is
a man who is fit for the place, a man who stands for clean
government and progressive policies." To Bryan this was
astonishing doctrine. It seemed to him that it would include
Republicans among those who might hope for appointments.
One of his most curious anomalies was his continued support
of the spoils system, in which he was in entire agreement
with Andrew Jackson. He was, without knowing it, to make
many missteps in carrying out his policy, and even the
later publication of a latter in which he avowed his intention of filling all the appointive offices in his jurisdiction with
"deserving Democrats" did not shake his equanimity.[9]

The afternoon of the day the first Cabinet meeting was
held, he asked Secretary Houston if he could find a place in
his Department for "Coin" Harvey![10] Harvey was not appointed.

William Jennings had a difficult problem on his hands.
Only a few in the Cabinet had actively engaged in politics,
and men like Houston had, in fact, no experience whatever
with practical politics. William Jennings, on the contrary,
had six million followers, and it was inevitable that he would
have to do something for the more "deserving." His apart-
ment at the New Willard took on the aspect of an employment agency, with Mrs. Bryan as directress. The day following the Inauguration she writes, "I spent the time making

notes of the wishes of various seekers and lists of their qualifications. One point which seemed particularly in evidence
was that they had 'been with Bryan from the beginning'
. . . it suddenly became the acme of respectability to have
supported him in 1896."[11]

So great was the press that his wife was unable to ad-
company William Jennings when he was sworn in as Secretary of State. But a huge bouquet of American Beauties
from Philander Knox was there to greet him, and his son-in-
law stood by his side. The latter received the pen with which
Bryan formally signed his name in the presence of several
members of the permanent staff. It was the second Federal
office that Bryan had held. When he had been elected to the
first in 1890, he had hardly expected to have to wait so
long for the next.

The round of social festivities quickly engulfed the Bryans.
As a measure of precaution William Jennings always ate a
dinner at home before going out to a public banquet. The
pace was a bit trying on both of the Bryans, and they were
not sorry when it eased off. William Jennings was working
hard. Mrs. Bryan went up to bed at ten, but William Jen-
nigs stayed up late. Nevertheless he was up and about at
seven.[12] He was putting in long days at the office, too, and
while the President took time off to play golf, Bryan stuck
doggedly to his duties.[13] He did not lose any of his infor-
mality under the strain of holding office, and as the hot
weather came an observer discovered him "shirt-sleeved
(literally), with handkerchief tucked in collar, and
a big palm-leaf fan in hand, he sat in the Secretary's
high-backed chair like a Hottentot chief on his tropical
throne."[14]

At the first luncheon given by Bryan to the diplomatic
corps, he arose, looking "pale but handsome," and announced
that family tradition and principle made it impossible for
him to sanction the serving of intoxicating liquors at any
table over which he presided. No wines, therefore, would
be served. The guests took the announcement in good part
and the Russian Ambassador, having been forewarned and

fortified, was particularly agreeable. At the suggestion of the hotel steward they drank grape juice.

When the story got out William Jennings was the butt of the derisive as well as the righteously indignant, and the stir created was out of all proportion to the significance of the incident. He may have been comforted by Bernard Shaw's observation that his only mistake had been to serve anything but water.[15] At any rate, whatever its effect on others may have been, it seemed to do him no harm with the gentlemen of the embassies, with most of whom he was always a favourite. Some of them "went out of their way to express their admiration of Mr. Bryan's simplicity, of his absolute candor, of the sincerity he showed in official intercourse. They saw that he was a dreamer, an idealist; that his heart ran away with his head; that he was lacking in guile; that he spoke to them truthfully; and these qualities they appreciated because they [were] so rare in their experience."[16] And if there was a quality of indulgence in their liking, it was none the less real for that.

He proved more offensive to American snobs than to foreign diplomats.

As early as the second Cabinet meeting, held on March eleventh, Wilson read a statement, prepared by himself, regarding the Latin American situation. "It clearly indicated that the President was going to be his own Secretary of State," thought Houston. "Bryan listened with a smile on his face and nodded approval as the President read."[17] It may have been something of a relief to Bryan—this strong formulation of ideas he could endorse—for when he was asked for a statement on his foreign policy he had nothing more specific to offer than the sentiments of his Indianapolis speech of 1900[18]—a pæan of praise to the moral superiority of our country over every other.

The fact that the Secretary of State found himself in agreement with the President on the questions first arising to trouble the administration helped to maintain his sense of power. An early problem was about a loan to China. The Morgan banking interests had tentatively arranged to take part in a Six-Power loan to that country, with the assent of the previous administration. When they called upon Bryan to find out what the stand of the Democrats would be, he first asked them for time to inform himself more fully, as he had "no very clear notion of the proposal."[19] Having informed himself in consultation with the President, he issued the decision that the government could not support the loan, whose terms involved the possibility of policies unacceptable to it. The Morgan banks in consequence refused to take part in the loan. The move was in effect a repudiation of Knox's dollar diplomacy. "The crucifixion of China upon a cross of gold," wrote the *Literary Digest* approvingly, "would naturally be repugnant to an administration whose foreign affairs are in the hands of our present Secretary of State."[20] Curiously enough Wilson's method of dealing with this matter was later admitted to be a mistake. He released the administration's statement from his own office instead of through the State Department. This method gave an erroneous impression of the part the President was playing in foreign affairs at the moment. It helped those hostile to Bryan to conclude he was a mere figurehead when it came to really important matters. On this occasion, and to an even greater extent later, President Wilson took an active part at crucial moments, but his control was not constant, and while it may have been decisive was not sufficiently active until well into 1915 to get Colonel House's entire approval.

But the project nearest to Bryan's heart was that of arranging a world-embracing series of peace treaties. Like most of his policies this one can be traced back to remote beginnings. It originally was an extension of his scheme for composing labour disputes through arbitration. One of Bryan's earliest public references to the idea was made on the occasion of the Russo-Japanese Treaty of 1905, when he had suggested that Roosevelt make the concluding of such treaties the next step in his foreign policy. He had returned to the matter in London in 1906. It was natural, therefore, that he should seek to make his programme as Secretary of State revolve around the conclusion of such treaties. Fortunately Wilson was sympathetic to such an arrangement. The plan was also approved by the State Committee on Foreign Relations before being submitted to foreign governments.

In one very important respect the Bryan treaties were revolutionary in conception.

Inspired by a belief that any dispute could be amicably settled, given sufficient time and calm for deliberation, he went a step farther in these treaties than any previous worker for peace. "The plan differed from that of Secretary Root's arbitration treaties, not only in the procedure called for but in the fact that it applied to all kinds of questions, not excepting those of national honour and vital interests."[21]

Previous to Bryan's advent in international diplomacy, national honour and vital interests had been reserved as good and sufficient causes for war, no matter how willing nations might be to arbitrate their disputes on lesser matters.

In a little memorandum, entitled "Mr. Bryan's Plan," the President laid the matter before the Cabinet at an early meeting, and the Cabinet approved its provisions.[22] Thus encouraged, William Jennings set to work. He summarized the scheme as follows in *The Commoner:*

(1) Investigation is to follow in all cases where diplomacy fails.
(2) The contracting parties reserve the right to act independently after the investigation.
(3) There is to be no appeal to force until after the investigation.
(4) The commission of investigation is to consist of five members.
    a. One chosen for each country by its citizens.
    b. One chosen by each country from another country.
    c. One chosen by agreement of the two countries.
(5) The investigation must be made and reported upon within a year, unless the contracting parties agree to extend the time.

On April 24, 1913, the proposal was laid formally before the foreign diplomatic representatives at the Department of State and was well received.

Bryan eventually arranged twenty-eight treaties embodying these principles. When eighteen had been concluded he sent them to the Senate for ratification. "I remained in the office of the Clerk of the Senate two days while the treaties were being discussed," he wrote in his memorandum on the subject, "answering questions as they arose."[23] From this ordeal he emerged victorious in all but two cases, and even after the World War broke out he persisted in his efforts to get new countries on his roll. Great Britain and France signed after they went to war. Germany persistently refused—a fact which had an important bearing on later events.

On the occasion of the signing of one of his treaties Bryan gave the representative a paperweight fashioned of steel in the form of a ploughshare. Not even the jeers of Roosevelt, who persisted in saying that no country would observe the treaty should its interests be involved, could diminish Bryan's pleasure. Roosevelt, Bryan pointed out, was abnormal on the subject of war."[24]

Before long Bryan found himself in his old position of ideals versus practice. California had thrown the Japanese question into politics. The Japanese were acquiring too much land for their truck farming to please her politicians and a bill, designed to curtail their rights of purchase, was presented to the Legislature. It provided that aliens not eligible to citizenship might acquire land only according to the terms of the treaty existing between the United States and their country, and, since this move made the issue an international one, the Secretary of State was obliged to take notice of it.

The Cabinet decided that Bryan should go to California and make an investigation on the ground, and somewhat reluctantly William Jennings departed for the West. He found the situation complicated by state politics and, after a series of consultations with local leaders, he met the Legislature behind closed doors and presented the government's case. Bryan acquitted himself well under the ordeal and revealed his diplomatic skill in his cautious reply to a question regarding the use of a certain phrase in the bill: "I would oppose the insertion of that phrase, unless the President has a different opinion. In that case I might have another opinion."

He doesn't seem to have accomplished very much, for the bill was passed and Japan, deeply resentful, sent a note of protest, demanding that the Federal government declare the California bill invalid on the ground of discrimination and violation of the existing treaty. Certain members of the Cabinet were up in arms, and so high did the feeling run that the possibility of war with Japan was debated.

Secretary of War Garrison suggested the strategic movement of ships in the Eastern waters, declaring that his board of army and navy officers were the people competent to pass upon such matters. Then Bryan "flared up . . . red in the face . . . and thundered that we were discussing not how to wage war but how not to get into war."[25] The President settled the dispute by ruling that the ships in Eastern waters should stay where they were, and Bryan was authorized to see the Japanese Ambassador unofficially and ask that the note be modified. This he did and at the end of the interview Mr. Chinda remarked: "I suppose, Mr. Secretary, this decision is final." With a smile, William Jennings arose and extending his hand answered: "There is nothing final between friends."

This characteristic reply made an excellent impression.

At a White House garden party a few days later he thanked Secretary Garrison for keeping his temper on the occasion of their recent difference and told him that there wasn't going to be any war.

"I've seen the Japanese Ambassador," he said, "and I'm letting the old man down easy."[26]

The old man must have appreciated it, for the Japanese note was revised and at Wilson's request (so David Lawrence alleges), the British government used its influence under the Anglo-Japanese treaty to allay Japan's indignation against the United States.[27]

The Secretary of State did not feel it beneath his dignity

to make some Chautauqua engagements for that first summer during which he held office, and he was certainly un-
prepared for the storm of derisive criticism brought down
on his head by what seemed to him the most natural step
in the world. He was an Antæus whose reviving contact
was the great mass of the common people. Give up his lectures? Nothing in the situation seemed to demand that.
Secretary Redfield, with whom he had discussed the point,
later made the talk a text for a discussion of the niggardli-
ness of the government. And it was indeed true that "No
concourse of ambassadors, however splendiferous, no Washington company, however brilliant, and no mere desk job,
however distinguished, could compensate Mr. Bryan for
continued absence from these beloved scenes."[28]

His opponents might laugh at him for "a barnstormer,
playing one-night stands, preceded by the magic lantern
and followed by the hurdy-gurdy man and his dancing
bear."[29] They might find him a sufferer from "a violent attack
of his old complaint, foot-and-mouth disease,"[30] but they
didn't budge him!

"I find it necessary to lecture in order to supplement the
salary which I receive from the government, the salary not
being sufficient to cover my expenses."

Senator Bristow of Kansas introduced a resolution, calling
upon the President to find out what salary would enable
the Secretary of State to cover his expenses; and the New
York *Sun*, an old enemy, remarked that with an income of
$12,000 a year a man worth from a quarter to half a million
might manage to live in Jeffersonian simplicity, if he tried.[31]

In replying to his critics, William Jennings ignored the
thrusts at his accumulated wealth (which was not in very
productive enterprises), maintaining the discussion on a
loftier level. "In aristocratic circles the common ways of
the common people are regarded with contempt, but among
the masses the earning of a living is not a disgrace, and min-
gling with the multitude is not a cause of reproach.... The
forum is not below the level of official life, it is not stepping
down to go from the desk to the platform."[32]

But he did not play his trump card then—another example of his consideration of Woodrow Wilson. He did not let it be known that the President approved of his Chautauqua work. Nor did he become petty and point out that Vice President Marshall and Speaker Clark also appeared on the Chautauqua platform while they were in office.

First Japan, now Mexico, harried the Apostle of Peace.

Bryan believed that all the undesirable phases of our policy in Latin America could be traced to intervention on behalf of private enterprise. Stop intervention, he said, and all would be serene. In his Madison Square Garden speech in 1906 he had protested the use of the United States Navy for the collection of private debts.

Mexico, as usual, was in a ferment. When Huerta, just as the Taft administration closed, resorted to violence and seized the reins of government, the question of his recognition by the United States arose. The Cabinet was divided, but Bryan agreed with Wilson that no stable rule could be established under his leadership, and recognition was refused, despite the pressure brought to bear by England and other foreign powers.

Sir William Tyrrell (sent over especially to deal with the Mexican affair) emerged from his interview with Bryan convinced that he was a sincere emotionalist but entirely misinformed about British policy.[33] But Bryan was not so much misinformed as too thoroughly convinced that British policy was absolutely controlled by the oil interests. As it turned out, the British were ready to follow the American lead, if they could admit the point Wilson wished to make. Colonel House arranged that Sir William discuss the matter with Wilson and the upshot was that the British withdrew their support from Huerta—a final blow to his prestige.

A much more exacting test of Bryan's generalized policy toward Latin America came with regard to Santo Domingo and Nicaragua. Perhaps he was really oblivious of where his course led. Perhaps he believed that the beneficial end justified the questionable means. Perhaps he was overridden by the will of his chief. Perhaps it was a combination of all these things. At any rate, the unhappy country of Santo Domingo was never unhappier than during his tenure of office. He sent there as minister one James Mark Sullivan, a "deserving Democrat" of shady character, who was hand in glove with a financial adventurer named Jarvis, in control of the Banco Nacional. Such complete havoc did they make of the financial and economic situation, resulting in bloodshed and misrule, that Bryan violated the sovereignty of the state by sending there a group of American agents—dubbed by the Dominicans "the twenty-nine tourists"—to supervise the elections of December, 1913. "The step so taken constituted the first evidence of formal intervention."[34] Eventually, matters reached such a pass that Sullivan was recalled and an investigation ordered, that brought to light a career so scandalous as to reflect painfully on Bryan's judgment in making the appointment.

For Nicaragua the Secretary of State blandly arranged a treaty called the Bryan-Chamorro Treaty of 1914, putting that country on the same basis, so far as financial transactions went, with the States of the Union. Previous American diplomacy in that region, according to the *Times*, looked like "ten-cent" diplomacy by comparison. "If all goes well, we shall soon see the dawn of a new era in our Latin American relations. But it will be due to a cheerful acceptance and amplification by President Wilson's administration of the much condemned dollar diplomacy of his predecessors."[35] The treaty was negotiated with American marines in the country and not only concerned financial matters but also secured to the United States the rights to the Nicaragua canal route. Even so conservative a Senator as Elihu Root condemned the affair. When Honduras and Salvador objected to the treaty, Bryan believed it was from motives of envy and magnanimously offered to negotiate similar treaties with them. To their explanation that their objections arose from the fact that the treaty abrogated the sovereignty of a sister state, his reply is not recorded. The protesting states carried their objections to the Central America Court of Justice, which sustained their position. But the treaty remained in force. The whole affair served to register upon the mind of the people the impression that Bryan was yielding on matters of principle. Perhaps he was aware of it himself and made minor concessions deliberately in order not to jeopardize his unique opportunity for high and holy service to the people in other fields—the field of peace, for example.

He was pleased with the tariff bill signed in October, and he won a nominal triumph in the matter of currency reform. The necessity for a new system of monetary control had long been recognized—something that would give greater flexibility to the money market. The collaboration of House, Houston, McAdoo, Senator Owen of Oklahoma, and Carter Glass of the House of Representatives finally produced the Federal Reserve Act. It was known that Wilson favoured the idea of having the banks issue notes but regarded with apprehension the effect of such a move on Bryan and his following. He was not left long in doubt.

At the Cabinet discussion William Jennings insisted that all notes should be issued by the government: that any other course would encounter opposition from the Democrats in the House as being contrary to recent political platforms. Having made his point, he added that if his position embarrassed the administration he was willing to resign and refrain from public criticism of the act.[36] After the meeting Wilson summoned Glass to the White House and to the latter's astonishment told him that he wanted "Federal Reserve notes to be obligations of the United States." When Glass pointed out that no government obligation was indicated in the bill, Wilson answered: "Exactly so, Glass, exactly so. If we can hold to the substance of the thing and give the other fellow the shadow, why not do it and thereby save our bill?"[37]

Bryan was delighted. "Mr. President," he said, "we have settled our differences, and you may rely upon me to remain with you to the end of the fight." He was as good as his word. Congressman Henry of Texas led the revolt against the bill and invoked the still magic name of Bryan to sustain his argument. While he was in full swing a letter arrived

Secretary of State William Jennings Bryan
at His Desk in the State Department

(*Photograph from Wide World Photos*)

Brother Charley upon His Formal Acceptance of the Nomination for Vice President by the Democratic Party, 1924, Shaking Hands with Senator E. Hull of Salem, Illinois, a Boyhood Friend of the Bryan Boys.

from Bryan for Glass, who read it aloud to his agitated colleagues:

You are authorized to speak for me and say that I appreciate profoundly the service rendered by the President to the people in the stand he has taken on the fundamental principles involved in currency reform, that I am with him in all the details. If my opinion has influence with anyone called upon to act on this measure, I am willing to assume full responsibility for what I do when I . . . stand by the President and assist in securing the passage of the bill.

It was a direct blow to the Henry group who now shouted that "Bryan doesn't know a damn thing about the provisions of this currency bill."[38] Further to prove his good will, Bryan also, having grown "by degrees into the harmless habit of issuing companion pieces to the public proclamations of the President, gave out a statement to the press which . . . very likely helped to confirm several of his zealous disciples . . . in their purpose to support the bill."[39] When it was passed, Glass wrote Bryan a letter of thanks and congratulation.

Again, in the opinion of the more stiff-necked among the Democrats, Bryan went over to the enemy on the Panama Canal Tolls issue. In 1910 he had advocated that the tolls, if applied to American vessels at all, should do no more than cover operation and maintenance. In 1912 a law had been passed exempting American coastwise vessels from payment of the tolls, and Great Britain attacked it as a violation of the Hay-Pauncefote treaty. Wilson soon grew convinced of the justice of her stand and when Colonel House visited England in July, 1913, he assured Sir Edward Grey privately that the President would work for the repeal of that section of the Panama Canal Act.[40] But since both the Republican and the Democratic platforms had endorsed the principle of exemption for American vessels, the situation was an extremely delicate one to handle. Bryan at first stood solidly on the platform, but was finally persuaded that to preserve international harmony a plank might be ignored.

Besides, he argued, in justifying his change of front, a poll had since been taken of the delegates attending the 1912 Convention and of the 845 answering 682 had been in favour of repeal.[41] Repeal won the day, but only after a debate of twenty hours in the House and a stiff fight that split both parties.

Before very long Mexico began making trouble again. A number of American naval officers landed at Iturbide Bridge in Tampico, in violation of regulations with which they were not acquainted. They were arrested by subordinate Mexican army officials and subsequently released with an apology from the local military commander. The incident, however, was interpreted by Admiral Mayo as a deliberate affront directed by the Huerta party against the United States and he demanded that the Mexicans salute the American flag by way of discipline. Instructed by Huerta, they refused. An account of the affair was telephoned by the State Department to Bryan, who lay sick at home, and he dictated a message supporting Mayo's action.

"Remember," he said, "that the United States can always be depended upon to stand upon its dignity and honour."[42] He then telephoned the message to the President at Hot Springs and was rewarded with the answer: "Exactly what I should have said."[43]

Things had reached this pass when a most untoward incident brought matters to a head. Tumulty, the President's secretary, received a cable at two-thirty in the morning of April twenty-first announcing that a German vessel with arms and ammunition for Huerta would land at Vera Cruz at ten o'clock. Tumulty called up Bryan and Daniels, and after a three-cornered conversation, Bryan telephoned to the President for his opinion.

"Of course, Mr. Bryan," said Wilson, "you understand what drastic action in this matter might ultimately mean to our relations with Mexico." Bryan answered that he did, but still felt that the German steamer should be prevented from landing its cargo for Huerta.[44] Wilson then instructed Daniels to send a wire to Admiral Fletcher saying: "Take

Vera Cruz at once." It may be that Bryan relied too heavily on the assurances of John E. Lind and others who had been sent to Mexico to investigate conditions and who had assured the United States government that Mexicans would resist no move hostile to Huerta. If this had been true, a blow struck at Huerta was a blow struck for both countries. If such was Bryan's belief, he was doomed to disappointment. The Mexicans, despite John Lind, did offer an unorganized resistance at Vera Cruz, the Americans made a confused and awkward landing, and the adventure resulted in relatively heavy fatalities on both sides. To make matters worse, the German ship landed her cargo at another port, and the loss of life accomplished nothing.

Peace treaties to the contrary notwithstanding, William Jennings, to his great dismay, had been involved in something very like war.

But he was comforted. Argentina, Brazil, and Chile arranged a conference between the United States and the Mexican factions at Niagara Falls. As a result of the pressure brought to bear upon him by this conference, coupled with the withdrawal of British support, Huerta was forced into retirement and General Carranza was given a chance to see what he could do with the government of the country. Bryan heaved a sigh of relief when the American troops evacuated Vera Cruz and congratulated himself that war was averted.

During the first half of 1914 he prosecuted his prohibition campaign and came out in favour of Woman Suffrage. "Does woman lack either intelligence or morality?" Evidently not, for the churches were full of them, and the prisons mainly occupied by men.[45] He helped defeat Roger Sullivan's aspirations to the Senate, thereby evening old scores; and his chief pronounced this blessing upon him: "Not only have Mr. Bryan's character, his justice, his sincerity, his Christian principle, made a deep impression upon all with whom he has dealt, but his tact in dealing with men of many sorts, his capacity for business, his mastery of the principle of each matter he has been called upon to deal with, have cleared away many a difficulty. . . . I cannot say what pleasure and profit I myself have taken from close association with Mr. Bryan, or how thoroughly he has seemed to all of us who are associated with him here to deserve not only our confidence but our affectionate admiration."[46]

There is little doubt that William Jennings Bryan and Woodrow Wilson would have continued to travel along the same road had not the World War come to part them. To Bryan its outbreak was absolutely inexplicable in the light of the fact that he had negotiated so many peace treaties. His first reaction was unqualified horror. To Wilson it was both less unexpected and less inexplicable. Colonel House and he had agreed a year before that a war was possible and Wilson explained the fact on the basis of deep-seated economic, racial, and politico-military rivalries. But he did not regard it with any less jaundiced eyes than Bryan. It was the evolution of their standpoints from somewhat common beginnings that parted them. Bryan's first move was to support neutrality; his second, to support all chances for bringing about mediation.

In September he presented his views in a fair and lucid letter to the President:

The European situation distresses me. The slaughter goes on and each day makes it more apparent that it is to be a prolonged struggle. All parties to the conflict declare they did not want war, that they were not responsible for it and that they desire peace —and to make their positions more nearly identical they desire an enduring peace.

. . . The responsibility for continuing the war is just as grave as the responsibility for beginning it, and this responsibility, if pressed upon the consideration of the belligerent nations, might lead them to consent to mediation. . . . The world looks to us to lead the way, and I know your deep desire to render every possible assistance. . . . Both sides seem to entertain the old idea that fear is the only basis upon which peace can rest.

It is not likely that either side will win so complete a victory as to be able to dictate terms, and if either side does win such a victory, it will probably mean preparation for another war. It would seem better to look for a more rational basis of peace.

I believe that a compulsory investigation of disputes before hostilities begin, such as our treaties provide for, would go far toward preventing war; but the most potent of all influences for the promotion of peace is the substitution of friendship for hatred. . . . Mediation would give opportunity for the consideration of all plans, and I see no other way in which these plans can be considered or even proposed, for complete success by either side will make that side feel that it is in a position to compel peace by the exercise of superior force. . . .[47]

Throughout his tenure of office Bryan never ceased to maintain his efforts toward a strict neutrality, while step by step he was forced from his position by the rapidly growing pro-Ally sentiment in the administration and the country, and by his constant inability to cope with the subtler minds and more powerful influences surrounding him. His first concession was in the matter of the Declaration of London. The State Department, in an effort to define the privileges of a neutral, proposed that the warring powers agree to abide by the declaration, a document drawn up in 1909, which, among other things, defined contraband and so made clear what articles might legitimately be exported by a neutral to a belligerent nation. It had been ratified only by the United States, but now the Central Powers agreed to accept it as a basis of action, provided the Entente would do as much. Great Britain refused. She was not going to have the usefulness of the blockade, always her most powerful weapon in waging war, impaired. She maintained that the technique of war had developed so rapidly that many articles would have to be added to the existing list of contraband, and only if she were permitted to make such additions as in her judgment seemed necessary, would she agree to the plan.

Under these terms, the contraband list would eventually include whatever the British Orders in Council chose to define as such, even to foodstuffs for enemy civilians. This proposal did not meet with the approval of Washington, and four times Ambassador Page was most reluctantly compelled to ask Great Britain to accept the declaration unconditionally. Four times Great Britain refused. Page was in despair. Sir Cecil Spring-Rice, British Ambassador to the United States, refused to deal with the State Department. At length, through the good offices of Colonel House, a so-called compromise was arrived at, which gave Great Britain exactly what she wanted. The American government agreed to waive the Declaration of London as originally drawn up, and to defend the rights of neutrals on the basis of existing treaties and the recognized code of international law. Great Britain made her own contraband list and arbitrarily extended, even beyond the limits defined by America in Civil War times, the interpretation of the doctrine of "continuous voyage," as a means of preventing all materials sent by neutral countries to Germany from reaching their destination.

Bryan had been away on political missions while most of the correspondence was going on, but he put his signature to the final papers.[48] He was giving ground under pressure, and if he realized that in so far as he yielded he betrayed his cause, somehow he managed to justify the process to himself.

The only alternative to compromise was resignation, a step he was loath to take. Retirement from the field meant leaving a cause unchampioned. What would happen, for example, to his beloved peace treaties, in which no official but himself seemed especially interested? Despite the carnage, he retained a touching faith in their efficacy. France and England had signed since the outbreak of war, and he never let slip a chance to advance their cause with the Central Powers.

"Every time we met," wrote Count von Bernstorff, "he used to remind me of his arbitration treaty. . . . Later I often regretted that we did not fall in with Mr. Bryan's wishes."[49] No, he would not resign. Better to stay and fight with a blunted sword than not at all.

And he did fight. He was foremost in insisting that England should be held equally accountable with Germany for her sins against neutrality, which were many. She interfered with United States mails. She flew the American flag on her own ships to protect them from attack. She forced American vessels into English ports and held them there so long that the shippers were glad in the end to sell their cargoes to the British at British prices. She did more than any other combatant to destroy the fabric of international law and practice governing neutrals, and Bryan signed the protest against each infraction—a protest so vigorous that in those days of beclouded issues and hysterical partisanship it wasn't long before he was being pelted with cries of "Pro-German!" But he did not accomplish much against the diplomatic negotiations being carried on behind his back by Colonel House and the Anglophile Ambassador to Great Britain, who apparently looked upon Bryan as a semi-imbecile and had trouble in mentioning his name without foaming at the mouth.

Bryan's position with regard to England's culpability was shared by other members of the Cabinet. Franklin K. Lane wrote to a friend on January 22, 1915: "England is making a fool of herself by antagonizing American opinion, insisting upon rights of search she never had acknowledged as to herself. If she persists she will be successful in driving from her the opinion of this country, which is ninety per cent in her favor. . . . We have some ambition to have a shipping of our own, and England's claim to own the seas, as Germany puts it, does not strike the American mind favorably."

And T. W. Gregory, Wilson's Attorney General, has said: "Up to the time that Germany began its atrocious submarine warfare culminating in the sinking of the *Lusitania*, we had far less cause of complaint against her than we had against Great Britain. . . . Her acts were substantially the same acts that brought on the War of 1812."[50] But the President's all-powerful influence was placed squarely behind leniency for the British. Mr. Gregory goes on to say: "A Cabinet meeting was held, at which several of Mr. Wilson's advisers expressed great indignation at what they considered violation of our international rights, and urged a more vigorous policy on our part. . . . After patiently listening, Mr. Wilson said . . . that the ordinary rules of conduct had no application to the situation; that the Allies were standing with their backs to the wall, fighting wild beasts; that he would permit nothing to be done by our country to hinder or embarrass them in the prosecution of the war unless admitted rights were grossly violated, and that this policy must be understood as settled."[51] Powerful protests? Yes. Action? No.

It must have irked Bryan to sign some of the official communications, which could of course contain no hint of what was going on behind the scenes but must be so drafted as to uphold with complete loyalty the ostensible policies of the government whose spokesman he was. He received from Senator William J. Stone of the Committee on Foreign Relations a letter charging, under twenty heads, discrimination of the United States as between Germany and Great Britain. Why, for example, were public war loans wrong and (as Bryan had ruled) the sale of ammunitions right? Bryan answered:

War loans in this country were disapproved because inconsistent with the spirit of neutrality. There is a clearly defined difference between a war loan and the purchase of arms and ammunition. The policy of disapproving of war loans affects all governments alike, so that the disapproval is not an unneutral act. The case is entirely different in the matter of arms and ammunition, because prohibition of export . . . would not operate equally upon the nations at war. . . . A war loan, if offered for popular subscription in the United States, would be taken up chiefly by those who are in sympathy with the belligerent seeking the loan. The result would be that great numbers of the American people might become more earnest partisans, having material interest in the success of the belligerent whose bonds they hold. . . .[52]

This was bad enough. But when, to the charge of wilful blindness to England's high-handed seizure of the ocean, he countered with the following words, it is hardly conceivable, in view of proven facts, that they were written in a willing spirit:

The fact that the commerce of the United States is interrupted by Great Britain is consequent upon the superiority of her Navy on the high seas. History shows that whenever a country has possessed that superiority our trade has been interrupted, and that few articles essential to the prosecution of the war have been allowed to reach its enemy from this country.

Petrol and other petroleum products have been proclaimed by Great Britain as contraband of war. In view of the absolute necessity of such products to the use of submarines, aeroplanes and motors, the United States government has not yet reached the conclusion that they are improperly included in a list of contraband. Military operations to-day are largely a question of motive power through mechanical devices. It is therefore difficult to argue successfully against the inclusion of petroleum among the articles of contraband.

If any American citizens, partisans of Germany and Austria-Hungary, feel that this administration is acting in a way injurious to the cause of those countries, this feeling results from the fact that on the high seas the German and Austro-Hungarian naval power is thus far inferior to the British.[53]

Then there was the "working agreement," its terms devised by Ambassador Page and Sir Edward Grey, whose true significance Bryan may have missed. It provided that American manufacturers, "using raw material obtained in part from Allied territories," should be assured of their supplies on condition that they should not reëxport to "countries at war with Great Britain or to neutral European countries from which Great Britain has not secured satisfactory guarantees against reëxportation of such articles."[54] It was a fine thing, to be sure, for the American manufacturers to have certain access to what they needed, but it was a still finer thing for the British government, since it rendered American industry more than ever dependent upon continued peaceful relations between the two countries and automatically created in influential American circles a strong prejudice against the creation of any ill feeling between them.

However Bryan may have been befuddled by himself or others, he was, after all, neither fool nor knave. He "became restive under the criticism he received. . . . The continued charges that he was unable to comprehend the business of the State Department, that he did not know what was going on under his nose, that he did not read the dispatches, and that, reading them, he could not understand them,"[55] were perhaps getting under his skin. Besides, the issues were growing too clear to be mistaken, sympathies too obvious to be denied.

In February, 1915, Germany announced unrestrained submarine warfare, in reprisal against Great Britain's self-made laws of the seas; a step to which America's passive concurrence with England's stand had certainly contributed. It was decided that a note should be sent to Germany demanding strict accountability, and in a letter to Wilson, dated April twenty-third, Bryan protested this move without a similar move in the direction of England:

> The note which you propose will, I fear, very much inflame the already hostile feeling against us in Germany, not entirely because of our protest against Germany's action . . . but in part because of its contrast with our attitude toward the Allies. If we oppose the use of the submarines against merchantmen, we will lay down a law for ourselves as well as for Germany. If we admit the right of the submarine to attack merchantmen but condemn their particular act or class of acts as inhuman, we will be embarrassed by the fact that we have not protested against Great Britain's defence of the right to prevent foods reaching non-combatant enemies.[56]

Then he wistfully offered his familiar panacea:

> I venture to suggest an alternative, namely, an appeal to the nations at war to consider terms of peace. We cannot justify waiting until both sides, or even one side, asks for mediation. As a neutral, we cannot have in mind the wishes of one side more than the wishes of the other side.

His first suggestion bore no fruit. The disputed note to Germany was sent, while England received so weak a protest against her misuse of the American flag that it might better have been left unwritten. As for mediation, Bryan knew that Wilson had sent Colonel House abroad as his peace emis-

sary. "Bryan was distinctly disappointed when he heard
I was to go," writes House. "He said he had planned to go
himself." But Bryan swallowed his disappointment and told
his rival graciously that since he could not go in an official
capacity House was the one person fitted to go unofficially.
He must have realized to some extent his lack of prestige
in British diplomatic circles, though he could hardly have
been aware of the utter contempt in which his capacities were
held. Perhaps he classed the British among "those supercilious persons who will constantly be looking down upon
me,"[57] as he had once plaintively described a suggested ap-
pointee to House.

On May 7, 1915, the United States was amazed by the
news that a German submarine had sunk the British liner
Lusitania in the Irish Sea and that among others one hundred and twenty-four Americans—men, women, and children
—had been lost. The blaze of war sentiment, already burning steadily in certain sections of the country, leaped high.
Colonel House in London abandoned his hopes for mediation and said to Page: "We shall be at war with Germany
within a month."

But this time the President's *alter ego* spoke too soon. Wilson was not so ready for war as many of his advisers would
have liked. Fully alive to the political implications of what
had occurred, he still remained unconvinced that he had
grounds for an immediate declaration of hostilities. The
Lusitania was an auxiliary cruiser of the British Navy and
carried a large quantity of ammunition.[58] Whether or not
she was armed is still a question for debate. The Americans
who had sailed aboard her, while not officially warned against
taking passage, were well aware of the risks they had assumed. To an impartial mind, Germany had a case.

To the mind of William Jennings Bryan the case was a
very clear one. "Germany has a right," he wrote to President Wilson on the ninth, "to prevent contraband going to
the Allies, and a ship carrying contraband should not rely
upon passengers to protect her from attack—it would be like
putting women and children in front of an army."[59] And he

pressed upon his chief the necessity for action that would prevent United States citizens from sailing aboard vessels carrying explosives. On the same day the President received a cable from House, urging war.

Two days later Wilson laid before the Cabinet his note to Germany. The crucial passage read:

This Government has already taken occasion to inform the Imperial German Government that it cannot admit the adoption of such methods [those incident to the unrestricted submarine campaign] or such a warning of danger [advising Americans not to sail on Entente ships] to operate as in any degree an abbreviation of the rights of American shipmasters or of American citizens bound on lawful errands as passengers on merchant ships of belligerent nationality; and that it must hold the Imperial German Government to a strict accountability for any infringement of those rights, intentional or incidental.

Bryan was appalled, not so much by the strong language used as by "the actual intention of the American government . . . to develop the correspondence with Germany to a climax which might result in war."[60] The Cabinet approved the note but the Secretary of State in great agitation suggested the advisability of a supplementary note that would convey to the German government the assurance that matters had not gone beyond a point where they could be settled by arbitration.

"The words, 'strict accountability,'" wrote Bryan, "having been construed by some of the newspapers to mean an immediate settlement of the matter, I deem it fitting to say that that construction is not a necessary one. In individual matters friends sometimes find it wise to postpone the settlement of disputes until such differences can be considered calmly and on their merits. So it may be with nations. The United States and Germany, between whom there exists a long-standing friendship, may find it advisable to postpone until peace is restored any disputes which do not yield to diplomatic treatment."[61]

The President was disposed to heed the advice of his Secretary. "It would not be wise, I think, to give out a direct statement; but I think the same purpose would be served by such a 'tip' as the enclosed, accompanying the publication of the note."[62] The enclosed tip read:

A frank issue is now made, and it is expected that it will be met in good temper and with a desire to reach an agreement, despite the passions of the hour—passions in which the United States does not share—or else submit the whole matter to such processes of discussion as will result in a permanent settlement.[63]

Bryan was satisfied. The idea was to release this tip to the press. It would then be transmitted to Germany as news, where the semi-official character of the utterance would be emphasized. But between the time he expressed agreement with Bryan and the time chosen for releasing the tip to the correspondents, Wilson was pressed to reconsider the step. Whether through conviction or the force of opposition, he yielded and withdrew his sanction. "Since I expressed my approval of the statement you suggested for the press, I have heard something, indirectly from the German Embassy, which convinces me that we would lose all chance of bringing Germany to reason, if we in any way or degree indicated to them, or to our own public, that this note was merely the first word in a prolonged debate."

The tip was not released, and the next day Bryan, prophet of peace, sent off to Germany a note that held the seeds of war.

He must have known that the end was near and the knowledge must have made him thoroughly miserable. To give the last unhappy touch to an unhappy day, he received another note from the President, setting forth his final views on the subject of warnings to American citizens to avoid the ships of belligerent nations. "My feeling is this," wrote the President: "the request is unnecessary. . . . It weakens the effect of our saying to Germany that we mean to support our citizens in the exercise of their right to travel both on our ships and on belligerent."[64]

One misfortune followed upon another and the savage

attacks to which he was subjected by the famous Dumba affair must have seemed to Bryan wholly gratuitous. On May twentieth, before Germany's reply to the *Lusitania* note had been received, Ambassador Dumba of Austria-Hungary expressed to William Phillips, Third Assistant Secretary of State, the opinion that the country was not unanimously behind the President in his note to Germany. Next day Bryan, having been informed of the conversation, talked with Dumba himself. What they said nobody knows, but on May twenty-third Bryan received a telegram from Ambassador Gerard, which read in part:

Zimmermann told me yesterday that Dumba, Austro-Hungarian Minister, had cabled that you had told him *Lusitania* note was not meant in earnest and was only sent as sop to public opinion.[65]

Bryan replied:

Will secure from Dumba and cable you statement denying the reported communication to Zimmermann or correcting the construction placed upon it. I need not tell you that there is absolutely no justification for his report, and you will please so notify the government at once. The government must not for a moment misunderstand the language or intent of the note regarding the submarine attack on the *Lusitania*.[66]

The promised statement from Dumba followed later in the day:

Secretary of State just advised me of a cable of Mr. Gerard purporting that I had sent to Berlin a telegram which, according to Mr. Zimmermann, said in substance the *Lusitania* note was not meant in earnest and "was only sent as sop to public opinion." I do not understand how my telegram could produce such an erroneous impression. Mr. Bryan emphasized the difference between the destruction of human lives and material damage, the high tension of public opinion and the correspondent earnestness of his protest, which does not exclude a friendly tone and spirit. It would be a great mistake to minimize the earnestness of this protest.[67]

Officially, Dumba's statement closed the business, but it was long before Bryan heard the last of it. The cries of "Pro-German!" were redoubled, and wholly unfounded rumours spread abroad that Bryan had been asked to resign. He may have been the soul of prudence at the Dumba interview —or he may not—but once the story was told, the public needed neither evidence nor confirmation, to believe the worst—it needed only desire, of which there was plenty.

Mexico must have been another thorn in William Jennings's flesh during this period, though an inconsiderable one compared with the poisoned barb of Europe. Carranza had been unable to form a government satisfactory to the United States, and Secretary Garrison, acting on the opinion of General Hugh Scott, had advanced the cause of Villa. On June first President Wilson announced to the Cabinet that he had prepared a message to Mexico, stating that unless the warring factions could settle their own differences, the United States would proceed to give "active moral support" to one of them. Bryan opposed the note as smacking of intervention. He was less tractable nowadays to the reasoned persuasions of his chief; or perhaps his chief, seeking to hasten the inevitable, took less trouble to persuade him. At any rate, he was overruled and compelled to telegraph the message to Mexico City next day.

Meantime, in the early morning of May thirty-first, the German reply to the *Lusitania* note had been received. It was inconclusive, a statement of the facts of the affair as they appeared to the German government and a request for a statement from the American government as to whether it was in agreement with the correctness of the German statement, and continued: "The Imperial Government begs to reserve a final statement of its position with regard to the demands made in connection with the *Lusitania*, until a reply is received from the American Government. . . ."[68]

This play for time displeased the President. He was in no mood for debate, and he proceeded to draft a second note, which was a virtual demand that Germany abandon submarine warfare. When this note was submitted to the Cabinet Bryan grew heated. What about England? he wanted to know. Why were we so ready to send notes to Germany and so reluctant to demand our rights of England, who was preventing our exports from going where we sent them? There was an immediate protest. Germany's action had involved the loss of human life. What were our material interests by comparison? Bryan, in the heat of the moment, charged that certain members of the Cabinet were pro-Ally; but he was not permitted to go far in that direction.

"'Mr. Bryan,' said the President with a steely glitter in his eye, 'you are not warranted in making such an assertion. We all doubtless have our opinions in this matter, but there are none of us who can justly be accused of having been unfair.'"[69]

Mr. Bryan apologized and the discussion was renewed, with the Secretary of State pulling one way and all his colleagues the other. If he had retained any smallest spark of hope up to that time, it now went out.

On Friday, June fourth, he announced that he could not sign the new note to Germany unless its severity were moderated.[70] No such assurance was forthcoming, and on Saturday McAdoo, who was acting as mediator between Bryan and the President,[71] found him in the throes of composing his note of resignation. McAdoo took the news to Wilson, whose only fear was that Bryan's step might create the impression both at home and in Germany that America was readier for war than was actually the case. On Monday, Wilson and McAdoo visited Bryan together and attempted to dissuade him, but it may safely be guessed that the effort lacked any great enthusiasm. Secretary of Commerce Redfield, who had an appointment with Wilson that afternoon writes:

He soon came in, visibly disturbed, and expressed his regret for the delay, saying that he had just left a conference with Mr. Bryan, who had resigned and insisted on leaving the Cabinet. The President had done his best to dissuade him, but fruitlessly, for Mr. Bryan felt that he could not conscientiously remain Secretary of State under conditions which might make him a responsible participant in the war.[72]

On Tuesday there was a Cabinet meeting, and when the members assembled Bryan was missing. Presently a messenger appeared with a note for the President. Wilson read it and turned to the Cabinet officers: "Gentlemen," he said, "Mr. Bryan has resigned as Secretary of State, to take effect when the German note is sent." Without waiting for comment, he added that Bryan had asked permission to attend the meeting, if his presence would entail no embarrassment upon his erstwhile colleagues. They agreed that it would not, and in a few moments he entered. His associates rose to greet him and the President welcomed him with his customary courtesy.

Bryan, apparently exhausted and suffering under an emotional strain, leaned back in his chair with closed eyes. He was again the centre of a dramatic situation, painful, but not without its minor compensations. The interrupted discussion was resumed.

At the close of the meeting he invited all the Cabinet members to lunch with him, and Lane, Garrison, Daniels, Burleson, and Houston accepted. Throughout the meal he was "preoccupied and seemed to be communing with himself."[73] Finally he arose and bade his guests a formal farewell. He said that Wilson and he were both right from their respective viewpoints, and that they were both striving toward the same goal: peace. He hoped to be of greater service to the President outside the Cabinet than he could be within.

Then Franklin Lane, apparently moved, said to him: "You are the most real Christian I know." This was too much for Bryan. Having been so long buffeted by opposition and bruised by scorn, Lane's kind words completely unnerved him.

"I must act according to my conscience," he said brokenly. "I go out into the dark. The President has all the prestige and power on his side." But after a few seconds he collected himself. He was not entirely bereft. After all, there were better things in the world than prestige and power. And suddenly, flinging back his head, he cried: "I have many friends who would die for me!"

That night the President read to House over the telephone the message to Germany as it had been tempered and revised by the suggestions of the Cabinet. But that night also, as the Bryans were going in to dinner at the home of friends, they heard the newsboys shouting an extra in the streets.

A paper was brought in and, streaming in huge black letters across the width of the sheet, they saw the words:

BRYAN RESIGNED

CHAPTER XXVIII

THE LONELY LEADER

IN A war-mad world in which treaties were scraps of paper, Bryan's frantic efforts for peace seemed but shrill anæmic cries. It was a lonely voice, less golden than of yore. His opinion was his own, not that of millions.

Bryan, Henry Ford, Jane Addams, Crusaders for Peace, an ill-assorted company tenuously in agreement on peace, not at all on fundamentals. Bryan, the man with millions of followers, when his cause collapsed, found himself standing rejected and alone. His efforts to regain contact with the sources of his strength were desperate and pathetic. Out of office and free to orate for any or all of the numerous causes which had engaged his passionate attention, he seized upon old issues with their convenient Biblical tags and tried to pump them into life—Peace, Woman's Suffrage, Prohibition, and God!

Peace! With seeming generosity he gave lip-service to Wilson, while, in reality, he opposed him.

In August the *Arabic* was sunk, giving Bryan a chance to dilate in public on what had been a private bone of contention between himself and Wilson. "The question just now is whether an American citizen should put his convenience or even his rights above his nation's welfare. If American citizens refuse to consider their own safety or the safety of the nation, then a second situation arises, namely: whether the government should permit a few persons to drag this country into an unparalleled war." He was hardly serving the President as the President would have liked to be served, but at least he was experiencing the satisfaction of saying what he thought.

Would he go abroad as the great unofficial ambassador of

peace and single-handed end the war? He considered this
for a time. "If I decide to go," he wrote, "it will be at my
own expense and not as the spokesman of any special
group." Colonel House, preparing Ambassador Page for
Bryan's descent upon Europe, thought that it might be a
good thing for him to go. "He would probably come back
a sadder and wiser man. I take it that no one in authority
in England would discuss the matter seriously with him, and
in France I don't believe he could even get a hearing."

Never mind about Bryan [Page answered]. Send him over here
if you wish to get rid of him. . . . If he had come while he was Secretary, I should have jumped off London Bridge and the country
would have had one ambassador less. But I shall enjoy him now.
You see, some peace crank from the United States comes along
every week—some crank or some gang of cranks. . . . He can't
hurt Europe—nor help it; and you can spare him.[1]

Bryan decided that he was needed at home. "The real
question is not what the President THINKS the people want;
but WHAT THE PEOPLE ACTUALLY WANT," he as-
serted;[2] and he felt that he, above all people, knew what
they wanted. The preparedness advocates captured the
President. In November, at the Manhattan Club, Wilson
announced his conversion to the cause. Bryan was shocked
and alarmed. When the President made his tour of the West
advocating preparedness, W. J. hurried in his wake, en-
deavouring to hold them firm to what he thought their
opinion really was.

The people had a choice of rhetorics. It was not Bryan's
that they chose!

If he was aware of how little headway he made against the
giant strides of his opponents, he gave no evidence of it.
"The reports that come to me," he wrote Jane Addams on
January 22, 1916, "all indicate a growing sentiment against
preparedness. The papers which formerly spoke of preparedness as a matter of course are now discovering that there
are all kinds of reasons why there is going to be difficulty."[3]

Meantime, the government grew more and more complacent to England's iniquities on the seas, and tended more and more to pursue, with regard to Germany, such tactics as antagonized and embittered her.

It was of course on the peace issue that Bryan gave Wilson his support in his second campaign for the Presidency. His wife, always the wise and devoted counsellor, was kept in Florida by illness but continued to sustain his spirit through the mails. "I believe your speech in Washington is of great importance," she wrote to him in March. "I *do want* you to show the so-called 'practical side' of your nature. Discuss it [peace] as you would if you were a lawyer arguing a case, and *please* answer the 'peace at any price' accusation. Don't grin now and take this matter lightly. I know some things, little and black as I am."[4]

Mrs. Bryan apparently recognized that it was becoming increasingly necessary to advise her husband to put weight as well as wind into his speeches.

He went to the 1916 convention as a newspaper correspondent, since the liquor interests had prevented his election as delegate-at-large, as successfully as they had kept his brother Charley from the governorship of Nebraska. When he appeared in the press gallery at St. Louis, the men on the floor went mad. They cheered and cheered, and he finally had to take refuge "under the speaker's platform," that he might record the proceedings in peace. Martin Glynn made the keynote speech, "paying such eloquent and beautiful tribute to Mr. Wilson that Mr. Bryan wept from emotion." Then at the request of the delegates, Bryan mounted the rostrum amid deafening plaudits and spoke in praise of Wilson, "in the same deep, penetrating voice, the same rounded periods, the same oratorical effects, so entrancing to his adherents, so effective in casting a spell over the multitude":[5]

I join the rest of the nation in gratitude that at a time like this we have a President who is trying to keep us out of war. . . . I believe that the American people, grateful for what this administration has done, grateful that we have peace in this country while war stalks throughout the world, will not be unmindful of the fact that it was a Democratic president . . . who has thus saved the country from the horrors of war.

Nor did he miss the occasion to give himself and his peace treaties a little boost:

When the day comes for the world's peace to be restored and for the treaties to be written that will guard against future wars, what administration is more worthy of the honor than the administration that has given to three quarters of the world a treaty plan that makes war a remote possibility between us and nearly all the principal nations of the earth?[6]

During the months that followed, he spoke early and late for the President, using with telling effect the dominant campaign slogan, "He kept us out of war!" He spoke chiefly in that section of the West where his views were most popular, and only one state out of those he covered went Republican.

"His mood is the mood of the West," wrote the Chicago *Tribune*. "He is more responsible for Wilson now than he was four years ago. He is the most powerful living American—" and continued ruefully: "Our only wish is that he had been a German or a Japanese or even a Canadian or a Mexican."[7] Despite the harsh criticism he had suffered on resigning from the Cabinet, despite his failure of election as a delegate to the convention, despite the scorn in which he was held by "supercilious persons" who were always "looking down" on him, he was still a force to be reckoned with.

Woodrow Wilson gracefully acknowledged his support:

May I not say how much I have admired your part in the campaign and what a vast deal of effective work you seem to me to have done in the very part of the country which has now aligned itself with the forces of progress. I think all Democrats are grateful to you. Certainly I am.

But it wasn't possible even for Bryan to close his eyes much longer to the terror that threatened. The tide of war hysteria rose daily higher, engulfing one landmark after another, and slowly the realization was forced upon his soul that this incredible thing which he had pushed away from his sight and refused to believe in might actually come to pass. A certain frantic quality entered into his activities. After congratulating Wilson on the note in which he had asked the warring nations under what terms they would consider peace, he himself sent off a peace note to Lloyd George:

As a friend of all the nations at war, as a Christian and a lover of humanity, I respectfully but most earnestly appeal to you to use your great influence to secure your government's consent to negotiations.

There is no dispute that must necessarily be settled by force. All international disputes are capable of adjustment by peaceful means. . . . Do not, I pray you, by refusing an exchange of views assume responsibility for a continuation of the unspeakable horrors of this unparalleled conflict. Your decision may mean life or death to millions.

Lloyd George remained unimpressed and, mumbling something about a premature peace, continued to fight.

On February third diplomatic relations were broken off between Germany and the United States. On February seventeenth, in an open letter to Jane Addams in *The Commoner*, Bryan gave his first intimation of what he would do in case war should be declared: "We shall support the government in the event of war, but as friends of peace we are in duty bound to do all in our power to save our country from war's horrors." The same issue ran a plea to his readers: "Send telegrams, letters and petitions to the President, to your Senators and to your Congressmen, giving your views on going to war. If opposed to entering this war on either side, say so at once. If you favor a referendum on a declaration of war, tell your representatives so and tell them immediately." Editorially he said: "I believe to go into this war would be a crime against our nation and the world," and again he spoke of his peace treaties and the possibility of using them as a guide for action.

On March fourth he received the following curious telegram from the ordinarily sober Judge Parker:

If you and your friend Senator LaFollette and all of your joint followers and sympathizers had gone to heaven three years ago, Germany would not have attempted to drive the United States from the seas or to conspire to make war upon her. . . . Nor would you have had occasion to sneak out of Washington upon the discovery of the German plot. While you can never undo the mischief you have planned, yet if you act quickly you may be able to persuade those now ambitious to become the Benedict Arnolds of Congress to end the shameful scene now being enacted.[8]

William Jennings couldn't quite make out what Parker was driving at and commented only that he had answered him once and for all, four years ago—and couldn't be bothered with him now. But once more Bryan said, this time in the Miami *Herald*, "I shall live up to a patriot's duty, if war comes."

And when war came, he lived up to a patriot's duty by telegraphing the President:

Believing it to be the duty of the citizen to bear his part of the burden of war and his share of the peril, I hereby tender my services to the Government. Please enroll me as a private whenever I am needed and assign me to any work that I can do. Until called to the colors, I shall, through the Red Cross, contribute to the comfort of soldiers in the hospital and through the Y. M. C. A. aid in safeguarding the morals of the men in camp.

Wilson wearily replied:

Thank you very warmly. I am sure that the whole country will believe that you are ready to serve in any way that may set its interests forward.

Mars must have smiled at this exchange of formalities.

"Whatever the country does is right," Bryan told reporters who waited for him on the steps of the White House after he had visited the President on April sixteenth. And yet the country was beating its ploughshares into swords. In *The*

Commoner he intensified this astounding position. Conscription was right. Suppression of free speech was right. Jailing of conscientious objectors was right. But even in this amazing shift of front he did not become a good hater. While he did not actively oppose German-baiting, he did not indulge in it.

William Jennings Bryan committed intellectual suicide "for the duration of the war" along with thousands of other peace-loving Americans. Like the emotional Democracy of which he is a symbol, he felt that the patriot should not play pacifist when the fight was on. Yet neither in the Spanish War nor in the World War did he fight with his whole heart. While his old enemy T. R. made his last tragic gesture of jingoism, William Jennings guiltily applauded.

The climactic compromise in a life of compromises. Faced with the enemy in person Bryan always refused to raise his fist to strike a physical blow. War was his enemy. His fists hung by his side. His tongue rattled on. Surrounded by women as a child he had never learned that a body blow is frequently more effective than a jawing. He was a moralist and not a moral hero. The logic of his position was conscientious objection. Instead, he became the pacifist in arms.

The peace issue eliminated, there remained to Bryan prohibition and woman suffrage, and the very war that blotted out peace was a powerful factor in driving the others through to success. The economic freedom toward which women had been slowly forging was suddenly brought within reach by the country's shortage of men, and the folly of denying the vote to so indispensable a section of the nation's citizenry was revealed with peculiar force. To Bryan the issue remained a moral one and on that basis he campaigned for it, although he was never more than mildly interested; but moral or economic, he was pleased when the amendment was adopted and the mothers of the land were free to exercise their elevating influence through the medium of the ballot box.

Prohibition was another story. That involved his political ambitions as well as his ethical beliefs, and his interest was more keen. Immediately after Wilson's election, he had announced: "My work during the next four years will be to contribute whatever I can toward making the national democracy dry."

He probably had his eye on the passage of a law as the 1920 campaign issue, but as it happened, prohibition wasn't going to wait for him.

It has been generally conceded that the Eighteenth Amendment rode into port on the wave of the "Help win the war" hysteria, shrewdly manipulated by the drys. But it cannot be said that it slipped in through the back door, for it had been an agitated question since 1880, and William Jennings had been grooming it for appearance in national politics since 1910. Conservation was being talked and practised all over the country, and the Anti-Saloon League found ready to its hand a formidable weapon. Pamphlets were issued, proving that if food would win the war prohibition would do much to conserve food. "Food, Labor, Life. These are the three factors in winning the war and the liquor men are wasting all three."[9]

In the struggle for ratification of the Eighteenth Amendment Bryan was active, despite the fact that all was not well between himself and the Anti-Saloon League. He harangued receptive audiences, he wrote thunderous editorials, he even forswore party lines. "Vote only for legislative candidates who favor ratification. A Republican legislator who will vote to ratify the National Prohibition Amendment is better than a Democratic legislator who will vote to defeat the Amendment and retain the saloons."[10] Eventually forty-six states ratified the Amendment and on January 16, 1919, Bryan's successor in office, Secretary of State Lansing, declared national prohibition the law of the land, to take effect one year from that date.

Meantime, William H. Anderson, leader of the Anti-Saloon League in New York, was out for the blood of Bryan. He had committed the crime of invading Anderson's own state to fight in the Legislature for prohibition. He had, besides, accepted the presidency of the Dry Federation after he had promised not to, unless the Dry Federation in-

cluded all prohibition societies within its compass.[11] And it
didn't. Two of the most powerful, the W. C. T. U. and the
Anti-Saloon League, were well outside. Bryan needed discipline and Anderson was going to see that he got it.

He came forth with the assertion that beneath its righteous mask the Dry Federation's dark purpose was to boom
Bryan for the Presidency in 1920.[12] He conceded that William
Jennings was an eloquent speaker, but "as a leader and supposed strategist, as a general, as one charged with responsibility for planning, Mr. Bryan is frankly a joke." He asked
that the Anti-Saloon League repudiate Bryan and disclaim
responsibility for the statements he had made in the New
York Legislature. The New York *World* found his indignation quite just. Why should Bryan reap the reward, when
others had "borne the heat of the day and the burden of the
struggle long before his conscience was awakened?"[13]

On May twenty-ninth, at a session of the league in Al-
bany, Anderson was upheld by both the State Board and the
National Executive Committee. "It is our judgment that
the facts justify the Superintendent in taking any steps
necessary to relieve the Anti-Saloon League of any responsibility of utterances of Mr. Bryan in New York."[14] As a
further mark of their displeasure his name was omitted from
the Prohibitionists' Hall of Fame.[15] He drew what comfort
he could from the Dry Federation, which, to commemorate
the signing, presented their president with a gold and
silver loving cup in the ratio of 16 to 1.[16] And as a matter of
fact, even the little tiff with the Anti-Saloon League ended
happily. Apparently suffering pangs of remorse, they passed
a resolution designed to smooth down the feathers of both
combatants. Certainly Anderson had the right to jurisdiction within his own state. But with equal certainty William
Jennings Bryan had performed invaluable service to the
cause they all had at heart.[17] Therefore, bygones should be
bygones, and the eloquent tongue of the president of the
Dry Federation should be employed by the Anti-Saloon
League for the furtherance of its purposes.

Peace had been welcomed with wonder and frenzy, with

bells and whistles, with weeping and prayer. *The Commoner* carried, boxed across its front page in huge black letters, the words

> PEACE
> GLORY TO GOD IN THE HIGHEST,
> ON EARTH PEACE, GOOD WILL TO MEN.

And William Jennings hastened to cry "Friend!"—if with a note of fatherly patronage—to the conquered enemy:

The world rejoices as it never rejoiced before, and no people more than the people of Germany, who are at last free to share with other civilized nations in progress toward more and more popular government. There is glory enough for all.

But 1919 was not a happy year. Mrs. Bryan's health had grown steadily worse and she was paralyzed with a form of arthritis from which she never fully recovered. "I must wait till God gives me strength," Bryan wrote to his brother Charley in March, "before I undertake anything in the way of leadership. Be patient with me. I have never felt so helpless before, so without strength. Poor Mary is struggling away at Baltimore with her braces and her crutches."[18]

Poor Mary's letters to her husband, who had gone to Washington to be treated for facial erysipelas, were pathetic. "My foot drags in a pitiful way." "My back has almost killed me. . . . Last Sunday I cried nearly all day. . . . My legs are all right in my dreams."[19] She was a brave woman, and such cries of distress to the husband she always tried to spare could have been wrung from her only in an agony of pain. The relationship between the two was probably the most appealing thing in Bryan's life. "I wish I could be there in person," he wrote, "to receive the welcome which your eyes have spoken to me for so many years."[20]

The years that took health from the Bryans gave them fortune. William Jennings seemed to be acquiring a taste for money as healthy as any plutocrat's. In 1919 he worked for the

Anti-Saloon League when he was able, for the handsome fee of $250 a day, spot cash, and expenses.[21] Before the year was over they had paid him $11,000[22]—no fabulous sum, to be sure, but still only $1,000 short of his salary as Secretary of State. Only the New York *World* was always taking the joy out of life. How much of his income was derived from the Anti-Saloon League—it wanted to know. What was he doing to earn it? Was it earned in part by his promised efforts to get a prohibition enforcement plank into the 1920 platform?[23]

Bryan made a sweeping and high-minded rejoinder. He pointed out that for nine years he had worked for the cause and had "received no compensation whatever, and nearly always paid my own traveling expenses. . . . My refusal, however, to accept compensation was not due to any thought that it was improper—God forbid that the defenders of this only, and not its opponents, should be worthy of their hire—but because I knew the foe I was attacking, and was not willing to have my efforts discredited by the criticism of those . . . who could not conceive of unpurchased services in a righteous cause."[24] Once the amendment was passed, however, and the issue no longer political (forgetting for the moment that the question of enforcement versus repeal threatened to create more excitement even than the original passage of the law), he saw no reason why he should not help in the work of raising funds, for which work he received "a little more than half as much per speech as I usually receive for my lectures."[25]

The Scotch in him again spoke out that the workman is worthy of his hire—and perhaps a little more.

The year 1919 saw also the beginnings of another profitable enterprise, which terminated only with Bryan's death. While he had been in the Cabinet he had met in Washington Charles A. Douglas, then representing Carranza's interests in the United States. Douglas decided that he could use to advantage Bryan's gift for words and his prestige as a former Secretary of State, and they drew up an agreement whereby Bryan, with the title of "Counsel in International

Matters," was to serve as the special representative of
Latin American countries in Washington,[26] appearing before
"tribunals of any character at home and abroad in international controversies which affect American citizens."[27]
The arrangement was kept dark until May, 1921, when it
was announced that Bryan had joined the law firm of
Douglas, O'Bear & Douglas.[28]

The chief business of the firm was the arrangement for
Latin American countries of loans in the United States.
We had loaned billions to Europe, said William Jennings;
we might spare millions for Latin America. But there were
other matters as well that took their attention. They were
retained, for example, to support the candidacy of Chamorro,
the conservative President of Nicaragua, in 1920, and William Jennings Bryan, patron saint of liberalism, presented his
case to the State Department.[29] Despite the influence of the
American minister on the side of the liberal candidate,
Chamorro was elected and Douglas and Bryan received for
their services the sum of $10,000.[30] Perhaps it was too much
to expect of Bryan that he should master the intricacies of
Latin American politics. Perhaps he didn't realize that
liberal and conservative meant the same thing in Spanish
as in English. Perhaps it was another case—as with the
Ryan-Belmont contribution in 1904—of ignoring with
benign complacency matters that might not bear too close
an investigation.

Anyway, he was far more interested in American than in
Nicaraguan politics, and the 1920 battle promised plenty of
excitement. As early as March 1919 he had written to his
"darling girl": "Senator Kenyon, the leader of the Progressives, is to call this afternoon. I regard him as the best
man in the Republican party of presidential size. I think I
can give Senator Kenyon some points that will help him
in the present situation. If he were President, my position
with the Administration would be much better in every way
than it has been with the present Administration."[31] What
he hoped to gain from the presidency of Kenyon is not
clear; but there was evidence here of a resentment against

his former chief that he had never acknowledged, and more than a hint that his devotion to the party was an incident compared with his devotion to William Jennings Bryan.

The two issues that were tearing the country apart were prohibition and the League of Nations. Hardly had the Eighteenth Amendment been passed than the hubbub arose for modification or repeal. Bryan regarded the issue lovingly for the 1920 campaign, but in order that all its possibilities should be realized, it must stand preëminent. The Treaty, with the League of Nations incorporated, brought home by Wilson from Versailles, threatened to dwarf it. It would be well to get that out of the way first.

Woodrow Wilson was the fighter for his ideals, no matter how mistaken. Where Wilson fought, Bryan would have compromised, and Bryan saw him, not a hero, but an autocrat.

Wilson was pleading that the League should be ratified without reservations, Article X, and all, and Bryan at first supported him. "No matter in what form the President gets it adopted, it is better that we should have the League than that we should fail to organize." But when the hopelessness of getting it through Congress in its original form grew daily more apparent, Bryan veered.

"The situation that confronts the President and the country is that the Senate will not ratify the Treaty save with reservations." Very well, said Bryan. The important thing is ratification—ratification as soon as possible, ratification in time for the first League session on January 16, 1920. And since the Senate representing the will of the people, would not endorse the League save with reservations, the only thing left was for Wilson to abandon his own stubborn insistence and allow ratification as the people wanted it. Bryan "would rather forego the establishment of an effective League to preserve world peace," wrote the Omaha *World-Herald*, "than surrender his ambition to lead his party this year."[32]

The discord between the two men was crystallized in a dramatic scene at another Jackson Day Dinner, just eight years after the one that had made them friends. Wilson sent a message to the diners, urging that the ratification of the League without reservations be made the 1920 campaign issue—exactly what Bryan was trying to avoid. The election, said Wilson, would then be a great and solemn referendum.

Josephus Daniels must have made his old friend's heart swell with pride when he observed at the dinner that "the principle and spirit of the Bryan treaties, expanded and enlarged, are embodied in the Treaty of Peace." Bryan was one of the last to be called on, and nothing much was expected of him. The company was tired and sleepy and anxious to get home. When he arose they regarded him with apathy but hardly had he uttered his first words than they sat up and began to listen. His speech resolved itself into a savage attack upon the President's stand, and it is safe to guess that the "asperity of his manner" and the "severity of his tone"[33] were accounted for less by the heat of his convictions than by the accumulated bitterness that for years he had been striving to deny even to himself.

At last he was giving vent to the spleen that had been fermenting within him against the man who had elevated him to the highest place among his councillors and then proceeded in such a manner as to drive him out of that place; the man who had won the prize he coveted and for which he had striven in vain all his life long.

Our nation [he concluded] has spent 100,000 precious lives and more than $20,000,000,000 to make the world safe for democracy, and the one fundamental principle of democracy is the right of the majority to rule. It applies to the Senate and to the House as well as to the people. A majority of Congress can declare war. Shall we make it more difficult to conclude a treaty than to enter war?

He spoke till half-past two and left his hearers in such agitation that many of them stayed up all night discussing the possible consequences of what had happened. Had a mortal blow been dealt to Wilson's leadership, or could he recover? "There were men who went out into the fog and rain who cursed the very name of Bryan, calling him Belial or worse; but there were others who nodded their heads in satisfaction, saying that Bryan was right and the time had come to put an end to his [Wilson's] mastery."[34] He has "thrust his knife home," said the Baltimore *News*, "and turned it round in the heart of the single great issue on which Mr. Wilson sought to prove the control of his party."

Bryan continued to turn it round and round. He began an intensive campaign against Wilson's autocracy, taking care to disclaim all desire for the candidacy himself, though he observed with a wide smile that "Democratic prospects are so poor that it would be perfectly natural for the party to want to draft me."[35] In April, Wilson had written to the Oregon Democrats, asking them to select delegates who would back up his position on the League.

"'Forgive them, Father, for they know not what they do,'" Bryan prayed. "Broken down in health by the weight of cares and anxieties such as have fallen to no other occupant of that high office, the chief executive has been denied the information essential to sound judgment and safe leadership."[36]

Meantime the Eighteenth Amendment had taken effect. On the eve of its enactment John Barleycorn was buried with impressive ceremonies in the First Congregational Church of Washington. At one minute of twelve Bryan arose with the tears streaming down his cheeks and uttered the words: "They are dead who sought the young child's life."[37]

And since they were dead, he decided that he might safely leave their burial to others. He refused to represent the Anti-Saloon League at San Francisco before the conventon. He was not anxious to provoke at this critical stage any such attentions as the *World* had been showering on him. "It would be unwise for me to go . . . as the representative of the Anti-Saloon League. My political work for prohibition has been crippled to some extent by the fact that I received compensation from the League. If I had had any idea of the activity of the wets, I would not have done so."[38]

He defeated a bitter opposition in Nebraska and went to the convention as a delegate at large with two ambitions:

to nominate a dry candidate and to kill the League as a party issue.

He failed to do either. He found the convention a gathering of "idolators—office-holding and non-office-holding—whose chief object was to glorify the President and obey his commandments."[39] Carter Glass, one of the idolators, introduced the League of Nations plank and it was accepted.

But the big fight came on prohibition. His opponent in oratory was Bourke Cockran, an ancient enemy, who inveighed with "his customary vehemence against any attempt to promote temperance by law." Bryan, according to an Associated Press dispatch, turned the convention "upside down with the magnetism and force of his oratory." When a heckler asked him what interests he represented, he cried: "I represent the women and children of America whom your damnable traffic would slay." But it was no use. The Democrats, like the Republicans, dodged the issue and the platform carried neither a wet nor a dry plank. Bryan did succeed, however, in subduing the wets somewhat, for Governor Cox of Ohio, the nominee and an acknowledged wet, declared himself in favour of strict enforcement of the law.

"My heart," mourned William Jennings piteously, if a trifle inaccurately, "is in the grave with the dry plank and I must pause until it comes back to me."[40]

He lost on the League, he lost on the dry plank, on a plank against profiteering, on a plank against military training, on a plank against political corruption, on the issuance of a national non-partisan bulletin, and on the investigation of labour disputes. He went home routed, and for the first time in forty years he didn't make a single speech during the campaign. Bryan now had one active adherent.

He relieved his feelings in fierce onslaughts upon the President. One barbed shaft after another he hurled at Wilson, while he strove to maintain his air of impartial justice. "You cannot call me an enemy of Woodrow Wilson. It was my peace plan that he took to the Conference. I have helped him to become immortal."[41] Was it his fault if Wilson couldn't profit by his teaching? "The ideal candidate," he cried bitterly, "is a man who will let the President direct him on every question excepting finance and liquor, and who on those two questions will submit his views to the liquor interests and Wall Street for revision." And again: "When the United States aided in attacking the arbitrary idea of government in Germany, it was with the hope of banishing it from the world, not for the purpose of transplanting it on American soil."[42] And finally: "I believe in God. Some day I shall stand before His Judgment bar, and when I appear there, there shall not be upon my head the blood of people slaughtered while I talked politics."[43]

In November, still true to the party, he made a special trip from Florida to Lincoln to vote for Cox. When the expected defeat materialized, he charged Wilson with having "laid the foundations for the disaster. . . . The President attempted to drive out of public life every Democrat who dared to differ from him even in minute details, while he made no effort to strengthen the Democrats who made him the keeper of their conscience."[44]

He also suggested in all seriousness that Wilson should resign at once, "now that the voters have rendered their verdict." Vice President Marshall would then become Chief Executive, and after appointing Mr. Harding Secretary of State he could also resign. Harding would then be President. The verdict of the country would be made effective immediately.

To protests against the virulence of his attacks on a sick man, Bryan answered somewhat illogically that he had earned the right, having given Mr. Wilson the peace plan that was the "heart of the covenant."[45] Besides, he argued, "if the President is too sick to be criticized, he is too sick to hold office."

And so the good Christian who interpreted the Bible literally forgot the teachings of his Master, in the heat of passion, and emptied the vials of his wrath over his adversary's head.

CHAPTER XXIX

SIXTY YEARS OLD

WHEN midnight struck on March 19, 1920, William Jennings Bryan was sixty years old. Although an elaborate public party had been arranged by the New York drys for next day, he decided to celebrate privately beforehand. He routed his old friend Henry T. Rainey out of bed and asked him over to the Lafayette Hotel. Rainey found Bryan sitting among a group of old-time newspaper men, most of whom had been through the '96 campaign with him. At midnight Bryan's health was drunk in ginger ale, and then Bryan made a confession. He spoke of '96, and later Rainey recalled that he said: "You all remember that at that time the argument used against me was that I was a young man. I always replied that . . . my opponent was sixty years of age, and that when I attained the age of sixty years I expected to retire from public life. I have sent for all of you to-night to tell you that when I said that I was mistaken. I will be at the San Francisco Convention, and I hope also at other conventions."[1]

With an energy quite remarkable, Bryan resolved to function to the end. However weak the body, the spirit remained willing.

1920. . . . The Methodists voted to permit dancing. . . . Emotional America indulged in acute hysterics over "the Reds." . . . Radio broadcasting started to throw its shadow across the Chautauqua. . . . Sinclair Lewis borrowed five hundred dollars and wrote *Main Street*. . . . Europe made official peace, with civil war in Ireland and Russia, hysterical demands to hang the Kaiser and bitter recriminations among the erstwhile Allies. . . . The successful candidate for the

Presidency of the United States had epitomized the spirit of the times with the word "normalcy." . . .

What had William Jennings Bryan to do in this world? The word "normalcy" was anathema to W. J. When he had first become a national figure there were no movies to while away the time and no radio to compete with the appeal of public speech making. Main Street was the centre of the world, the human norm, and not an object of derision. This new world! It required an effort to keep up with it! Bryan had not even noticed its coming.

For twenty-four years he had worked on a national scale to make the world a better place to live in. A severe moralist, he had never been at a loss as to where the right of disputed matters lay. Nor was he entirely a leader of lost causes. The majority of his reforms were on the statute books. But his fatal weakness was that the bases of his judgment were fixed and immutable. However much the outer forms changed, he could not believe that one must recast one's fundamental ideas in the light of later information. As a Christian moralist he was horror-stricken when modern learning began to question the foundation of his whole world outlook. In the twinkling of an eye he was changed from a moralist seeking change to a moralist defending what was. A radical all his life, William Jennings was to end his days an ultra-conservative.

But the whole situation was so confusing that Bryan ran hither and thither approving here and denouncing there, with no clear thread of purpose to integrate his life. He became an enraged blind man, contradicting his whole scheme of life on occasion and passing from the trivial to the profound with no sense that his actions were incongruous.

One thing, however, seemed to him beyond question. Morality and religion were synonymous, and religion meant orthodox Christianity and a literal belief in the Bible. At forty he had taken down Darwin's books and "found several important contradictions. The theory has no support in nature and paralyzes religious activity in many intellectuals."[2] That was his story and he stuck to it. Evolution was the devil's doctrine and the Bible was the Word of God. The Word of God must be true in every particular, every miracle, every explanation of man's nature and origin.

"There is more science in the twenty-four verses of the First Chapter of Genesis ... than in all that Darwin wrote."[3]

Incontestable proof of the superior validity of the Bible lay in the fact that it had been delivered by God to the people once and for all. It had endured forever, the centuries had not been able to shake it, while scientific works were "guesses strung together," that had "to be revised and corrected every few years."[4] Religion and morals were static, not progressive. That was axiomatic.

No one who has observed Bryan's mental habits closely will be astonished to notice that he saw the "error" in Darwinism at forty, but put off speaking on the issue for twenty years. For one thing, he did not feel that the question had reached an acute stage until 1920. By that time he detected the pernicious doctrine at work on the faith of the masses. In earlier days it had been the property of the intellectuals, then of the college educated, finally it reached the public school teachers and through them Tom, Dick, and Harry.

It was time to strike.

Furthermore, as he grew older and his place in politics became more insecure, he found more occasion to be a moralist pure and simple. Prohibition was a moral issue. So, to him, was woman suffrage. And from morals to religion, was, to Bryan, not even a step. Lastly, as old age crept on, Bryan wrestled with the spectre of death. He was afraid of death. For some reason or other he lived in mortal fear of dying of pneumonia.[5] After a careful examination, the doctors warned him that unless he took care he would die of diabetes. Taking care meant regulating his ferocious appetite—an exceedingly difficult thing to do. And as death crept upon him his hope of heaven became a ruling hope. But where would he stand, if that hope were snatched from him—and those who were like him—by the impious hands of scientists?

Yet he was hardly able to hew a line, and his last years were exceedingly disordered. Only by sheerest accident did his life rise to a grand climacteric. He began to talk against evolution in 1921, asking rhetorical questions and uttering resounding generalizations. Bryan went in for celestial politics. "Was Christ conceived of the Holy Ghost and born of a Virgin? Or was he the illegitimate son of an immoral woman?"[6]

Bryan, in his characteristic fashion, introduced a specious sort of logic into his campaign against evolution. He aimed his blows at the teaching of it in the publicly supported educational institutions. These schools, he reasoned, were the indirect creations of the mass of citizens. If this were true, those same citizens could control what was taught in them. Bryan assumed that the masses were thoroughly Christian and consequently against anything having a deleterious effect on Christianity. Since they had, quite rightly, insisted that no particular variety of Christian dogma be taught, had not they the right to bar a doctrine that struck at the roots, not of a variety of dogma but of Christianity itself? They certainly did have that right. In essence: "The hand that writes the paycheck rules the school."[7]

The necessity was, then, to convince the masses—or their servants, the legislators—that evolution was a destructive doctrine. If evolution were freely taught, Bryan argued, the masses would cease to believe in the Bible. That sense of God's constant presence that the Bible gave them would inevitably be lost, the bars against sin would be lowered, and the pasture of the soul inevitably defiled and destroyed.

What had evolution to offer in exchange for what it took? Nothing. Neither a watchdog for the conscience nor any other check on the evil inclinations of mankind. Indeed, since its promulgators taught that man was descended from the apes, one might reasonably conclude that the morals of the jungle were acceptable to them. Certainly the lofty ideals of believing Christians were beyond their understanding. Had not Mr. John H. Williams of the Chicago Law Enforcement Commission stated that five out of six criminals in the Illinois Penitentiary were college educated?[8] Did not Mr. Harry Elmer Barnes declare, at the University of North

Carolina, that "the great periods of cultural efflorescence have been those characterized by a large amount of freedom in sex relations, and . . . those of the greatest cultural degradation . . . accompanied with . . . sex repression and purity"?[9] "It is worth while to inquire," wrote Bryan, "why those in charge of a great institution of learning allow such filth to be poured out for the stirring of the passions of its students." But retribution might be left for the Lord.

"Nietzsche carried the Darwinian theory to its logical conclusion and died in an insane asylum."

So he inveighed against evolution in *The Commoner*, and delivered stirring speeches in various states where anti-evolution bills had been presented to the Legislature. In Kentucky he attacked Darwinism and the state university for teaching it. In West Virginia he addressed the Legislature on Science versus Evolution. At Dartmouth he spoke to one of the largest and most excited audiences that had ever crowded into Webster Hall, and later appeared before members of the college Round Table to continue the controversy. For one persistent heckler he offered to buy a Bible; but when the offer was accepted on condition that Bryan take $5.00 in exchange and buy a copy of *The Golden Bough* for himself, the Commoner backed down.[10] His influence helped in the passage of both the Florida and the Tennessee anti-evolution law, though he urged in each case that no penalty be attached to infractions. The moral force of public disapproval, he thought, would be punishment enough.

*   *   *   *   *

In 1921, because of Mrs. Bryan's ill-health, the family had taken up permanent residence in Florida, and Bryan had transferred his citizenship to that state. His passage from the scene of Nebraska politics brought peace to the Democratic party there, and Gilbert Hitchcock wrote a valedictory editorial:

. . . There are thousands of the graying generation . . . who will delight to think of and remember him . . . as the Bryan of the Nineteenth Century with raven locks, frame of oak, clarion voice, the shining face of an archangel when his hopes were high and his ambition pierced the heavens.[11]

The following year Fairview was turned into a Methodist hospital.

Bryan's ardour for the salvation of his fellow men flamed as high in Florida as in Nebraska. He established an open-air Bible class at Royal Palm Park, Miami, to which thousands flocked each Sunday. The thought that he was reaching men and women who did not customarily go to church delighted him. He felt the evangelist's joy in making conversions. He told his audience that the Bible was the repository of all wisdom. It was true in all its parts. It must be accepted without reservation. "I would dread to be compelled to set forth upon this sea with nothing but the light of my reason to aid me." Nor must it be subjected to the scrutiny of the intellect. "The sin of this generation is mind worship."[12] The heart came first, the intellect was secondary.

It gratified him to know that in addition to those within hearing of his voice he was reaching four million people through his syndicated talks in the press. It doubtless also gratified him that the syndication was bringing him close to $2,000 a month.[13]

Bryan always had a shrewd business sense. The step from orator to realtor was hardly a long one. In Florida his talents as a speaker had been engaged to help boom the market. "What shall we do with the city that Mr. Flagler conceived and of which he laid the foundation? What is our vision of what Magic Miami should be? We can best honour the name that will be forever dear to the people of Miami by giving this beautiful spot a wholesome environment which will attract the best citizenship of the nation, and thus make permanent the city's growth and progress."[14] He talked daily at Coral Gables during the height of the fever. "His subject was not real estate," says Mrs. Bryan, "but he spoke of Florida generally, of its advantages and pleasures. This was a sparkling little speech which Mr. Bryan enjoyed making, for he was full of enthusiasm for his state."[15]

For these sparkling little speeches he was paid at the rate of $100 a day.[16]

This was a trifle compared with his returns from speculation in the Florida land market. In 1920 he had admitted to a fortune of between $250,000 and $300,000. During the next five years he increased it by $500,000 and brought himself perilously close to the millionaire class. Things finally reached a point where he felt it necessary to defend his accumulation of wealth.

"Can a man ... amass one million dollars in a lifetime and still return an equivalent? I believe so. Ten millions? Yes. Can a man amass five hundred million in a lifetime and return an equivalent service? I believe it possible. I am not willing to set any maximum and still set a limit on a man's possible service to society."[17] He must have felt that his services to mankind were easily worth the paltry hundred thousands he had salted away.

As he grew wealthier he tended to agree with his old friend, Andrew Carnegie, on the accumulation of wealth and the justification a wealthy man should offer to society.[18] As he grew wealthier he also had shirts made to order on Fifth Avenue and discarded his humdrum overcoat for the more dashing and romantic cloak, though he still walked along the street eating peanuts and leaving a trail of shells.[19] And as he grew wealthier, his pure passion for the welfare of the masses seemed to grow a little muddy.

Bryanism again compromised by events.

He deplored the action of the workers during the 1922 labour strikes, pointing out that the hardships endured by at most five million strikers and their families were as nothing compared with the suffering their selfishness entailed on ninety-five million.[20] The workers had no more right than the plutocrats to dictate the policies of the country. "Neither capitalism backed by an army, nor a class government in the control of labor is suited to our institutions. . . . All classes ought to join together, each individual acting according to his judgment and his conscience." There was a note of caution apparent here, which had been absent from Bryan's early pronouncements on capital versus labour.

His children worried him. He and his wife had adopted their daughter Ruth's boy, John Baird Bryan, who received letters from his grandafther, exhorting him to say his prayers and read his Bible every day. The family was grieved by the domestic difficulties of William Jennings, Jr., brought on, the doctor said, by the younger Mrs. Bryan's lack of health.

My Dear Ones All [wrote young William], I am not going to take any action unless it is the only way out. . . . I am enclosing letters to and from Dr. J. which will inform you of what has transpired since you left. My last letter from Helen was very encouraging, in that she expressed appreciation of my loyalty to her and her desire to live in harmony with me.[21]

The trouble between them was never adjusted, and though Bryan tried hard to effect a permanent reconciliation the marriage was finally broken up. One of his favourite lectures at this time, which may have been induced by his son's unhappiness, was called: "Is the young man Absolom safe?" and dealt with the anxiety of a father's heart as he watches his children mature and become involved in life's perplexities.

He entertained Venizelos, the Greek leader, and Harding motored over to see him. He had liked Harding ever since the days when, as Lieutenant Governor of Ohio and Chairman of the Marion Chautauqua, the less eminent man had offered the distinguished Chautauquan speaker the hospitality of his home. They understood each other, these two, and Bryan commended Harding publicly as a believer in the inspiration of the Holy Scriptures.

For a time William Jennings toyed with the idea of going to the Senate. "If the Democrats of Florida feel that as a Senator I could render sufficient service to the state, party and nation to justify calling upon me to represent them at Washington . . . I would consider the matter from the standpoint of duty in connection with other claims upon me. But I have no thought of entering into a contest for the office. . . .

No friend will expect me at my period of life, when my political record is known to all, to solicit support."[22] George A. Garden, a winter resident of Florida, wrote to Bryan's daughter Ruth: "The movement is now started. . . . There will be sufficient petitioners to induce your father to announce his candidacy." But apparently there weren't, for nothing came of it. Or perhaps Bryan knew that he couldn't be elected and had enough on his hands to keep him busy anyway. For in 1923 he suspended publication of *The Commoner*, giving as his reason that it interfered with work "into which circumstances have led me."

It was probably his anti-evolution work to which he referred, though he may also have had in mind his activities in connection with Latin America. In 1922 he signed an agreement, to run for two years, with Boaz Long, who had been head of the Latin American Division in the State Department under Bryan. By the terms of this agreement they associated themselves for "the securing for the Central American Republics of Guatemala, Salvador, Honduras and Nicaragua, or either of them, loans from the United States Government for internal developments or the refunding of existing loans, and in securing for Salvador and Honduras the sale of naval bases in Fonseca Bay to the United States Government."[23] To promote the plan it was necessary for William Jennings to share with his partner the task of visiting the Central American countries, and pleasant a task as it might be, still it took time.

Moreover, he continued to labour conscientiously as a member of the firm of Douglas, O'Bear & Douglas. The firm was paid $4,000 a month to represent Panama's interests in her boundary controversy with Costa Rica, and Bryan's share was a third of the fee.[24] They were also engaged by the Cuban Ambassador, De la Torriente, in the settlement of the Isle of Pines Treaty. And they supported the dictatorship of Tinoco of Costa Rica in Washington—Tinoco, who was said to be the creature of the big oil and banana men.

Their chief concern at the moment was with Mexico, where they represented certain Standard Oil subsidiaries and were trying very hard to get the business of the Guffey oil interests.[25] For they hoped that the resulting prestige would attract to them the patronage of British oil companies with holdings in Tampico. There were many claims growing out of the revolutions that were being pressed against the government by English and Americans alike, and the field offered excellent opportunities to an ambitious law firm. So here was Bryan soliciting, as a member of the firm, the dollars of the hated capitalists to line his own pockets.

The days of his immaculacy lay behind him.

Yet, whatever part these affairs played in crowding his daily routine, they occupied only the edge of his real interest. Latin America was alien and far away. Religion was close and precious and gave him besides an opportunity for dialectic on the plane where he felt most at home. A meeting of the General Assembly of the Presbyterian Church was to be held at Indianapolis in May of 1923. Bryan, appalled to think that the General Assembly apparently winked at evolution by permitting it to be taught in church schools, went to the meeting with a resolution in his pocket that was designed to put an end to this outrage.

The first business before the delegates was the election of a new Moderator, and the issue that split them into two raging mobs, fundamentalists versus modernists. The choice of the fundamentalists was William Jennings Bryan.

"I ask you to rally for the consecrated Christian layman, William Jennings Bryan, and thus to help bring the world to the foot of the cross."

But the liberals lobbied zealously against him and a one-time friend of Bryan's, Dr. Martin D. Hardin, put the opposition candidate, Dr. Charles Wishart, into nomination.

"I refuse to touch the hand of a man," said Bryan of Hardin later, "who prefers the blood of the beast to the blood of the Lamb."[26]

When the balloting began Bryan withdrew and "sat outside in the front hall, fanning himself. He appeared to be extremely nervous."[27] He ran ahead for the first three ballots, but on the fourth his opponent passed him, and when the hard-won victory of Wishart was finally announced it was greeted with deafening cheers and salvos of applause. Bryan must have recovered from the nervousness which the *Times* correspondent had detected in him, since he endured without apparent emotion the demonstration for his rival and listened calmly while his election was made unanimous. But when a post on a minor committee was offered him he declined peremptorily.

⌒ In introducing his temperance resolution he took a whack at the Eastern newspapers, those instruments of Satan who were trying to howl down prohibition: "I think the only Bible verse they know is, 'The wise men came from the East.' They think that if a reform does not start in New York it does not amount to anything. But no reform ever does start in New York."[28] Without troubling to reconcile the last two statements, he presented the resolution and had the satisfaction of seeing it unanimously passed. Then came the proposal to ban the teaching of evolution from the church schools. He held forth for an hour, in a speech described by Dr. William P. Merrill as "fiery, witty, impassioned, keen and given with all his unrivaled skill as a popular speaker," but "undignified, unfair, and unintelligent . . . a regrettable exhibition of unrestrained fanaticism."

It produced a sensation. The assembled Presbyterians yelled and shook their fists, while the Moderator pleaded for Christian decorum and reminded them that they were gathered together in a "court of Jesus Christ."

"I am trying to save the Christian Church from those who are trying to destroy her faith," cried Bryan, bewildered that here in the very stronghold of religion he should be so little understood. But in spite of his high, God-guided purpose, he failed. His resolution was defeated. When he realized it, wrote the *Times* correspondent, "he sank into his chair and looked so pale as to appear almost ill."

He recovered sufficiently to present another resolution condemning the views of Harry Emerson Fosdick, which was adopted. He comforted himself further by ascribing his failure at the convention to machine politics. It had been dominated by a powerful minority, he asserted, who had steam-rollered the anti-evolution resolution, much as a political group might have done.[29]

He was sure that ninety per cent. of all Christians disapproved of evolution. What made him so sure, he never bothered to tell.

"I don't think there is a busier man than I am," William Jennings had told the assembly delegates, with more than a trace of Messianic delusion. "I have got to keep the Democratic party straight, and I have got to see that prohibition is enforced, and I have got to see that religion is defended." He had just done what he could for the last. His labours on behalf of the second didn't meet with the appreciation they merited. In fact, an official of the Anti-Saloon League had said that he really wasn't much use because he shied away from the League every time a political convention drew near.[30]

With one in sight now, the time was drawing near when he must give all his energies to keeping "the Democratic party straight." It was generally conceded that he was still a power in the party, but an indeterminate one. No one could predict how deeply his influence would affect the platform or the nomination. He had declared, in 1920, that if McAdoo would join the drys, he could easily make himself the leading candidate in 1924. McAdoo *had* joined the drys, and Bryan talked kindly of his chances. But before long he was back at his old tricks. In January he announced that Dr. A. A. Murphree, president of the University of Florida, was his candidate. More astonished than anyone else by the announcement was Dr. Murphree, to whom Bryan's tactics were a closed book. But his brother politicians, having mastered something of his own technique, saw in the move a scheme to swing Alabama's twenty-four votes from the wet Underwood to the dry and progressive Murphree. Little did he know the toughness of Alabama loyalty.

McAdoo's chances were believed by many to have been ruined because of the Tea Pot Dome scandal that had broken six months earlier. He had been retained for five years at

$50,000 a year by E. L. Doheny, one of the principal figures in the affair, and though he had publicly stated that his work had no slightest relation to the Tea Pot Dome business and though he had immediately severed his connection with Doheny and returned a year's fee, he couldn't quite get rid of the reek of oil. But he remained in the race.

On Saturday, the twenty-second of a sizzling June, Bryan arrived in New York and was immediately engulfed in conferences. He emerged from an hour and a half with McAdoo with a definite statement: "I am for him. The same forces that are lined up against me are lined up against McAdoo."[31] He predicted that the liquor and religious issues would be disposed of peacefully, and that the real fight would come on taxation and the tariff. It was probably his wish rather than his belief, but Oscar Underwood threw a wrench into the works and brought the Klan question into the light of day by denouncing that organization in very plain language in Monday's *Times*. It was impossible longer to evade the issue.

McAdoo went into the fight with the support of the drys, the Klan, and William Jennings Bryan!

And to judge from the sheer volume of enthusiasm that greeted Bryan's appearance at the dinner that night at the Commodore Hotel, his support should have been worth having. So busy was he kept shaking hands that he scarcely got a chance to eat, which must have been a trial to him. And when the feasting was over, the guests stood up on their chairs and shouted "B-r-y-a-n! B-r-y-a-n! B-r-y-a-n!" How much was sentiment and the moment's contagion and how much rock-bottom faith in the leader, events were to prove. The recipient of this tribute smiled in response but said nothing.

On Tuesday the sessions began. "It was a hot day and Madison Square Garden began to give forth once more, if faintly, the atmosphere of the long-vanished circus."[32] Senator Pat Harrison made the keynote speech and his eulogistic mention of Woodrow Wilson drew the heaviest applause of the day.

The most important developments of the following day were the artificially stimulated ovation for McAdoo, the beginning of work by the Resolution Committee, of which Bryan was chairman, and the loss of Byran's watch. The committee went into session that day and emerged only as the sun was rising Saturday morning. They agreed on a League plank with satisfactory reservations. They agreed on a prohibition plank that declared for enforcement. Bryan and Senator King lost their fight for an immediate declaration on the independence of the Philippines, but the Commoner succeeded in getting in an anti-war plank that was the most progressive of the platform.

What they could not agree on was the Klan. Should it be denounced by name or tacitly included in a general resolution for religious tolerance? Certainly the former course would constitute a more powerful corrective against this pernicious growth on the body of society, and should have recommended itself to so firm a believer as William Jennings Bryan in the freedom to worship as one pleased. But by some curious phenomenon, the Klan flourished most vigorously among just that element of the population that acknowledged Bryan leader. These were the people from whom he drew his strength; these were the people who were passing his anti-evolution bills. They were his friends and he didn't want to call them names. He didn't want to make bad blood. He liked them too well and they were too important to him. So he fought against the denunciation of the Klan by name.

By Friday the members of the committee were "drowsy from lack of sleep and overwrought." Early Saturday morning, in a "most fervid and tense atmosphere," with the deadlock unbroken, they decided to present to the convention a majority and a minority report—the first declaring for a plank to uphold the old constitutional principles of freedom of religion, of speech, of press, and of assembly, without specific reference to the Klan; the second advocating denunciation of the Klan by name. As the day broke, William Jennings asked John H. McCann, a Catholic, to lead them in the Lord's Prayer, after which he prayed a prayer of his own:

Our heavenly Father, we come unto Thy presence conscious that Thou art infinite in wisdom, love and power, while we are limited in knowledge and prone to err.

Thou dost care for Thy children and hast promised to reveal Thyself and Thy will to those whose hearts are open to divine suggestion.

We need Thy counsel, Lord. We are carrying great responsibilities and dealing with mighty problems that vex and trouble us. We are subject to prejudice and passion and unconscious bias.

Cleanse our minds of all unworthy thoughts and purge our hearts of all evil desires. Show us Thy ways and help us to know what Thou wouldst have us say and do and be.

We would consecrate ourselves wholly unto Thee and Thy service. "Thy Kingdom come, Thy will be done on earth as it is in heaven."

Help us to advance in our day and this day the brotherhood Thou didst establish; may it include all mankind.

So guide and direct us in our work to-day that the people of our party and of our country and of the world may be better for our coming together in this convention and in this committee.

Bless us, not for ourselves, but that we may be a blessing. We ask in Jesus' name. Amen.

That day the platform was presented to the convention. There was a five-hour debate on the League plank. Newton D. Baker argued for ratification without reservations, Bryan for the opposite. Bryan won.

At ten minutes of four he mounted the platform to present the Klan plank. Chairman Thomas J. Walsh introduced him as "the revered Democrat, William Jennings Bryan." Most of the delegates rose and "cheered him to the echo, but when the cheering died away a few hisses were heard."

He was a tired man. He had had but three hours' sleep the night before and not more than an average of three or four hours for a week. "All that was left of the old Bryan," a spectator remembered later, "was the fire in his fanatical eyes."[33] But that was enough. It proved the survival of his fighting spirit. He precipitated a battle as stormy as any he had fought in his long and stormy career.

"The only difference between those who favored the majority report was three words: Ku Klux Klan," began William Jennings. . . . He got no further. The galleries, packed not with the small town crowds that he understood but with city scoffers, wouldn't let him go on. Shrieks, boos, hisses! He waited for a lull. When it came he threw at them again the three offending words: "Ku Klux Klan."

The result was pandemonium. They hated him—the man from the sticks, the small town America, he whose adherents were responsible for the Klan, he who refused to allow its name to be pilloried. They defied him, they scalded him with epithets, they wouldn't be quieted until Chairman Walsh threatened to put them out. Then Bryan was allowed to continue with his speech:

In this country it is not necessary to protect any church. I have such confidence in the Catholic Church, which was for fifteen hundred years my mother church as well as yours, that I deny it needs political aid. . . .

The Jews do not need this resolution. They have Moses, they have Elijah, and they have also Elisha, who drew back the curtain and revealed upon the mountain top an invisible host greater than a thousand Ku Klux Klans.

I am not willing to bring discord into my party. . . . Now when we are united . . . these people tell us that we must divide our party on a religious issue and cease to be a great political force.

My last objection is that I am not willing to divide the Christian Church, because if it is destroyed there is nothing to take its place.

Jew and Gentile, Catholic and Protestant stand for God, on whom all religion rests, and Protestant and Catholic stand for the Christ. Is it possible that . . . at this time, in this great land, we are to have religious warfare? . . . I cannot believe it. God forbid! I call you back in the name of our party. I call you back in the name of the Son of God and Saviour of the world. Christians, stop fighting. Banish the Hymn of Hate; our song must be "Blest be the tie that binds our hearts in Christian love."

It probably didn't matter what he said. The reasoning of a Socrates would hardly have moved his hearers from their passionate convictions. When the vote was taken Bryan won—won by an appallingly close margin; a fraction of a single vote. When the result was made known such a bedlam of "unearthly noises" broke out as drowned even the patriotic melody that the band was trying to play. It was the wildest scene that the Garden had witnessed in the memory of the generation that took part in it.

At one-fifty Sunday morning the convention adjourned.

On Monday the balloting for the Presidential candidate began. When the session ended McAdoo had 479 votes, Al Smith of New York 305½. Next day there was a drift toward John W. Davis of West Virginia, which Bryan was determined to stop. With this object in view he approached the Mississippi delegates.

"This Convention must not nominate a Wall Street man," he said firmly. "Mr. Davis is the lawyer of J. P. Morgan."

"And who is Mr. McAdoo the lawyer for?" a woman delegate asked.

"McAdoo never got close enough to Doheny," retorted Bryan, "to get the friendship of Wall Street." Moreover, he told them that Davis couldn't carry the West, and McAdoo —presumably with his (Bryan's) help—could. The Republicans would certainly carry the East, which left only the South for Davis. And the South, however solid, wasn't enough to elect a President.[34]

But the tide was beyond his control. McAdoo's strength slowly declined, as Al Smith's and Davis's increased.

"Why don't you support Al Smith?" he was asked. "He's certainly a progressive."

He answered "coldly and curtly: 'I am opposed to Smith, not because he is a progressive, but because he is wet,' and turned his back."[35]

Wednesday, on the thirty-eighth ballot, Bryan rose to explain his vote. It was the signal for action from the crowd. He was still their best butt. He pointed out that the country was rich in candidates. There was Murphree of Florida—

laughter from the galleries. There was Ralston—E. T. Mere-
dith—Charles Bryan—hoots and jeers and laughter unrestrained. There was Walsh of Montana——

"Come across!" yelled the galleries. "Who's your man?"

He told them that the candidate must be dry and progressive, he told them that McAdoo had made the progressive platform possible.

"Ku, ku, McAdoo—Oil!" they shouted. But when they
had shouted their heads off he went on.

"Mr. McAdoo's retainers had to do with oil in Mexico. If
any oil has ever tainted William Gibbs McAdoo, the intense,
persistent, virulent opposition of Wall Street washes all the
oil away."

"Who's paying you for this?" they wanted to know. "A
thousand dollars a minute! Roll call!"

"What this nation wants—" he thundered against them—

"Is a good five cent cigar," suggested some blasphemer
from above.

"—is a man whose heart beats with the common people,
and we don't care where he was born or where he lives."

But he couldn't do for McAdoo what he had done for
McAdoo's distinguished father-in-law. By Saturday night
77 ballots had been taken and the deadlock held: McAdoo,
513; Smith, 368; Davis 76½.

William Jennings hoped that the telegrams would pour
in from the common people on Sunday and break the deadlock, as had happened in 1912.[36] He was disappointed. The
leaders, with the exception of Bryan, who refrained from
political activity on the Sabbath, conferred all day, and all
the candidates but McAdoo agreed to release their delegates.

On Monday the shift began. McAdoo dropped below
Smith and released his delegates on Tuesday to E. T. Mere-
dith. Meantime a hurried message to Wayne Wheeler had
brought the information that Davis was satisfactory to the
League and would be still more so if the Vice Presidential
candidate were in favour of law enforcement.[37]

Bryan was in his room at the Waldorf-Astoria, sorting clippings, when Davis was nominated on Wednesday. He was

still a party regular and announced that he would support the candidate. In a midnight conference it was arranged that Charley Bryan should be Davis's running mate, and amid angry protests he was so nominated at two A. M. Thursday morning. It may have been a graceful gesture in William Jennings's direction, but it was not a trade for his support. *That* he had definitely pledged several hours before.

On Thursday he saw McAdoo off for Europe and left New York to join his wife in St. Louis. The treatment he had received at the hands of the New Yorkers rankled in his soul. He had been not "applauded, but hissed; not carried on shoulders, but in danger of being booted; not smiling, young, trim, inspiring and inspired, but hard, set of mouth, dogmatic, shrivelled, old and malicious."[38]

It was growing more and more dismal as the years piled up this going home from conventions with shattered hopes, to pick up the threads of his routine existence again.

But presently he was again the good political sport, campaigning for Davis, certainly with a better will in that he was campaigning for Charley at the same time.

So he invaded California, Oregon, and Washington and did what he could; which, judging from results, wasn't much. Davis was defeated and Bryan found consolation in the fact that Coolidge and Dawes were men of high character, though he went through the familiar motions of assuring the liberal politicians that the Democratic party was still the only hope of the masses.

The campaign over, he returned to Florida. Mrs. Bryan's condition was no better. The doctor had pronounced her incurable and in desperation she turned to faith healers.[39] William Jennings continued his operations in Florida real estate and, with a smile, sparkled and profited each day at Coral Gables. It must indeed have been profitable, if he was accurate in his letter to E. L. Lambright, editor of the Tampa *Tribune*, written in April, 1925, in which he estimated his fortune at less than half a million. His will disposed of over $800,000. Did Florida real estate so prosper him?

The world had changed. It had pilloried Bryan when it

discovered him beneficiary of $50,000 from Philo Bennett's will. It laughed sarcastically when he became a prosperous realtor.

Material things could not lighten their depressing days. His own health, Mrs. Bryan's plight, his loss of political adherents, led him for the first time to rest.

On July fifth William Jennings Bryan made his will!

CHAPTER XXX

REDEMPTION

In the name of God, farewell.

Trusting for my salvation to the blood of Jesus Christ, my Lord and Redeemer, and relying on his promise for my hope of resurrection, I consign my body to the dust and commend my spirit to God who gave it.

So William Jennings Bryan opened his will.

No conviction or passion in his life had been so important to Bryan as his idea of God. He came nearer physical combat in his defence of his brand of Christianity than he ever did for anything else. Ridicule may have eaten into his soul and hastened his death, but even those who shouted loudest that he was a fool paid tribute to his sincerity.

And they shouted!

To keep in touch with developments in evolution, he joined the American Association for the Advancement of Science, curiously enough forgetting to sign his check when he sent it in.[1] At the society's annual meeting he was roundly denounced by Edward L. Rice of Ohio Wesleyan as a menace not to science but to religion, for he provoked the students to a defiant choice between evolution and Christianity and they invariably chose the former.

"It is precisely because I am a follower of Christ," said Mr. Rice, "that I most resent the attitude of Mr. Bryan."[2]

Even Luther Burbank took a turn at him. "Mr. Bryan is an honoured friend of mine," he said, "yet this need not prevent the observation that the skull with which nature endowed him visibly approaches the Neanderthal type. Feeling and the use of gesticulation and words are more according to the nature of this type than investigation and reflection."[3]

In Tennessee the Anti-Evolution Law he had helped to pass was causing an upheaval. Like millions of other people in the country, the majority of the population had been ignorant of the existence of the evolution theory until Bryan had called their attention to its dangers. They had then elected to the Legislature on an anti-evolution platform John Washington Butler, a slow-moving, slow-thinking mountaineer, and he had averted the danger by composing and sponsoring the enactment of the Anti-Evolution Bill:

Be It Enacted, by the General Assembly of the State of Tennessee, that it shall be unlawful for any teacher in any of the universities, normals, and all other public schools in the State, which are supported in whole or in part by the public school funds of the State, to teach the theory that denies the story of the divine creation of man as taught in the Bible, and to teach instead that man has descended from a lower order of animals.

That the law might provoke opposition never entered their heads. It was aimed to preserve what everybody valued—the Bible and the beliefs grounded therein. Who could find anything to object to in that?

Apparently George Rappleyea of Dayton could. He was a civil engineer of considerable repute and such general culture that "visiting scientists sought him out and found pleasure in his company."[4] He saw that a violation of the law, brought to the attention of the court, would expose its folly and he pointed out to town boomers what a lot of priceless publicity the case might bring to Dayton.

His friend, John Thomas Scopes, a teacher in the local high school, admitted violation of the law and was indicted. The American Civil Liberties Union had offered to provide counsel for any teacher willing to test the law; the state provided counsel of its own.

On May fourteenth the state counsel wrote a letter to William Jennings Bryan:

We have been trying to get in touch with you by wire, to ask you to become associated with us in the prosecution of the case of the State vs. J. T. Scopes, charged with violation of the anti-evolution law, but our wires did not reach you.

We will consider it a great honor to have you with us in this prosecution. We will have no difficulty in obtaining the consent of the attorney general and the circuit judge for you to appear in the case.[5]

William Jennings hastened to signify his eager willingness to help and spent the next two months in preparation, giving particular attention to a summing-up speech that was to be the flower of his anti-evolutionary eloquence.

Dayton was agog with excitement. It is a pleasant town, lying "in a fat and luxuriant valley. . . . The homes are surrounded by pretty gardens, with cool green lawns and stately trees. The two chief streets are paved from curb to curb. The stores carry good stocks and have a metropolitan air. . . . A few of the town ancients still affect galluses and string ties, but the younger bucks are nattily turned out."[6] It was the counterpart of a thousand American small towns.

Over this one on the eighth of July hovered an air of festive anticipation, for Bryan was coming to town. Its buildings were adorned with banners, signs decorated every available flat space. One of them read:

THE SWEETHEART LOVE OF JESUS CHRIST AND PARADISE STREET IS AT HAND. DO YOU WANT TO BE A SWEET ANGEL? ITEMIZL YOUR SINS AND INIQUITIES FOR ETERNAL LIFE. IF YOU COME CLEAN GOD WILL TALK BACK TO YOU IN VOICE.

Clarence Darrow's agnosticism was an open secret. The famous criminal lawyer had volunteered his services to the Civil Liberties Union for Scopes's defence. Friends for years, he and Bryan had been finally alienated in 1908. As they fought at Dayton it seemed fabulous to remember that Darrow had ever supported Bryan. A heaven-sent opportunity for William Jennings to battle against a worthy opponent for God and Genesis.

The ears of the whole civilized world were turned to Dayton. Europe was enjoying the joke on America and the antics of its great politician who had "taken personal charge of God."

Had England forgotten W. E. Gladstone?

It was an orgy for the modern publicity mongers. They made every use of the humorous and dramatic spectacle of Blind Justice holding God and the gorilla on her scales. Every device for the recording of word and deed had been provided—telegraph instruments, radio microphones, motion picture men, and America's foremost journalists.

Associated with Darrow were Dudley Field Malone, an Assistant Secretary of State under Bryan and now an eminent divorce lawyer; Arthur Garfield Hays, official attorney for the Union and prominently identified with liberal legal battles; Dr. John Randolph Neal of Tennessee, formerly Dean of the University of Tennessee Law School; and later, T. B. McAlwee, also of Tennessee. On the side of Bryan and the state were A. T. Stewart, Circuit District Attorney; General Ben G. McKenzie of Dayton; County Judge J. Gordon McKenzie; his son, William Jennings Bryan, Jr.; and Sue and Herbert Hicks, local lawyers.

By wagon, by car, and afoot, the town and country folk streamed toward the court house. Mountain farmers and small shopkeepers, with their wives and children, "silent, gaunt men and women,"[7] who feared God and respected themselves, filled the benches long before the hour set for the opening. John Washington Butler, author of the bill, his big frame squeezed behind a press table, breathed a calm confidence characteristic of these people.

They loved and understood Bryan as only kindred souls could; they trusted him as they trusted God. They might not be able themselves to cope with these fine city gentry who had invaded their lives unasked, and threatened all that they held most dear, but the Lord had raised up a righteous man in their need, to defend them against the inexplicable attack of an alien host. And they made holiday to watch him do it.

The jammed court room had "the atmosphere of a blast

furnace." Judge Raulston came in, smiling, accompanied by his wife and daughters, who carried flowers. The girls were pretty and had their stockings rolled.[8]

Young Scopes was a slight, inconspicuous figure. Blond and good looking, his collar open and his forearms bare, he might have been "any college senior on a vacation." His childhood had been spent in Paducah, Kentucky, and a clergyman who had known the family there wrote to Bryan: "His father . . . was a rank socialist and confirmed infidel . . . his influence was all against God, the Bible, Society and the United States Government." It was his day and it was not. Two old giants overshadowed him.

Counsel for the defence was gathered on one side of the room and counsel for the prosecution, barring its most distinguished member, on the other.

All were informally coatless as the weather demanded, Darrow conspicuous in pongee shirt and blue suspenders.

Only Malone, conceding nothing of his elegance to the heat, shone in double-breasted coat and sartorial perfection. Throughout the trial he continued a source of wondering admiration to his simple audience, who followed his course about the room with craning necks and excited nudges of one another's ribs.

No stage entrance could have been more carefully prepared. William Jennings entered late, in a burst of applause. Like heavy-weights before the prize fight, Bryan and Darrow "stood for a moment chatting, with their hands on each other's shoulders."[9]

William Jennings Bryan on this, the twenty-ninth anniversary of his Cross of Gold speech was "an elderly man in baggy trousers . . . mostly bald except for a few stringy strands of graying hair that hang, a little untidily, over his . . . collar; that once superbly clear voice . . . a little marred by a slightly hissing sound that comes from age's imperfect teeth; the eyes, though they still flash, flash now with rather the cold hardness of an old fighter who has been denied success rather frequently."[10]

Every day of the trial Mrs. Bryan was carried into the

court room, to sit near her husband. Her presence seemed to transform him.

The court was opened with prayer by the Reverend Mr. Cartwright, and while he besought that the Holy Spirit might be "with the jury and with the accused, and with all the attorneys interested in this case . . . Mr. Darrow, Mr. Malone, and Mr. Hays looked steadily through the windows to where a slight breeze stirred the trees."[11]

The judge then read the charge and the first chapter of Genesis.

The charge against the defendant was that he had taught his pupils that man was descended from a lower order of animal, in violation of a state statute forbidding such teaching. The penalty was the payment of a fine of not less than $100 or more than $500 for each offence.

Scopes pleaded not guilty. Technically, the prosecution must prove only that Scopes had taught a theory of creation that contradicted the Bible. A flaw in the indictment was quickly corrected.

Darrow sought to determine whether expert witnesses on the meaning of evolution might be introduced for the defence, consideration of which point was postponed until Monday. A child, perched on the corner of the judge's bench,[12] drew names for the panel from a hat, and the jury was quickly chosen. It was comprised of six Baptists, four Methodists, one member of the Church of the Disciples of Christ, and one man who belonged to no church.[13]

Ten were farmers and one of the ten a teacher as well, one was a wealthy landowner, and one a shipping clerk. One of the Methodists was passed despite his confession that he didn't read the Bible as regularly as he should; but he remained suspect throughout the trial and was later accused of reading the *Literary Digest* and of owning a banjo. Another admitted that he couldn't read at all. Such as it was, however, the jury was chosen and court adjourned over the week-end.

Dayton was in an uproar, "half a street fair and half a religious revival meeting." Hot dogs, lemonade, and peanuts. Hawkers of religious tracts: "Hell and the High Schools,"

"God or Gorilla?" Minstrels, black and white, competed for the attention of the crowds. When a blind man sang: "How Beautiful Heaven Must Be," the men's faces softened and the women closed their eyes in ecstasy.

At night, by flaring lantern light, dozens of itinerant evangelists expounded God's word with ingenuity and fervour, offered to perform miracles, and called upon Him to blast all infidels.

Salvation was promised through a dozen magic formulæ. No sinner but could be saved. One holy man wore a sign on his back, proclaiming himself the Bible champion of the world; ". . . he had studied the Bible four hours a day for thirty-three years and . . . devised a plan of salvation that would save . . . even a scientist, a theatre actor, or a pirate on the high seas in forty days."[14]

Their day of glory was short-lived. On Monday most of the licences were revoked, on the ground that these brethren were going a trifle too far in their efforts to bring sinners to Jesus.

On Saturday the prosecution issued a statement through the press, withdrawing Friday's agreement to consider the admission of scientific evidence. Each side regarded the other with growing resentment and "sad incredulity that man should be so obtuse."

Bryan spent most of the day on the court-house lawn, coatless and collarless, receiving the hordes of the faithful who wanted to shake him by the hand. But he took time to issue an independent statement:

There is no doubt that evolution asserts man's descent from some lower form of life, and no scientific specialists could change the law or its meaning, no matter who these specialists might be or how many there might be. . . . The people of Tennessee have a right to protect the Bible as they understand it. They are not compelled to consider the interpretation placed upon it by people of other states, whether Christians or scientists or both.

Moreover, he continued, if witnesses had been brought from Tennessee to tell New Yorkers what was harmful for their children, such a step would have been regarded as "offensive as well as improper." The inference was clear.

Darrow, lying in wait on his bed at the Big House for whatever breath of air might stir the sultry atmosphere, read the stinging indictment and answered:

Mr. Bryan's statement about the rights of Tennessee to protect its religion is ambiguous, if he means that any state has the right to pass a law which prohibits the teaching of a theory that is contrary to any religion, and in doing so he is flying in the face of every state constitution. . . . Whether the scientists come from Tennessee or outside, the meaning of evolution cannot matter. Science is the same everywhere. The Constitution does not permit the Legislature to put a Chinese wall around the State of Tennessee, as Mr. Bryan seems to think should be done.[15]

On Sunday morning Bryan preached in the Methodist Episcopal Church South, where he was introduced as "the ambassador of Jesus Christ Our Lord."[16] In the afternoon he said to three thousand on the court-house lawn:

I am an enthusiast for education, but we have to deal with conditions as they are. A religion that didn't appeal to any but college graduates would be over the head or under the feet of ninety-nine per cent. of the people. The God I worship is the God of the ignorant as well as the God of the learned man. Thank God I am going to spend the latter days of my life in a locality where there is a belief in God, and in the son of God, in a civilization to be based on salvation through blood.[17]

A microphone had been installed in the court house with a loud speaker on the lawn, preparatory to Monday's session, which started off with a bang. Darrow offered an objection to opening court with prayer and Hays suggested that the Reverend Mr. Cartwright be substituted by a non-fundamentalist minister—a rabbi would do. This drew a horrified gasp from the spectators, who were beginning to refer to Darrow familiarly as "the infidel." A daily entry in the court record resulted, at Darrow's request that his objection had been duly made.

At intervals the high school band of fifty boys and girls played selections for the spectators. Bryan was wearing a shirt with no sleeves or collar but a stiff bosom, a shirt designed by Mrs. Bryan and executed by a competent seamstress. H. L. Mencken examined it closely, assuring Bryan that he proposed to have one made for himself.

Ignoring for the moment the question of scientific evidence, the defence, given an opening by McKenzie, moved to quash the indictment on the ground that the law was unconstitutional and too vaguely worded to be applicable to any specific case. Dr. Neal made the motion, but Darrow undertook the burden of support. Beginning with the legal technicalities involved, he was soon launched on a discussion of the Bible, its origins and interpretation. He was terribly in earnest.

Facing Bryan and a court room bristling with hard-eyed antagonism, his shoulders humped and a thumb hitched into his blue suspenders, he proceeded to confound every belief that his audience held sacred.

William Jennings "sat silently fanning himself . . . his eyes darting fire"[18] at his insolent foe.

The natives listened in stunned amazement, wondering perhaps why the Lord in His infinite wisdom hesitated to strike the blasphemer dead at their feet. Before he had finished, Darrow's sleeve was ripped out of his sweat-soaked shirt, and his eyes were filmed with exhaustion. The court adjourned to consider the motion and rendered its decision in the negative late next day.

They settled down to business again on Wednesday. The young attorney, Stewart, presenting the case for the prosecution, created a sensation by the brilliance and passion of his argument. It was a "cry of anguish from a man who clings to a raft of faith in a surging sea of doubt."

"I want to know," he cried, his arms raised above his head and his voice shaken, "that beyond this world there is happiness for me and for others. Would they have me believe that I was a worm and writhed in dust, and that I will go no farther when the breath has left my body?"

"The Sun may be eclipsed but the Democratic
Party never." Bryan at the Eclipse of the Sun in
1925 in Washington.

(Photograph from Wide World Photos)

The Judge's Bench at the Scopes Trial

Malone presented the case for the defence. He quoted a passage from an introduction that Bryan had written to a volume of Thomas Jefferson's:

He said in the first place that to attempt to compel people to accept a religious doctrine by act of law was to make not Christians but hypocrites. . . . He said, too, that there was no earthly judge who was competent to sit in a case and try a man for his religious opinions, for the judgment of the court, he said, would not be a judgment of law but the personal opinion of the judge. What could be more true? . . .

Tell me that Jefferson lacked reverence for religion. He rather lacks reverence who believes that religion is unable to defend itself in contest with error. He places a low estimate upon the strength of religion, who thinks that the wisdom of God must be supplanted by the force of man's puny arm.

"These words," said Malone, "were written by the gentleman referred to as the evangelical leader of the prosecution, and the defence appeals from the Fundamentalist Bryan of to-day to the Modernist Bryan of yesterday."

Stewart was on his feet with an objection, in which the Court sustained him. But Bryan rose and, speaking for the first time since the trial had begun, said:

"I require no protection from the Court. At the proper time I shall be able to show that my position now differs not at all from my position in those days."[19]

The wildest applause the court room had yet heard greeted this statement.

Witnesses were then examined to determine the nature of Scopes's teaching. When the fourteen-year-old Howard Morgan was questioned by Darrow as to just what his teacher had taught him, the audience was frankly enthralled and Bryan, cupping his ear to catch every word, "leaned forward, the lines on his square face deepening, his deep-set eyes under the arched, imperious eyebrows sparkled with determination." Darrow smiled sardonically.[20]

Having established by Howard's testimony that Scopes had indeed taught him the theory of evolution, Darrow called to the witness stand Dr. Maynard M. Metcalf of Johns Hopkins.

"Are you an evolutionist?" asked Darrow. Hardly had the words been spoken before Bryan jumped from his seat and "planked himself directly in front of chubby Dr. Metcalf . . . his gaze fixed immovably on the witness. Now and then his face darkened and his eyes flashed, but he never uttered a sound."[21]

The chief purpose in the examination of Dr. Metcalf and other experts was to test the admissibility of their evidence, and after it had been taken court adjourned.

Next day Bryan, in his only court room speech during the trial, argued against the admission of scientific evidence. He addressed himself not to the Court but to the simple country folk who listened to him in awed reverence. Whatever he was to the world at large, charlatan, time server, or simply a pitiful figure that had outlived its day, to the people of Tennessee he was still the "flawless, peerless leader," the shining champion of all the virtues.

I want the Christian people to know [he said], that I am not afraid to defend the Christian faith against agnostics. . . . The people of this State passed this law. The people of this State knew what they were doing when they passed the law, and they knew the dangers of the doctrine that they did not want taught to their children. And, my friends, it isn't proper to bring experts here to try to defeat the purpose of the people of this State.

The question is, can a minority in this State come in and compel a teacher to teach that the Bible is not true and make the parents of these children pay the expenses of the teacher to tell their children what these people believe is false and dangerous.

On page 194 [of Hunter's *Biology*] we have a diagram, and this diagram purports to give someone's family tree. Not only his ancestors but also his collateral relations. We are told just how many animal species there are. . . . We have circles differing in size, according to the number of species in them, and we have the guess that they give. . . .

And then we have mammals, 3500, and there is a little circle, and a man is in the circle. Find him; find Man!

There is the book. There is the book they were teaching your

children, teaching that man was a mammal and so indistinguish-
able among the mammals that they leave him there with other
mammals. . . .

Talk about putting Daniel in the lion's den! How dared those
scientists put man in a little ring like that, with lions and tigers
and everything that is bad?[22]

The audience applauded him madly when he sat down, and
Darrow shrugged in despair.

Malone rose to the defence.

"What is this psychology of fear?" he cried. "Why does
the prosecution demand that the other side should not be
heard?" Then, his voice softening, "I do not understand it
in my old chief. I have followed him in many a battle, and
he never ran away before."

But he didn't linger long on bathos. He pleaded for freedom of education. He pleaded for the right to introduce testimony which would prove that evolution was not hostile to
the Bible, and he finished on a note so stirring as to draw
from his reluctant audience a burst of applause as mad or,
according to some witnesses, madder than that which they
had accorded Bryan:

There is never a duel with truth. The truth always wins and we
are not afraid of it; the truth is no coward. The truth does not
need the law. The truth does not need the forces of government.
The truth does not need Mr. Bryan. The truth is imperishable,
eternal and immortal, and needs no human agency to support it.
We are ready. We feel we stand with progress. We feel we stand
with science. We feel we stand with intelligence. We feel we stand
with fundamental freedom in America. We are not afraid. Where
is the fear? We defy it. We ask your Honor to admit the evidence
as a matter of correct law, as a matter of sound procedure, and as
a matter of justice to the defence in this case.[23]

When the Court decided next day in a short and stormy
session that scientific evidence should not be admitted, Darrow's anger blazed uncontrollably. Gone was his urbanity,
gone his clear-sighted grasp of the situation. He seized
violently on technicalities. Then, when Judge Raulston

threatened to hold him in contempt of court for one of his reflections, he told him to go ahead. Having lost on every point he tried to make, he left the courtroom with lips grimly set. It was evident that he felt he had suffered these fools long enough.

Now, come what would, they should get their deserts as soon as he could mete them out!

Bryan, magnanimous in triumph, expressed his regret that the law precluded the introduction of scientific evidence. The truth, replied Darrow, was that Bryan didn't dare put his views to the test in the open court. The champion, he declared, "who blew the loud trumpet calling for a battle to the death has fled from the field."

On Sunday Bryan spoke at Sequatchie Valley, twenty miles out of Dayton, telling his listeners that the trial had proceeded far enough "for us to uncover a gigantic conspiracy among atheists and agnostics against the Christian religion."[24]

Darrow spoke at Chattanooga before the Y. M. C. A. on Bryan's old friend, Tolstoy.

Scopes went swimming.

On Monday Darrow, cooled off, apologized to the Court and avowed that he had been treated with the fullest courtesy. The scientific evidence was read into the record for use in a higher court in case of an appeal.

In the afternoon the proceedings were moved to the lawn, for greater comfort and to prevent the collapse of the court house under the eager pressure of the crowds. "A rough platform had been erected. . . . On one side . . . were the attorneys for the defence, on the other the prosecution; in the middle, the Judge's bench. Below, under the spreading trees, was the audience."[25]

A perfect setting for the trial's most dramatic scene. Mrs. Bryan's chair had been wheeled out to a place from which she could watch her husband's every move, and her body's rigidity contrasted strangely with the quick lighting and darting of her eyes.

Suddenly, and without consulting his colleagues, Mr.

Hays asked the Court if the defence might question Mr. Bryan.

The Court regarded him in dismay, then turned to Mr. Bryan.

By all means, agreed Mr. Bryan heartily, provided he might question Mr. Darrow in his turn. Mr. Darrow bowed. He would be delighted.

The jury was excused. An aëroplane whizzed overhead, and the Tennessee Christians leaned forward to hear. After a momentary confusion—due to the suddenness with which the task had been thrust upon him—Darrow began to question Bryan. Bryan's first answers were given with the sweetness of a "cooing dove."

"You have given considerable study to the Bible, haven't you, Mr. Bryan?"

"Yes, sir, I have tried to."

"Do you claim that everything in the Bible should be literally interpreted?"

"I believe everything in the Bible should be accepted as it is given there. Some of the Bible is given illustratively. For instance: 'Ye are the salt of the earth.' I would not insist that man was actually salt, or that he had flesh of salt; but it is used in the sense of salt as saving God's people."

"Do you believe . . . that He made . . . a fish . . . that was big enough to swallow Jonah?"

"Yes, sir. Let me add: one miracle is just as easy to believe as another."

The crowd whooped for its champion.

"You believe the story of the flood to be a literal interpretation? When was that flood?"

"I wouldn't attempt to fix the date."

The Court intervened, but Bryan refused to be rescued. "These gentlemen," he said, looking down upon them benignly, "have not had much chance. They did not come here to try this case. They came here to try revealed religion. I am here to defend it, and they can ask any questions they please."

But it wasn't long before both he and his interrogator began to lose their tempers. They had been on edge for many days. What seemed to Darrow the sheer incredible folly of his opponent got under his skin.

"Don't you know that there are many old religions that describe the flood?"

"No, I don't know. The Christian religion has satisfied me, and I have never felt it necessary to look up some competing religion."

Too much for Darrow! He started to make hash of Bryan. He pelted him with queries like whiplashes. He mocked, sneered, buzzed at his ears like a gadfly. From benignity Bryan was moved to irritation. From irritation, to bewildered defiance. As the questioning proceeded Darrow leaned over his table, straining his blue galluses, Bible in hand, and shot his questions with all the force he could command.

"Mr. Bryan, could you tell me how old the earth is?"

"No, sir; I couldn't."

"Could you come anywhere near it?"

"I wouldn't attempt it—I could possibly come as near as the scientists do, but I had rather be more accurate before I give a guess."

He clung to the props of his faith. But he was forced to admit that he knew nothing of geology, philology, or comparative religions, that the days of creation might really be millions of years, that he didn't know where Cain got his wife.

He glared at Darrow and sought encouragement from the throngs scattered open-mouthed over the grass.[26]

Young Stewart could stand the strain no longer. He jumped to his feet and condemned the whole procedure as illegal.

"What is the purpose of this examination?" he cried.

Both men sprang forward, hurling their answers not at the questioner but at each other.

"The purpose is to cast ridicule on everybody who believes in the Bible!" shouted Bryan.

"We have the purpose," roared Darrow, "of preventing

bigots and ignoramuses from controlling the education of the United States! And you know it—and that is all!"

Stewart couldn't stop them. The Court couldn't stop them. Darrow was speeding ahead, his eyes intent on his goal, and he dragged Bryan with him. With each question their passions rose visibly higher. With each answer they came nearer the breaking point. Bryan was the first to crack.

"The only purpose Mr. Darrow has," he cried, his voice trembling, his eyes misty with pain as they sought to fix themselves on his tormentor, "is to slur at the Bible."

"I object to your statement," shouted Darrow in a fury of anger. "I am examining you on your fool ideas, that no intelligent Christian on earth believes."[27]

Bryan's own faith could be questioned but not shaken. It defied analysis. He had intellectualized the tariff, but he shook with powerful rage when asked to question the soul. Bryan and Darrow, dog's tooth to bone, fought over God.

The Holy Bible was buffeted between two fits of temper!

They leaped at each other. The crowd bellowed in excitement, and Judge Raulston, pounding violently on his table, adjourned the Court.

Bryan sank into his chair, muttering over and over again, "slur the Bible—slur the Bible!"[28]

Next day came anti-climax. Darrow and Bryan were ready to go on where they had left off. But Stewart refused to allow it, and the Court ruled that yesterday's testimony be stricken from the record as irrelevant. The defendant was being tried on a charge of teaching that man was descended from a lower order of animal, a fact which had somewhere been lost sight of by all concerned.

Darrow waived his right to a summing-up address, and so added the final fillip to Bryan's discomfiture by depriving him of the chance to make the big speech he had been working on for two months, and which he had hoped would cover him with glory.

Scopes was found guilty and fined $100.

In an unsteady voice but with a natural dignity that won for him the respect of friend and foe alike, he said: "Your

Honor, I feel that I have been convicted of violating an unjust statute. I will continue in the future as I have in the past
to oppose this law in any way I can. Any other action would
be in violation of my ideal of academic freedom, that is, to
teach the truth as guaranteed in our Constitution of personal
and religious freedom."

Bryan had to content himself with a few words:

Human beings are mighty small, your Honor. We are apt to
magnify the personal element and we sometimes become inflated
with our importance, but the world little cares for man as an individual. He is born, he works, he dies, but causes go on forever,
and we who participated in this case may congratulate ourselves
that we have attached ourselves to a mighty issue.[29]

Court was dismissed. The lawyers made polite speeches
to the Judge and to each other, offering and receiving thanks
for hospitality and courteous treatment.

Only Bryan sat apart, "looking grim as the tombstone
of a forgotten king. . . . Presently he rose and moved about
among the attorneys and the ringside spectators. As he talked
he smiled, but only with his lips. There was no merriment in
his eyes."

Perhaps he had been counting on the miracle which he
had dreamed of as off-stage for him all his life.

No miracle at Dayton.

Only heat and a disappointed old man, and the futile
waving of a palm-leaf fan.

The show was over, but the fight for Bryan had just begun.
On Wednesday and Thursday he dictated the undelivered
speech. On Friday he went to Chattanooga to see George
Fort Milton to arrange for its printing. It was set up at once.
And that evening William Jennings read the first proof.

"I feel," he said, "that this is the mountain peak of my
life's efforts."[30]

He met Mrs. Bryan on Saturday morning just outside
Chattanooga. She had motored from Dayton and found him
waiting for her by the roadside, "vigorous and smiling."[31]
They went on to Winchester, Judge Raulston's home town,

where they lunched with him and other local celebrities, and where Bryan made a speech in the afternoon.

Then he returned to Chattanooga to correct page proofs,[32] while Mrs. Bryan went on to Dayton. There was a place in the text that didn't quite suit him. He inserted:

"With hearts full of gratitude to God."

These were the last words he ever wrote.

On Sunday morning he returned to Dayton. At eleven he and Mrs. Bryan went to church, where William Jennings offered a public prayer. During the noonday meal he told his wife that a doctor had examined him the day before and found him in excellent condition.[33]

"I never felt better in my life," he remarked, not once but several times. After dinner he made several long distance telephone calls, arranging for a vacation in the Smoky Mountains the following week. At three he called George Fort Milton, to arrange the release date of the speech.[34] All his heart and soul were in the details of that speech. He had found the perfect note on which to end it:

Faith of our fathers—holy faith,
We will be true to Thee till death.

Then Mr. Bryan lay down to take a nap. Mrs. Bryan was in her wheel chair on the porch. They were alone.

About half an hour later Mrs. Bryan heard her husband breathing heavily and became worried. But she could not move to go to him.[35]

Presently, McCartney, the chauffeur, came and she sent him to waken Mr. Bryan. McCartney found his master sleeping quietly, as he thought, and did not attempt to waken him. Mrs. Bryan was not reassured. She told him to go in again and to feel Mr. Bryan's pulse.[36]

There was no faintest stir at the wrist. Mr. Bryan was dead. He had died as he slept, of apoplexy accompanied by cerebral hemorrhage.

*　　*　　*　　*　　*

When William Jennings Bryan had stood before Napoleon's tomb in Paris, his eye was caught and held by a stained-glass window from which Christ looked down upon the scene.

"I do not know," he commented, "whether it was by accident or design that this god of war thus sleeps at the feet of the Prince of Peace, but to me it symbolized the victory of love over force."

What does it symbolize that the humble follower of the Prince of Peace lies buried in Arlington Cemetery, that tragic shrine dedicated to the memory of those who gave up their lives on the altar of the god of war?

BIBLIOGRAPHY

407

BIBLIOGRAPHY

E. H. Abbot: "William Jennings Bryan," *The Outlook*, August, 1925.

Willis John Abbot: "The Battle of 1900," Chicago, 1900. "William Jennings Bryan," *The American Review of Reviews*, August, 1896.

C. F. Adams: "1835–1915: An Autobiography," Boston, 1916.

Leslie H. Allen: "Bryan and Darrow at Dayton," New York, 1925.

American Church History Series, Vol. II and Vol. V, New York, 1893–1897.

American Issue, April, 1918.

American Mercury.

"American Secretaries of State and Their Diplomacy," Vol. X: "Bryan." New York, 1929.

A. T. Andreas: "History of Chicago," Vol. I, II, III, Chicago, 1884.

Annual Cyclopædia, New York, 1898.

Atlanta *Constitution.*

Atlantic Monthly.

J. H. Atwood: "William Jennings Bryan—A Well-Rounded Man."

Ray Stannard Baker "Woodrow Wilson: Life and Letters; Youth." Garden City, N. Y., 1927.

"Woodrow Wilson" in New York *Herald Tribune*, Jan., Feb., 1929.

Baltimore *Evening Sun.*

Harry Elmer Barnes: "Genesis of the World War" (third ed.), New York, 1929.

Harvey E. Bartholomew: "Bryan (the Boy of the Platte) Unveiled," Chicago, 1908.

J. S. Bassett: "Our War with Germany," New York, 1919.

Newton Bateman and Paul Selby: "Historical Encyclopedia of Illinois," Chicago, 1905.

Charles A. Beard: "Contemporary American History," New York, 1914.

Charles and Mary Beard: "Rise of American Civilization," New York, 1927.

Beloit *News*.

Count Johann von Bernstorff: "My Three Years in America," New York, 1920.

John Bigelow: "Retrospections of an Active Life," Vol. I, New York, 1909.

Joseph Bucklin Bishop: "Presidential Nominations and Elections," New York, 1916.

"Theodore Roosevelt and His Times," New York, 1920.

Frederick H. Blodgett: "Evolutionary Democrat," *Scientific Monthly*, July 1925.

Richard Boeckel: "Labor's Money," New York, 1923.

Ernest Ludlow Bogart and Charles Manfred Thompson: "The Industrial State" (Centennial History of Illinois, Vol. IV), Springfield, 1920.

Bogus Programme, Illinois College, Jacksonsville, Ill., 1881.

Boston *Herald*.

Claude G. Bowers: "Life of John W. Kern," Indianapolis, 1918.

William W. Brewton: "Life of Thomas E. Watson," Atlanta, Ga., 1926.

J. H. G. Brinkerhoff: "History of Marion County, Illinois," Indianapolis, 1909.

Sidney Brooks: "Mr. Bryan," *Living Age*, August 7, 1925.

Florence Whiting Brown: "Alcott and the Concord School of Philosophy."

John H. Brown: "Bryan, Sewall and Honest Money Will Bring Prosperity," New York, 1896.

Mary Baird Bryan: Scrapbook, 1896.

William Jennings Bryan: "Christ and His Companions of the New Testament," New York, 1925.

"Famous Figures of the Old Testament," New York, 1923.

"The Future of the Democratic Party," *The Outlook*, Vol. LXXVIII, New York, 1904.

"Guaranteed Banks," Chicago, 1908.

"Heart to Heart Appeals," New York, 1917.

"In His Image," New York, 1922.

"The Last Message," New York, 1925.

"Library of Congress Papers."

"Memoirs," New York, 1925.

"The Price of a Soul," New York, 1914.

"The Prince of Peace."

"Speeches," Vol. I, II, New York, 1913.

Speeches, articles and editorials printed in *The Commoner*, 1901–1923.

"A Tale of Two Conventions," New York, 1912.

"Under Other Flags," Lincoln, 1904.

William Jennings Bryan and Arthur Sewall: "Life and Speeches of William Jennings Bryan and Arthur Sewall," New York, 1896.

James Morgan Buckley: "A History of Methodism in the United States"; New York, 1896.

William Vincent Byars: "An American Commoner: The Life and Times of Richard Parks Bland," Columbus, Mo., 1900.

H. H. Caldwell: Articles in *Illinois College Alumni Quarterly*, 1925.

Andrew Carnegie: "Autobiography of Andrew Carnegie," Boston, 1920.

"Centennial History of Illinois," Vol. II, III, IV, Springfield, Ill., 1918–1920.

French Ensor Chadwick: "The Relations of the United States and Spain," New York, 1911.

Godfrey Rathbone Benson (Lord) Charnwood: "Abraham Lincoln," New York, 1917.

Joseph C. Chase: "Famous Sitters," *Saturday Evening Post*, August, 27 1927.

Chicago *Tribune, Record-Herald, Times*.

Richard Washburn Child: "Mr. Bryan Says, 'Boo!'" *Collier's Weekly*, July 13, 1912.

Champ Clark: "My Quarter Century of American Politics," New York, 1920.

Frederick Lyman Cobb: "Prohibition," New York, 1922.

Arthur C. Cole: "The Era of the Civil War," (Centennial History of Illinois, Vol. III), Springfield, 1919.

Collier's Weekly.

The Commoner.

John R. Commons: "Races and Immigrants in America," New York, 1920.

Congressional Globe.

Congressional Record.

Royal Cortissoz: "The Life of Whitelaw Reid," New York, 1921.

Herbert Croly: "Marcus Alonzo Hanna," New York, 1919.

Shelby M. Cullom: "Fifty Years of Public Service," Chicago, 1911.

George William Curtis: Orations and Addresses, New York, 1892–1893.

Josephus Daniels: "Life of Woodrow Wilson," Philadelphia, 1924.

Elmer Davis: Articles on 1924 Convention in the New York *Times*.

H. P. Davis: "Black Democracy," New York, 1928.

Current History.

Denver *News*.

Davis Rich Dewey: "National Problems," New York, 1907.

John Dewey: "America's Intellectual Frontier," *The New Republic*, May 10, 1922.

Arthur Wallace Dunn: "From Harrison to Harding," New York, 1922.

"Gridiron Nights," New York, 1915.

"How Presidents Are Made," New York, 1920.

Charles M. Eames: "Historic Morgan and Classic Jacksonville," Jacksonville, 1885.

Charles H. Eggleston: "When Bryan Came to Butte," Butte, Mont., 1912.

El Paso *Times*.

Milo Erwin: "The History of Williamson County, Illinois," Marion, Ill., 1876.

Emily Faithful: "Three Visits to America," Edinburgh, 1884.

L. E. Fitch: "Lincoln's Growth," Lincoln, Neb., 1889.

Joseph Benson Foraker: "Notes of a Busy Life," Cincinnati, 1916.

Henry James Ford: "Explaining Mr. Bryan," *World's Work*, May, 1908.

Carter Glass: "An Adventure in Constructive Finance," Garden City, N. Y., 1927.

Foreign Relations of the United States: 1898-1914: Supplement, The World War: 1915.

Harry E. Fosdick: "Evolution and Mr. Bryan," Chicago, 1922.

Glenn Frank: "William Jennings Bryan," *Century*, September, 1923.

Edward A. Freeman: "Some Impressions of the United States," London, 1883.

Albert L. Gale and G. W. Kline: "Bryan The Man," St. Louis, 1908.

A. G. Gardiner: "Prophets, Priests and Kings," London, 1917.

Gilson Gardner: "The Sunrise Conference," *McNaught's Monthly*, June, 1925.

Weston Arthur Goodspeed: "History of Cook County," Chicago, 1911.

BIBLIOGRAPHY 413

C. Hartley Grattan: "St. Andy," *The American Mercury*, July, 1928.

"The Walter Hines Page Legend," *The American Mercury*, 1925.

Viscount Grey of Fallodon: "Twenty-five Years," New York, 1925.

William Bayard Hale: "Mr. Bryan," *World's Work*, June, 1913.

Norman Hapgood and Henry Moskowitz: "Up from the City Streets," New York, 1927.

Arnold B. Hall: "Popular Government," New York, 1921.

William Hard: "What About Bryan?" *Everybody's Magazine*, April, 1916.

Harper's Weekly.

Mrs. J. Borden Harriman: "From Pinafore to Politics," New York, 1923.

D. H. Harris: "A Brief Report of the Meeting Commemorative, of the Early St. Louis Movement in Philosophy, Psychology, Literature, Art and Education," St. Louis, 1921.

Frederic Harrison: "Autobiographic Memories," London, 1911.

W. H. Harvey: "Coin's Financial School," Chicago, 1894.

Joseph Hatten: "Henry Irving's Impressions of America," Boston, 1884.

Paul L. Hawarth: "The United States in Our Own Times," New York, 1920.

A. B. Hayes and Samuel D. Cox: "History of Lincoln," Lincoln, Neb., 1889.

Arthur Garfield Hays: "Let Freedom Ring," New York, 1928.

John L. Heaton: "Cobb of 'The World,'" New York, 1924.

Burton J. Hendrick: "The Life and Letters of Walter Hines Page," Garden City, N. Y., 1923.

"The Training of an American," New York and Boston, 1928.

Mrs. Genevieve and J. O. Herrick: "The Life of William Jennings Bryan," Chicago, 1925.

Ida Hinman: "The Washington Sketch Book," Washington, 1895.

Paxton Hibben: "Henry Ward Beecher: An American Portrait," New York, 1927.

George F. Hoar: "Autobiography of Seventy Years," New York, 1903.

Richard Hooker: "Story of an Independent Newspaper," New York, 1924.

Charles F. Horner: Articles in *Lyceum Magazine*, November, 1925.

Edward M. House: "Intimate Papers," arranged as a narrative by Charles Seymour, Boston, 1926.

David Houston: "Eight Years with Wilson's Cabinet," Garden City, N. Y., 1926.

Frederic C. Howe: "Confessions of a Reformer," New York, 1925.

Henry Howe: Historical Collections of Virginia, Charleston, S. C., 1852.

Illinois College Alumni Quarterly, Vol. III, Jacksonville, Ill.

Illinois College Catalogue, 1878–1881, Jacksonville, Ill.

Illinois *State Register.*

India.

Indianapolis *Star.*

Jacksonville *Courier-Journal.*

Jacksonville Female Academy Catalogue, Jacksonville, 1878–1881.

Leland H. Jenks: "Our Cuban Colony," New York, 1928.

Tom L. Johnson: "My Story," New York, 1911.

Davis Starr Jordan: "Imperial Democracy," Boston, 1898.

Journal of the American Akádémé.

Judge.

Frank Richardson Kent: "The Democratic Party," New York, 1928.

J. K. Kinney: "A Scholar's View of Mr. Bryan," *North American Review,* February, 1914.

Joseph Kirkland: "The Story of Chicago," Chicago, 1892.

A. Kitson: "William Jennings Bryan," *Fortnightlly Review,* October, 1914.

M. M. Knight: "The Americans in Santo Domingo," New York, 1928.

Herman H. Kohlsaat: "From McKinley to Harding," New York, 1923.

Robert M. LaFollette: "LaFollette's Autobiography," Madison, Wis., 1913.

John Holladay Latané: "America as a World Power," New York, 1907.

David Lawrence: "The True Story of Woodrow Wilson," New York, 1924.

James Lawrence Laughlin: "Bi-Metallism in the United States," New York, 1896.

Leslie's Weekly.

Alfred Henry Lewis: "Life of Richard Croker," New York, 1901.

Lincoln *State Journal.*

BIBLIOGRAPHY 415

Literary Digest.

London *Times.*

J. C. Long: "Bryan, the Great Commoner," New York, 1928.

Edward G. Lowry: "Washington Close-Ups," Boston and New York, 1921.

Maurice F. Lyons: "William F. McCombs—President Maker," New York.

William Gibbs McAdoo: "Prohibition, Nullification and Lawlessness," U. S. Govt. Printing Office, 1927.

"Williams Jennings Bryan," New York *Times*, Aug. 5, 1925.

Samuel W. McCall: "Life of Thomas B. Reed," Boston, 1914.

William F. McCombs: "Making Woodrow Wilson President," New York, 1921.

B. W. McDonald: "History of the Cumberland Presbyterian Church," 1888.

J. L. McDonough: "Combined History of Randolph, Monroe and Perry Counties, Illinois," Philadelphia, 1883.

Robert McNutt McElroy: "Grover Cleveland," New York, 1923.

Thomas H. McKee: "The National Conventions and Platforms," Baltimore, 1906.

William McKinley: "Speeches and Addresses," New York, 1893.

Frank L. McVey: "The Populist Movement," New York, 1896.

Manila *Libertas.*

Thomas R. Marshall: "Recollections," Indianapolis, 1925.

Edgar Lee Masters: "The Christian Statesman," *The American Mercury*, December, 1924.

H. L. Mencken: Dayton Articles in the Baltimore *Evening Sun*, 1925.

Charles E. Merriam: "The American Party System," New York, 1922.

"Four American Party Leaders," New York, 1926.

Richard L. Metcalfe: "The Real Bryan."

"Victorious Democracy," Chicago, 1900.

"Mirrors of Washington," New York, 1921.

Samuel E. Moffett: "Mr. Bryan's Election," *American Review of Reviews*, Vol. XXXVIII.

J. B. Moore: International Law Digest, Vol. VII.

Albert T. Morgan: "On Our Way to the Orient," Denver, 1909.

Henry Morganthau: "All in a Life-Time," Garden City, N. Y., 1922.

David Muzzey: "An American History," New York, 1911.

The Nation.

National Encyclopedia of American Biography.

Nebraska *State Leader.*

Harvey E. Newbranch: "William Jennings Bryan," Lincoln, Neb., 1900.

New Republic.

New York *American, Herald Tribune, Evening Post, Sun, Times, Tribune, World, Evening World.*

Nineteenth Century and After, July, 1915.

George K. Norris: "Bryan as a Political Leader," *Current History*, September, 1925.

North American Review.

Peter H. Odegard: "Pressure Politics," New York, 1928.

John S. Ogilvie: "Life and Speeches of William J. Bryan," New York, 1896.

Charles S. Olcott: "The Life of William McKinley," Boston, 1917.

Omaha *Bee, World-Herald.*

Henry Fairfield Osborn: "The Earth Speaks to Bryan," New York, 1925.

"Evolution and Religion," New York, 1923.

Richard V. Oulahan: "Campaign Rigors That Try Candidates," the New York *Times Magazine*, Sept. 16, 1928.

George F. Parker: "Recollections of Grover Cleveland" New York, 1909.

Frederick Logan Paxson: "History of the American Frontier," New York and Boston, 1924.

"The Last American Frontier," New York, 1910.

"Recent History of the United States," New York and Boston, 1928.

T. C. Pease: "The Frontier State" (Centennial History of Illinois, Vol. II, Springfield, 1918.

Harry Thurston Peck: "Twenty Years of the Republic," New York, 1906.

R. F. Pettigrew: "Imperial Washington," Chicago, 1922.

James K. Pollock: "Methods of Raising Campaign Funds," New York, 1925.

Arthur Ponsonby: "Falsehood in War Time," New York, 1928.

Perley Poore: "Perley's Reminiscences, or Sixty Years in the National Metropolis," Philadelphia, 1886.

Prairie Farmer.

Puck.

Joseph Gilpin Pyle: "Life of James J. Hill," Garden City, N. Y., 1917.

Julian Ralph: "Our Great West," New York, 1923.

The Rambler, Jacksonville, Ill., 1876–1881.

William C. Redfield: "With Congress and Cabinet," Garden City, N. Y., 1924.

Review of Reviews.

Edward L. Rice: "Darwin and Bryan," *Science*, March 6, 1925.

James D. Richardson: "A Compilation of the Messages of the Presidents," U. S. Govt. Printing Office, 1899.

James Ford Rhodes: "History of the United States," Vol. IV, VII, VIII, IX, New York, 1906, 1919, 1923.

J. Fred Rippey: "The United States and Mexico," New York, 1926.

Corinne Roosevelt Robinson: "My Brother, Theodore Roosevelt," New York, 1921.

Theodore Roosevelt: "Theodore Roosevelt's Diaries of Boyhood and Youth," New York, 1928.

Elihu Root: "Speech of Elihu Root at Furland's Riding Academy," Washington, 1908.

J. J. Russell: "The Next Political Battle," New York, 1898.

George Augustus Sala: "America Revisited," London, 1882.

Carl Sandburg: "The American Song Bag," New York, 1927.

   Abraham Lincoln: "The Prairie Years," New York, 1926.

Saturday Evening Post.

James W. Savage and John T. Bell: "History of Omaha," Omaha, 1894.

Don Seitz: "Joseph Pulitzer," New York, 1924.

Albert Shaw: "William Jennings Bryan," *The American Review of Reviews*," September, 1924.

Lloyd Shaw: "The City of Lincoln," Lincoln, Neb., 1889.

L. B. Shippee: "Recent American History," New York, 1924.

Sigma Pi Records: Unpublished MSS., Jacksonville, Ill.

Esther Singleton: "The Story of the White House," New York, 1907.

Arthur D. H. Smith: "The Real Colonel House," New York 1918.

T. V. Smith: "Bases of Bryanism," *Scientific Monthly*, May, 1923.

Sigmund Spaeth: "Read 'Em and Weep," Garden City, N. Y., 1927.

J. A. Spender: "Life, Journalism, and Politics," New York, 1927.

Edward Stanwood: "American Tariff Controversies in the Nineteenth Century," Boston, 1903.

"History of Presidential Elections," Boston, 1888.

Orlando Oscar Stealey: "Twenty Years in the Press Gallery," New York, 1906.

G. W. Steevens: "The Land of the Dollar," New York, 1898.

Justin Steuart; "Wayne Wheeler, Dry Boss," New York, 1928.

Marietta Stevenson: "William Jennings Bryan as a Political Leader," in University of Chicago Library (unpublished).

William M. Stewart: "Reminiscences," New York, 1908.

Henry L. Stimson, "American Policy in Nicaragua," New York, 1926.

F. P. Stockbridge: "Bryan, the Great Commoner," *Current History*, September, 1925.

H. L. Stoddard: "As I Knew Them: Presidents and Politics from Grant to Coolidge," New York, 1927.

Mark Sullivan: "Our Times," Vol. I, II, New York, 1926, 1928.

William Roscoe Thayer: "Life and Letters of John Hay," Boston, 1915.

Augustus Thomas, *North American Review*, CLXXXVII.

Charles Willis Thompson: "Party Leaders of the Time," New York, 1905.

Times, of Bombay.

Toledo *News*.

Frank Basil Tracey: "Menacing Socialism," *The Forum*, May, 1893.

"Rise and Doom of the Populist Party," *The Forum*, Vol. 16.

Payson J. Treat: "Japan and the United States," Stanford University, 1928.

Julius A. Truesdall: "Our Statesmen: Who They Are, How They Look," New York, 1888.

Joseph P. Tumulty: "Woodrow Wilson as I Know Him," New York, 1921.

F. J. Turner: "The Problem of the West," *Atlantic Monthly* September, 1896.

"The Frontier of American History," New York, 1921.

Charles R. Tuttle: "Illinois Currency Conventions," Chicago, 1895.

United States Congressional Record: 35th Congress, first session; 52nd Congress; 53rd Congress; 69th Congress, first session. U. S. Govt. Printing Office.

United States Senatorial Campaign Investigations: Govt. Printing Office.

Oswald Garrison Villard: "Prophets True and False," New York, 1928.

Wall Street Journal.

Washington *Post.*

Sumner Welles: "Naboth's Vineyard," New York, 1928.

Everett P. Wheeler: "Sixty Years in American Life," New York, 1917.

Andrew B. White: "Autobiography of Andrew B. White," New York, 1905.

Horace White: "Life of Lyman Trumbull," Boston, 1913.

William Allen White: "The End of an Epoch," *Scribner's*, June, 1926.

"The Great Political Drama at St. Louis," *Collier's*, July 12, 1904.

"Woodrow Wilson," Boston and New York, 1924.

Brand Whitlock: "Forty Years of It," New York, 1925.

Edwin Wildman: "Famous Leaders of Character in America," Boston, 1922.

Wayne C. Williams: "William Jennings Bryan: A Study in Political Vindications," New York and Chicago, 1923.

Henry Lane Wilson: "Diplomatic Episodes in Mexico, Belgium and Chile," Garden City, N. Y., 1927.

Woodrow Wilson: "Cleveland as President," *Atlantic Monthly*, March, 1897.

"A History of the American People," Vol. V., New York, 1903.

John Kennedy Winkler: "W. R. Hearst," New York, 1928.

David Ward Wood: "Chicago and Its Distinguished Citizens," Chicago, 1881.

World's Work.

NOTES

NOTES

NOTES

CHAPTER I

(1) Andreas, II, 225-6; (2) Bigelow, I, 196; (3) N. Y. *Tribune*, March 22, 1860; Rhodes, II, 461.

CHAPTER II

(1) Beard, I, 140-1; (2) Brinkerhoff; Mrs. Anna Torrence, p. 411; (3) Henry Howe, p. 239; (4) Commons, p. 37; (5) A. Torrence, p. 412; (6) Brinkerhoff, p. 822; (7) Buckley, V, 529; (8) Brinkerhoff, p. 172; (9) Erwin, p. 490; (10) Brinkerhoff, p. 107; (11) Erwin, p. 62; (12) *ibid*; p. 63; (13) *ibid*., p. 49; (14) *ibid*., p. 57; (15) Brinkerhoff, p. 136; (16) *ibid*., pp. 137-8; (17) *ibid*., p. 127; (18) *ibid*., pp. 121-2.

CHAPTER III

(1) Perley Poore, p. 330; (2) Cole, p. 400; Erwin, pp. 267-8; (3) Erwin, p. 257; Chicago *Tribune*, Jan. 14 and 22, 1862; (4) Erwin, p. 258; (5) *ibid*., p. 261; (6) *ibid*., p. 305; (7) *ibid*., p. 302; (8) *ibid*., p. 301; (9) Miss Davenport, Rhodes, IV, p. 235; (10) Cole, p. 303; Erwin, pp. 275-6; (11) Cole, p. 315; (12) *ibid*., p. 306; (13) *ibid*., p. 297; (14) *ibid*., p. 298-9; (15) *ibid*., p. 300; (16) *ibid*., p. 307; (17) Anna Torrence, p. 412; (18) Mrs. Baird; (19) W. J. B. "Memoirs," p. 40; (20) *ibid*., p. 43; (21) *ibid*., p. 44; (22) *ibid*., p. 26; (23) *ibid*.

CHAPTER IV

(1) *Congressional Globe*, 35th Cong. 1st Sess., Part II, 962; (2) Proceedings, p. 552; (3) *ibid*., p. 83; (4) *ibid*., pp. 545-6; (5) *ibid*., pp. 311-2; (6) *ibid*, p. 745; (7) *ibid*., p. 139; (8) *ibid*., p. 453; (9) *ibid*., p. 428; (10) *ibid*., p. 425; (11) Green; (12) Brinkerhoff, p. 412; (13) "Mem." p. 18; (14) Joseph Schwartz; (15) Mrs. Baird; (16) Brinkerhoff, p. 412; (17) Bogart and Thompson, p. 34; (18) Cole, p. 251; (19) Perley Poore, p. 310; (20) Dr. William Hill quoted by Mark Sullivan in "Our Times," I, 116-7.

CHAPTER V

(1) "Mem." p. 44; (2) *ibid.*, p. 35; (3) *ibid.* p. 45; (4) Bogart and Thompson, p. 39; (5) Chicago *Tribune*, Jan. 1 and 12, 1875; (6) Bogart and Thompson, p. 49; (7) Green; (8) *American Church History Series*, Vol. II, 1894, p. 265; (9) *ibid.*, p. 271; McDonald; (10) *ibid.*, p. 303; (11) Green; (12) "Mem." p. 49; (13) *ibid.*, p. 52; (14) *ibid.*, p. 53; (15) Jacksonville *Courier*, June 3, 1925; (16) Bateman and Selby, p. 859; (17) Torrence, p. 414; (18) Green; (19) *Prairie Farmer*, Aug. 30, 1873; (20) Brinkerhoff; McDonough, p. 195; (21) *ibid.*

CHAPTER VI

(1) Illinois *Register*, April 16, 1857; (2) Rhodes, VII, 183-5; (3) *Congressional Record*, Jan. 10, 1876, p. 324; (4) N. Y. *World*, June 29, 1876; (5) Paxson, p. 70; (6) Democratic National Platform, 1876, N. Y. *World*, June 29, 1876; (7) Illinois *State Register*, Feb. 19, 1873; (8) Bogart and Thompson, pp. 85-6; (9) *Congress. Record*, March 30, 1874, pp. 2617-8; (10) Rhodes, VI, 162; (11) June 15, 1877; (12) *Congress. Record*, April 6, 1874, p. 2825; (13) Poland Report, p. 10; (14) *Congress. Record*, March 23, 1874, p. 2354; (15) Bogart and Thompson, p. 115; (16) *Nat'l. Cyclopedia of Am. Biog.* III, 390; (17) N. Y. *World*, June 23, 1876; (18) "Mem." p. 97; (19) N. Y. *World*, June 29, 1928.

CHAPTER VII

(1) "Mem." p. 98; (2) Stevenson, p. 8; (3) *Journal of the American Akádémé*, I; (4) "Mem." p. 52; (5) *ibid.*, p. 53; (6) Bateman and Selby, pp. 741-2; (7) *Journal of the American Akádémé*, I, 47; (8) Brown, p. 5; (9) *ibid.*; (10) "Mem." p. 53; (11) Dr. Carl E. Black: Statement; (12) "First Battle," p. 38; "Mem." p. 58; (13) W. J. B. Speeches, II, 283; (14) "Prince of Peace," pp. 11-2; (15) Allen, pp. 133-56; Stevenson, p. 10; (16) Mary Baird Bryan's Scrapbook; Article by James Barton; (17) Albert Mordell: Interview; (18) *ibid.*; (19) Sigma Pi Records, p. 15; (20) *ibid.*, 55; (21) *ibid.*, 71-2; (22) Abbot, "William Jennings Bryan," p. 162; (23) "Mem." p. 59; (24) *ibid.*, p. 85; (25) Scrapbook; (26) "First Battle," p. 39; (27) Sigma Pi Records, p. 83; (28) *ibid.*, pp. 71-2; (29) Eames, p. 183; (30) Hulett: Letter; (31) "Mem." p. 223; (32) *ibid.*, p. 53; (33) July 11, 1896; (34) "Mem." p. 56; (35) Article

by James Barton, M. B. B.'s Scrapbook; (36) "Mem." p. 91; (37) *Rambler*, II, 9; (38) Illinois College Catalogue; (39) Caldwell, *Illinois College Alumni Quarterly*, III, No. 4, Oct. 1925, p. 5; (40) *ibid.*, p. 6; (41) "Mem." p. 222; (42) *ibid.*, p. 86; (43) Sigma Pi Records, p. 20; (44) *ibid.*, p. 84; (45) *ibid.*, p. 116; (46) *ibid.*, p. 83; (47) *ibid.*, p. 76; (48) *Rambler*, II, 52; (49) Sigma Pi Records, p. 161; (50) Toledo *News* Aug. 30, 1896; (51) Scrapbook, p. 20; (52) *ibid.*; (53) "Mem." pp. 222–3; (54) *Rambler*, II, 92; (55) Sigma Pi Records, p. 173; (56) "Mem." p. 88; (57) *ibid.*, p. 86; (58) *ibid.*, p. 91.

CHAPTER VIII

(1) Rhodes, VIII, 115–27; (2) "First Battle," p. 40; (3) Jacksonville *Courier-Journal*, June 4, 1925; (4) Dunlap: Statement; (5) "Mem." p. 244; (6) J. F. A. Catalogue 1879–80; (7) *ibid.*; (8) *Rambler*, IV, 4; (9) *ibid.*, p. 12; (10) Sigma Pi Records, pp. 136–7; (11) "Mem." pp. 41, 57, 87; (12) Hulett: Letter; (13) Rammelkamp: Statement; (14) "Mem." p. 223–4; (15) Caldwell, p. 6; (16) Ill. Coll. Catalogue; (17) Caldwell, p. 6; (18) *Rambler*, III, 74; (19) Bogus Programme; (20) Sigma Pi Records, P. 208; (21) Allen, p. 153; (22) Caldwell, p. 7; (23) *Rambler*, IV, 66; (24) *ibid.*, p. 42; (25) *ibid.*, p. 74; (26) Speeches, II, 376–8; (27) H. W. B., p. 105; (28) "Mem." p. 230.

CHAPTER IX

(1) *Leslie's*, Nov. 19, 1881; (2) N. Y. *Times*, Sept. 9–16, 1881; (3) Wood, p. 5; (4) Kirkland, III, 127; (5) Wood, p. 328; (6) Kirkland, III, 868; (7) N. Y. *Times*, Oct. 7, 1881; (8) Kirkland, III, 166; (9) *Leslie's*, Sept. 10, 1881; (10) *Leslie's*, Sept. 5, 1881; (11) N. Y. *Times*, Sept. 22, 1881; (12) Kirkland, III, 868; (13) Horace White, p. 418–9; (14) *ibid.*, pp. 424–5; (15) *ibid.*, pp. 146–7; (16) Brinkerhoff, p. 604; (17) "In His Image," p. 45; (18) Horace White, p. 431; (19) "In His Image," p. 112; (20) Talbot: Statement; (21) "Mem." p. 228; (22) Hulett: Letter; (23) Thomas: Statement.

CHAPTER X

(1) Brown, p. 48; (2) Bateman and Selby, p. 742; (3) *Journal of the Akádémé*, I, 1; (4) Block quoted in Harris, pp. 23–4; (5) Hulett: Letter; (6) "Mem." p. 76; (7) Wayne Gard: Letter; (8) "First

Battle," p. 47; (9) "Mem." p. 65; (10) *ibid.*, p. 66; (11) *ibid.*, p. 63; (12) Scrapbook, p. 5, "Mem." p. 226; (13) *ibid.*, p. 65; (14) *Congress. Record*, LXVII, 5897; (15) Y. M. C. A. Records, II, 298; (16) N. Y. *Herald*, July 10, 1884; (17) "Mem." pp. 98–9; (18) N. Y. *Herald*, July 9, 1884; (19) *ibid.*, July 10, 1884; (20) 9, VII; (21) Mordell: Interview; (22) "Mem." p. 259; (23) *ibid.*, p. 230; (24) Jacksonville *Journal*, June 4, 1925; (25) Washington *Post*.

CHAPTER XI

(1) Rhodes, VIII, 277; (2) Omaha *Bee*, Sept. 29, 1888; (3) *ibid*; (4) "First Battle," p 49; (5) Omaha *Bee*, Sept. 28, 1888; (6) Omaha *World-Herald*, Aug. 6, 15, 18, 1888; (7) Gordon; (8) Dahlman, "Mem." 248–9; (9) Metcalfe-Boell; (10) Metcalfe, p. 57; (11) *Bee*, Oct. 20, 1888; (12) Gale and Kline, p. 136; (13) N. Y. *Times*, June 7, 1888; (14) Rhodes, VII, 313; (15) *ibid.*, p. 316; (16) N. Y. *Times*, June 27, 1888; (17) Lloyd Shaw, p. 24; (18) *ibid.*, (19) Omaha *Bee*, July 31, 1890; (20) Omaha *World-Herald*, Sept. 24, 1890.

CHAPTER XII

(1) Prof. Robbins: Statement; (2) "First Battle," p. 50; (3) Omaha *Bee*, Nov. 28, 1927; (4) Metcalfe, pp. 97–8; (5) McVey, p. 137; (6) Omaha *Bee*, Oct. 1, 2, 1890; (7) Omaha *World-Herald*, Oct. 9, 1890; (8) Omaha *Bee*, Oct. 19, 31; Nov. 1, 1890; (9) Post to Dr. Stevenson, Apr. 18, 1926; (10) Jan. 29, 1890; (11) Quoted in Rhodes, VIII, 353; (12) Scrapbook, p. 90; (13) Rhodes, VIII, 354; (14) McKinley, Speeches and Addresses, p. 492; (15) Chicago *Times*, Nov. 27, 1894; (16) Omaha *Bee*, Sept. 18, 1891; (17) Orations and Addresses, II, 435; (18) Clipping, Scrapbook, p. 7; (19) Dec. 7, 1891, Scrapbook, p. 100; (20) Clark, p. 273; (21) "Mem." p. 238; (22) *Congress. Record*, 52d Cong. 1st Sess., p. 181; (23) Scrapbook, p. 18.

CHAPTER XIII

(1) Scrapbook, pp. 9, 32; (2) *ibid.*, p. 53; (3) *Congress. Record*, 52d Cong. 1st Sess., p. 78; (4) Abbot, p. 164; (5) Scrapbook, p. 32; Jan. 29, 1892; (6) "Mem." p. 233; (7) Abbot, "William Jennings Bryan," p. 164; (8) Mar. 20, 1892; (9) Speech, Jan. 8 1892,

Scrapbook, p. 15; (10) "Mem." (11) N. Y. *Times*, Mar. 17, 1892; (12) Scrapbook, p. 37; (13) N. Y., *Times*, Mar. 17, 1892; (14) Speeches, I, 45; (15) Washington *Post*, Mar. 17,1892; (16) Sullivan, I, 119, Footnote; (17) Scrapbook, p. 30; (18) *ibid.*, p. 31; (19) *ibid.*, p. 91; (20) Omaha *Bee*, Scrapbook, p. 61; (21) Scrapbook, p. 31; (22) Omaha *World-Herald*, June 21, 1892; (23) Omaha *Bee*, June 21, 1892; (24) *Nation*, May 21 and June 11, 1896; (25) John F. Miller in Stealey, pp. 221–2; (26) Scrapbook, p. 20; (27) Omaha *World-Herald*, Sept. 23, 1892; (28) Robbins: Statement; (29) *World-Herald*, Talmage meeting, Sept. 29, 1892; (30) Robbins, *World-Herald*, Sept. 23, 1892; (31) Washington *Post*, Mar. 20, 1892; (32) *World-Herald*, Sept. 7, 1892; (33) Letter: July 16, 1928; (34) Rhodes, VIII, 322; (35) N. Y. *Times*, July 28, 1928; (36) "Mem." p. 256.

CHAPTER XIV

(1) McElroy, II, 34; (2) Rhodes, VIII, 400; (3) McElroy, II, 80–1; (4) Rhodes, VIII, 397; (5) McElroy, II, 29; (6) Paxson, p. 190; Rhodes, VIII, 384; Masters, p. 385–6; (7) Rhodes, VIII, 404; (8) *ibid.*; (9) McElroy, II, 21; (10) McElroy, II, 27; (11) Kitson, p. 562; (12) Rhodes, VIII, 250; (13) McElroy, II, 31; (14) Speech in U. S. Senate, Aug. 25, 1893; (15) McElroy, II, 34; (16) Speech in H. of R., Feb. 9, 1893; (17) McElroy, II, 21; (18) Speech of February 27, 1893; (19) *Congress. Record*, Speech of Aug. 16, 1893; (20) *ibid.*, (21) Whitlock, p. 80; (22) Tuttle, p. 46; (23) Steevens; Bryan and Sewall, p. 26; (24) Washington *Post*, Aug. 18, 1893; (25) Scrapbook, II, 37; (26) McElroy, II, 33, 93; (27) Scrapbook, II, 39; (28) *ibid.*, 45; (29) *ibid.*, 37; (30) *ibid.*, 157; (31) Parker, p. 214; (32) Beard, II, 217; (33) Rhodes, VIII, 403; (34) Nebraska *State Leader*, Oct. 14, 1893; (35) Metcalfe, p. 146; (36) *ibid.*, pp. 142–3;(37) Omaha *Bee*, Oct. 5, 1893; (38) *ibid.*, Oct. 15, 1893; (39) Metcalfe, p. 163; (40) *ibid.*, p. 142; (41) *ibid.*, p. 135; (42) Kitson, 563; (43) Speech, Aug. 16, 1893; (44) Speech, Jan. 9, 1894; (45) Johnson, p. 109; (46) Con Backley to the Hon. Clinton Babbit, in the Beloit *News*; (47) Jan. 13, 1893; (48) Speech, Jan. 20, 1894; (49) Jan. 31, 1894; (50) Jan. 30, 1894; (51) N. Y. *World*, Feb. 2, 1894; (52) *ibid.*; (53) N. Y. *Sun*, Feb. 2, 1894; (54) *ibid.*; (55) Washington *Post*, Mar. 20, 1892; (56) Dan Bride; (57) *ibid.*; (58) *Rev. of Rev.*; (59) "Mem." p. 98; (60) "First Battle," p. 121; (61) McElroy, II, 77; (62) *Congress. Record*, Dec. 22, 1894.

CHAPTER XV

(1) "First Battle," p. 59; (2) House and Senate Journals; (3) McElroy, II, 80–1; (4) Cf. Rhodes, VIII, 458; (5) Speech: H. of R., Feb. 14, 1895; (6) Steevens, p. 83; W. W. in *Atlantic*, Mar. 15, 1897; (7) Tom Johnson; Abbot, p. 161; (8) Dodd in Stevenson, p. 96; (9) Metcalfe, p. 198; "First Battle," p. 150; (10) Boell; Lee Herdmann; (11) McElroy, II, 225–6; (12) *Congress. Comm. Report*, quoted in Stevenson, p. 48; (13) Wm. Allen White, p. 565; (14) McElroy, II, 36; (15) Steevens, p. 242; (16) Abbot, "William Jennings Bryan," p. 165; (17) *ibid.*; (18) Boell: Letter, Aug. 18, 1928; (19) Prof. H. Alexander: Letter, June 18, 1928; (20) *Journal*, 1895; (21) Horace White, p. 415; (22) Abbot, (23) Cf. McElroy, II, 36; (24) Metcalfe, pp. 201; (25) N. Y. *World*, May 15, 1904; (26) Kitson, p. 560; (27) Speeches and Addresses, p. 492; (28) Albert Shaw: *Rev. of Rev.* LXXII, 260; (29) Sydney Brooks, p. 90; (30) "First Battle," p. 160; (31) Kohlsaat, p. 52; (32) Houston, p. 36; (33) Abbot, p. 170; (34) "First Battle," p. 157; (35) Tuttle, pp. 100–7; (36) Letter: Aug. 10, 1928; (37) Byars, p. 232; (38) El Paso *Times*, Jan. 23, 1896; (39) "First Battle," p. 126.

CHAPTER XVI

(1) *Atlantic*, Mar. 15, 1897; (2) Stevenson, p. 121; (3) Gale and Kline, pp. 179–80; (4) Charnwood, p. 146; (5) *Congress. Record*, XXI, Part 5, 51st Congr., 1st Session, p. 4702; (6) Stevenson, p. 70; (7) McElroy, II, 218–20; (8) Dunn, p. 175; (9) Clark, p. 401; (10) "Mem." p. 102; (11) Dunn. p. 182; Chicago *Tribune* and Chicago *Record*, July 3, 1896; (12) May 21, 1896; (13) "Mem." pp. 99–100; (14) Dunn, p. 141; (15) *ibid.*, p. 181; (16) Dunn, p. 184; (17) "Mem." pp. 105–6; (18) *ibid.*, pp. 108–9; (19) Abbot, "William Jennings Bryan" p. 164; (20) Chicago *Times*, June 26, 1896; (21) Frederic Howe, p. 134; (22) "Mem." p. 31; (23) *ibid.*, p. 101; (24) *ibid.*, p. 106; (25) N. Y. *Tribune*, July 13, 1896; (26) "Mem." p. 111; (27) *ibid.*; (28) Chicago *Tribune*, July 10, 1896; (29) Stevenson, p. 127; (30) "Mem." p. 112; (31) Masters, p. 387; (32) Peck, p. 498; (33) Masters, p. 387; (34) Peck, p. 502; (35) N. Y. *Tribune*, July 11, 1896; (36) *Congress. Record*, LXVII, No. 79, p. 5732; (37) N. Y. *Herald*, July 10, 1896; (38) Chicago *Tribune*, July 11, 1896; (39) "First Battle," pp. 216–7; (40) Tuttle, p. 54; (41) N. Y. *Tribune*, July 12, 1896; (42) Byars; (43) N. Y. *Tribune*, July 7, 1896; (44) Byars, pp. 296–7.

CHAPTER XVII

(1) Olcott, p. 321; (2) Byars, p. 206; (3) "First Battle,"p. 474; (4) *ibid.*; (5) Thayer, II, 145; (6) McKinley: Letter of Acceptance, Aug. 26, 1896; (7) "First Battle," p. 272; (8) *ibid.*, pp. 276–9; (9) *ibid.*, p. 297; (10) Speech, Oct. 31, 1908; (11) *Judge*, Aug. 11, 1896; (12) *ibid.*, Sept. 19, 1896; Andrew B. White, I, 206; (13) Thayer, II, 145; (14) "First Battle," p. 492; (15) Quoted in Sullivan, I, 180–1; (16) Pyle, I, 496; (17) Croly, p. 219; (18) *Nation*, Oct. 8, 1908, p. 328; (19) Rhodes, IX, 11; (20) McKinley: Letter of Acceptance; (21) Hendrick, p. 251; (22) Dunn, I, 187; (23) John Temple Graves in Brewton, p. 269; (24) Brewton, p. 271; (25) July 11, 1896; (26) White papers in Cornell University Library, Frederick William Holls to Andrew B. White, Aug. 5, 1896; (27) Cf. *Nation*, May 21, 1896; (28) N. Y. *World*, Mar. 30, 1908; (29) Rhodes, IX, 22; (30) Peck, p. 511; (31) Croly, p. 217; (32) *ibid.*, p. 219; (33) Stevenson, p. 145; (34) Cortissoz, II, 210; (35) Johnson, p. 109; (36) "First Battle," p. 303; (37) *ibid.*, p. 344; (38) *ibid.* p. 303; (39) T. V. Smith, pp. 506–7; (40) Lewis; (41) T. V. Smith, pp. 506–7; (42) "First Battle," p. 344; (43) *ibid.*, p. 300; (44) Edward C. Little in "First Battle," p. 257; (45) Stockbridge, p. 867; (46) Toledo *News*, Aug. 30, 1896; (47) *ibid.*; (48) "First Battle," p. 300; (49) Byars, p. 297; (50) Lowry, p. 34; (51) *ibid.*, p. 36; (52) *ibid.*; (53) Oulahan: N. Y. *Times Magazine*, Sept. 16, 1928; (54) Lowry, p. 40; (55) Thayer, II, 151; (56) Peck, p. 506; (57) Lowry, p. 36; (58) Foraker, p. 1, 494; (59) Steevens, pp. 83–6; (60) Thayer, II, 152; (61) Oulahan: N. Y. *Times Magazine*, Sept. 16, 1928; (62) p. 511; (63) Peck, p. 508; (64) Kitson, p. 565; (65) Kohlsaat, p. 52.

CHAPTER XVIII

(1) "First Battle,"p. 605; (2) Kohlsaat, p. 53; (3) p. 296; (4) "First Battle," p. 626; (5) W. J. B. to Wm. E. Brady, Dec. 3, 1920; (6) N. Y. *Times*, Feb. 28, 1897; (7) Stevenson, p. 160; (8) N. Y. *Times Magazine*, Oct. 21, 1928; (9) McElroy, II, 248–9; (10) *ibid.*, pp. 250–1; (11) Atlanta *Constitution*, Mar. 4, 1897; (12) McElroy, II, 252; (13) Cortissoz, II, 318; (14) *World's Work*, Sept., 1923; Muzzey, p. 571; (15) N. Y. *World*, July 11, 1926; (16) N. Y. *Herald*, July 11, 1896; (17) *Rev. of Rev.*, Sept., 1925; Stevenson, 75–6; (18) C. W. Bryan: Statement; (19) Bartholomew, p. 15; (20) Sullivan, I, 304–5, Footnote; (21) Col. Mahr: Statement; (22)

Winkler, p. 124; (23) Lewis, p. 331; Dodd in Stevenson, p. 38; (24) Dan Bride: Statement; (25) Stevenson, p. 106; (26) Dunn, I, 237; (27) *Rev. of Rev.* XIV, 173; (28) "Mem." p. 286; (29) N. Y. *Times*, Feb. 11, 1897; (30) Merriam, **p.** 71; (31) N. Y. *Times*, Feb. 25, 1897; (32) *ibid.*, Feb. 28, 1897; (33) *ibid.*, June 13, 1897; (34) Bartholomew, p. 16; (35) N. Y. *Times*, July 16, 1897; (36) Merriam, p. 74; (37) Thayer, II, 156; (38) Moore, p. 75; (39) Winkler p. 144; (40) "Foreign Relations," 1898, p. 1007; (41) Roosevelt, p. 232; (42) "Foreign Relations," 1898, p. 684; (43) Rhodes, IX, 59; (44) Peck, p. 642; (45) "Foreign Relations," p. 732; (46) *ibid.*, pp. 746-7.

CHAPTER XIX

(1) To Lodge, Sept. 21, 1897; (2) "Foreign Relations," LIV; (3) Grover Cleveland in McElroy, II, 284; (4) Lodge to T. R., May, 1896; (5) Annual Cyclopedia, 1898, p. 739; (6) Olcott, II, 83; (7) N. Y. *Times*, June 2, 1898; (8) Gen. Vifquain in Lincoln *State Journal*, Sept. 23, 1898; (9) N. Y. *Times*, May 7, 1898; (10) T. R. Diary, June 3, 1898; (11) N. Y. *Times*, May 17, 1898; (12) Bryan Papers; (13) *ibid.*; (14) N. Y. *Times*, June 15, 1898; (15) *ibid.*; (16) *ibid.*, May 29, 1898; (17) *ibid.*, May 25, 1898; (18) *ibid.*, June 1, 1898; (19) *ibid.*, June 2, 1898; (20) Bartholomew, p. 20; (21) N. Y. *Times*, Apr. 14, 1898; (22) "Mem." p. 277; (23) N. Y. *Times*, June 15, 1898; (24) *XIX Century and After*, CCCCLXI, July 1915, p. 96; (25) W. J. B. Speeches, II, 385-6; (26) McElroy, II, [?]; (27) Boston *Herald*, Sept. 29, 1921; (28) Robinson, p. 169; (29) Dan Bride papers; Original letters; (30) Dan Bride papers, N. Y. *Times*, Sept. 7, 23, and 28, 1898; (31) *ibid.*, (32) Bryan papers, II; (33) N. Y. *Times*, Nov. 8, 1898; (34) from May 7 to Sept. 15; (35) Chadwick, II, 116; (36) Richardson, X, 131; (37) McElroy, II, 280; (38) Olcott, II, 110-1; (39) W. J. B. Speeches, II, 8; (40) *ibid.*, 13; (41) N. Y. *Times*, June 15, 1898; (42) W. J. B. Speeches, II, 9; (43) *ibid.*, p. 39; (44) *ibid.*, p. 37; (45) *ibid.*, p. 38; (46) *ibid.*, p. 29; (47) Hoar, II, 322; (48) Pettigrew, p. 271; (49) Beard, II, 380; (50) Speeches, II, 46; (51) "Reminiscences," p. 325; (52) Masters, *Am. Mercury*, Dec., 1924; (53) *North American Review*, June, 1900.

CHAPTER XX

(1) Roosevelt, p. 399; (2) Wheeler, p. 219; (3) House, I, 39; (4) Post to Stevenson, (5) Latané, p. 123; (6) Frederic Howe, pp.

131-4; (7) p. 51; (8) p. 52; (9) "Life of Croker," p. 350; (10) Thayer, II, 153; (11) Chicago *Record-Herald*, July 2, 1900; (12) Letter: June 14, 1928; (13) Stevenson, p. 95; (14) *Kenyon Committee Hearings*, I, 537; (15) P. H. Callahan: Statement; (16) T. R. "Letters," I, 474; (17) *ibid.*; (18) *ibid.*, 478; (19) *American Mercury*, Dec., 1924; (20) Thayer, II, 253; (21) Boeckel, p. 655; (22) N. Y. *Times*, Nov. 11, 1900; (23) Jan. 10; 1901; (24) N. Y. *Herald*, Jan. 8, 1901; (25) Augustus Thomas: *North American Review*, CLXXXVII, 802; Richard Hooker, p. 173; (26) C. F. Adams, p. 51; (27) Stevenson, pp. 165-6; (28) N. Y. *Tribune*, July 31, 1901; (29) Sullivan, I, 519-20; (30) Stanwood, II, 78; (31) Sullivan, I, 516; (32) N. Y. *Herald*, Jan. 10, 1901; (33) N. Y. *Tribune*, Jan. 25, 1901; (34) Merriam, p. 80.

CHAPTER XXI

(1) Letter: June 14, 1928; (2) Sermon: Ithaca, N. Y., March 12, 1922; (3) *Commoner*, April 15, 1904; (4) M. F. Dunlap: Statement; (5) *Commoner*, Feb. 5, 1904; (6) "Mem." p. 135; (7) Bryan papers, XXVI; (8) Bryan testimony: N. Y. *Times*, Oct. 22-23, 1903; (9) N. Y. *Times*, Oct. 4, 1903; (10) Dr. Grace Dewey: Statement; (11) C. W. Thompson, N. Y. *Times*, Aug. 2, 1925; (12) "Mem." p. 273; (13) Bride papers, Letter of July 20, 1898; (14) "Under Other Flags," p. 82; (15) *ibid.*, p. 89; (16) *Commoner*, Feb. 19, 1904; (17) "Under Other Flags," pp. 98-9; (18) *ibid.*, p. 107; (19) Stevenson, p. 90; (20) "Under Other Flags," p. 122; (21) *ibid.*, p. 52; (22) *ibid.*, p. 121; (23) *Commoner*, April 8, 1904; (24) Thompson, pp. 244-5; (25) *ibid.*, p. 366; (26) "Mem." p. 147; (27) p. 369; (28) Post to Johnson, July 24, 1904, in Stevenson, p. 177; (29) "Mem." pp. 149-52; (30) Thompson, pp. 374-8; (31) *ibid.*, p. 377; (32) William Allen White, *Collier's*, July 12, 1904; (33) Speeches, II, 50-60; (34) *Collier's*, July 12, 1904.

CHAPTER XXII

(1) N. Y. *Tribune*, July 9, 1904; (2) Denver *News*, July 11, 1904; (3) *Commoner*; July 15, 1904; (4) *ibid.*; (5) Peck, p. 715; (6) N. Y. *Tribune*, Feb. 15, 1906; (7) *Commoner*, April 12, 1907; (8) *ibid.*, July 12, 1907; (9) Hawarth, p. 310; (10) N. Y. *Tribune*, Aug. 31, 1904; (11) N. Y. *Sun*, Sept. 2, 1904; (12) *ibid.*, Sept. 7, 1904; (13) N. Y. *World*, June 1, 2, ff., 1908; (14) *ibid.*, June 11, 1908;

(15) *Commoner*, Sept., Oct., Nov., 1904; (16) N. Y. *Tribune*, Sept. 7, 1904; (17) *Commoner*, Oct. 21, 1904; (18) *ibid.*, Nov. 11, 1904.

CHAPTER XXIII

(1) Stevenson, p. 183; (2) N. Y. *Tribune*, Jan. 22, 1905; (3) Stevenson, p. 102; (4) *ibid.*, p. 184; (5) N. Y. *Tribune*, Jan. 22, 1905; (6) Peck, p. 732; (7) Rammelkamp; (8) *Commoner*, April 14, 1905; (9) Rammelkamp; (10) *ibid.; Commoner*, April 14, Aug. 4, 1905; (11) Bryan to Rammelkamp, June 3, 1905; (12) *Commoner*, June 23, 1905; (13) Rammelkamp; (14) *Commoner*, Aug. 11, 1905; (15) Schilling statement to Stevenson; (16) *Commoner*, Sept. 15, 1905; (17) *ibid.*, Sept. 29, 1905; (18) Hendrick, "Page," I, 236; (19) Herrick, p. 212; (20) *Commoner*, Jan. 26, 1906; (21) *ibid.*, Feb. 2, 1906; (22) Manila *Libertas;* (23) *India*, July 20, 1907; (24) *Puck*, Aug. 8, 1906; (25) N. Y. *Tribune*, June 8, 1906; (26) *ibid.*, June 5, 1906; (27) *ibid.*, July 8, 1906; (28) *ibid.*, July 5, 1906; (29) N. Y. *World*, July 5, 1906; (30) Spender, I, 177; (31) Post to Bryan, Aug. 4, 1906; (32) London *Times*, July 25, 1906; (33) Cortissoz, I, 333; (34) Dunlap; (35) *ibid.*; (36) N. Y. *Tribune*, Aug. 3, 1906; (37) *Commoner*, Sept. 7, 1906; (38) N. Y. *World*, Aug. 31, 1906; (39) Dunn, II, 18.

CHAPTER XXIV

(1) *Commoner*, Dec. 14, 1906; (2) *ibid.*, Feb. 14, 1908; (3) *ibid.*, Jan. 18, 1907; (4) *ibid.*, March 29, 1907; (5) *Wall Street Journal*, April 10, 1907; (6) Dunn, II, 50; (7) Kent, p. 371; (8) *Harper's Weekly*, May 2, 1908; (9) N. Y. *Sun*, July 5, 1907; (10) Don Seitz, p. 323; (11) Dunn, II, 48; (12) *Literary Digest*, May 23, 1908; (13) N. Y. *World*, June 27, 1908; (14) *ibid.*, June 28, 1908; (15) *ibid.*, June 28, 1908; (16) *Commoner*, July 10, 1908; (17) Claude G. Bowers: Statement; (18) *Commoner*, Aug. 28, 1908; (19) Pettigrew, p. 257; (20) *ibid.*, p. 258; (21) *Commoner*, July 24, 1908; (22) *ibid.*, (23) Stevenson, p. 196; (24) Bowers: Statement; (25) *Literary Digest*, Oct. 10, 1908.

CHAPTER XXV

(1) *Commoner*, March 25, 1910; (2) *ibid.*, Aug. 12, 1910; (3) *ibid.*, March 15, 1912; (4) Kent, p. 317; (5) *Commoner*, Jan. 6,

1911; (6) *ibid.*, (7) *Literary Digest*, July 29, 1911; (8) Clark, II, 396; (9) Baker, House, II, 277; (10) *ibid.*, I, 48, 49; (11) "Mem." p. 326.

CHAPTER XXVI

(1) House, I, 49, 50; (2) *ibid.*, pp. 50, 51; (3) *ibid.*, p. 52; (4) Tumulty, p. 95; (5) *ibid.*, p. 96; (6) N. Y. *Tribune*, Jan. 9, 1912; (7) *ibid.*; (8) Tumulty, p. 97; (9) Washington *Post*, Jan. 9, 1912; (10) Tumulty, p. 97; (11) *Commoner*, Jan. 26, 1912; (12) Clark, II, 398; (13) *Commoner*, Feb. 2, March 8, 1912; (14) *ibid.*, March 22, 1912; (15) Mullen: Statement; (16) *Commoner*, April 26, 1912; (17) Harriman, p. 99; (18) *Commoner*, June 22, 1912; (19) "Mem." p. 166; (20) Harriman, p. 108; (21) *ibid.*, p. 104; (22) Omaha *World-Herald*, June 26, 1912; (23) C. W. Bryan, N. Y. *Times*, March 6, 1921; (24) "Mem." p. 174; (25) N. Y. *Times*, March 6, 1921; (26) *Commoner*, July 12, 1912; (27) N. Y. *World*, June 28, 1912; (28) *ibid.*; (29) Child; (30) N. Y. *American*, July 2, 1912.

CHAPTER XXVII

(1) *Commoner*, Nov. 8, 1912; (2) House, I, 84; (3) *ibid.*, I, 98; Lawrence, p. 67; (4) Marshall, pp. 160–1; (5) House, I, 108; (6) *ibid.*, I, 84; (7) A. P. dispatch quoted in *Commoner*, March 5, 1913; (8) Houston, I, 38; (9) The letter, N. Y. *Times*, Jan. 15; Bryan's comment, Jan. 16, 1915; (10) Houston, I, 43; (11) "Mem." 346; (12) Dan Bride papers; (13) N. Y. *Tribune*, Aug. 3, 1913; (14) Stoddard, p. 285; (15) *Commoner*, May 9, 1913; (16) Lowry, p. 46; (17) Houston, I, 43; (18) *Commoner*, March 14, 1913; (19) Houston, I, 43; (20) *Literary Digest*, March 29, 1913; (21) "American Secretaries of State," X, 9; (22) Library of Congress papers, XXIII; (23) *ibid.*; (24) *ibid*; (25) Houston, I, 50; (26) *ibid.*, p. 67; (27) Lawrence, p. 101; (28) Lowry, p. 41; (29) J. K. Kinney; (30) Boston *Herald* in *Literary Digest*, July 26, 1913; (31) *ibid.*; (32) *Commoner*, Oct., 1913; (33) Hendrick, "Page," I, 203; (34) Welles, p. 726; (35) N. Y. *Times*, July 21, 1913; (36) Tumulty, p. 178; (37) Carter Glass, p. 125; (38) *ibid.*, p. 138; (39) *ibid.*, p. 142; (40) Hendrick, "Page," I, 244–5; (41) *Commoner*, May, 1914; (42) Dan Bride papers; (43) *ibid.*; (44) Tumulty, pp. 151–2; (45) *Commoner*, Nov., 1914; (46) Lowry, p. 44; (47) "Mem." pp. 388–92; (48) "Am. Sec. State," X, 30; (49) Von Bernstorff, p. 37; (50) N. Y. *Times*, Jan. 20, 1925; (51) *ibid.*; (52) "Foreign Relations," 1915,

p. xii; (53) *ibid.*, pp. vi, viii, xx; (54) *ibid.*, p. 356, supplement; (55) Lowry, p. 47; (56) "Mem." p. 396-7; (57) House, I, 179; (58) Barnes, p. 399; (59) "Mem." p. 399; (60) Lawrence, p. 148; (61) "Mem." p. 399; (62) *ibid.*, p. 400; (63) *ibid.*, p. 401; (64) "Mem." p. 403; (65) "Foreign Relation" 1915, p. 407, supplement; (66) *ibid.*, p. 407; (67) *ibid.*, p. 408; (68) *ibid.*, p. 420; (69) Houston, I, 137; (70) "Amer. Sec. State," X, 41; (71) N. Y. *Times*, Aug. 2, 1925; (72) Redfield, p. 102; (73) Houston, I, 145.

CHAPTER XXVIII

(1) Hendrick, "Page," II, 13-4; (2) *Commoner*, Nov. 15, 1915; (3) Stevenson; (4) Library of Congress papers; (5) Dunn, II, 276; (6) *Commoner*, June, 1916; (7) *ibid.*, December, 1916; (8) *ibid.*, March, 1917; (9) Odegard, p. 67; (10) *Commoner*, Sept. 1918; (11) *American Issue*, April 18, 1918; (12) *ibid.*; (13) N. Y. *World*, April 4, 1918; (14) N. Y. *Times*, May 30, 1918; (15) *American Issue*, Feb. 15, 1919; (16) *Commoner*, Feb., 1919; (17) *ibid.*, June, 1918; (18) Dan Bride papers; (19) *ibid.*; (20) *ibid.*; (21) N. Y. *World*, March 1, 1920; (22) "U. S. Senatorial Campaign Expenditures," p. 1406; (23) *American Issue*, March 6, 1920; (24) *ibid.*; (25) *ibid.*, March 21, 1920; (26) Charles A. Douglas: Interview; (27) N. Y. *Times*, May 26, 1921; (28) *ibid.*; (29) Douglas: Interview; (30) *ibid.*; (31) Dan Bride papers; (32) *Literary Digest*, Jan. 17, 1920; (33) N. Y. *World*, Jan. 9, 1920; (34) N. Y. *Sun*, Jan. 9, 1928; (35) N. Y. *Tribune*, quoted in *Commoner*, Jan. 1920; (36) *Commoner*, May, 1920; (37) Dan Bride: Interview; (38) Justin Steuart, pp. 159-60; (39) *Commoner*, May, 1920; (40) *ibid.*, July, 1920; (41) *ibid.*; (42) *ibid.*; (43) *ibid.*; (44) *ibid.*, Nov., 1920; (45) *ibid.*

CHAPTER XXIX

(1) *Congress. Record*, LXVII, 5065-6; (2) Mordell: Statement; (3) *Commoner*, April, 1921; (4) *ibid.*; (5) Dan Bride papers; (6) *Commoner*, Dec., 1921; (7) *Commoner*, Jan., 1923; (8) *ibid.*, May, 1922; (9) "Last Message," p. 64; (10) Willey: Letter; (11) *Commoner*, June, 1921; (12) *ibid.*, Aug., 1921; (13) Lib. of Cong. papers, XXIII; (14) *Commoner*, Feb., 1921; (15) "Mem." p. 475; (16) N. Y. *Times*, Aug. 11, 1925; (17) *ibid.*, July 10, 1921; (18) Grattan, *Am. Mercury*, July, 1928; (19) Dan Bride papers; (20) *Commoner*, March, 1922; (21) Letter from William Jennings Bryan, Jr., Nov.

24, 1922; (22) *Commoner*, Feb., 1922; (23) Lib. of Cong. papers, XXIII; (24) *ibid.*, IX; (25) Douglas: Interview; (26) Stevenson, p. 281; (27) N. Y. *Times*, May 8, 1923; (28) *ibid.*, May 28, 1923; (29) *ibid.*, May 23, 1923; (30) *ibid.*, June 25, 1923; (31) N. Y. *American*, June 23, 1924; (32) Elmer Davis, N. Y. *Times*, June 25, 1924; (33) H. L. Mencken to Pettigrew, Oct. 8, 1925; (34) N. Y. *Times*, July 2, 1924; (35) Hapgood and Moskowitz, p. 304; (36) N. Y. *American*, July 9, 1924; (37) Steuart, p. 291; (38) Masters; (39) N. Y. *Times*, Aug. 30, 1925.

CHAPTER XXX

(1) N. Y. *Times*, Dec. 28, 1925; (2) *ibid.*, Dec. 31, 1925; (3) *ibid.*, Dec. 18, 1925; (4) H. L. Mencken, Baltimore *Evening Sun*, July 20, 1925; (5) "Mem." p. 483; (6) Mencken, Balt. *Eve. Sun*, July 9, 1925; (7) N. Y. *Times*, July 11, 1925; (8) *ibid.*; (9) *ibid.*; (10) Mark Sullivan, N. Y. *Herald-Tribune*, July 19, 1925; (11) N. Y. *Times*, July 11, 1925; (12) Hays, p. 36; (13) Allen, p. 7; (14) Mencken, Balt. *Eve. Sun*, July 10, 11, 1925; (15) Allen, p. 7; (16) N. Y. *Times*, July 13, 1925; (17) Allen, p. 9; (18) N. Y. *Times*, July 15, 1925; (19) Allen, p. 51; (20) N. Y. *Times*, July 16, 1925; (21) Mencken, Balt. *Eve. Sun*, July 16, 1925; (22) Allen, pp. 63-79; (23) Hays, p. 65; (24) Allen, p. 109; (25) Hays, p. 69; (26) N. Y. *Herald-Tribune*, July 21, 1925; (27) Allen, pp. 133-56; (28) N. Y. *Herald-Tribune*, July 21, 1925; (29) N. Y. *Times*, July 22, 1925; (30) Milton, Preface to "Last Message," p. ii; (31) "Mem." p. 484; (32) Preface, "Last Message," p. ii; (33) "Mem." p. 487; (34) Preface, "Last Message," p. ii; (35) Milton: Letter; (36) "Mem." p. 487.

INDEX   437

INDEX

Abbot, Jacob, 69.
Abbott, Willis John, on Bryan, 208.
Adams, Charles Francis, on Bryan, 225.
Adams, Henry, 199.
Addams, Jane, open letter to, 355.
Akádémé, founded, 99.
Alcott, Bronson, 67, 82.
Aldrich plan, 301.
Allen, T. S., 256.
Altgeld, John Peter, 113, 182.
American Association for Advancement of Science, 388.
American Civil Liberties Union, 389.
Anderson, William H., 358.
Anti-Saloon League, Bryan on, 358.
Arabic, 351.

Babcock, Orville E., 47, 56.
Bailey, Joseph W., 136.
Baird, John, 83.
Baird, Mamie (*see* Bryan, Mamie Baird).
Baltimore, Democratic convention in, 308 *et seq.*
Baltzell, George, 14.
Baltzell, Jane Bryan, 14, 29.
Barnum, P. T., 46.
Bayard, Thomas F., 65.
Beecher, Edward, 55.
Beecher, Henry Ward, 63, 66, 106.
   Tilton scandal, 44, 56.
Belknap, William W., 47, 58.
Belmont, August, 46, 63, 104, 150.
   Bryan's denouncing of, 312.
Bennett, Philo Sherman, philanthropies, 239 *et seq.*
   will, 241 *et seq.*
Bernstorff, Count von, on Bryan, 338.
Beville, Mrs. A. V., 40, 100.
Bibliography, 409 *et seq.*
Bigelow, John, 8.
Bill of Rights, 26.
Black, James C. 100.
Blaine, James, G., 46, 119.

Bland, Richard Parks, 177, 192.
   silver issue, 141.
Boyd, James E., governorship campaign, 123.
Breese, Sidney, 19.
Bride, Dan, 207, 215.
Bristow, Benjamin H., 329.
Broady, J. H., 133, 164.
Brooks, Sydney, on Bryan, 216.
Bruce, Blanche K., 55.
Bryan, Charles, 96, 284, 310, 386.
   poverty, 106.
Bryan, Fannie, 30, 48.
Bryan, Jane (*see* Baltzell, Jane Bryan).
Bryan, John (grandfather), 12.
Bryan, John Baird (son), 375.
Bryan, Mamie Baird (wife), 82, 84, 153.
   aid to Bryan, 137, 272.
   at the Scopes trial, 392.
   conception of life, 88.
   fears for Bryan, 218, 243.
   first meeting with W. J., 75.
   graduates, 84.
   ill health, 319, 353, 386.
   paralyzed, 360.
   partnership with husband, 129.
Bryan, Mariah Elizabeth (mother), appearance, 20, 31.
   character, 29.
   death, 182.
   loss of children, 20.
   religion, 31.
Bryan, Martha, 14.
Bryan, Nancy Lillard, 12.
Bryan, Ruth, 157.
Bryan, Silas Lillard (father), 55, 65, 86, 100.
   ambition, 12, 15.
   ancestry, 11, 35.
   appearance, 35.
   arrest, 25.
   birth, 12.
   childhood, 13.
   compact with God, 17.
   court session, 34.

Bryan, Silas Lillard—*Continued.*
defeated for Congress, 42.
education, 14 *et seq.*
election to state Senate, 20.
first public office, 18.
law studies, 18.
made a judge, 27.
marriage, 20.
on the classics, 57.
opposed to women's rights, 37.
opposition to Lincoln, 5 *et seq.*
oratory of, 35.
political faith, 36.
poverty, 17.
religion, 12, 13, 17, 49.
success, 15.
support of Douglas, 23.
teaching experience, 17 *et seq.*
Bryan, William (uncle), 14.
Bryan, William Jennings, ambitions,
81, 93.
ancestry, 12.
appearance, 73, 97, 116, 136.
appreciation of publicity, 101.
arrogance, 282.
as congressman, 136 *et seq.*
at 1884 convention, 104.
at first convention, 62 *et seq.*
attitude toward health, 98.
attitude toward life, 69.
attitude toward science, 67, 74.
at Whipple Academy, 65 *et seq.*
attempts to secure public office, 107.
birth, 9, 23.
birthday party, 368.
Chautauqua lectures, 209.
childhood, 28 *et seq.*
children, 137.
church membership, 49.
class president, 73.
college, 50, 67 *et seq.*
compared to Lincoln, 10.
conservatism, 250.
conversion, 49.
courtship, 78, 82.
death, 405.
debating ability, 70 *et seq.*
dreams of glory, 101.
early library, 57.
economics, 97.
education, 38 *et seq.*
effort to escape home, 52.
engagement, 82.
enters politics, 108.
family discipline, 30.

Bryan, William Jennings—*Continued.*
family troubles, 224, 241, 375.
fear in make-up, 51.
fight for Hearst, 247 *et seq.*
finances, 207 *et seq.*, 239 *et seq.*, 255
et seq.
first court speech, 101.
first meeting with wife, 76.
first political campaign, 42, 80.
first Presidential candidacy, 187 *et
seq.*
friends, 96, 226.
graduation, 84.
illness, 218.
in Chicago, 89.
in the Spanish War, 214 *et seq.*
in Trumbull's office, 94.
lack of sex interest, 45.
last days, 404.
law studies, 92 *et seq.*
marriage, 105.
memories of youth, 44.
mother's teachings, 32.
never first, 78, 84.
on temperance, 47.
opinion of his father, 35.
oratorical development, 70 *et seq.*, 77.
parentage, 82.
patriotism, 356.
personality, 65, 116, 148.
personal triumph, 204 *et seq.*
political education, 10, 59, 65, 79.
prizes, 72, 74, 77.
reading, 69, 233, 237.
religion, 31, 33, 41, 46 *et seq.*, 95,
369 *et seq.*, 377 *et seq.*,
routine of life, 237 *et seq.*
second-hand opinions, 100.
settles in Jacksonville, 99.
shipwrecked, 298.
support of Wilson, 353 *et seq.*
unpopularity, 96, 102.
weakness for food, 120.
wealth, 106 *et seq.*, 360, 386.
will, 388.
women's influence on, 71.
youth, 45, 57.
Bryan, William Jennings, Jr. (son),
375, 391.
Bryan, Bryan, Bryan, Vachel Lindsay,
xii.
Bryan-Chamorro Treaty, 331.
Bryant, William Cullen, 8, 52.
Bullard, Erastus F., 83.
Burbank, Luther, on Bryan, 388.

Burnside, General, 26.
Butler, Benjamin F., 104.
Butler, Nicholas Murray, 42.

Cabinet, Bryan in, 319.
  Bryan's resignation from, 349.
  under Wilson, 321 *et seq.*
Cameron, Simon, 92.
Campaigns, Political, 1858, 5.
  1876, 60 *et seq.*
  1888, 116 *et seq.*
  1896, 175 *et seq.*, 189 *et seq.*, 190 *et
    seq.*
  1900, 202 *et seq.*, 222 *et seq.*
  1904, 250 *et seq.*
  1908, 259, 276 *et seq.*
  1912, 295 *et seq.*, 301 *et seq.*, 306 *et
    seq.*
  1916, 353 *et seq.*
  1920, 362 *et seq.*
  1924, 378 *et seq.*,
  discomforts, 194.
  expenses, 193, 227.
  finances, 145, 255 *et seq.*, 285.
  in the enemy's country, 197 *et seq.*
  methods, 192, 229, 285.
  muck-raking, 281.
  rallies, 117.
Canfield, President, on Bryan, 127.
Carlyle, Thomas, xiv.
Carnegie, Andrew, 119.
Centennial Exposition, 63.
Chance, Jackie, 45.
Charleston, S. C., founding, 22.
Chautauqua lectures, Bryan's, 209.
Chicago, in 1881, 89 *et seq.*
  1896 convention, 182 *et seq.*,
Chicago University, 55, 94.
Civil War, 24.
  draft riots, 25.
Clark, Champ, 178, 248.
  bitterness against Bryan, 320.
  Bryan on, 297.
  campaign of 1912, 302 *et seq.*
  candidacy, 296.
  on Bryan, 141.
Clark, William A., 165.
Clay, Henry, 22.
Cleveland, Grover, attack on Bryan,
  154 *et seq.*
  bolting, 177.
  compared with Bryan, 149 *et seq.*
  death, 289.
  disadvantages, 148.
  in the 1896 campaign, 175 *et seq.*

Cleveland, Grover—*Continued.*
  nomination, 103.
  silver issue stand, 149 *et seq.*, 163.
Cockran, Bourke, 104.
Colfax, Schuyler, 47.
Commoner, The, 237.
  established, 230.
  quoted, 252, 253, 258, 263, 277, 279,
    326, 355, 360.
Congress, Bryan in, 124 *et seq.*
  business of, 128.
  members of the Fifty-second, 136.
  speeches, 139.
  Ways and Means Committee, 134.
Congressional Record, 153.
Conkling, Roscoe, 79, 91.
Connell, W. J., 123, 126.
Constitution, Atlanta, 184.
  on Bryan, 170.
Constitutional Convention, Illinois,
  petition presented, 37.
  proceedings, 38.
Conventions, Political, 8, 103, 222 *et
  seq.*
  St. Louis, 118, 179 *et seq.*
Cooper, Peter, 62.
Cortelyou, George, 254.
Courier, Jacksonville, 107.
Courtship of Miles Standish, The,
  Longfellow, 3.
Cozzens, Phœbe, 63.
Crampton, Rufus, 85.
Crédit Mobilier, 47.
Cuba, annexation, 219 *et seq.*
  political possibilities, 205.
  rebellion, 203 *et seq.*

Dahlman, James C., 176, 272, 291.
  Bryan's fight against, 293.
Daly, Marcus, 165.
Daniels, Josephus, 307.
Darrow, Clarence, 42, 182.
  in the Scopes case, 390 *et seq.*
Darwinism, Bryan's position on, 370 *et
  seq.*
Davis, Jefferson, 23.
Davis, John W., 382.
Dawes, Charles G., 116.
Day, William R., 189.
Dayton, Tenn., Scopes case, 389 *et seq.*
Debates, Bryan with Darrow, 390.
  prohibition, 290.
  silver issue, 183 *et seq,*
  with John M. Thurston, 163.
  with W. J. Connell, 126.

Democratic party, 22.
  brighter prospects, 294.
  Bryan abdicates, 230.
  campaigns (*see* separate item).
  conservatism, 250 *et seq.*
  conventions (*see* separate item).
  crisis of 1897, 166.
  in Civil War, 25.
  issues of 1908, 270 *et seq.*, 274.
  money issue in, 62.
  plan for a radical, 253.
  oppose prosecution of war, 27.
  triumph, 319.
  victory in 1862, 27.
  free soil (*see* Free Soil Democrats).
Denver, Democratic convention in, 284.
Dixon, Thomas, on Bryan, 189.
Doheny, E. L., 380.
Douglas, Charles A., 361.
Douglas, Stephen A., 4, 55.
  defeat of Lincoln, 6.
  Presidential ambitions, 22.
Douglas, O'Bear & Douglas, Bryan a member of, 376.
Dow, Lorenzo, 16.
Dumba affair, 346.
Dunlap, Millard Fillmore, 10, 80, 88.

Edward VII, Bryan presented to, 272.
Egypt, Illinois, 3.
  draft riots, 25.
  effect of, 24.
  1860, 22 *et seq.*
  war on war politics, 24.
Eighteenth Amendment, 358, 365.
Eliot, Charles W., Bryan on, 321.
Emerson, Ralph Waldo, 67.
England, war relations with United States, 338 *et seq.*
Estabrook, Experience, 23.
Evolution, Bryan's campaign against, 371 *et seq.*, 377, 388 *et seq.*

Fairbanks, Charles W., 178.
Fairfax, Lord, 12.
Fairview, building of, 238.
  Democratic National Committee, 285.
  turned into a Methodist hospital, 373.
Federal Reserve Act, Bryan's stand on, 332.
Fell, Jesse, 7.
Field, Allen W., 143.
Field, Marshall, 46.
First Battle, The, Bryan, 207.

Fisk, Jim, 47.
Florida, Bryan's residence in, 372.
Flynn, Timothy, 81.
Foraker, J. B. 103.
Fosdick, Harry Emerson, Bryan on, 378.
Freeman, Edward A., 89.
Free Soil Democrats, 7.
Free Trade, 55.
Frémont, John C., 22.
Fundamentalism, 65.

Garfield, James A., 79.
  death, 90.
Gazette, Jonesboro, 26.
George, Henry, 113.
Germany, submarine warfare, 342.
Gibbons, Cardinal, 308.
Gillespie, Joseph, 19.
Gold standard issue (*see* Silver issue).
Golden Hours, 16.
Grange Movement, 60.
Grant, Ulysses S., 47, 56.
Greeley, Horace, 6, 63.
Green, Judd, 31, 47.
Greenback party, 42, 62.
Gregory, T. W., 339.
Gulliver's Travels, xv.

Hamill, Professor, 70.
Hammond, James H., 36.
Hancock, Winfield Scott, 81.
Hanna, Marcus Alonzo, 103, 119, 192, 204, 210.
Hardin, Dr. Martin D., 377.
  on Bryan, 237.
Harper's Weekly, 3.
Harrison, Benjamin, 119.
Harrison, Carter, 90.
Harrison, William Henry, 14.
Harvey, George, backing of Wilson, 305.
Haskell, C. N., 280.
Hay, John, on Bryan, 189, 199, 200, 228.
Hays, Arthur Garfield, 391.
Hearst, William Randolph, 316.
  candidacy, 246 *et seq.*
  offer to Bryan, 243.
Henricks, Rev., 48.
Hepburn Railway Bill, 260.
Herald, Lincoln, on Bryan, 127.
Herald, Miami, 356.
Herald, New York, 3, 105.
Herndon, William, 59.
Hewitt, Abram S., 63.

Hibben, Paxton, tribute to, xiii.
Hill, David B., 63, 226.
1904 campaign, 253 et seq.
silver issue stand, 152, 184.
Hill, James J., 191.
Hitchcock, Gilbert, 229.
on Bryan, 372.
Hoar, Senator, 57.
Holcomb, Silas A., 167.
House, Colonel E. M., 298.
campaign of 1912, 301 et seq.
in Wilson's Presidency, 320 et seq.
letters to Bryan, 301 et seq.
on Bryan, 224, 352.
peace mission, 342.
Houston, David, on Bryan, 169.
Howell, Clark, 184.
Hughes, Charles Evans, 42.
Hulett, Granville, 72, 82, 96.
in Chicago, 89.
Huntington, Collis P., 46.

Illinois, Currency Convention, 170.
Illinois College, 50, 79.
commencement address, 262.
financial difficulties, 261.
standard of, 55.
Illinois Woman's College, 75.
Income-tax law, Bryan's proposal of, 156.
Industrial University, Illinois, 55.
Ingersoll, Robert Green, 68, 71, 104.
Bryan compared to, 118.

Jackson, Andrew, 12, 13.
Jacksonville Female Academy, 75.
Jamaica, Bryan's visit to, 298 et seq.
James, Ollie, 310 et seq.
Japanese question, Bryan's handling of, 327.
Jennings, Charles Edgar, 19, 93.
Jennings, Israel, 19, 31.
Jennings, Mariah Elizabeth, (see Bryan, Mariah Elizabeth).
Johnson, Andrew, 23.
Johnson, William "Pussyfoot," 125.
Jones, Charles H., 181.
Jones, Dr. George, 71.
Jones, Dr. Hiram K., 50, 66, 85, 99.
lack of classical education, 67.
lectures, 73.
Jones, Lizzie, 71, 83.
Journal, Jacksonville, 73, 101.
Judge, on Bryan, 230.

Kagy, Dan, 95, 96.
Kelly, John, 63, 104.
Kenyon, Senator, Bryan on, 362.
Kern, John W., 309.
Kirby, Edward P., 100.
Knights of the Golden Circle, 26.
Knights of Pythias, Bryan Chancellor Commander of, 114.
Know Nothing party, 22.
Ku Klux Klan, 26, 32.
political issue, 381 et seq.

Labour, Bryan's position on strikes, 374.
problems, 114.
Ladies' Repository, 16.
LaFollette, Robert M., 306 et seq.
Lane, Franklin K., 339, 349.
Latin America, Bryan's policy toward, 330.
Bryan's relations with, 362, 376.
League of Nations, an issue, 363 et seq.
Lemon, Mary Putnam Reed, 39, 100.
support of Negroes, 40.
Lenin, Nikolai, xiv.
Leslie's Weekly, 3.
on Bryan, 246.
Lewis, Alfred Henry, on Bryan, 225.
Life of Ben Harrison, Gen. Lew Wallace, 119.
Lincoln, Abraham, election to Senate, 6.
legend of, 9.
popularity in West, 8.
Presidential aspiration, 7.
running for Senate, 5.
Lincoln, Thomas, 15.
Lincoln-Douglas debates, 6, 20.
Lincoln, Neb., in 1888, 121.
state convention at, 119.
Little Rock and Fort Smith Railroad, 56.
Lloyd George, David, Bryan's peace note to, 355.
Lodge, Henry Cabot, 103.
war attitude, 213.
Logan, Gen. John A., 24, 27, 61, 114.
Lowrie, Ted, on Bryan, 197.
Ludendorff, Erich, xiv.
Lusitania, 343.
Germany's position on, 347.
sinking of, 343.
Lynch, John R., 103.

McAdoo, William, campaign of 1924, 379 et seq.
McCormick, Cyrus, 46.
McGuffey, William Holmes, 32.

McKendree College, 16.
McKenzie, Ben G., 391.
McKenzie, J. Gordon, 391.
McKinley, William, 103, 119, 144.
    as President, 202 et seq.
    death, 233.
    election, 200.
    in the Cuban situation, 219 et seq.
    Presidency nomination, 189.
    war issue, 211.
McShane, John A., 108, 119.
Madison Square Garden, Byran's
    speeches in, 199.
    Democratic convention in, 380 et seq.
    1908 speech, 273.
Maine episode, 211.
Malone, Dudley Field, 391.
Marble, Manton, 59, 63.
Martin, Gen. John, 24, 27, 42, 43.
Masters, Edgar Lee, on Bryan, 184,
    186, 228.
Medill, Joseph, 91.
Memoirs, William Jennings Bryan, 34.
Merrill, William P., on Bryan, 378.
Methodist Church, temperance work,
    47.
Mexican situation, 330, 334.
Miami, open air Bible class, 373.
Money, 61.
    greenbacks, 60 et seq.
    Wall Street, 61.
Moody, Dwight L., 46.
Morgan, J. Pierpont, 46, 191.
    Bryan's denunciation of, 312.
Morning News, Savannah, on Bryan,
    170.
Morton, J. Sterling, 115.
    attack on Bryan, 154 et seq.
    Bryan a henchman of, 122.
Morton, Oliver P., 62.
Mott, Lucretia, 100.
Mullen, Arthur, 306.
Murphree, Dr. A. A., in 1924 campaign,
    379 et seq.
Murphy, Charles F., 312, 314.

National Democrat, on Bryan, 139.
National Farmers' Alliance, 90.
Neal, John Randolph, 391.
Nebraska, Bryan in, 108, 115 et seq.
    county option bill, 291.
    Democratic Free Coinage League,
    164.
    senatorial campaign, 166 et seq.
    state convention, 291.

Negroes, in Kansas, 8.
    in the Senate, 55.
    overran Middle West, 28.
News, Baltimore, on Bryan, 364.
New York, Democratic convention in,
    380 et seq.
North American Review, Bryan in, 301.

O'Leary, John, 119.
Omaha, Nebraska, state convention at,
    123.

Page, Walter Hines, on Bryan, 352.
Panama Canal, 289.
    Bryan's position on tolls, 333.
Panic of 1873, 47.
Parker, Alton B., Bryan's support of,
    255 et seq.
    candidacy, 250 et seq.
    in the 1912 campaign, 307 et seq.
    telegram to Bryan, 356.
Payne-Aldrich Bill, 294.
Peace, Bryan's single-handed fight for,
    325 et seq., 351 et seq.
Peck, Professor, on Bryan, 139, 153.
Pettigrew, R. F., 54.
    on Bryan, 221.
Phillips, Wendell, 9, 66.
Pioneers, marriage among, 16.
    modes of travel, 14.
    types, 7, 15.
Poland, Senator, 62.
Politics, age of corruption, 47, 56.
Populist party, amalgamation tactics,
    166.
    Bryan's support of, 131 et seq.
    1896 campaign, 190 et seq.
    silver issue, 142 et seq.
Post, Louis, 231.
Post-Dispatch, St. Louis, 181.
Presbyterians, Cumberland, 48.
    1923 assembly meeting, 377 et seq.
Prohibition, Bryan's position on, 122
    et seq., 323, 335, 378.
    destruction of liquor, 41, 47.
    issue of, 290 et seq., 366, 380 et seq.
    political possibilities, 263.
    Republican assessments, 123.
    struggle for, 357 et seq.
Pryor, Roger A., 63.
Publishing ventures, campaign books,
    207.
    pamphlets, 169.
Pulitzer, Joseph, 282.

Railroads, financing, 58.
land grants, 59.
political issue, 253, 274, 276 et seq.
Rainey, Henry T.., on Bryan, 368.
Randall, Samuel Jackson, 136.
Rappleyea, George, 389.
Redfield, on Bryan, 348.
Reid, Mayne, 69.
Reid, Whitelaw, on Bryan, 204.
Republican party, 22.
campaign of 1912, 306 et seq.
1896 campaign, 179 et seq.
conventions (see separate item).
finances, 254.
Rice, Edward L., on Bryan, 388.
Rockefeller, John D., 46.
Roosevelt, Theodore, 42, 114, 211, 306.
Bryan's relations with, 259 et seq.
in the Spanish War, 213 et seq.
1900 campaign, 227.
1904 campaign, 251 et seq.
1908 campaign, 276 et seq.
1912 campaign, 306 et seq.
on Bryan, 224, 274.
Presidency, 233, 262 et seq.
Root, Elihu, 331.
Ross, E. A., on Bryan, 226, 237.
Rothschild, House of, 150.
"Russ, Uncle," 41.
Russell, John E., 184.
Ryan, Thomas F., Bryan's denouncing
of, 312.

St. Louis, Democratic convention in,
118.
Republican convention in, 179 et seq.
Salem, Ill., Bryan's home in, 34 et seq.
Scopes case, 389 et seq.
Senate, Bryan's candidacy for, 162
et seq., 375.
1894 campaign, 166 et seq.
Seward, William H., opposed in West, 8.
Sherman, John, 79, 119.
Sherman, William Tecumseh, 26.
Shields, James, 5.
Silver issue, Bryan's stand on the, 131
et seq., 141 et seq., 167 et seq.
business depressions, 156.
Cleveland's stand, 149 et seq., 163.
1896 campaign, 175 et seq.
influence on senatorial campaign,
167 et seq.
leagues, 175.
Nebraska conference, 164.
passions of, 191.

Silver issue—Continued.
platform debates, 183 et seq.
revival, 252.
under McKinley, 202 et seq.
Slavery, 8.
abolition discussion, 4, 55.
not destroyed, 36.
Smith, Alfred E., 384.
Smith, Mollie, 29, 41, 71.
marriage, 39.
postmistress of Salem, 39.
Socialism, Bryan against, 268.
South America, Bryan's interest in,
289 et seq.
Spanish War, 214 et seq.
forerunners, 210, 211.
means of averting, 212.
yellow fever, 218.
Sparks, Jared, xv.
Speech making, acceptance, 225, 285.
"Character," 86.
commencement, 279.
congressional, 139, 153, 157 et seq.
"Cross of Gold," 195.
first success, 117.
free-silver, 133, 153, 169.
Illinois College, 262.
in the East, 209.
in Florida, 373.
in the West, 210.
Madison Square Garden, 199.
nausea, 177.
on physiology, 73.
oratory defined, 118.
peace conference, 271.
political, 126 et seq., 248, 278, 319.
power in, 117.
preparations, 137.
tariff, 140.
themes, 87, 96, 103.
Spoils system, Bryan's support of, 322.
Springer, William McKendree, 80, 135.
Standard Oil Company, 301.
Stephens, Alexander, 36.
Stevens, G. W., on Bryan, 200.
Stewart, A. T., 391.
Stone, William J., 340.
Stuyvesant, Peter, 65.
Sullivan, James Mark, 331.
Sullivan, John L., 46.
Sun, New York, on Bryan, 329.

Taft, William Howard, candidacy, 282
et seq.
Presidency, 294.

Talbot, Adolphus, 96, 108.
Talmage, T. De Witt, 46.
Tammany Hall, at convention of 1876, 63.
 Bryan's speech in, 143.
Tanner, Professor, 83, 85.
Tariff issues, Bryan's position on, 128.
 speeches, 140.
Tea Pot Dome scandal, 379.
Teller, Henry M., 177, 179.
Temperance (see Prohibition),
Tennessee, Anti-Evolution Law, 389.
Thomas, Charles S., Bryan's letter to, 171.
Thomas, H. W., 90.
Thurston, John M., 115, 163.
Tilden, Samuel J., 64.
Tilton, Theodore, 66.
Tilton scandal, 56.
Times, Chicago, 26.
Times, New York, on Bryan, 142.
To a Waterfowl, William Cullen Bryant, 52.
Tolstoy, Count Leo, Bryan's visit to, 244.
Travels, Bryan's, Cuban, 243.
 European tour, 243 et seq.
 home-coming, 273.
 South American tour, 290.
 world tour, 264 et seq.
Tribune, Chicago, 62, 73.
 on Bryan, 354.
Tribune, New York, 3, 6.
 on Bryan, 159, 172, 230.
Trotter, James M., 107.
Trumbull, Henry, 94 et seq., 121.
Trumbull, Lyman, 5, 19.
 ancestry, 91.
 death, 181.
 philosophy, 95.
 professor of law, 94.
 public service, 92.
Trust issue, 282 et seq., 301.
Twain, Mark, 46.

Underwood, Oscar W., 1924 campaign, 379 et seq.
Union College of Law, 93.
United States, background of Bryan's career, 130, 368.
 brink of war, 129.
 new century movements, 231 et seq.
 political background, 267, 289.
 (see also Spanish War and World War).

Van Wyck, C. H., 114.
Villard, Henry, 9.
Voorhees, Daniel, 63.

Wall Street Journal, The, conciliated, 278.
Walsh, Thomas J., 382.
Washington, D. C., Bryan's life in, 136 et seq., 160.
 Conference of Natural Resources, 283.
 Jackson Day Dinner, 303, 363.
 White House reception, 138.
Watson, Tom, 192.
Watt, James, xiv.
Watterson, Henry, 63.
 on Bryan, 190.
Weaver, James Baird, 144.
Webster, Henry, 44.
Wentworth, Erastus, 16.
Wheeler, Joe, 216.
Whig party, 22.
Whipple Academy, 50.
 Bryan at, 65.
 lecturers at, 66.
White Cloud, 4.
Whitman, Walt, 68.
Whisky ring, 56.
Williams, "Blue Jeans," 64.
Wilson, Woodrow, 294.
 Byran's break with, 363 et seq.
 campaign of 1912, 301 et seq.
 candidacy, 295 et seq.
 illness, 367.
 1920 campaign, 363 et seq.
 nomination, 317.
 on Bryan, 174.
 Presidency, 319 et seq.
 reëlection, 353 et seq.
Wilson tariff, 159, 163.
Wishart, Dr. Charles, 377.
Woman suffrage, 37.
 Bryan's position on, 335, 357.
 discussed at Democratic convention, 63.
World, New York, 63, 361.
 on Bryan, 139, 159, 256.
World-Herald, Omaha, Bryan editor-in-chief of, 165.
 on Bryan, 363.
 quoted, 172.
World War, America in, 356.
 Bryan's position in, 336 et seq.

Yates, Richard, 102.
Young Men's Christian Association, 102.

DATE DUE

NO 9'82		
NO 23'82		
DE 6 '82		
DE 13'82		
JA 31'84		
AR 27'84		
		PRINTED IN U.S.A.
GAYLORD		